Micro Aspects of Development

edited by
Eliezer B. Ayal

The Praeger Special Studies program—utilizing the most modern and efficient book production techniques and a selective worldwide distribution network—makes available to the academic, government, and business communities significant, timely research in U.S. and international economic, social, and political development.

Micro Aspects of Development

PRAEGER SPECIAL STUDIES IN INTERNATIONAL ECONOMICS AND DEVELOPMENT

Praeger Publishers New York Washington London

Library of Congress Cataloging in Publication Data

Main entry under title.

Micro aspects of development.

(Praeger special studies in international economics and development)

Selected papers from a conference held at the University of Illinois at Congress Circle and sponsored by the National Science Foundation.

1. Economic development—Congresses. 2. Microeconomics—Congresses. I. Ayal, Eliezer B., ed. II. Illinois. University. University at Congress Circle, Chicago. III. United States. National Science Foundation.

HD82.M457 330 72-89641

PRAEGER PUBLISHERS
111 Fourth Avenue, New York, N.Y. 10003, U.S.A.
5, Cromwell Place, London S.W.7, England

Published in the United States of America in 1973
by Praeger Publishers, Inc.

Printed in the United States of America

To Livia and Dahlia

PREFACE

The papers in this volume were presented at the Conference on Micro Aspects of Development, held November 19-22, 1970, at the Chicago Campus of the University of Illinois. They have been revised and updated for publication here. Due to limitations of space, only a little more than half the papers presented at the conference could be included in this book. The editor wishes to emphasize that this carries no implication whatsoever that the excluded papers are in any way inferior to those retained for publication. Selection was dictated by the requirements of the publisher and the need to focus on relatively few themes.

I acknowledge with gratitude the encouragement and financial help supplied through Grant GS-3288 by the National Science Foundation, and the assistance of the University of Illinois, Chicago Circle, in providing facilities and honoraria for the participants.

CONTENTS

Page

PREFACE vii

LIST OF TABLES xiv

LIST OF FIGURES xvii

INTRODUCTION xix
by Eliezer B. Ayal

Chapter

1 SOCIAL AND ECONOMIC DEVELOPMENT AT THE MICRO LEVEL—A TENTATIVE HYPOTHESIS
Irma Adelman 3

Comment by Marvin Frankel 13

2 NOTES ON X-EFFICIENCY AND TECHNICAL PROGRESS
Harvey Leibenstein 18

Some Reasons for the X-Efficiency Approach to Growth 18
X-Efficiency and Output 19
X-Efficiency Versus "Technical Efficiency" 25
X-Efficiency and Technological Shifts 27
Localized Technological Change and Technological Stagnation 31
X-Efficient Technological Change and Innovational Diffusion Sequences 33
Conclusions 37

Comment by Larry A. Sjaastad 38

Chapter | Page

3 COMPARATIVE CONSUMPTION PATTERNS, THE EXTENT OF THE MARKET, AND ALTERNATIVE DEVELOPMENT STRATEGIES
Albert Fishlow 41

Introduction 41
Historical Expenditure Levels Derived from Household Surveys 45
Comparative Demand Structures 64
Origins of American Industrial Demand 74
Implications for Current Problems of LDCs 78

Comment by Jeffrey G. Williamson 80

4 EXPERIENCE IN GENERATING MICRO DATA IN LATIN AMERICA
Robert Ferber and Jorge Salazar-Carrillo 84

The Framework 84
Consumer Expenditure Survey 85
Industrial Wage and Labor Cost Survey 95
Conclusions 98

5 GENERATING MICRO DATA IN LESS DEVELOPED COUNTRIES THROUGH SURVEYS: SOME EXPERIENCE IN ASIA
Eva Mueller 101

Kinds of Economic Data to Be Collected 103
Purposes of Data Collection 111
Sample Size and Feasibility 115
Data Organization and Dissemination 116

Comment by Irwin Friend 118

6 DOMINANCE AND ACHIEVEMENT IN ENTREPRENEURIAL PERSONALITIES
Reeve D. Vanneman 122

Introduction 122

Chapter | Page

Case Studies 127
General Motors 127
Carnegie Steel 130
Examples of Specialization within Top Management 133
Examples with Long Periods of Dominance by Empire-Builders 135
Two Exceptions 138
Examples from Less Developed Countries 139
Discussion 140
Conclusions 142
Need Achievement and Entrepreneurial Behavior 143
Schumpeter, Sombart, and Weber 144

Comment by Bert F. Hoselitz 145

7 EFFECTS OF POLICIES ENCOURAGING FOREIGN JOINT VENTURES IN DEVELOPING COUNTRIES
Louis T. Wells, Jr. 149

Introduction 149
Investment Patterns 153
Changes in Ownership 153
The Pattern of Foreign Investment 154
Retreating from the Policy 156
Determinants of the Enterprise's Attitude toward Joint Ventures 159
The National Interest 164
Balance of Payments 166
Skills and Training 173
The Supply of Capital 174
Control and Political Factors 175
Conclusion 176

Comment by Stephen Hymer 177

8 INDUCED INNOVATION IN AGRICULTURAL DEVELOPMENT
Yujiro Hayami and Vernon W. Ruttan 181

Chapter | Page

Introduction 181
Induced Innovation in the Private and Public Sectors 183
Induced Innovation in the Private Sector 183
Induced Innovation in the Public Sector 184
Institutional Innovation 188
An Operational Model of Induced Innovation in Agriculture 189
Testing the Induced Innovation Hypothesis 193
Conclusion 202
References 205

Comment by Patrick Yeung 208

9 MICRO FUNCTIONS IN A MACRO MODEL: AN APPLICATION TO AGRICULTURAL EMPLOYMENT AND DEVELOPMENT STRATEGIES
Lawrence J. Lau and Pan A. Yotopoulos 212

Introduction 212
The Micro Model 214
Factor Demand Function and Output Supply Function as Derived from Profit Function 214
The Labor Supply Function 219
Micro Equilibrium 220
The Macro Models 221
Specification of Functional Forms 222
An Application to Indian Agriculture 227
Conclusions and Caveats 233
Appendix A: Structural Equations 234
Appendix B: Partial Macro Equilibrium Relationships 236
Appendix C: General Macro Equilibrium Relationships 237
References 239

10 THE EMPLOYMENT PROBLEM IN DEVELOPMENT
Benjamin Higgins 241

Chapter | Page

Introduction 241
Causes of Unemployment 245
The Role of Microeconomics 246
The Modern Sector 247
The Traditional Sector (Poor Region) 249
Case 1: The Capitalist Landlord 250
The W-L Curve 252
Introducing Monopoly Power 254
Variable Output Per Hour 254
The Low-Level Employment Trap 257
Case 2: Peasant Proprietors 257
The Production Function 260
The Constant Wage Gap 263
Case 3: The Village Landlord 265
The Transitional Sector in Developing Countries 268
Transitional Regions in Advanced Countries 269
A Three-Region Model 270
Conclusion: Need for an Integrated Approach 274

Comment by Nathaniel H. Leff 275

11 MICROECONOMIC THEORY AND ECONOMIC DEVELOPMENT: REFLECTIONS ON THE CONFERENCE
Richard R. Nelson 278

Neoclassical Price Theory and Economic Development 278
Key Questions in a Dynamic Microeconomics of Economic Development 281
How Much Psychology and Sociology Does Development Economics Need? 284

Chapter | Page

12 CURRENT STATE AND DESIRABLE DIRECTIONS IN ECONOMIC DEVELOPMENT RESEARCH (SUMMARY OF EXCHANGES BY PARTICIPANTS) 286

The Role of Microeconomic Theory 286
The Role of Government 287
Desirable Directions for Research 288
Conclusion 290

NOTES 291

ABOUT THE AUTHORS 312

LIST OF TABLES

Table		Page
3.1	Consumption Patterns of "Normal Families," 1888-91 (United States, Great Britain, and France)	46
3.2	Consumption Patterns in Industrial Towns (United States, 1909; United Kingdom, 1904; and France, 1907-8)	49
3.3	Savings Ratios by Industry	56
3.4	Regional Food Expenditure Ratios, 1901	60
3.5	Expenditure and Scale Elasticities	65
3.6	Specific Food Consumption Scales	72
4.1	Likely Effect of Errors on Means and Variances of Three ECIEL Studies	99
7.1	Ownership of Manufacturing Subsidiaries Entered in 1960-67 by Area, Less Developed Countries	152
7.2	Ownership of Manufacturing Subsidiaries in Japan	153
7.3	Manufacturing Subsidiaries in Spain, Ceylon, India, Mexico, Pakistan, and Other Less Developed Countries, Classified by Willingness of the Parent to Enter Joint Ventures Elsewhere (1960-66)	157
7.4	Manufacturing Subsidiaries in Spain, Ceylon, India, Mexico, Pakistan, and Other Less Developed Countries, Classified by the Parent's Holding of Joint Ventures Elsewhere (1966)	158
7.5	Average Ownership of Manufacturing Subsidiaries in Spain, Ceylon, India, Mexico, and Pakistan, by Parent's Ownership of Manufacturing Subsidiaries Elsewhere	159

Table		Page
7.6	Advertising Expenditures and Joint-Venture Entries	161
7.7	Organizational Structures and Use of Joint-Ventures	162
7.8	R&D Expenditures and Joint Ventures	163
7.9	Use of Joint Ventures by Extractive Firms	164
7.10	Use of Joint Ventures by R&D-Oriented Diversified Firms	165
7.11	Size of Firm in Industry and Use of Joint Ventures	166
7.12	Percent Overpricing of Imports in Colombia by Subsidiary Ownership and Industry	167
8.1	Fertilizer-Rice Price Ratios and Rice Yields Per Hectare in Selected Asian Countries and in Japan, 1883-1962	194
8.2	Changes in Output, Productivity, and Factor-Factor Ratios in Agriculture: the United States and Japan, 1880-1960	198
8.3a	Regressions of Land-Labor Ratio and Power-Labor Ratio on Relative Factor Prices: United States, 1880-1960 Quinquennial Observations	200
8.3b	Regressions of Land-Labor Ratio and Power-Labor Ratio on Relative Factor Prices: Japan, 1880-1960 Quinquennial Observations	201
8.4a	Regressions of Fertilizer Input Per Hectare of Arable Land on Relative Factor Prices: United States, 1880-1960 Quinquennial Observations	203
8.4b	Regressions of Fertilizer Input Per Hectare of Arable Land on Relative Factor Prices: Japan, 1880-1960 Quinquennial Observations	204

Table		Page
9.1	Reduced Form Coefficients of the Micro Equilibrium Model	225
9.2	Reduced Form Coefficients of the Partial Macro Equilibrium Model	226
9.3	Reduced Form Coefficients of the General Macro Equilibrium Model	228

LIST OF FIGURES

Figure		Page
1.1	Expected Return Versus Risk	15
2.1	Performance Variation and Choice	22
2.2	Utility-Effort Relation and the Inert Area	22
2.3	X-Efficient and X-Inefficient Switches in Techniques	30
2.4	Innovational Diffusion and Technological Stagnation	33
2.5	The Push and Pull Boundaries	36
3.1	Demand with Given Endowment of Factors	43
3.2	Demand Again, but with Different Initial Preferences than in Figure 3.1	44
3.3	Engel Curves for Consumption of Foodstuffs	53
3.4	Savings-Income Ratios	58
3.5	Engel Curves for Food by Immigrant Group, United States	63
4.1	Time Schedule for Field Work on Consumption Study	86
7.1	Percentage of Subsidiaries that Were Wholly-Owned by per Capita GNP of Host Country	155
8.1	Induced Innovation and the Innovation Possibility Curve	185
8.2	Shift in Fertilizer Response Curve along the Metaresponse Curve	191
8.3	Factor Prices and Induced Technical Change	192
8.4	Fertilizer and Arable Land, United States and Japan, 1880-1960	196

Figure		Page
9.1	The Labor Market	231
9.2	The Output Market	232
10.1	The Labor Market, Modern Sector	248
10.2	Marginal Productivity and the Wage-Labor Curve, Traditional Sector	251
10.3	Wage-Labor Equilibria in the Production Function, Peasant Proprietors	258
10.4	The Wage-Labor Curve in a Two-Dimensional Production Function	259
10.5	Employment by Village Landlord	266
10.6	A Three Region Model	271

INTRODUCTION

Eliezer B. Ayal

The motivation for organizing the Conference on Micro Aspects of Development was the realization that significant forward strides in the understanding of economic development are unlikely without substantial research on the micro level. The study of micro aspects is, of course, important in its own right. Here, however, we are primarily interested in the contribution that such study can make to the understanding of the process of development.

There is no precise definition for "micro aspects of development."* The term may encompass the whole range between sectoral models and project analysis. The former blend with macro models, and the latter are often reduced to engineering cost studies. Our pragmatic definition would be: a disaggregated study of development, especially the study of nongovernmental decision-units, in the less developed countries (LDCs), the interactions among them, and between them and the aggregate economy.** With some exceptions, most notably in agricultural economics, the study of these basic building blocks of the economies of the LDCs and of the processes of development associated with them has not been at the center of attention of development literature. My contention is that, at this stage, theoretical and empirical work on the micro level may be a more rewarding approach to the development process than the hitherto prevalent macro approach, as well as a necessary complement to such macro work. The macro implications are of great importance, of course, and the hope is that through detailed micro work a better understanding of some aggregate indicators and the policies required may be attained.

Students of economic development are familiar with the success of the Marshall Plan for Europe and the contrast between its achievements and the far less impressive results of the subsequent aid programs to LDCs. Not least among the factors contributing to the relative failure of the latter has been our incomplete understanding of the causes of underdevelopment and how to overcome it. This is not surprising in view of the fact that this field of study was essentially

---

*In fact, there is disagreement even about the precise definition of microeconomics, in spite of its having been at the core of economic theory for so long.

**The fact that some micro units are owned by government need not exclude them from our definition.

developed after World-War II and had few intellectual antecedents in the mainstream of economic analysis. For such antecedents we have to go back to the pioneers of classical economics, especially Adam Smith. Given such a background and the prevalence of Keynesian economics, it is not surprising that theorizing and empirical research in the development area were focused primarily on macro aspects of development. Due to the paucity of data and the urgent need to devise policies and development plans, this was probably unavoidable. Great strides were made initially, but during the last decade or so the rate at which new insights have emerged has slackened. This has been sometimes accompanied by an atmosphere of disillusionment with development plans in countries which had put great stock in macro planning.*

The scant attention given to the study of the workings of the private sector and its component units, or their relationship to the overall performance of the economy, has often been the cause of the unsatisfactory results of development plans. In the study of development problems, macro analyses, usually based on less-than-reliable official data, often obscure more than they reveal. The plateau at which economic development research now finds itself has resulted primarily from the shortage of systematically assembled and analyzed empirical data on the forces which determine the functioning of underdeveloped economies, as well as of suitable theories to guide such research. Our conference, and the further work it may encourage, should contribute to narrowing this gap in our knowledge.

WIDESPREAD CONCURRENCE

The recognition that economic development has entered a period of relative stagnation is shared by pioneers in this area of study, some of whom we were privileged to have with us at the conference. The overwhelmingly favorable response to this conference was one indication of this recognition. Needless to say, it has also been expressed in recent surveys of the literature. For example, in the revised edition

---

*A case in point is India where planning had been almost an article of faith. During the second half of the 1960s, Indians both inside and outside of government have undergone what for many was a traumatic experience of losing faith in the efficacy of national development planning as it had been applied in their country. Not surprisingly, the plans had failed particularly in their misjudgment of the expected performance of the private sector.

of his Economic Development, Problems, Principles, and Policies, Benjamin Higgins writes:

> There has not been any dramatic progress in the general theory of economic development. The lack of "break-through" in this respect has been no surprise to this writer. The chief barrier to economic development is still our ignorance of the process, and we face a long period of painful accumulation of the relevant empirical knowledge before general theory can be much improved.[1]

A similar opinion was expressed more recently by another writer on economic development, Stephen Enke:

> A recent survey of . . . contributions (subsequent to the late fifties and early sixties) to the theory and practice of development reveals less that is new and important. Meanwhile poverty persists in the less developed countries (LDCs).[2]

The conclusion that micro analysis of development has not received the attention it deserves and that research in this field holds substantial promise of significant results is also gaining ground. A good recent example is a paper surveying the current status of development economics by Lloyd Reynolds, former director of the Yale Growth Center (which had been largely concerned with macro aspects of development).[3] Reynolds also maintains that the field provides an almost limitless opportunity for doctoral dissertations which are "more interesting scientifically, more important practically" than most other dissertation topics.[4]

Similar trends have appeared in other areas of economics. In fact, there is evidence that a certain degree of soul-searching is evolving in other social sciences as well. A good example is the Program of East Asian Local Systems (PEALS) developed recently at Stanford University. This program was an attempt to break out of the "malaise that afflict[s] area studies . . ."[5] which in the case of East Asian studies was marked "by a preoccupation with the center and with macro-level analysis."[6]

Economic Development still has a long way to go to become a well-structured field, like, for example, the field of International Trade. It may well be that the subject matter is such that no "general theory" is possible. Not the least problem for such a theory is the necessity that it incorporate noneconomic factors, at least for analysis of the early stages of development. Persistent disaggregated studies would help the field to achieve a better structure and better theories. At the very least, such studies would facilitate the identification, measurement, and analysis of relevant variables.

The differences in degree between LDCs and MDCs are so large that they often amount to differences in kind. This means that scholars in the field would find new uses for existing analytical tools as well as being forced to develop new tools. To some extent this is already happening. The study of development problems is also influencing work in other branches of economics. The great interest in technological progress and investment in human capital are current examples.

THE SELECTION OF PANELS AND SUMMARY OF PAPERS

Ideally, the conference should have had panels covering all the most important areas where disaggregated analysis can contribute to the understanding of the development process. However, like other human endeavors, conferences are imperfect. Though we succeeded in attracting a most distinguished gathering of development scholars, we still fell short of comprehensive coverage. The constraints have been the usual ones: time, the availability of pertinent research work, and, to some extent, budget restrictions. Consequently, certain areas had to be excluded, such as the development implications of urbanization, education, and population control.

There were eight conference panels, each focusing on an important research area. The first—Micro Analysis and Economic Development—was an obvious choice. This was clearly confirmed by the rather heated and all-embracing discussion that it provoked. The issues were those which have been bothering students of economic development since the early stages of this field of study. What are the appropriate micro models? Should noneconomic factors be included, and how? What are the macro implications? These questions arise from the uncomfortable feeling that the analytical tools usually applied by economists have proved to be insufficient for the analysis of the development problems faced by LDCs. To be sure, we have progressed beyond the stage of uncomfortable feelings, and many attempts have been made to improve our analysis, partly by incorporating noneconomic factors. These efforts, such as those pursued by E.E. Hagen, Irma Adelman and her colleagues, and others, are well known to development economists.

In her paper here Adelman makes a further effort in this direction. She presents a tentative hypothesis that goes beyond the widely accepted realization that economic development and modernization involve the transformation of the entire patterning of the social and economic system. She maintains that this transformation leads to or at least "permits the switch in the rules of operation and modes of interaction from risk reduction to surplus maximization."

Her thesis is that in traditional societies risk minimization is a major goal designed to meet their extreme vulnerability to various disasters. In order to reduce the risks, clientele relationships are evolved to provide the kind of insurance which in developed countries is taken over by explicit institutions devoid of kinship and kindred relationships.

Many economists have noted the apparent reluctance of farmers in traditional societies to respond to change in technology and the relative prices of agricultural products. The Adelman hypothesis would ascribe this reluctance to fears of losing the "insurance" arrangement and social status in their traditional societies. Huge returns, however, would compensate for their losses and thus bring forth a "rational" supply response.

Policy conclusions from the above can be reduced to the necessity of providing alternative modes of insurance if the government intends to guide the economy from a traditional structure to one focusing on profit ("surplus") maximization.

The second panel was devoted to the application of Harvey Leibenstein's X-efficiency theory to development analysis. The discussion following the presentation of his paper, "Notes on X-Efficiency and Technical Progress," was long and vigorous, testifying to the topicality of his now famous concept of X-efficiency, especially as it relates to the problem of development.

The focus of the paper is on the choice of technique and the diffusion of technological change. After presenting the essence of his X-efficiency theory, including the notion of inert areas for both groups and firms, he challenges maximization and minimization applications of standard micro theory with its assumptions of an exogenously given state of the art.

His concept of "decisions" follows from the above—the action or inaction which results from the interactions of individuals with differing objectives and constraints. It follows that there is no distinct single-minded entity such as "management," nor a single valued function between labor purchased and the degree of effort that enters into the production process. There are "inert areas" where a move from one position to another (e.g., exerting more effort) would not be undertaken without a clear gain in utility over the cost of the shift in terms of utility. This utility includes such things as the social approval of co-workers, the set of values and ambitions which enters one's incentive system, etc.

The implications include a departure from the usual analysis of technological shifts. Changes in input prices may or may not produce an expected shift in technique, since in an X-efficiency world there are no unique "recipes" of factor proportions and the specific choice or pace of adjustment would be guided by the X-efficiency or X-inefficiency involved.

A major problem for technology borrowing countries is that the "recipes" available to them were developed in capital intensive countries. Partly because of this, techniques which are X-efficient in developed countries often are X-inefficient in LDCs. A shift to a technique that is X-inefficient may cause an industry to be locked-in on that technique which perpetuates technological backwardness.

The chief reservations advanced by Sjaastad are: 1) that LDCs do little research of the R and D kind because they are poor and have given low priority to this activity; 2) that Leibenstein's theory is so general as to be consistent with almost any outcome.

The third panel was designed to show what economic history and economic historians can contribute to our understanding of micro determinants of growth. Ever since Adam Smith, the importance of the "extent of the market" and demand structure has been recognized. However, an analysis of the relationship between demand and patterns of growth has been largely neglected. Albert Fishlow's contribution takes up these issues with the aid of historical data.

The paper begins by sketching the various theoretical issues involved, especially the determinants of demand elasticity. It then proceeds to investigate the differential demand elasticities which can be determined from historical data for the United States, Britain, and France. Comparative demand structures are analyzed, utilizing for the most part micro household data. The implications for the American experience, and the extension of such implications to the current problems of developing countries then follow.

Fishlow pays special attention to the observation that the proportionate expenditure on food by American families has been lower than by British and French families. He utilizes not only aggregate income, but also its distribution, as well as price effects, to explain this pattern. Half of the lesser American expenditure is explained by a combination of higher incomes and an elasticity of demand of less than one. But even at identical levels of income the above American consumption patterns prevailed, in large part due to lower relative food prices.

The concomitant of the above has been higher American expenditures on nonfood items. Moreover, important differences in the rural sector contribute to this consequence. The independent, geographically dispersed, and relatively affluent American farmers (in contrast to the large numbers of tenants and hired workers in Britain and France) did not spend so much on food as their European counterparts. In addition, they were receptive to standardized, low priced, and less durable commodities. This structure of demand sheds light on the process of industrial growth as it relates to consumer goods in the United States in the nineteenth century.

Both an extensive market for manufactures and a continuing supply of foodstuffs have been missing in most LDCs. Fishlow suggests that policies directed toward improvement in both should be pursued. The apparent inconsistency of such analysis and prescription with dual economy models, with their emphasis on reinvested surplus, is largely mitigated by the more effective channeling of resources which a vigorous market demand can evoke.

Williamson's comment highlights the significance of Fishlow's findings to present-day LDCs by focusing attention primarily on the possible effect on demand structure and development of the changing rural-urban distribution of population in the presence of significant variance in commodity price structure (between food and nonfood products).

The fourth panel—Generating Micro Data on LDCs Through Surveys—was designed to shed light on what can and is being done about the problem of unreliable and insufficient data on LDCs. The emphasis on surveys was largely motivated by the realization that a shortage of well-executed surveys is the weakest link in this data problem. Few outsiders realize the tremendous difficulties encountered by anyone engaged in generating data on LDCs. The papers in this panel give the reader the benefit of the experience and analysis of veterans in this field.

The Ferber and Salazar-Carrillo paper builds on the experience derived by the authors from recent surveys conducted across eleven Latin American countries and coordinated under the sponsorship of the Brookings Institution. It provides a general framework for evaluating data collecting problems in LDCs and suggests the most likely errors of means and variances in estimates based on such survey data.

The paper reviews three surveys in urban areas of Latin America: 1) Consumer Expenditure; 2) Price and Purchasing Power Parity; and 3) Industrial Wage and Labor Cost. It finds that numerous types of errors are likely to be encountered in such work and that the probable direction and magnitude of the effects of particular types of errors are not easily generalized. Indeed, the same source and even type of error may produce opposite effects on means and variances, depending on the particular study.

The types of errors likely to be most important in studies of this nature are no different from those to be found in comparable studies in the United States. Namely, sample selection bias, difficulties of interviewer training and supervision, and conscious or unconscious modifications in the data collecting process.

From the standpoint of international comparisons, there is some indication that the nature of these errors tends to be much the same in all countries for a particular study. Hence, the multicountry nature of these studies helps to offset biases encountered in survey work and to make international comparisons more reliable than absolute estimates of means or variances in a particular country.

Eva Mueller begins her paper by presenting the case for empirically tested generalizations, based on scientifically drawn samples of sufficient size, about the experiences and behavior of representative groups of households, producers, and firms in LDCs. With the help of her experience in India and Taiwan, she challenges the common preconception that satisfactory surveys are impossible in LDCs. Between them, the interviewers and the interviewees generate much of the required data. Difficulties arise when questions are based on Western concepts and abstract notions meaningless to the interviewees.

The author then relates the specific problems connected with the collection of data that are of special interest to economists—quantitative micro data on income, saving, consumption, and business operation. The most unreliable of all series is saving. In fact, Mueller maintains that to collect saving data through surveys is not worth the effort given the extremely poor results and the high opportunity costs. She is almost as pessimistic about quantitative data on business operations, a view not necessarily shared by other investigators. In her opinion, the most useful surveys for LDCs are those pertaining to studies of income and asset distribution, to the determination of functional relationships, and to program planning and evaluation. There are still various pitfalls, especially in attempting to quantify functional relationships.

Mueller concludes by expounding the merit of professional survey organizations and medium-sized samples in LDCs in the interest of increased efficiency and reliability. Her paper leaves little doubt about the overriding importance of survey work for the micro analysis of development problems.

Irwin Friend's comment is devoted largely to challenging Mueller's warning against "excessive quantification" from survey data in general, and household saving in particular.

The fifth panel was devoted to the insights of other social scientists into the process of economic development. Some of the issues raised in earlier papers, in particular those of Adelman and Leibenstein, can be better understood by bringing to bear recent research by noneconomists, especially psychologists and sociologists. The matter of entrepreneurial behavior is taken up in Reeve Vanneman's paper. His focus is on the importance of the firm's environment and of social and interpersonal relations in determining entrepreneurial success, both aspects having been neglected in McClelland's famous Need Achievement analysis. Two different types of entrepreneur can be said to have been identified in the early stages of industrial development—(1) the dominant, expansive empire builder, and (2) the rationalizing organization builder. The success of each is dependent on environmental factors affecting the firm. The paper reviews examples of both types of individuals, primarily nineteenth-century American entrepreneurs, to indicate the distinctiveness of the two patterns, botn as to their role in the growth of a firm and their interpersonal styles. The author maintains that within the development of a firm there is usually specialization in one or the other role and this specialization is consistent throughout the entrepreneur's life, which suggests a personality basis for the specialization. The types of behavior examined also correspond closely with two general but orthogonal dimensions of behavior as revealed by small group studies—dominance and task-oriented achievement. Since it is thus unlikely that one personality variable could predict predispositions to these two different patterns, a more contingent model is required.

In his comment on Vanneman's paper Hoselitz wonders, among other things, whether capitalism, and the personality types associated with its development, are not unique to Western Europe and North America. If so, examples taken from these cultures and the associated analysis may be irrelevant to present-day LDCs.

The sixth panel—The Development Role of the Multinational Firm—grew out of the realization that one of the most dynamic forces in the world's economy today is the expanding role of the multinational firm (MNF). International transactions include an increasing volume of transfers of working and investment capital guided by the interests of MNFs, whose operations straddle national boundaries. This fact has important implications both to the host and home countries of these companies.

To students of development, the most interesting aspect of the operations of multinational firms is their impact on the host economy. That impact involves a number of issues, not all of which can be analyzed with standard economic models. The basic argument in favor of MNF operations in LDCs is that they supply certain key factors necessary for the development process—for example, entrepreneurial initiative, technology, capital, and other components of modernizing economies. Different stages of development call for different levels and combinations of imported resources. On the other hand, there are those who would argue that MNFs distort the host economies and retard their long-term growth.

It is difficult to determine the contribution of foreign companies to the host economy. Most governments appear to believe that such potential contribution is substantial enough to warrant the enactment of various incentives and concessions to attract foreign firms. At the same time many countries insist on certain levels of local participation in ownership and/or employment. The responsiveness of MNFs, which are often reluctant to engage in substantial local participation, depends on a variety of considerations, including their bargaining powers.

Louis Wells's paper focuses on an important but seldom analyzed policy question: what happens when the host government insists on local participation in the equity of foreign subsidiaries? After presenting empirical evidence from countries pursuing different policies in this regard, he points to the uncertain conclusions that can be drawn regarding the alternative benefits accruing to the host economy from different policy courses. Data limitations confine his analysis essentially to tabulation of the number of companies responding in certain ways to different policy challenges by the host countries. The uncertainty of the conclusions stems not so much from doubts over the impact of certain policy measures, but from the problem of how to weigh and aggregate the "costs and benefits."

The low tolerance of MNFs for local partners springs from the contradiction that often exists between maximizing the profits of the whole system of subsidiaries as against the profits of a single subsidiary. On the other hand, smaller firms and those experimenting with new products and markets tend to favor local participation.

The notion that a joint venture is always preferable to the host country over a fully-owned subsidiary is not necessarily valid, due to the discriminatory pricing policies and other extra charges (e.g., for know-how, trademarks) which the parent company may impose on joint ventures. The balance-of-payments effect might also be more favorable to a host country with fully-owned rather than joint-venture subsidiaries because of the higher incentive to export connected with the former.

Similar uncertainty prevails concerning contributions to the training of local managers or the gain of the host country in inflow of capital. On the political side, however, joint ventures are more appealing to the nationalist spirit prevailing in many LDCs. In general, the choice will depend on the assumptions and development strategy of the host government. Since these often change, a flexible policy would appear advisable.

Hymer challenges the arguments presented in this panel both on the ground that the evidence presented is inconclusive and because he seems to doubt whether the author is sufficiently committed to the interests of the LDCs. Hymer favors joint ventures over fully-owned subsidiaries, since with access to inside information of the subsidiary firms, the nationals will be in a better position to assess the benefits and costs of the subsidiaries' operations. His doubts about the role played by MNFs lead him to conclude that they are part of the problem, rather than the solution, of underdevelopment.

The seventh panel—Technology and Innovation in Agriculture—deals with the all-important question of technological progress and transfer of innovations. There is no implication that this is more important in agriculture than, say, in manufacturing. But since more research has been done on these questions in agriculture, the panel focused on experience in that field.

The process of agricultural development and its importance in the general development process is only beginning to get the attention it deserves. Specifically, both technical and institutional change in agriculture have been treated as exogenous to most development models. The Hayami-Ruttan (H-R) paper is a pioneering effort to evolve and test an induced innovation model for agriculture. The paper is itself innovative in that the model is applied to the public sector's role in releasing the constraints on agricultural production through research investment, adaptation and diffusion of agricultural technology, and the provision of the supportive institutional infrastructure.

H-R's theoretical base is Ahmed's elaboration of the Hicksian theory relating the direction of induced innovation to changes or differences in the relative prices of factors of production. H-R's extension is the inclusion of research scientists and administrators in public institutions as respondents to the inducement mechanism. The sequence of responses is conceived as follows: Supply limitations raise the relative prices of scarce factors. This induces farmers to seek technical alternatives and press research institutions and agricultural supply firms to come up with such cheaper alternatives. If the latter are perceptive, they provide the farmers with cheaper and increasingly abundant alternative inputs which allow lower unit cost. Moreover, even though part of such scientific innovation is not of an induced character, and unrelated to changes in factor proportions, the rate of adoption of such innovations is strongly influenced by the factor and product markets. Similarly, institutional change, such as changes in land tenure and the socialization of agricultural research, can also be viewed as an effort to internalize the gains and externalize the costs of innovative activity.

The hypothesis that emerges from the above is that adaptation of the agricultural sector to changes in factor-factor and factor-product price ratios involves both movement along a fixed production surface and also innovations leading to a new production surface. As an illustration they cite the following: The increased use of fertilizer resulting from a decline in its price relative to land and farm products is partly contingent on the development of new crop varieties which are responsive to high levels of biological and chemical inputs.

The authors then test their hypothesis with data from Japan, other Asian countries, and the United States. H-R ascribe the considerable difference in rice yields between Japan and the Southeast Asian countries to their being at different positions on the "metaproduction-function" (an envelope of individual response curves, each representing a different variety of the same crop characterized by a different degree of response to fertilizer). The consistent rise in rice yield per hectare in Japan, on the other hand, is interpreted as reflecting movement along the metaproduction function.

The essentially identical relations between fertilizer input per hectare and the fertilizer land price ratio in Japan and the United States is explained, say H-R, by shifts in individual response curves along a common metaproduction function. In short, each country developed its own fertilizer-responsive crop varieties. Further tests with land-labor and power-labor ratios satisfy H-R that, subject to some statistical-methodological reservations, their induced innovation hypothesis is confirmed.

In his comment, Yeung points to some circularity in H-R's argument, since relative factor scarcities may themselves be consequences of technological change. He also takes issue with the appropriateness of the term "metaproduction function," the shape of the curve designed to present it, and the identification problem which may arise due to its definition by the prices of both fertilizer and output. These reservations need not negate the eminent plausability of the market-induced innovation hypothesis.

The eighth panel—Development and Employment—was designed to offer fresh methods for analyzing supply and demand for labor. There is growing concern among economic observers over the increasingly serious problem of unemployment in LDCs, a problem often accompanying economic growth.

The Lau-Yotopoulos (L-Y) paper uses an econometric approach with a household micro-equilibrium model incorporating demand and supply of labor in agriculture as endogenous variables, a model for the agricultural sector as a whole ("partial macro-equilibrium model") where factor prices are also endogenous, and a macro model for a whole economy (with an aggregate demand function for agricultural output).

In the micro model the labor demand function is estimated jointly by what L-Y call the UOP (Unit-Output-Price) profit function, the assumption being that agricultural households maximize their profits, given the level of their fixed (non-labor) inputs. As for the household supply of labor, it is visualized in the context of a block recursive model where the choice between leisure and work is made after the profit minimizing production decisions are taken.

L-Y maintain, however, that this micro model is not directly useful for analysis of many policy issues. For this they need the macro models mentioned earlier. The government may impose agricultural taxes, control farm prices, etc., and the models help compute the results of such policies, especially after the inclusion of a demand function for agricultural products. There is no need in this brief summary to get into a discussion of the specifications of the functions. Testing the models with Indian data revealed some problems which highlight the need for better data and familiarity with institutional arrangements.

Since the L-Y model is a general equilibrium one in the neoclassical tradition, it makes no provision for unemployment. At the same time, it provides a novel approach for analyzing demand and supply of labor.

In the first paragraphs of his paper, Benjamin Higgins voices the growing concern among development specialists and government officials about the high and rising rates of under- and unemployment in LDCs. The problem is aggravated by the large influx into urban areas (where traditional "shared poverty" systems are not operative), the failure of the industrial sector to provide sufficient employment, the very high dependency ratios in LDCs, and the apparent failure of respectable rates of growth of GNP to mitigate the problem.

After presenting the possible reasons for the unemployment crisis, including the irrelevancy of the Keynesian model, Higgins proceeds to examine the possible contribution of microeconomics. Like Irma Adelman, he emphasizes the importance of including noneconomic factors.

He then presents models for a few micro units in the traditional sector with wages, hours of work, and productivity as variables. All the examples end on a note of pessimism regarding employment prospects. In the course of his analysis, Higgins develops the concept of the transitional sector and ends with a three-sector analysis. The conclusion is that for an increase in both welfare and employment to take place there must be a modern sector or modern implantations in the traditional and transitional regions. But doubts remain as to how this can be done.

Nathaniel Leff points out, among other things, that as it turns out, in both approaches macro factors determine employment, while Higgins has not taken into account the determinants and effects of population growth.

As already indicated, the conference could not possibly have covered all important subjects or analytical approaches. Nor was the purpose of the conference exhausted by the subject matter of the panels. The bringing together of scholars with differing experience and approaches for an exchange of views was deemed to be of equal importance. Some of the recurring themes in the conference papers and discussions, especially as these pertain to the applicability of microeconomic theory, are put in perspective by Richard R. Nelson's concluding paper. The volume ends with a summary of exchanges by the participants on the current state of, and desirable directions in, economic development research.

Micro Aspects of Development

CHAPTER

1

SOCIAL AND ECONOMIC DEVELOPMENT AT THE MICRO LEVEL—A TENTATIVE HYPOTHESIS

Irma Adelman

This paper presents a fundamental but tentative hypothesis concerning the relationships between economic and social institutions during the course of economic development and modernization. This hypothesis is suggested by (but not based solidly upon) empirical analyses of village India,[1] and by the anthropological literature on peasantries throughout the world. It is still tentative in that references to empirical phenomena are selective and illustrative, rather than exhaustive, and rigorous tests of the hypothesis have not yet been undertaken.

Empirical analyses of economic development in the agrarian sectors of traditional societies indicate that the early stages of the development process are characterized by an intimate relationship between economic and social modernization.[2] Anthropologists studying primitive and peasant communities have tended to stress two complementary propositions: 1) in traditional societies, virtually all economic transactions are based upon social relationships; 2) in traditional societies, many social transactions have an economic content. These propositions arise because both economic and social institutions in traditional societies have evolved in response to a common objective—the need to guarantee the survival of the society.

The author is indebted to F. L. Adelman for his incisive comments and to George Dalton and Cynthia Taft Morris for many suggestive discussions. The comments of Marvin Frankel, Benjamin Higgins, Vernon Ruttan, Richard Savage, Reeve Vanneman, and Jeffrey Williamson have also been most helpful. The research in this program was supported by a NSF postdoctoral fellowship and by a fellowship at the Center for Advanced Study in the Behavioral Sciences.

More specifically, traditional economic and social organizations and the patterns of interactions among them are so structured as to reduce to a reasonably low value the risk of societal and individual disaster, subject to an adequate income constraint. By contrast, economic institutions in the modern sectors of developed economies are organized to maximize (more or less) the overall social value added, subject to a maximum risk constraint. In capitalist systems, this is accomplished by profit maximization at the micro level; in Communist systems, the maximization of the national surplus is carried out through a system of quotas, allocations, and specialized managerial incentives. In both types of systems, social institutions are organized in such a way that they do not significantly interfere with economic performance. As might be expected, the modern sectors of developing economies are transitional; the more developed the sector, the more surplus- or profit-oriented their economic institutions and the smaller the economic role of social institutions. In short, economic development and modernization involve transformations in the entire patterning of the social and economic system which permit the switch in rules of operation and modes of interaction from risk reduction to surplus maximization.

There are several points of potential confusion which need to be clarified at this point. The thesis advanced relates to the rules of operation and structure of institutions <u>for the system as a whole</u> rather than to the decision rules of individuals within the system. It relates to the institutional economic and sociocultural setting within which individuals or subgroups in the system exercise their choices, rather than to the criterion by which micro-unit decisions are made. A typical individual within the traditional sector can be a profit maximizer or a risk minimizer (indeed, he may even switch decision rules!), provided he does his optimization within the social, cultural, economic, and institutional constraints proposed by the system's mode of operation. Thus the thesis is designed to draw attention to important differences in the setting in which micro behavior occurs in modern and traditional socio-economic systems. It should also be noted that the risk minimization features of traditional societies are designed to protect the individual against the "normal" kinds of adversity as well as to reduce the threat to the survival of the society of the "normal" class of economic and social failures.

The thesis can be stated more forcibly with the aid of some notions relating to group decisions which are borrowed from game theory.[3] Consider a group of people placed in a situation in which they must choose, acting in concert, an act (or a patterning of modes of acting, i.e., institutions) f from a set of available acts F. The acts can relate to choices of technology; to choices of institutions for, say, credit; to the patterning of markets for factors of production or for outputs; to the rules relating economic interactions among different social strata and among different members of the kinship group, etc. For each particular decision the expected payoff to a member of the group can be characterized by a mean value, a variance, and an expected loss. Given the collective choice of f, there exists a conditional expected loss L to individual or subgroup i. This conditional loss can be expressed as

$$L\ (i, f) = \int_{-\infty}^{\infty} P\ (r_i \mid f) \times U\ (r_i)\ dr_i$$

where $P\ (r_i \mid f)$ is the conditional probability of a loss of r for individual (or subgroup) i given the collective choice of f, and $U\ (r_i)$ is the disutility of the loss of r to individual i. Our thesis here asserts that f is chosen in such a manner that the expected loss L(i, f) over all classes of individuals is a minimum for the normal types of choices facing the collectivity and its typical member. More precisely, the thesis states that the choices of f in traditional societies are made in accordance with the group minimax rule. Formally stated, the rule says that decision f' is made if it satisfies the condition

$$L\ (f', i) = \min_{f \in F} \max_{i \in I} L\ (f, i)$$

Since f relates to the choice of social and economic structure, our thesis states that the traditional social and economic systems are organized so as to reduce the conditional expected loss to both the society and its typical member. This can be done either by altering the joint probability density $P\ (r_i, f)$ relating the payoff r_i and the choice of collective decision f, or by altering the probability of f.

The conditions of life among traditional tribes and peasantries are such that the risk of hunger and starvation tends to be exceedingly high. Their use of primitive technology entails great dependence on weather; relative isolation and fragmentation of markets means that trade cannot be relied upon to iron out the fluctuations induced by the effects of local weather, ecology, and other local events; the dependence on one or two staple foodstuffs, which is typical of such societies, makes the economy more vulnerable to calamity; and the almost complete reliance of the society on primary activities (hunting, fishing, herding, and farming) resulting from the limited scope of reasonable alternative means of securing livelihood contributes to the inherently high-risk character of life in the traditional sector. Not only is the absolute level of risk in traditional agrarian systems greater than that with modern agriculture, but risks are also considerably more interdependent. The smallness, isolation, and lack of economic, social, and political integration of traditional villages into the national scene which characterize underdevelopment entail significant local interdependence among economic payoffs to various subgroups.

It would therefore not be surprising to find that the traditional economic and social systems that have survived have been organized so as to reduce the risk to both the individual participants and to the society and economy stemming from the ecological and technological conditions under which traditional communities operate. Part of this risk reduction is accomplished by imbedding measures for the transfer of risk among individuals and subgroups into various economic transactions. This would appear to be a rational economic adaptation to the fact that risks to individual members of traditional systems have significant externalities.

The pattern of transactions in traditional communities is based on the establishment of reciprocal relationships among the participants. For instance, membership in a tribe, clan, or kinship unit establishes a claim by the individual upon communal economic resources, as well as a communal claim upon individual resources. The amounts and types of resource flows in both directions are dependent upon the individual's social role, as well as upon the contingencies he and the community face. Similarly, a transfer of labor among households for harvesting and such practices as the habitual performance of menial services by the low-caste Hindus for the upper-class families to which they are attached, establish claims upon the resources of the other parties to the transaction. The "credits" thus earned have the character of a promissory note, with an unspecified due date and an unspecified face value. The redemption value of the note bears some positive relationship to the needs of the owner of the claim and to the social roles of the participants in the transaction, as well as the value of the services originally performed by the claimant. In other words, an economic transaction in a traditional society has implicit within it the basic elements of a social contract, with payments in both economic and social terms.

What is more important, however, at least for the purposes of the present argument, is that economic transactions (along with the pattern of social roles in the traditional sector) include an insurance feature for which there is no institutional equivalent in the analogous exchange in the market sector. The insurance aspects arise from the relationship of the nature, amount, and timing of the payment to the needs of the payee. In anthropological terms, the insurance is an integral part of the clientship relationship established or maintained through the transaction.

As a result, economic models which describe transactions among micro units in traditional societies in terms of reinsurance markets may be more appropriate than purely competitive models for characterizing micro behavior and for describing "markets" in traditional economies.

The degree of social security that can be provided by such insurance institutions in traditional societies is strikingly demonstrated by the caste structure of village India. By specifying the occupational structure and the economic relationships among castes, the system provides a way of sharing overall poverty, and converts what might be overt unemployment into ritually specified underemployment combined with socially enforced minimum income guarantees. Insurance features of this nature (but not necessarily of this strength) are embedded in the economic and social institutions of virtually all traditional societies. The absence of this type of flexibility in market interactions may help explain why attempts to extend agricultural credit in the traditional sectors of developing countries have not been uniformly successful, and why, despite the availability of modern types of credit, many farmers prefer to pay the higher rates of interest attaching to traditional modes of credit.

Naturally, risk reduction also plays a role in the modern sectors of developed societies. The manner in which this function is performed, however, is radically different. In general, in developed countries, the insurance functions have become differentiated from both the social nexus and from most economic transactions. Instead, these functions have been taken over by a combination of specialized economic institutions designed specifically to sell insurance against various economic risks and by self-insurance through savings against most personal and familial risks. In addition, the polity is assuming more and more collective responsibility for assuring minimum standards of living to all members of society and for protecting most economic groups against the normal risks of the system. As a result, economic institutions have become able to perform more nearly in a profit-maximizing mode. The role of kinship and of the social network is becoming increasingly emasculated, especially for the middle- and upper-income groups.

One condition for the traditional socio-economic insurance system to be stable is that, under constant risk conditions, there be no alternative opportunities which are sufficiently profitable to make self-insurance a reasonable proposition (considering all costs, not only the economic). For such an opportunity would permit significant numbers of households to break away from the system profitably, without sacrificing too much of their security. Further, the threat posed to the stability of the system by individual accumulation makes plain why conspicuous consumption activities (such as religious feasts, lavish family entertainment, burning possessions on death, potlatch) are frequently institutionalized in traditional economic and social modes of organization. Furthermore, stability requires that there be no comparably secure or superior alternative for insurance outside the social and economic structure of the community. Otherwise, if the social and other noneconomic costs are not excessive, there will be an automatic flow of people from the original community to any reasonably attractive competitor.

The threat to the maintenance of the mutual insurance pattern of the socio-economic organization also suggests why relatively severe economic and social sanctions (in particular, noneligibility for future insurance) accompany the manifestation of certain kinds of self-reliant traits, "uppity" behavior, and economic or social transgressions by the individuals in a traditional society. Further, the stability of the system is usually increased by the cultural enforcement of aversion toward risk, by inculcation of the view that life is full of risks beyond the control of individual societies, and by various social and cultural devices (strong kinship ties, religion, etc.) designed to enhance the psychic value of belonging to the system.

A reasonable question to ask at this point is: What is the mechanism of selection of socio-economic modes of operation? Obviously, these choices are not the product of conscious decisions by "the system." Rather, at any point of time, a variety of mechanisms for accomplishing a given function are possible in principle; furthermore, there are often several functions which a new or modified institution can serve. A variety of institutional or organizational modes (e.g., ad hoc organizations, assignment of new functions to old groups, assumption of new roles by old players, new organizational modes) are formed; those that survive in the long run are those which are most nearly consistent with overall goals and constraints of the system. Moreover, in a society whose ethos is well entrenched, certain modes for fulfilling purposes and certain kinds of objectives tend to be ruled out by social innovators on _a priori_ grounds as being inconsistent with the "style" of the society. This process tends to reinforce the results of past "natural selection processes" for those institutions which have survived in the society.

It is also pertinent to note some of the mechanisms of intergenerational transfer of social institutions and values. The major methods appear to be through the processes of education and socialization of the individual. These processes impart an overall knowledge of "the way things are done," the rights and obligations accompanying various kinds of social and economic roles and transactions, which types of goals are "good" and which are "bad," etc. The process of socialization in traditional societies is usually carried out by some combination of kinship units and larger groupings of the society. This process is often supplemented by attempts by the individual (consciously or otherwise) to experiment with alternative ways of accomplishing his own objectives. Those ways which tend to succeed (in the sense of achieving the intended goals) are those which are the most nearly consistent with the overall social structure and culture.

When the system faces a totally new contingency (e.g., major technological change, a new road, contact with a totally different culture, etc.), there may be no generally accepted guidelines within the society. At such a point, the opportunities for significant institutional change are generally increased, as both the stresses and the scope of possible modifications are enhanced. The solutions adopted are, like biological mutations, only sometimes successful.

The test of any hypothesis, of course, is the extent to which it agrees or disagrees with empirical evidence. In the present case, the existing empirical evidence relates generally to the question of whether individual farmers in traditional agriculture maximize profits or use some other decision rule. The question at issue here, however, is whether the society as a whole is risk-minimizing rather than profit-maximizing. Evidence at the micro level cannot validate the present hypothesis, as it appears to be just as consistent for individuals within a risk-minimizing society to profit-maximize within the constraints of the economic and social system as to use a risk-minimizing decision rule themselves. However, if it can be shown that individual micro units do not profit-maximize, it would follow that the society as a system cannot itself maximize profits.

Empirical observations on the economics of traditional agriculture at the micro level in the face of technological change suggest that response to very profitable innovations (such as new wheat strains in India and Pakistan) is qualitatively different from the response to innovations from which the expected rate of return is only moderate. In the former case, where the net rate of return may be as high as 200 percent or 300 percent, there seems to be little concern, among the farmers who adopt the innovations, about the social repercussions for themselves or their families arising from the adoption of the innovation; when the anticipated net rate of return is only 20 percent to 30 percent, on the other hand, the lower-caste and poor farmers tend to wait for sanction from the upper-class and wealthy farmers before they dare even explore the proffered innovation. This difference in response pattern is very consistent with our hypothesis:* the very profitable innovation offers the possibility for self-insurance and thereby enables the household to dispense with the insurance features offered by the social scheme; the less profitable innovation does not promise sufficient return to justify defying the existing social order. Another empirical phenomenon which is consistent with our

---

*It is also consistent with a variety of other hypotheses.

hypothesis* is the phenomenally rapid spread of agricultural innovation schemes in the Ivory Coast, in which the cultivator enters into a "marriage contract"** with an agricultural processing factory. The cultivator agrees to devote a certain acreage to the cultivation of a given crop (e.g., pineapples) and to conform absolutely to planting, tending, weeding, and harvesting procedures and schedules set down by the agricultural extension agents of the processing firm. In return, the processing company provides seed, intermediate inputs, and extension services and agrees to purchase the entire output at a specified price; it thereby removes the entire market risk from the operation.† This scheme has been so successful that there are waiting lists for would-be participants.

Empirical analyses at the micro level, while mixed, lend some support for the position that individual micro units (and *a fortiori* the system as a whole) do not profit-maximize. One recent study[4] of cropping patterns in the Nyere region of Kenya suggests that the farmers there tend to play a minimax game against nature, rather than simply maximizing profits or maximizing some objective function that combines profit maximization with deductions for risk. On the other hand, a number of studies of economic behavior of micro units within the system indicate that these units select combinations of inputs and outputs in a manner consistent with the hypothesis of profit maximization.[5] Because of the apparent inconsistency of these micro analyses, it is not possible on the basis of micro data to rule out profit maximization as the decision criterion for the society as a whole.

At the macro level, the general conclusion has been to the effect that the system as a whole is riddled with a variety of economic, social, and institutional characteristics which are not conducive to overall profit maximization. These features, when identified, are usually considered "irrational" by the visiting experts.

It may be possible to obtain more conclusive information on the degree to which individual micro units profit-maximize or obey other decision rules and thereby to infer whether it is at all possible that traditional agricultural sectors *as systems* do indeed profit-maximize. A fruitful area in which to test this hypothesis is the manner of diffusion of agricultural innovations. A direct proof of the present hypothesis (or of any other hypothesis on the behavior of the society as a whole) is, however, not possible; the most one can hope for is a statement analogous to that of the study of Kenyan farmers cited above,

---

*But also, alas, with many other alternatives.

**This is the term actually used by the Ivorians to describe their relationships to the processing company.

†The risk due to weather is still there, of course.

in which the actions of the individual farmers were found to be more consistent with the minimax rule than with the profit maximization rule. But for the society as a unit, there are two additional complications. One is that a significant number of instances of the pertinent kinds of decisions must be accumulated for an approximately stable system. This means either the collection of significant amounts of historical data for a single society or, perhaps, cross-sectional studies over a range of societies in comparable states of economic and social development. Second, and more important, the kind of evidence that would have a bearing on the nature of the societal decisions is that associated with changes in economic or social institutions, rather than simply evidence on the totality of individual economic decisions by micro units within the system. These latter almost inevitably give the same information that direct micro studies provide. It appears to the author that the only reasonable way to try to test the hypothesis systematically is through the examination of historical data on change of institutions within a single society or, possibly, among a group of comparable societies (but each with a number of instances).

In summary, the purpose of this paper has been to call attention to a hitherto largely neglected feature of traditional agrarian societies, and one which has significant policy implications. Attempts to alter or replace institutions cannot be successful unless they are accompanied by a thorough understanding of the functions performed by the institutions one is trying to supplant. Development policies toward traditional agriculture have been based largely upon the more or less implicit premise that the primary economic function of the traditional system is the maximization of value added per unit of input (land, or labor, or capital). When farmers have failed to respond to presumably technically and economically sound innovations at a "reasonable" speed, they have been labeled traditional, irrational, or ignorant. But perhaps the main reason for this observed reluctance to change lies in the crucial importance (to the individual) of the insurance mechanisms which have been built into the traditional economic, cultural, and social system of which he is a part.

To be effective, a market instrument designed to supplant a nonmarket mechanism must cost enough less or pay enough more to compensate the participants for the loss of the insurance features attaching to the equivalent nonmarket transactions. This point is a direct reflection of the fact that the social insurance held by the individual is itself a valuable asset. A proposed course of action by the individual which reduces his insurability through the social community network requires a larger payoff than would be anticipated were the individual's action-determining calculus based solely on expected value-added considerations. Practical examples are various agricultural innovations whose adoption may offend the village elders, anger the wealthy farmers, or create trouble with the landlords. Another example may well be the general lack of success of population-control measures, which can be explained, under the present hypothesis, as a reaction to the loss of the old-age insurance provided by children (particularly males) in many traditional societies. The insurance character of traditional socio-economic modes may also explain why most recently independent African countries have adopted extensive risk-minimizing legislation (minimum wage laws, social equality management compensation) in their modern sectors surprisingly early (prematurely from a profit-maximizing point of view).*

Clearly, the insurance features of the social system need to be taken into account in the design of credit schemes, in the design of alternative institutions to market the input and output, and, indeed, in connection with all kinds of economic innovations in traditional economic sectors. It should also be recognized that, in the traditional milieu, a modern institution, such as a credit cooperative, may change its mode of operation so as to conform better with the overall systemic goals. For example, credit cooperatives may, when viewed with a Western eye, be judged to be inefficient to the extent that they do not enforce repayment schedules, are flexible about collection practices, and appear to be predicated upon the assumption that a loan, once made, will never be completely repaid. What the "inefficient" credit cooperative has attempted to do is to operate in the manner of a traditional institution—a perfectly plausible and quite probable social outcome.

The policy implications of this paper, then, call for devising market instruments that are more nearly akin in significant ways to the nonmarket instruments they are designed to replace. In particular, the considerations advanced suggest the great need to add insurance features to the market-based policy levers and institutions used to induce the modernization of agriculture. These are necessary not only in order to compensate individuals for the inherent risk which attaches to any kind of innovation, but also in order to compensate them for the loss of the insurance that they may forfeit by departing from the old ways. The provision of old-age insurance may well be considered in connection with future population control programs as well.

The present paper also has significant implications for a theory of economic development. It views economic development as a process of transition from a state in which socio-economic institutions are designed predominantly for risk minimization to one in which economic

---

*This observation, too, is subject to more than one interpretation.

institutions are designed mostly for profit maximization. During this transition, the insurance functions become differentiated from their socio-economic context; specialized economic and politico-legal structures for risk reduction are built up.

The transition among states is accomplished through several mechanisms: (1) the integration through commercialization of small isolated communities into the national markets and the buildup of national economic institutions to perform functions previously performed only locally (e.g., to provide credit), thus reducing interdependence, at the local level, among various economic risks, and spreading risk among more units operating under more diversified conditions; (2) the adoption of productivity-increasing innovations permitting the accumulation of surpluses and hence enabling individuals to rely to a greater extent on self-insurance; (3) the introduction of technology designed to reduce risk; (4) the creation of physical and socio-cultural linkages to decrease local risk by enabling adjustments to local calamities through temporary or permanent migration; (5) the spread of education to lower risk by enabling individuals to perform more diversified economic functions and by decreasing the probability of misapplications of technology (it also increases productivity and readiness to adopt innovations, thereby promoting self-insurance); (6) the emergence of specialized economic institutions designed to reduce risk (e.g., labor unions, trade associations, holding companies); (7) the emergence of specialised economic institutions designed to provide insurance (e.g., insurance companies, pension funds); (8) the emergence of specialized politico-legal institutions designed to protect the security of various economic groups and to reduce the risks attendant upon various types of economic activity (minimum wage laws, antitrust legislation, minimum welfare and income guarantees).

Most of the mechanisms enumerated above have long been recognized as important for economic development. However, their significance for permitting a switch in the mode of operation of economic and social institutions has tended to be ignored by economists.

* * *

COMMENT BY MARVIN FRANKEL

The central hypothesis advanced by Irma Adelman, narrowly stated, is that traditional societies tend to be risk-minimizing, subject to an income constraint, while modern societies tend to be profit-maximizing, subject to a risk constraint. In its broader version, the argument recognizes and emphasizes the role played by various security-oriented institutions in traditional societies and the need, if innovation is to be successful, to discover substitutes for the insurance features which these institutions provide. It is an argument with considerable appeal, being consistent with much that has been observed, and offering a plausible, if partial, explanation of the apparent differential response to economic opportunity of traditional and modern societies. It has the further virtue of drawing our attention to elements in the development problem that may be strategic for policy purposes.

Adelman emphasizes that her thesis relates to "the rules of operation and structure of institutions for the system as a whole" rather than to the decision rules of households and firms. This macro oriented thesis presumably carries implications for the behavior of the micro units and, accordingly, must be susceptible of interpretation at the micro level. That is, it should be possible to specify how the insurance features embedded in the socio-economic structure affect the actions of the micro units and cause them to differ from what they otherwise would be.

There are two possible interpretations. One centers on the attitudes of firms (and households) toward risk and the other on the way firms perceive economic opportunities. Consider first attitudes toward risk. The dichotomy inherent in Adelman's view of the one society as risk-minimizing and the other as profit-maximizing is probably too severe. These two objectives are sought by economic units in both traditional and modern societies, though presumably to differing degrees. Some units in a traditional society may seek profit aggressively, though the preponderant emphasis will be on security. In a modern society the reverse will be true. The "typical" firm in each society will recognize the trade-off possibilities between risk and profit, but the relative worths of these objectives, and hence the rates at which they will be substituted for one another, will differ.

Some aspects of the situation are illustrated in Figure 1.1. The segmented line connects a series of investment opportunity points, with each point characterized by an expected return (the abscissa) and by a risk or security measure (the ordinate). Instead of defining the latter by some familiar measure of dispersion, let us, in deference to the notion that firms are maximiners, define it as the (subjective) probability that the return will equal or exceed some threshold amount, as designated by the point z on the abscissa. Along with the investment opportunity frontier, two sets of indifference curves, one for the traditional and one for the modern society, are shown. In the traditional society the typical firm would choose point A on its investment

FIGURE 1.1

Expected Return Versus Risk

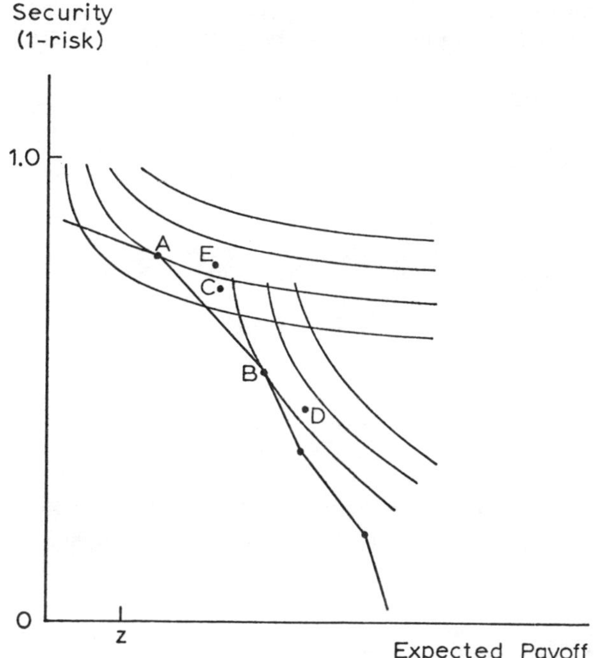

opportunity frontier, while its counterpart in the modern society would choose point B.*

The traditional firm's indifference curves are comparatively risk sensitive. Unlike the modern firm, it will resist opportunities that promise substantial gain in expected profit if they carry with them more than small increases in risk. Thus it would not respond to the opportunity at point C. Though C carries a substantially larger expected payoff than A, its slightly greater risk causes it to fall on a lower indifference curve. By contrast the modern firm would prefer point D to point B, indicating its readier acceptance of risk in exchange for expected profit.

---

*A single frontier is shown for convenience. Obviously the two societies do not share the same set of investment opportunities.

Note, however, that these responses relate to typical firms and reflect predominant tendencies. Every society is a mixed bag, and in the traditional society there will be some firms, whether because of their asset positions, managements, or otherwise, with outlooks more tolerant to risk. One would expect therefore that opportunities eschewed by most would nonetheless be pursued by a few. These few, if successful, would have shown the way, thereby reducing the risk for—and thus encouraging—emulators. Incidentally, the reduction in risk for followers in a follow-the-leader game provides an alternative (or complementary) explanation to that offered by Adelman of the behavior of lower-caste and poor farmers when faced with opportunities promising only modest gain (20 percent to 30 percent). She attributes their sluggish and reluctant response to a tendency "to wait for sanction from the upper-class and wealthy farmers before they dare even explore the proffered innovation."

Eventually, with modernization and an increasingly secure environment, we might expect changes in the shape of the traditional firm's indifference curves, toward a shape showing greater tolerance for risk. Other things being equal, the firm would then be led from point A to a position in the vicinity of point B.

Consider next the micro interpretation of Adelman's thesis on the firm's perception of economic opportunities. Suppose that certain socio-economic arrangements cause some opportunities to appear riskier to the firm than they would under different institutional conditions—perhaps, for example, because of awareness that their exploitation would disrupt family or social bonds. These opportunities, which otherwise might win a favorable response, may then be pushed outside the bounds of acceptability or may even fail to be recognized and seriously reviewed. In terms of Figure 1, using the indifference curves as originally drawn for the underdeveloped economy, an opportunity, otherwise the equivalent of point E, which is marginally superior to A, may be perceived as point C, which is marginally inferior to it. Or it may be perceived as like point D and unworthy of attention. In either case, note that it is not the shape of the indifference curves that is important but rather the way opportunities are seen in relation to them.

If the traditional firm's indifference curves are of a risk-averting shape, and/or if conditions cause it to attach additional risk to some opportunities, then policy must be directed to these circumstances. If the firm's attitude is especially negative toward outcomes at the lower end of the returns scale—if it is a maximizer, as our definition of risk implies—then policies intended to insure that the worst outcome will not fall much below the return currently enjoyed are apt to be especially useful. Among eligible types of policies are the following:

1. Crop insurance, perhaps with a deductible provision; relatedly loss-sharing arrangements;

2. Guaranteed markets, perhaps with the unit price scaled inversely with volume;

3. The establishment and support of demonstration farms and exemplar firms that lead the way and demonstrate success;

4. Supporting measures that get directly at one or more types of uncertainty, as through steps to assure reliable supplies of labor and intermediate inputs or extension services to provide strategic information and management know-how.

Subsidies at a given rate per unit of output, or exemptions from income or producers' taxes, will affect the perception of opportunities favorably but are likely to be less useful in dealing with risk-averting attitudes. Note that whatever the policy, it will generally need to be maintained only for a transition period, until the new method or other innovation has been established.

Adelman gives some instructive examples of ways in which insurance-like features become built into traditional societies, and she notes that this may explain why farmers seem sometimes to prefer familiar, though high cost, sources of credit to ostensibly lower cost sources. A fine illustration of this phenomenon, albeit in a commercial rather than an agricultural setting, is provided by Clifford Geertz in his study of Modjokuto, an Indonesian town. There exists in the bazaar-based commercial life of the town a complex, ramified network of credit balances that bind large and small traders together.

> These credit balances are only half-understood if they are seen only as ways in which capital is made available, for they set up and stabilize more or less persisting commercial relationships. If this element is taken into account, the seemingly anomalous fact that traders often prefer expensive private credit to cheap government credit becomes clearer. Private credit gives them more than simple access to capital; it secures their position in the flow of trade.[6]

In such a setting, given the objectives of larger scale and lower costs and prices, it is no mean challenge to devise policy substitutes for the insurance protection that the credit structure affords.

CHAPTER

2

NOTES ON X-EFFICIENCY AND TECHNICAL PROGRESS

Harvey Leibenstein

SOME REASONS FOR THE X-EFFICIENCY APPROACH TO GROWTH

Technical progress is unevenly distributed among the countries of the world. There is a sense in which different countries may be said to be located at different points in technological space. This allows less developed countries to borrow techniques from more developed ones. In addition, the "technological distance" between countries may create special problems for the diffusion of techniques from advanced to less developed countries. These matters will here be examined in relation to the concept of X-efficiency developed elsewhere by the author.

These notes are based on the belief that the conventional textbook microeconomic theory offers inadequate scope for some factors frequently believed to contribute significantly to economic growth. An important aspect not well treated within the theory is the increase in technological information and the diffusion of such information, as well as the sequence of adoption of new techniques and the reasons for the lack of adoption of such techniques. Perhaps of greater importance is that the standard theory does not handle changes in knowledge as events determined within the system. In the static version of the theory the state of the arts is presumed to exist. Firms choose on the basis of some maximizing assumption from a given spectrum of techniques presumed to be equally available to all. However, changes in the state of the arts are either presumed to

---

Research for this paper was financed by the National Science Foundation.

occur as an exogenously determined event or, in more recent theories, to be a function of the rate of capital accumulation. A broader theory should enable us to incorporate such phenomena in a more natural way.

An attempt will here be made to outline an X-efficiency theory of the firm and to consider briefly the application of this theory to some aspects of choice of technique and to the diffusion of technological change. Though some aspects of these problems have already been treated, in part, elsewhere, it may be advisable to restate some of the elements already published.[1] While the theory as such is not necessarily limited to the problems of developing countries, I do have such countries in mind in considering its applications to the diffusion of technical progress and the transmission of technological knowledge. In general, it can be stated that innovations do not take place in a developing country but that technology is borrowed from a technologically more advanced country. The process of innovation depends frequently on the numerous small decisions made by a great many individuals, often outside the group of supposed top decisionmakers in the larger firms.

The entrepreneurial role plays no part in existing microeconomic theory. This is because the nature of inputs is presumed to be given. Once we are in the presence of a specific production function, a set of prices for inputs, and an objective for the firm, the activities of the firm are entirely determined. Inputs as such do not have to be "managed" in any way. With input-output relations and prices given, there is almost nothing for entrepreneurs, as this term is generally understood, to do. Nor does the firm have to be alive to changes in technological knowledge, since this is already provided for by the other determinants within the system. Entrepreneurship will not be emphasized in this paper, but the theory here presented does give more play to this input.

While the increase and diffusion of technological information will not be examined in detail, we should keep in mind the fact that unused knowledge atrophies. Thus, the greater the degree to which new techniques are diffused in an economy, the greater the extent to which technical information and scientific knowledge may be presumed to persist and to have their existence supported. In other words, part of the interest in the process of diffusion of specific techniques is based on the presumption that any meaningful growth of knowledge in a country depends to a considerable degree on the extent of its use.

X-EFFICIENCY AND OUTPUT

Output does not depend on the number of man-hours combined with a given quantity of capital, but on the nature and degree of effort of the man-hours. While this assertion may seem obvious, quality-effort units are not usually employed as variables in the analysis of technological change.

The basic assumptions on which the X-efficiency theory rests are as follows: 1) labor contracts are vague and incomplete; 2) detailed supervision of labor is impractical and has been shown to be insufficient. Hence, there are many areas of choice within the work context, and there is no single valued function between labor purchased and the degree and nature of effort that enters the production process. This last is especially true of supervisory and management employees, but I suggest that it is true of all employees. The choices made by anyone attached to a firm (in any capacity) are unlikely to be the ones that maximize output for input units purchased. The result is that some degree of X-inefficiency almost always exists.

A development of this idea is shown in Figure 2.1. Curves A_1 to A_3 are indifference curves that reflect the tastes of an individual between two production activities α and β. Lines P_1 to P_3 are given pace of effort "budget lines" and indicate the combination of units of activity in α and β for a given pace of effort. Q_1 to Q_3 are the isoquants of value added to output. The locus OA of tangencies A_iP_i indicates the optimum activity distribution for different pace levels for an individual. The locus MQ of tangencies P_iQ_i indicates the activity bundles for different pace levels which maximize value added to the firm. The taste-for-activities locus and the maximum output locus are clearly not the same. What the individual wants to do does not lead to maximum output.*

It is likely that for many individuals who in one way or another become attached to a firm there are some minimum performance levels

---

*The activity indifference curves $A_1 \ldots A_3$ are drawn so as to reflect a preference for less pace rather than more, and the existence of a trade-off between a worse distribution of activities and a lower pace. It is to be noted, however, that for indifference curves close to the origin a greater pace may be preferred to a lesser one, and in that area of the chart the curves would be concave to the origin.

We ignore in the present paper the relation between pace and leisure, a complex problem which cannot be handled in the space alloted. However, it is to be noted that a low pace on the job is not the same as, or a substitute for, leisure in terms of time away from the job. Nor is utility a simple function of pace. For cooperating individuals, utility in the aggregate may not decline if pace is increased, since within some range individuals may be primarily concerned that their pace be equal rather than whether it is somewhat slower or faster.

explicitly or implicitly agreed upon; violators will believe themselves subject to some sort of discipline. In some cases this may mean being fired. Of course, there may be considerable vagueness in the implicit or even explicit agreements about minimum "required" performance levels. In Figure 2.1 the levels α^* and β^* are the minimum performance levels. The curve $\overline{\alpha_i}\,\overline{\beta_i}$ represents the maximum performance locus. Beyond the point $\alpha^*\ \beta^*$ and the locus $\overline{\alpha_i}\,\overline{\beta_i}$ there is an area (and it is frequently large) in which performance variation is allowed and in which choice takes place.

In Figure 2.2 the curve U(OA) indicates the utility-effort relation for the individual who operates on the locus OA. (The utility includes the utility of income.)* On OA every value of β is associated with a given α. (For simplicity we assume the ratio of α to β is constant for all points on OA.) The curve U(MQ) indicates the utility-effort relation for the individual if he were operating on the quantity maximizing locus MQ. For many points on U(OA), e.g., the point X_1, if there is a utility cost for shifting from one effort position to another, then the points in that set of effort points within the cost boundaries will be stable. The same will hold for points below the locus U(OA). Hence there are many activity bundles which do not maximize utility and which if they existed would persist. Also, under these circumstances, there is no reason for the effort point actually made to maximize output.

Similarly, the above will hold for the collection of individuals who make up the firm. Many nonoptimizing effort points will exist which are stable to some degree if we take into account the utility cost of a shift for both management and labor.

A logical complement to the notion of X-efficiency is a somewhat different conception of a production function. One can visualize a production function as a set of "recipes." Each recipe indicates most of the essential elements that enter into the production of the output, but like a real recipe, or a real blueprint, it does not truly indicate all of them. A given recipe may be carried out slowly or quickly or with careful or sloppy workmanship. (After all, different cooks will turn out meals of different quality on the basis of the same recipe.) Since a recipe may involve various amounts of labor in units of time, it would now be illustrated by a segment rather than a point on an isoquant map.

---

*It is easier to state and develop the theory on the basis that all employees are paid in terms of time. While some features change if we assume that some individuals are paid on a piece-rate system, the essentials of the model do not change. However, this assertion cannot be developed further here. See the author's paper in the Quarterly Journal of Economics (November 1969.)

FIGURE 2.1

Performance Variation and Choice

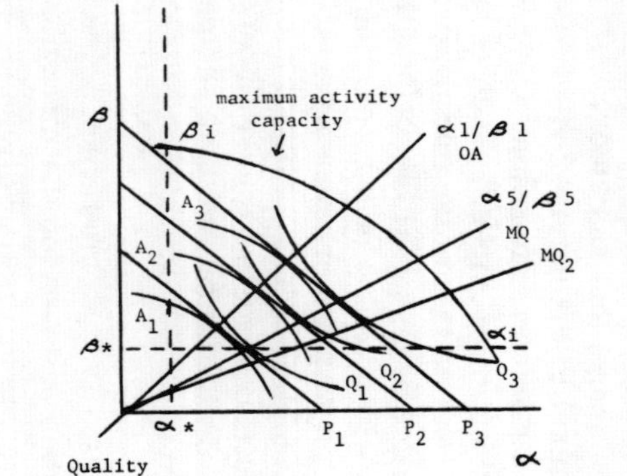

FIGURE 2.2

Utility-Effort Relation and the Inert Area

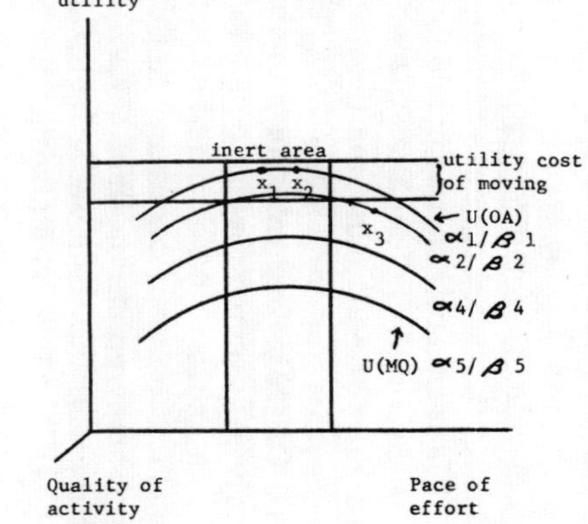

$\alpha\beta$ are activities from which indiv. choice is made
$\alpha^*\beta^*$ are min. activity levels in employment contract
P_1P_2 are constant pace of effort levels
A_1A_2 are indiv. indifference curves for activities
Q_1Q_2 are value added to product isoquants
OA is locus of indiv. opt. activity bundles
MQ is locus of firms max. value added activity bundles

For a given quality per activity each point in Fig. 1 ⟶ Fig. 2
Move from x_1 to x_2 leads to no change
Move from x_1 to x_3 leads to return to some point in <u>inert</u> area

The critical element in the theory just outlined leads to the related concept of inert areas. For the individual, the fact that there is a utility cost in a shift from one postition to another (see figure 2.2) implies that there is an area within the utility cost bounds which will not induce any change of position. It seems natural to refer to this area as an inert decision area. Briefly, opportunities for change which do not lead to a gain in utility (or an evident loss of utility) greater than the cost of the shift in utility will not be entertained seriously. The inert area idea could be transferred from one individual to a number of individuals where firm decisions depend on the initiative or approval of such a number of individuals. Inert areas can be said to exist for all individuals attached to a firm. If several individuals' activities are interconnected, such as is the case where there is a continuous flow of work, then the choices made must somehow be reconciled with the given interconnections between their work. Individuals cannot simply maximize their utilities in the choice of activity bundles without taking heed of the extent to which they might interfere with choices made by others, setting in motion the existing approval, disapproval, and social sanction mechanisms. If all individuals in a tightly interconnected work situation simply maximize the utilities in the choice of their activities, then all of their time might be spent in conflict rather than in productive performance. The inert areas avoid some of the more debilitating conflicts that might arise.

Thus, every individual chooses a set of activities, a pace of effort, and a set of quality levels at which activities are performed which maximize his utility, subject to the constraints imposed by his choices in relation to the disutility of interfering with other people's choices, as well as the disutility of moving from one position to another.

The fact is that individuals who become attached to firms (as employees, part owners, etc.) bring with them potential productive capacities and a set of direct and indirect incentive influences. That is, each person brings with him a set of desires and attitudes about the activities of others around him which, when combined with the attitudes of these others, determines the approval and disapproval atmosphere within the firm, and the nature of possible sanctions toward some types of behavior. The informal approval and sanction system, plus many of the activity choices made in official and unofficial capacities that suggest the system of financial and other payoffs to individuals under various circumstances, together determine the incentive system that exists in the firm. It is the basic fact that human inputs bring with them their incentive influence capacities, whether or not these capacities are wanted by the firm in any sense, that distinguishes human inputs from other inputs.

We shall ignore for the most part the interesting problem of whether increasing the number of individuals increases the inert areas of the component individuals or decreases them. In general, one might expect that this would depend on the nature of their relationships. Individuals sensitive to other individuals' tastes, and keen on achieving cooperation, would have inert areas that are larger than the independent inert areas involved. The existence of "boat rockers" may possibly reduce some of these areas. We should expect that in cases where the number of individuals involved in a decision is larger rather than smaller, the inert area would likewise be larger.

The concept of inert areas for the group allows one to see the firm itself as having inert areas within its decisionmaking process. That is to say, data may exist reflecting opportunities for change which lie within the inert areas of individual decisionmakers, and hence such data should also be viewed as within the inert areas of the firm as such. If firm decisions are made on the basis of a single variable—for example, profits—then we might view the matter of inert areas as being resolved into upper and lower decision bounds, within which opportunities for change do not result in any action. We shall refer to these bounds as the upper pull bound and the lower push bound.

While we assume the existence of some group responsible for making decisions for the firm, there may be others without official responsibility that influence decisions in a variety of ways. It is the activity of this augmented activity group, and the utilities they attach to gains and losses from such decisions, that will determine the nature of the decisions that actually take place.

It is to be noted that above and below the inert area bounds nothing is explicitly assumed (from the outside as it were) about the presumed objectives of the decisionmaking group. In other words, no assumptions are made about maximizing profits or sales revenues or any combination of such objectives. For the yes or no type of decision, no such presumed objective need be implied. For other types of problems, however, some types of objectives may be necessary, but in general one need not suppose that all firms pursue the same objectives beyond the inert areas.

To summarize briefly the basic elements of the X-efficiency theory of the firm: 1) It is assumed that there is no symmetry between human and nonhuman inputs, in the sense that all human inputs make performance choices. 2) Minimum levels of performance in some employment contexts exist, but beyond such minimum performance levels a frequently significant area of choice exists. 3) Each individual is assumed to choose an activity-pace-quality of activity bundle subject to the serious constraints of: a) the utility cost of not interfering with the choice of others; b) the utility cost of moving from one activity-pace position to another. 4) The consequence of the utility costs of moving implies that all individuals possess inert areas within which opportunities for utility gains will not result in any action. 5) Those who attach themselves to firms bring with them not only productive capacities, but also direct and indirect incentive influence characteristics which determine: a) degrees of approval and disapproval of others' choices; b) standards of rewards, promotions, career paths, etc.; c) attitudes toward authority; d) the appropriateness of possible disciplinary measures; e) the capacity to influence other people's standards of behavior and to be influenced by the standards of behavior of others. To a considerable degree these largely nonperformance characteristics determine the incentive mechanism and atmosphere within the firm. 6) Not all inputs used are purchased or purchasable—for example, the incentive system. 7) There is no externally determined objective for all firms that is assumed to exist even beyond the bounds of the inert areas. As a result, costs are not minimized, and profits are not maximized, within this model.

X-EFFICIENCY VERSUS "TECHNICAL EFFICIENCY"

X-efficiency, as I conceive it, is different from and broader in nature than what has been called "technical efficiency" or "productive efficiency" in the limited literature that exists in this area.[2] Technical efficiency implies that in some sense a factor called "management" maximizes the output from a given combination of inputs. The difference between maximum output and actual output is viewed as technical inefficiency. There are four points to be noted: 1) the phenomenon takes place entirely within the firm; 2) human inputs are treated symmetrically with other inputs; 3) all inputs are purchased; 4) there is a sense in which the firm has a clear-cut objective which it pursues by "management." I would deny the validity of all these assumptions. In the X-efficiency view, the firm does not *decide* to be technically efficient or not. Firm decisions are not made by some entity for the firm as though it were a person with a well-defined objective. Rather, "decisions" are seen as the result of a process of interaction among a variety of individuals who have objectives and feel constraints that differ from each other, but it is through such interactions that decisions are made when, and if, they are made at all. This last phrase is important since this view of the firm allows for a great number of potential decisions, probably the majority, to be "made" by *inaction*. For a variety of reasons, firms, as well as other organizations, do not take note of changes in data most of the time and hence do not make any decisions in accordance with such changes. In addition, the decisionmakers within the firm, whatever they may be called, are not necessarily a unique and unified group, and they are not inputs in the sense of being symmetrical with other inputs. To a considerable extent, they are individuals who, while carrying out other specified functions, participate in one way or another in the decisionmaking process. In fact, many such individuals may not be explicitly charged with this function, nor are they hired for this purpose. This includes individuals who frequently obstruct the adoption of new modes of behavior or new techniques, as well as those who take the initiative in such adoption. Thus, in an important sense, the "input" that makes decisions is not completely hired in the marketplace.

Finally, many of the elements that influence what I call X-efficiency do not manifest themselves in decisions taken entirely or even especially within the firm. They may be a consequence of interaction between firms,* or the interaction between firms and noneconomic units such as the family or the educational system.

The idea of the maximum output** from a given combination of inputs begs the basic question as to what it is that is different about human beings as production inputs. Individuals can be hired. But the inputs that enter production are not given. The critical units that enter production are the directed efforts of the individuals involved. These efforts are the activity-quality-pace-time bundles that determine output, but they are not viewed in this theory to be determined fully by "management," but are instead the result of the incentive system created by the interacting decisionmaking members of the firm, and in part are determined by forces outside the individual firm.

Interactions between firms are likely to influence a great many variables having to do with specific effort levels: responsiveness

---

*Such as the disciplinary effects of a high degree of competitive pressure. At present I consider it an open question whether competitive pressure can be sufficiently strong so as to eliminate all inert areas.

**The basic assumption of the standard theory is that there is an output frontier which involves maximizing output from given inputs. The view taken here is that such a frontier does not exist. There may, however, be a boundary of the following kind. There are unquestionably bounds which involve outputs above and beyond what we may ever expect to result from the inputs purchased. We can visualize that some minimal external bound may exist. An approximation to such a fictional minimal external bound may set a limit from which we may want to measure the degree of efficiency. However, for many instances it may be sufficient to measure relative degrees of X-efficiency without keeping in mind such a minimal external bound.

to incentives, types of personnel selection, patterns of authority, communication, communication breakdowns, repairs in employee relationships, degrees of inertia, etc. In part such interactions may be imitative, or influential in various ways in determining certain interfirm standards of behavior. Or they may be competitive.

The interaction between firms and such social units as the family, schools, governmental units, or social clubs, are also likely to be important—especially the nurture system (family, education, etc.) that determines the behavioral patterns of the individuals fed into the labor force. For example, diet patterns, the time pattern of meals and sleeping periods, physical stamina, and effort levels are likely to be related to each other, and to influence effort levels. In addition, the quality of the people who apply for different types of jobs, their attitudes toward risk, responsibility, novelty, career patterns, and the introduction of innovations, will all determine behavior patterns in and between firms.

In general, the view taken here is to see the firm as a group of interacting individuals of different degrees of importance in the variety of decisions that many of them help to make. This view differs from the one in which it is assumed that there is a distinct entity called "management," or "entrepreneurship," or something unspecified, which acts as though it were a single individual with a clearly specified firm objective that is able to control other people's decisions and actions in conformity with that objective. Thus no one can be said to be fully in charge or fully in control of the actions of the firm, though some individuals may be held accountable for the results of its activities. Such a view requires a broader and somewhat different set of questions about the nature of efficiency from the one implied by the words "technical efficiency."

X-EFFICIENCY AND TECHNOLOGICAL SHIFTS

X-efficiency can be seen from the standpoint of a given technique or recipe without consideration of other possible recipes. In such a case, we may conceive the degree of X-efficiency as the ratio of actual output to the minimal external bound output.

But where switches in technique are concerned, one may distinguish two types of X-efficiency: the first, transitional X-inefficiency; the second, the comparative degree of X-inefficiency. By transitional X-inefficiency we mean the degree of inefficiency which occurs as the consequence of a technical switch but is temporary in nature. By switch X-inefficiency we mean the ratio of the degree of X-inefficiency prior to the switch compared to what it is afterwards, inclusive of some allocation of the transition costs involved.

Two factors may account for transitional X-inefficiency: (1) individuals may be committed to traditional work habits or a traditional work code, and as a result resist work arrangements appropriate for the new technique; (2) if the new technique is expected to decrease employment opportunities for some people, then individuals assigned to it may attempt to use work-spreading tactics.

There are a great many reasons why the degree of X-efficiency should change when there is a change from technique T_1 to T_2, but for our purposes it is not necessary to cover all possibilities. The following might be mentioned: (1) Tastes for different activities may be further from the activity mix that maximizes output under T_2 than under T_1. This possibility is illustrated in Figure 2.1 where MQ is the output maximizing locus under T_1 and MQ_2 is the output maximizing locus under T_2. We would normally expect the distance between OA and MQ to differ for different techniques. (2) The degree of coordination and factory discipline required may be greater for the new technique than for the old. (3) The existing technique may be carried out fairly efficiently, but in a highly rigid manner, which may be detrimental to the synchronization of activities required under the new technique. (4) The system of personnel selection appropriate for $T1$ may not be suitable for $T2$. (5) The balance of fears and hopes existing in a certain job situation may change when the technique changes, and as a consequence the morale aspects of the work situation may change accordingly. (6) There may be a trade-off between effort and the increase in potential output under T_2 as compared to T_1. If the output standard per person remains constant, then the entire increased productive potential could be taken in less effort. On the other hand, the change to the new technique may suggest a share in the potential rewards of rising productivity and result in a higher effort level than would otherwise be the case. (7) The new technique may require a scale of operations different from the old one, but the skill mix available in the work force may be more appropriate to the smaller scale than to the larger. In general, there is little that can be said as to whether the new technique will be more or less X-efficient than the old one without examining the initial conditions in detail. There are a great many considerations that suggest the possibility that X-efficiency will change with a change in technique.

Figure 2.3 illustrates a shift from technique T_1 shown in the figure, to technique T_2. We assume that the budget line marked W_2 is consistent with the wage level that would make it worthwhile to shift to T_2. Let us now examine the X-inefficient switch possibility indicated in the figure as T_2'. The budget line tangent at this point will imply a lower wage level. This means that it is less likely for the shift in technique to take place if the wage level were lower than would be the case if the shift were to T_2, under which X-inefficiency does not decrease.* Similarly, at the other extreme, the point T''_2 implies an X-efficient shift and is associated with a potentially higher wage level. In this case, the shift would be worthwhile, not only at the existing wage level W_2, but even if the wage level rose.

A point on an isoquant no longer represents a technique, in the sense of a given recipe. Since any recipe can be related to varying quantities of labor to produce a certain output, a given technique is represented by <u>at least</u> a line segment. If techniques are continuous, the segments are continuous, and the isoquant is no longer a line but an area of varying degrees of thickness. There is significance, however, in an isoquant of the usual kind where a single point represents a technique, if we allow every point to represent the same degree of X-efficiency. A shift involving an increase in X-efficiency means a movement to a lower "equi-X-efficient" isoquant, and vice versa. Thus, for a given rate of wage increase, a firm will move more rapidly to more capital intensive techniques the greater the degree of X-efficiency associated with such techniques. Indeed, when there are discontinuities in technique, we may expect slow changes if the move is X-inefficient, and more rapid ones if technique switches are X-efficient.

In the simplified case here considered, every technique (or "recipe") is associated with a unique amount of capital but a variable quantity of labor.** Hence, every technique is represented by a line segment parallel to the labor axis. We shall not here consider the more likely situation in which somewhat variable amounts of capital may also be associated with a given recipe. It seems reasonable to presume that a given recipe need not specify the amount of capital with complete precision. Wastefulness in the use of capital is certainly possible and likely. Under such circumstances each recipe then becomes a sausage-shaped area in a two-dimensional diagram. The integral of such overlapping areas will then become a given isoquant. For present purposes we will ignore the implications of this version of the production function.

---

*Since minimization of costs is not assumed, we cannot rule out a taste for novelty on the part of decisionmakers and the adoption of T_2 despite the fact that it is X-inefficient and causes costs per unit to rise.

**The band Q'Q" should not be taken as the result of a stochastic process. In other words, the band in which labor requirements vary does not depend on some given probability distribution. Rather, the points depend on the overall internal incentive system and the nature of the inert areas determining the degrees of X-efficiency or X-inefficiency that will exist for a given technique.

FIGURE 2.3

X-Efficient and X-Inefficient Switches in Techniques

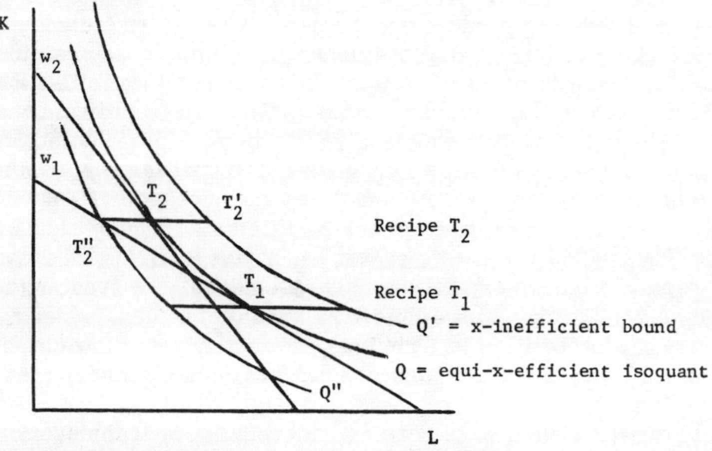

In general, an increase in X-efficiency operates in a way similar to learning by doing.[3] Furthermore, switches could be X-inefficient while there is no negative "learning by doing." Hence, a firm contemplating a shift in technique must take into account not only the change in the relative prices of inputs but also the degree to which the change will be X-efficient or X-inefficient. For instance, in Figure 2.3 the change illustrated by the new wage rate W_2 would not be worthwhile if the switch in technique was X-inefficient.

As in learning by doing, changes in X-efficiency may involve externalities. An innovation may pay even though it is X-inefficient, but if these X-inefficiencies spread to other firms because of the new but more slack standards of work in the innovating firm, then the social cost of the innovation will be greater than its direct private cost, and the innovation may not pay from a social viewpoint though it may appear to do so from a private one. Or, the introduction of an X-efficient technical change in some firms may raise the quality-effort standard and make efficient labor available to other firms. The policy implications of such an effect is that governments should encourage (subsidize) those technological changes which exhibit X-efficient external benefits and tax those whose externalities are X-inefficient.

LOCALIZED TECHNOLOGICAL CHANGE AND TECHNOLOGICAL STAGNATION

Atkinson and Stiglitz[4] have suggested the felicitous concept of "localized technological change," and have worked out some of its implications. The results are of interest for the theory of growth and the problems of developing countries. However, the labor variable is treated mechanically in their version, and therefore we should not assume that labor purchased per unit of time is the input that enters the production process. In essence, localized technological change implies that only a portion of the production function shifts at a time. In our language, only one—or a subset—of the recipes changes, never all of them.

Here the technological change involves not only the shift of a point or set of points on an isoquant, but one that can be associated with various degrees of X-efficiency. We think of this shift as the introduction of a new recipe into an existing set. The new recipe dominates at least one of the old ones in that for the degree of X-efficiency associated with the old recipe there exists a new one that is less costly per unit of output.

Parenthetically, one may note that localized technological progress may result in the creation of superior techniques—techniques which require less capital and less labor to produce a given output. Whether or not this happens will depend on the degree to which the new technique turns out to be X-efficient or X-inefficient. If the new superior technique is combined with no loss in X-efficiency, it will be chosen irrespective of factor scarcities. If X-efficiency is the critical variable in determining whether a new technique is totally superior to an old one then new techniques may be introduced in some cases but not in others, though it would always <u>appear</u> that there exists a recipe superior to the existing one.

A lack of technological change, or a slow rate of such change, may be explained to some degree by whether or not (and the extent to which) such changes are accompanied by improvements in X-efficiency. Firms and economies whose alternative technical options are X-inefficient may choose not to introduce them, or if they do, will discover them to be uneconomic and abandon them.

The main consideration to be kept in mind is the possibility that an industry may be <u>locked in</u> on a given technique if the shift in the direction required for adjustment is X-inefficient. Similarly, technological changes may not be introduced if such changes are localized[5] and X-inefficient. The basic idea is elementary. The loss from the X-inefficiency accompanying the change may be greater than the benefit that would otherwise have occurred as a consequence of the change. The implications of this possibility may be of considerable importance. For a given range of change in some variable (e.g., the wage rate), changes that would take place in response to a disequilibrium state may in fact not occur. This "locked in technique" concept may help to explain certain types of phenomena familiar in less developed countries.

Suppose that all innovations are visualized in terms of borrowing new recipes from more advanced countries and substituting them for some of the existing recipes. Suppose further that a new recipe is understood only to the extent to which it is reasonably close to an existing one. It will obviously make a difference whether the new recipes available are many or few compared to those currently in use. Thus, if research and technological change take place mostly in advanced countries, this would imply that new recipes are created in relatively high capital/labor ratio countries and are not generally available in the relatively low capital/labor ratio countries.

There is a sense in which a country may be said to be located in technological space. By this we have in mind the set of recipes appropriate to a country's capital stock, labor force, and skills. On an equi-X-efficient isoquant in the two input cases we would find the recipes appropriate to its capital/labor ratio. In this sense, we can readily think of countries as being located at different positions in technological space. The chief consideration for the technology borrowing country is how far or close it is in technological space to the lending countries and at what point in technological space inventions (i.e., new recipes) are being made.

Thus countries which find themselves in technological space at the relatively low capital/labor ratio end may also find that they have relatively few new recipes available to them for borrowing. Clearly their experience will be disappointing if in addition the few recipes they can borrow are X-inefficient in implementation.

This idea (which explains a possibility but not necessarily the <u>only</u> source of relative technological stagnation) is illustrated in Figure 2.4 where points representing high capital/labor ratios are shown to follow a path of localized and X-efficient innovations T_2 and T_3, while those with a low capital/labor ratio yield localized and X-inefficient innovations T_2' and T_3' (or no innovations at all). Under such circumstances low income countries would be technologically stagnant, while high income ones would show continued technological change. The borrowing country at position T_0 cannot benefit from the inventions T_2 and T_3 taking place in the lending country.

Or consider the following possibility. We start with a pair of economies A and B which are similar in almost every respect. The same rate of investment exists in both. Part of the investment is spent for capital widening and capital deepening, while another part is spent for the introduction of technological change. Suppose that in

FIGURE 2.4

Innovational Diffusion and Technological Stagnation

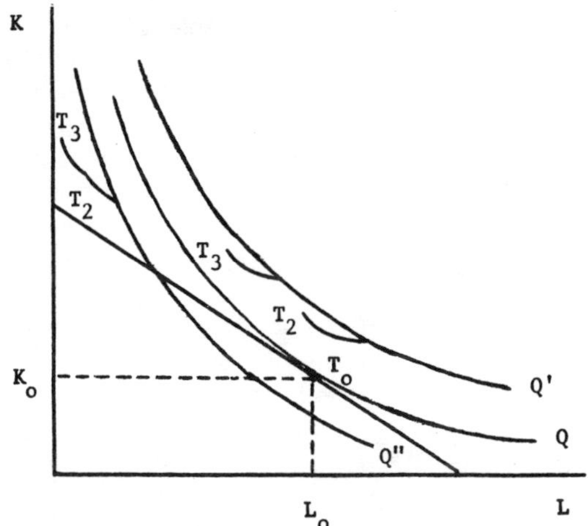

country A technological change is X-efficient while in B it is X-inefficient, though entrepreneurs in both countries expect the degree of X-efficiency to remain unchanged. In A the results will more than justify expectations in terms of output and profit, while in B the opposite will be the case. As a consequence A shifts more of its investment funds into technological change, while B moves in the opposite direction.

X-EFFICIENT TECHNOLOGICAL CHANGE AND INNOVATIONAL DIFFUSION SEQUENCES

Suppose that recipe T_2 is superior to the current technique T_1. Under what circumstances will T_2 be adopted? We must also consider the nature of the possible sequences involved. T_2 may be a superior technique in the sense that for the given degree of X-efficiency under T_1, T_2 requires both less capital and less labor. Alternatively, T_2 may not be a completely superior technique, but T_2 is more profitable (for all firms) than T_1 if it can be employed with the same degree of X-efficiency as T_1. Under the normal textbook assumptions in which X-inefficiency does not exist, and in which there are no inert areas, the problem is trivial. T_2 will certainly be adopted by all firms if under the circumstances it is profitable for them, but this is not necessarily the case under the X-inefficiency assumption.[6]

For convenience let us assume that there is a relatively large number of firms, each of equal size. Also assume that the adoption of T_2 implies an investment in proportion to the normal scale of the firm. Thus the essential decision is not a scale decision, but a yes or no decision. The basic considerations that determine (within the limited set of variables under consideration) whether or not an adoption sequence occurs are as follows: (1) The distribution of the anticipated relative degree of X-efficiency of T_2 over T_1 among the firms. (2) The extent to which profits change for innovating firms, given the point of adoption within the sequence of innovation. (3) The extent to which profits fall for the noninnovators, given the point of adoption within the sequence of innovation. (4) The distribution of the pull bounds for potential adopting firms when firms act _independently_. (5) The distribution of the pull bounds for potential adopting firms when firms act as _followers_ of other adopters. (6) The distribution of the push bounds for potential adopters when firms act _independently_. (7) The distribution of the push bounds of potential adopters when firms act as _followers_ of other adopters.

In what follows we will use "profit" as our index of what the decisionmaking group presumes to be important. The pursuit of "profits" or the avoidance of "losses" occurs only when opportunities imply "profits" or "losses" that fall outside the inert areas. In a more extensive analysis than that undertaken here, an attempt would be made to work out the relations between the income of firms, the gains to decisionmakers within the firm, the utilities that they attach to such gains, and the size of the pull-push bounds. To the extent that some individuals receive utility from the overall performance of the firm rather than their individual share in firm gains, this factor too has to be taken into account. Though the elements involved may be complex, this does not alter the plausibility of the hypothesis that inert areas with more or less given bounds exist for firms as well as for individuals who are members of these firms.*

---

*Along these lines one could reinterpret the neoclassical profit-maximizing function as the situation under which the management of the firm has completely internalized its welfare with firm profits, irrespective of its own share of the profits. Furthermore, the management as such is capable of knowing the activity bundles and the maximum pace for every point on the production function. Finally, the neoclassical theory would have to assume that managers of this type would be able to "force" individuals to shift from the activity bundle and pace which maximizes that utility to the activity-pace bundle which maximizes output. Once these assumptions are specified, it seems clear that they are unlikely to be fulfilled in practice.

The profitability of the adoption of a new technique will depend in part on whether the switch is X-efficient or not, and if it is X-inefficient then the degree of inefficiency will determine the result. Thus we visualize a distribution of degree of X-efficiency for a given switch for different firms. The upper and lower bounds of the firm decision mechanisms in juxtaposition with the innovating or noninnovating profit levels will determine whether or not T_2 is adopted. An important consideration is how firms that are nonadopters at some point react to firms that have made the switch to T_2. The following four-fold table illustrates the possibilities: (1) the independent adopters are those who make a technical switch irrespective of

	independent	follower
pull	PI	PF
push	Pui	Puf

whether others have done so; (2) the pull followers are those who make a switch only after a given number of firms have already done so. A given firm may be an independent adopter at a given profit level and a follower adopter at a lower profit level. In Figure 2.5 the independent pull bounds are shown by the curves PI and PF. The follower pull boundary will be the same or below the independent pull boundary. The implicit assumption is that any firm that is an independent adopter would not be dissuaded by others being adopters and might be persuaded to adopt at a lower profit level if a certain number of others have already adopted T_2.

The push boundaries (Pui and Puf in Figure 2.5) operate in a similar manner. As more firms make technical adoptions, the nonadopter profit level falls. At some point they may fall sufficiently to induce nonadopters to make the technical innovation in order to avoid further losses. Once again we can distinguish firms which make such a decision on an independent basis given only the fall in the profit level, and those which are additionally persuaded by the fact that others have made the adoption. Thus the follower push boundary (Puf) will be above the independent push boundary (Pui) or at the same level as, but not below, the independent push boundary.

In Figure 2.5 the basic behavioral curves for the firms are in order of the lowest profit level on the pull boundary. The initial adopter can only do so independently—thus the first firm is at the minimum profit level of an independent adopter. The second firm is the one which would adopt at the next lowest profit level whether or not this is done independently or on a follower basis. In a similar way, we can visualize the profit level for all subsequent adopters.

FIGURE 2.5

The Push and Pull Boundaries

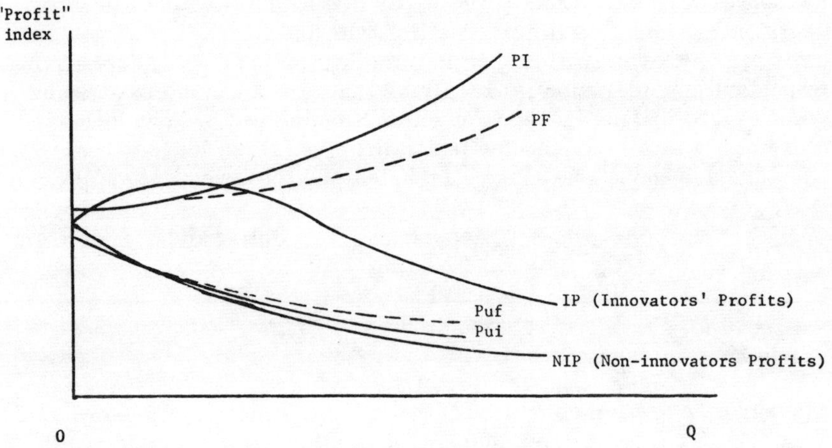

Thus every point on the lower pull boundary (the lower point of either Pui or Puf) identifies a given firm along the x-axis. The points (above the x-axis) on the push boundaries represent the identical firms and indicate their push profit levels.

The curves which help to determine the outcome are the lower bounds of the independent pull curve and the follower pull curve, and the upper bounds of the independent push curve and the follower push curve. If an adoption decision is already made on a follower basis, what the result would have been if it had to be made on an independent basis is of no consequence.

There are a number of possible outcomes depending on whether the pull and push boundary curves cross the curves that represent the innovation (IP) and noninnovation profit (NIP) levels. Some are as follows:

1. The pull boundary may be above the innovating profit level curve. In this case no adoption will take place.

2. The pull boundary intersects the profit curve but not initially. This means that the adoption process never gets under way because of a lack of initiators. In this case, the nonstarting firms represented by the portion of the pull curve above the innovating profit level could somehow be subsidized or bribed to carry out the adoption, whereupon the rest of the adoption sequence would take place. This would appear

to be a case where we have a valid "infant industry" type of argument to promote technological progress.*

3. The pull boundary starts below the actual profit level, in which case the innovation process does get underway, but it may be truncated if at some point the pull boundary is above the innovating profit level curve.

4. The push boundary crosses the NIP curve prior to the point where the pull boundary crosses the IP curve. In this case, the innovation process continues as a consequence of the push process.

5. The process may be truncated if the pull curve is above the innovating profit level prior to the completion of the adoption process and the push curve is below the NIP curve at that point. This would involve a situation in which the system is consistent with more than one technique. This could easily be the case where the advantage between the new technique and the old one is sufficiently close so that, given the differences in X-inefficiency in the new technique, it is possible for both techniques to exist in the industry simultaneously.

6. Under the situation consistent with the usual textbook theory in which there are no inert areas and in which T_2 is profitable, we would always expect the innovational diffusion process to be completed. This obviously contrasts sharply with some of the possibilities considered above.

CONCLUSIONS

1. The existence of X-inefficient technological change allows for the possibility of locked-in techniques of production, which in turn may help to explain some cases of technological backwardness and economic dualism.

2. The existence of X-inefficient technological changes may account for nonstarters in the process of technological diffusion.

3. Relative input scarcity and related prices are not sufficient to determine the desirability of shifting (or not shifting) from one technique to another.

---

*The IP curve (innovator's profit curve) is assumed to rise at first and then fall. This may be so (but, of course, need not necessarily be) for a variety of reasons. External economies may exist, repairs and maintenance costs by experts outside the firm may be cheaper if more firms are available to be serviced, other inputs (e.g., spare parts) may also be cheaper for the same reason, etc. In addition, firms may learn from each other's errors and experiences, i.e., interfirm learning by doing, which ceases to be significant beyond the existence of some minimum number of firms as innovators.

4. In contrast to the conventional theory, the availability of a superior technique does not necessarily lead to its adoption.

5. Two or more competing techniques may exist in the same industry even if the age structure of capital in different firms is the same.

* * *

COMMENT BY LARRY A. SJAASTAD

Leibenstein's basic proposition appears to be that workers' preferences may be inconsistent with the best interests of the firm, and that as a consequence the adoption of some or all innovations may be prevented or at best retarded, despite the fact that these innovations would improve intrinsic efficiency, because their adoption would result in changes in the conditions of employment so detrimental to workers' welfare that any potential savings would be more than exhausted by the additional compensation demanded by workers.

The first part of this proposition is both plausible and consistent with factual knowledge of the operation of the labor market. Indeed, Marshall himself devoted a great deal of attention to the role of conditions of employment in his treatment of the supply of labor, and the more recent work on discrimination takes this proposition as a point of departure. That worker resistance to technical change can effectively preclude that change is also apparent, at least in those industries where labor's share of output is large. One frequently wonders, for example, why capital is not used more intensively—on a two- or three-shift basis rather than just one. A rather small wage premium for second- and third-shift labor is sufficient, it turns out, to wipe out any gains from more intensive utilization of capital, particularly when labor's share is large. Hence it is not surprising that these premia do prevent multiple shifts except in highly capital intensive activities, such as the drilling of oil wells, or where multiple shifts are required by the process involved, such as in oil refineries. Thus I find Leibenstein's basic proposition to be interesting and reasonable, but I must take exception to the implications he derives from it.

Leibenstein is emphatic in his assertion that acceptance of his theory of X-efficiency implies rejection of the concept of a production function and much of the rest of neoclassical production theory. This rejection would seem to arise from an excessively <u>narrow</u> conception of the production function. It is widely recognized now that both labor and capital are multidimensional inputs—quality, for example, is repeatedly found to be a highly relevant consideration in the case of both labor and capital. Anne Krueger, writing in the Economic Journal a couple of years ago, found education as a proxy of quality to be highly important in explaining cross-country differences in per capita GNP.[7] Leibenstein seems to accept some elements of conventional production function theory, since his "isoquants" do exhibit the usual substitution properties and do become single-valued once the degree of X-efficiency (i.e., level of effort) is specified. One could formulate the quality argument in exactly the same manner. There is a difference, of course, in that quality is probably more amenable to measurement than effort.

Leibenstein places considerable emphasis on the twin observation that very little research and development is taking place in the less developed countries, and that the new technology coming out of the R and D process in advanced countries is frequently inappropriate to the factor price structure of the developing countries. At one point he suggests that failure of LDCs to undertake significant R and D may be due to a bias of the effect of technical change on X-efficiency in the LDCs—that is, new technology in the advanced countries may be X-efficient, but similar "progress" in the LDCs is X-inefficient and hence is not "progress" at all. Why this coincidence should occur is not all obvious, unless one is prepared to take the major step of attributing both the relatively low current rates of growth and low levels of income to such a bias in the effects of technical change on effort. A more promising approach was pointed out about ten years ago by Richard Nelson, who observed that knowledge has the attributes of public goods, hence adequate investment in the provisions of new knowledge is a responsibility that must be assumed by the state. Investment in R and D in the United States is currently estimated at about $30 billion, or $150 per person, annually. As this amount exceeds per capita income of many countries, and exceeds per capita investment, as conventionally defined in the various national accounts, in virtually every LDC, it is not surprising that comparable R and D efforts are not mounted in those countries. But it would seem that in Latin American countries investment in new knowledge is not even 1 percent of NNP, and on the average is much less than 1 percent. One is hesitant to attribute this poor performance to an X-inefficiency bias; indeed, it is doubtful that these countries have ever sponsored research on a scale sufficient to expose such a bias. Thus, while it may be true that R and D has a low payoff in the LDCs, the fact remains that the data which might refute this hypothesis have not yet been generated.

Any new technology coming into use in the LDCs is, unfortunately, largely imported. The Argentines, for example, claim to have been the first to have discovered hybrid corn, but it is only since 1960 that an organized effort has been made to develop hybrids appropriate to Argentine soil and climatic conditions, and that effort is modest indeed. It is generally true in the LDCs that little public attention has been given to organized research in agriculture, apart from efforts by major foundations. However, in Mexico and India, where such research has been underwritten by major foundations, there would seem to have been relatively little resistance to the new technology once its risks, or lack thereof, have become known.

In any case, the scattered evidence we have on the generation and diffusion of new technology does not support the X-efficiency bias hypotheses. Nor, of course, does it contradict it. But a theory with empirical content must be able to make testable predictions. Leibenstein would argue that the neoclassical production theory fails in that its predictions are not borne out, owing presumably to the omission of some important variables. There is a different problem with the X-efficiency theory (at least as described in his paper), particularly when it is applied to the problem of technical change. It is that the X-efficiency theory is sufficiently general to be consistent with any outcome, and is thereby inherently unable to predict.

CHAPTER

3

COMPARATIVE CONSUMPTION PATTERNS, THE EXTENT OF THE MARKET, AND ALTERNATIVE DEVELOPMENT STRATEGIES

Albert Fishlow

INTRODUCTION

An important question recurrent throughout discussions of development—whether historical or contemporary—is the extent of the market. The role of demand is regarded by some as central to the initial emergence of Great Britain in the industrial era, by others as crucial to the retardation of the American South in manufacturing, and remains today one of the important issues in Latin American development strategy.[1] Yet despite a considerable history of statistical investigation (it is, after all, to the nineteenth century that we trace Engel's Law), there has been relatively little carry-over to analysis of the relationship of demand structures to rates of growth.

Theoretical models have afforded much greater significance to alterations in supply conditions—the accumulation of capital and technological change, in particular. In these models, demand serves to determine the particular commodity composition of output, but—except for the savings-consumption decision—has little influence upon growth. Indeed, in open economy models, where international prices determine the composition of production, the role of demand is even more inconsequential, as is also the case under neoclassical growth conditions. Dual economy models have rectified the imbalance somewhat by attaching differential weight to the traditional and modern sectors. Since the development of the latter contributes more to aggregate growth (through capital formation and more rapid technological change), higher income elasticity of demand for the modern product can facilitate the transformation.[2]

If one adds such considerations as variable distribution of income, externalities, and internal economies of scale, the role of demand becomes potentially more powerful still. Uniquely associated with any production point is an income distribution reflecting the derived demand for factor inputs. Strong preferences for land-intensive goods, for example, will lead to higher rents and larger incomes for landowners. Income distribution, in turn, influences effective demand; the aggregate income elasticity is a weighted average of elasticities of different income groups. Thus one of the principal criticisms of trade-directed development, where trade occurs in tropical products, say, is that foreign demand shifts the income distribution in favor of landholders, who in turn prefer luxury imports. Domestic development, initially slower, may ultimately overtake exports, but is disadvantaged by the wealth accumulation in the rural sector.

The second factor, externalities, requires little elaboration. These may range from dependence of technological change upon the size of the industrial sector to positive stimulus of investment due to the existence of a more skilled labor force. Their explicit consideration would take us far afield. The essential condition is that certain types of products have differential growth impacts not capable of being fully captured by their producers. The third set of circumstances, internal economies of scale, operates to exclude domestic production in favor of imports when the size of the market is too small. This is much more likely to occur with specialized capital goods than with consumers' goods. Note, however, that variegated consumer durable demands resulting from an unequal income distribution can create a serious problem of excess capacity, as has been the case with multiple automobile firms in Latin American countries.

Some of these observations may be illustrated diagrammatically. Starting from an initial endowment of factors as portrayed in Figure 3.1a, the transformation frontier of Figure 3.1b results. The structure of demand is compatible with the equilibrium point E indicated in Figure 3.1b; this means that at such a point, the income distribution resulting from the wage-rental rate implicit in production at E, and shown in Figure 3.1a, generates demand for A and B that exactly clears the market. The net accumulation of capital inherent in such a structure of demand is shown in Figure 3.1c. For convenience, income distribution is assumed to be stable, and therefore demand shifts outward uniformly following the initial preference map.

Figures 3.2a through 3.2d repeat the story for identical endowments but different initial preferences. The result is an altered wage-rental rate ratio and income distribution associated with production point F. Consequent upon production of more B, more rapid capital accumulation occurs as in Figure 3.2c, and, in addition, production functions are shifted due to more rapid technological change. The outcome is a new production point F1, this time with a changing income distribution, and thus with alterations of the original indifference curve mapping.

FIGURE 3.1

Demand with Given Endowment of Factors

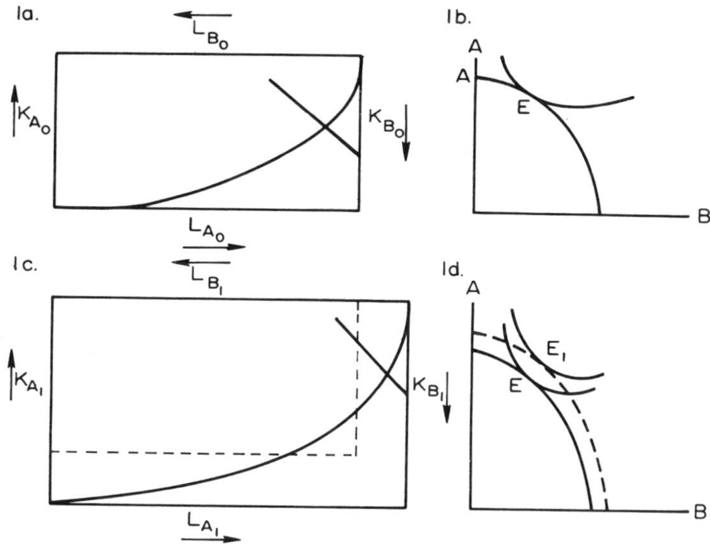

This is not the moment to elaborate upon such theoretical formulations. Rather, my intent is to illustrate how microeconomic household data may shed light upon the role played by forces of demand in historical development. I will be specifically concerned with the structure of consumption as found in nineteenth-century Great Britain, France, and the United States. One of the ready generalizations offered to explain the success of American economic achievement is the extent of the market. As H. F. Williamson has written, one significant explanation for American mass production is to be found "in the nature of the domestic market and market demand that by the latter half of the nineteenth century had stimulated or made possible a widespread development of methods of mass distribution."[3] Yet the precise attributes of that consumption structure and its causes remain largely _terra incognita_. Only in an explicitly comparative context can the question be adequately posed.

Such a theoretical discussion suggests that systematic differences in favor of nonsubsistence goods should characterize American demand. They can emanate from three distinct sources: underlying preferences, the distribution of income, or the structure of relative prices. The relationship between productive and demand patterns is interactive

FIGURE 3.2

Demand Again, but with Different Initial Preferences than in Figure 3.1

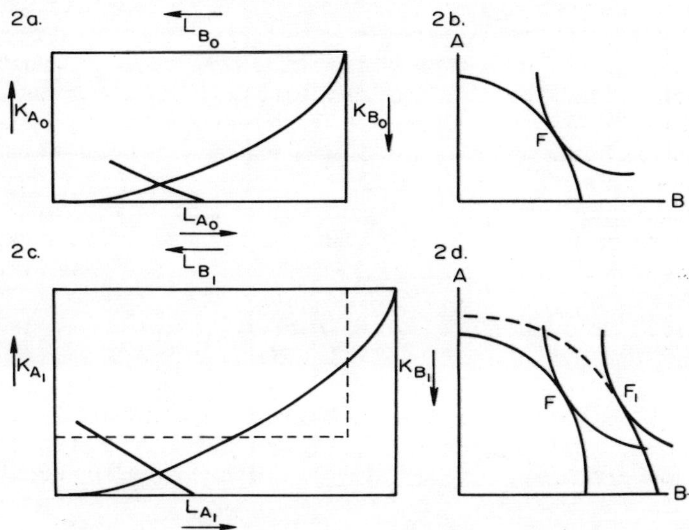

and endogenous in the last two eventualities, while unilateral in the instance of underlying tastes. I shall attempt to show that it was the existence of precisely such internal and reinforcing forces, rather than national character, that led to a more favorable American market in the nineteenth century.

The first section of this paper discusses the levels of American, British, and French expenditures on food, rent, clothing, and sundries, based upon data generated by urban household surveys at the end of the nineteenth and beginning of the twentieth centuries. It establishes the existence of smaller American expenditures on foodstuffs and ascribes them to international differences in their price. The second extends the analysis to statistical comparison of the demand structures in the three countries by examining demand and family size elasticities. It takes up the other side of the argument to maintain the consistency of the data with uniform tastes, at least insofar as changes in demand with changes in income are concerned. The third section goes beyong the basic household data to consider more fully the mechanism by which the more productive American agriculture contributed to industrial demand. A brief concluding section makes some extensions to problems of presently developing countries.

HISTORICAL EXPENDITURE LEVELS DERIVED FROM HOUSEHOLD SURVEYS

Corresponding to the neglect of interest in consumption patterns is the neglect of a considerable body of data. Here I can only scratch the surface. Comparisons in this section will be founded principally upon analysis of two sets of budget studies aimed explicitly at ascertaining international differences in the standard of living of industrial working-class families. The first goes back to 1888-91 and was conducted by the United States Bureau of Labor; the second was designed by the British Board of Trade and relates to the period 1904-9. Of course, the earlier and proliferating studies of household behavior after the 1850s had not failed to invoke international comparison. Indeed, while we associate Engel's Law with declining relative expenditures on food as income increases within nations, he himself was concerned with absolute standards and framed it more broadly: "The proportion of the outgo used for food, other things being equal, is the best measure of the material standard of living of a population."[4] And Carrol D. Wright's famous and erroneous restatement of Engel's Law in 1875 combined explicit reference to the habits of workers in Massachusetts and Germany. Yet it was not until the two studies in question that comparative inquiries were undertaken on any significant scale.[5] Their consistency with other later sources will become apparent.

Tables 3.1 and 3.2 show the allocation of expenditures for urban workers in the three countries for the dates indicated. The totals confirm the expectations set forth above. American families as a whole spend relatively much less on food than their British and French counterparts. This is true whether 1888-91 outlays are measured as a proportion of expenditures or of income. Nor are the larger American expenditures for rent sufficient to negate this same conclusion for both subsistence categories taken together. Correspondingly there is greater scope for American consumption of other manufactures and services, particularly nonclothing. The aggregate margin in Table 3.1, however, is smaller than that in Table 3.2, and for good reason: the disparities in income per capita are correspondingly narrower. The declining proportions of food expenditure abundantly bear out Engel's Law of less than unitary income elasticity (for rents the situation is less uniform) and thus the greater the absolute difference in income the larger the divergence in observed food consumption. Even if the two samples were accurately representative, such a result obviously confounds cause and effect; it cannot be argued on the basis of aggregate data that differential consumption patterns contributed to higher incomes.

TABLE 3.1

Consumption Patterns of "Normal Families"[a]

a. United States, 1888-91

	Annual Income											
	$200-299	300-399	400-499	500-599	600-699	700-799	800-899	900-999	1000-1099	1100-1199	1200+	Total
Number of observations	105	395	659	509	300	102	111	95	62	24	86	2,448
Average size of family	3.5	3.7	3.8	4.1	4.1	4.2	4.0	4.3	4.3	4.1	4.2	3.9
Average income	$ 266	351	447	538	635	739	836	935	1030	1136	1421	$570
Average expenditures	308	384	454	513	585	676	706	808	859	969	1186	$540
Average savings	-42	-33	- 7	25	50	63	130	127	171	167	255	$+30
Average income per capita	76	95	118	131	155	176	209	217	240	277	338	$145
Proportion of expenditures (percent)												
Food	44.3	45.6	45.1	43.8	41.2	38.9	38.1	34.3	34.7	30.6	28.6	41.1
Rent	14.6	15.0	15.3	15.2	15.5	15.6	16.1	15.0	15.1	12.2	12.6	15.0
Clothing	14.3	14.1	14.4	15.3	15.9	16.3	15.1	16.8	17.5	16.5	15.7	15.2
Other	26.8	25.3	25.2	25.7	27.4	29.2	30.7	33.9	32.7	40.7	43.1	28.6
Proportion of income (percent)												
Food	51.2	49.9	45.8	41.8	37.9	35.6	32.2	29.6	28.9	26.1	23.9	38.9
Rent	16.9	17.8	15.5	14.5	14.3	14.3	13.6	13.0	12.6	10.4	10.5	14.4
Clothing	16.5	15.4	14.6	14.6	14.6	14.9	12.7	14.5	14.6	14.1	13.1	14.5
Other consumption	31.0	27.7	25.6	24.5	25.2	26.7	25.9	29.3	27.3	34.7	36.0	27.1

[a]Normal families are those without boarders or relatives, with two adults and children 14 years of age and younger, and renting a home.

Source: U.S. Bureau of Labor, Sixth Annual Report, 1891, Part III; Seventh Annual Report, 1892, Part III. Averages calculated from subsample; percentages are as given and relate to all observations.

b. Great Britain, 1888-91

	Annual Income						
	$200-299	300-399	400-499	500-599	600-699	700-799	Total
Number of observations	68	177	105	46	24	21	441
Average size of family	3.4	4.1	4.6	4.8	4.2	4.6	4.2
Average income	$266	352	440	542	640	740	$413
Average expenditures	267	345	418	505	562	658	$393
Average savings	-1	7	22	37	78	82	$ 20
Average income per capita	78	86	96	113	152	161	$ 98
Proportion of expenditures (percent)							
Food	50.1	49.5	48.7	50.8	45.3	44.0	48.9
Rent	14.6	12.8	11.6	10.4	9.4	9.5	11.8
Clothing	12.1	13.8	14.9	14.5	15.6	19.0	14.6
Other	23.2	23.9	24.8	24.3	29.7	27.5	24.8
Proportion of income: (percent)							
Food	50.3	48.5	46.3	47.3	39.8	39.1	46.5
Rent	14.6	12.5	11.0	9.7	8.2	8.4	11.2
Clothing	12.1	13.5	14.2	13.5	13.7	16.9	13.9
Other	23.3	23.4	23.6	22.6	26.1	24.4	23.6

<u>Source</u>: See Table 3.1(a), except that no subsampling procedure was used.

(continued)

TABLE 3.1 (continued)

c. France, 1888-91

	Annual Income					
	Under $200	200-299	300-399	400-499	500-599	Total
Number of observations	9	67	54	13	5	148
Average size of family	3.6	4.0	4.2	3.6	3.2	4.0
Average income	$99	252	339	434	525	300
Average expenditures	106	261	312	346	404	282
Average savings	-7	-9	27	88	121	18
Average income per capita	28	63	81	121	164	74.91
Proportion of Expenditures (percent)						
Food	51.6	48.8	50.6	42.6	45.5	48.8
Rent	10.4	11.1	9.9	10.5	9.7	10.5
Clothing	15.6	14.7	13.8	16.6	20.1	14.8
Other	22.4	25.4	25.7	30.3	24.7	25.9
Proportion of income (percent)						
Food	55.2	50.5	46.6	34.0	35.0	45.9
Rent	11.1	11.5	9.1	8.4	7.5	9.9
Clothing	16.7	15.2	12.7	13.2	15.5	13.9
Other	24.0	26.3	23.6	24.2	19.0	24.3

Source: See Table 3.1(b).

TABLE 3.2

Consumption Patterns in Industrial Towns

United States,[a] 1909

	Weekly Income[b]								
	Under $9.73	9.73-14.59	14.60-19.46	19.47-24.33	24.34-29.20	29.21-34.07	34.08-38.94	Over 38.95	Total
Number of observations	67	532	1,036	545	437	224	131	243	3,215
Average number of persons	3.78	4.08	4.54	5.02	5.27	5.82	6.10	6.38	4.92
Average income	8.76	12.42	16.99	21.51	26.10	31.38	36.13	50.33	22.37
Average income per capita	2.32	3.04	3.74	4.28	4.95	5.39	5.92	7.89	4.55
Average food per capita	1.19	1.45	1.65	1.76	1.87	1.92	2.04	2.24	1.74
Proportion of income (percent)									
Meat	13.0	13.5	12.2	11.4	10.5	9.8	10.2	8.3	10.9
Other food	51.4	47.6	44.2	41.2	37.8	35.5	34.5	28.4	38.9
Rent	19.5	17.7	16.7	15.3	14.0	12.0	12.0	9.9	14.2

[a]Refers to American born, or descendent of British stock, and resident in Northern states.
[b]£ = $4.865, following conversion in Bureau of Labor Statistics, Bulletin No. 93, 1911.

Source: Great Britain Board of Trade, Cost of Living in American Towns (Cd. 5609), 1911.

(continued)

TABLE 3.2 (continued)

(United Kingdom, 1904)

	Weekly Income[a]					
	Under $6.08	6.09-7.29	7.30-8.51	8.52-9.73	Over 9.73	Total
Number of observations	261	289	416	382	596	1,944
Average number of persons[b]	5.1	5.3	5.2	5.4	6.4	5.61
Average income	5.20	6.56	7.77	8.39	12.66	8.87
Average income per capita	1.02	1.24	1.49	1.55	1.98	1.58
Average food per capita	.68	.82	.97	1.00	1.13	.96
Proportion of income (percent)						
Meat	18.0	18.1	18.7	17.6	16.4	17.4
Total food	67.4	66.2	65.0	61.0	57.0	61.1

[a]See note b, Table 3.2a.
[b]Number of children as given, plus two adults.

Source: Great Britain Board of Trade, Cost of Living of the Working Classes (Cd. 3864), 1908.

(France, 1907-8)

	Weekly Income[a]					
	Under $4.86	4.86-6.08	6.09-7.29	7.30-8.51	8.52-9.73	Over 9.73	Total
Number of observations	223	614	931	1,065	821	1,951	5,605
Average number of persons[b]	3.6	3.8	3.8	3.9	4.1	4.9	4.2
Average income	4.32	5.57	6.72	7.86	9.07	12 .86	9.20
Average income per capita	1.20	1.47	1.77	2.02	2.21	2.62	2.19
Average food per capita	.75	.89	1.04	1.17	1. 24	1.38	1.18
Proportion of income (percent)							
Meat	15.3	16.4	16.6	17.4	17.0	16.3	16.6
Total food	62.7	60.8	58.6	57.9	56.1	52.8	55.5
Rent	12.3	11.2	10.1	9.7	9.7	8.4	9.2

[a]See note b, Table 3.2a.

[b]See note b, Table 3.2b.

Source: Great Britain Board of Trade, Cost of Living in French Towns (Cd. 4512), 1909.

To evaluate this proposition requires us to focus on expenditures, while holding income constant. Happily, this liberates us from the requirement that the data portray exactly the income distributions of the three countries; all that is needed is accurate recording within income groups. In Figure 3.3 the Engel curves are plotted for the principal expenditures category, foodstuffs, to facilitate visual comparisons at fixed income levels. The first panel is confined to the 1888-91 inquiry and to the proportion of total outlays spent for food. Expenditures of American workers are consistently smaller than those in the other countries over the entire range of income per capita. None of the British observations lie below the freehand curve describing the American function. Of the three French data points overlapping the American income range, two clearly indicate higher expenditures for food as well. Because of the substantial variance in the French data, however, there is little reliable indication of how they compare with the British. Fortunately, it is possible to be more rigorous and to compare expenditures for individual cells of identical family income and size. Since these are "normal families," even age composition is thereby approximately standardized.

Utilizing all cells containing at least ten families, the American percentage is inferior to that of Great Britain in 18 out of 19 cases, and to that of France in 8 out of 9.* The average deviation is 3.8 percentage points for both comparisons. Similarly, the French expenditure is inferior to the British 6 times out of 8, but with a mean deviation of less than 1 percentage point. Thus, for reasons presently to be explored, American industrial laborers clearly spent less for food, after adjusting for income and scale factors. This paired comparison, with its average difference of less than 4 percentage points rather than the 8-point margin indicated in the totals, suggests that higher American per capita income in the sample accounts for approximately half the American differential. This impression is corroborated by an alternative aggregate calculation standardizing the three income distributions. By utilizing the European shares as common weights and the expenditure patterns for given income, the differences between the United States, France, and Great Britain, can be narrowed as follows:

---

*In the case of France, because of the paucity of observations, it was necessary to use one cell numbering nine families, and another with eight.

FIGURE 3.3

Engel Curves for Consumption of Foodstuffs

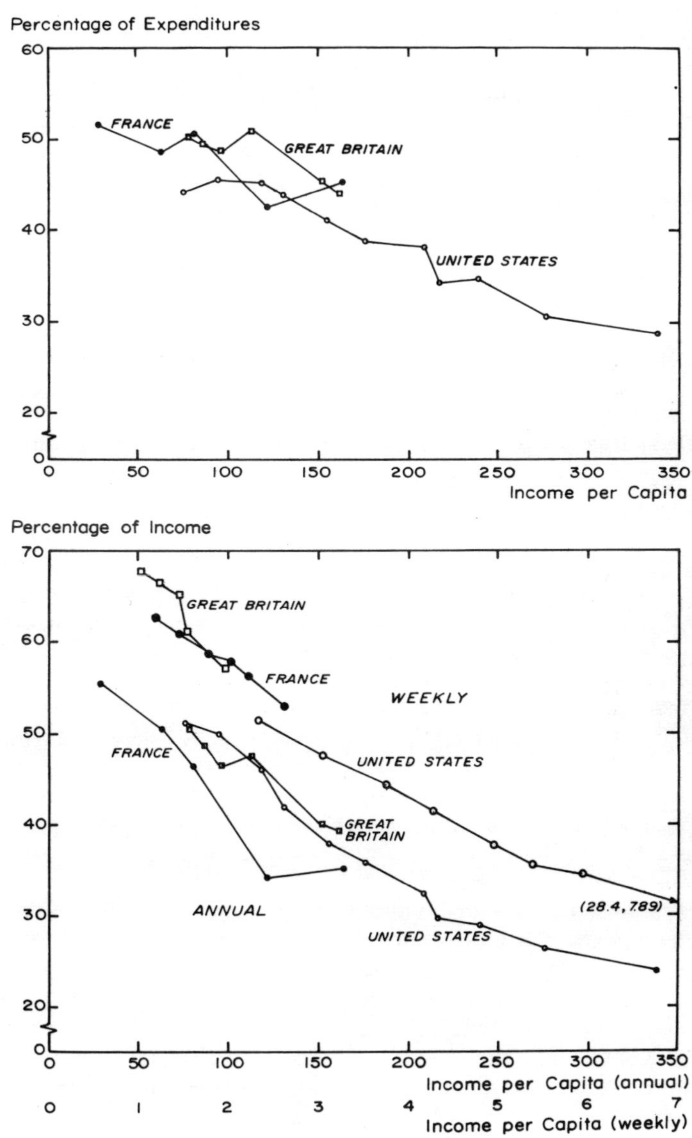

	French weights	British weights	United States weights
France	48.7		
Great Britain	49.8	48.9	
United States	44.8	44.3	41.1

The initial differences are measured along the diagonal;* the adjusted margins are obtained from the relevant columns holding the income weights constant. Again, something like half the lesser American aggregate expenditures are explained by the combination of higher incomes and an elasticity of demand less than one.

Panel B relates food expenditures to income rather than to total outlays. The 1890-91 survey results, shown on the lower left side, no longer present the neat order characteristic of Panel A. French food expenditures are now regularly below those for the United States and Great Britain, with the latter two countries indistinguishable over the relevant income range. The British Board of Trade inquiry, plotted higher in the chart, confirms the lesser French expenditures vis-à-vis the United Kingdom, but its limited overlap makes comparison with the United States hazardous. The one meaningful French observation lies above its American counterpart, contrary to the results reported by the Bureau of Labor. But this gives us precious little to go on.

These less-conclusive obrservations, relating as they do to income, do not detract from the earlier finding of consistent and significant differences. For there are good reasons to credit the relationship with expenditure rather more. Given certain plausible assumptions about consumer utility functions, it is perfectly appropriate to dichotomize the specific expenditure decision into one of total consumption versus savings, and from there to one of allocation of the consumption.** The difference between the 1888-91 expenditure

*Both the American and British percentages are as reported in Table 3.1. The French is slightly smaller because of the necessity to exclude families with income of less than $200 in order to make it comparable with the standardized averages.

**Technically what is required is either the strong separability or homogeneity of the utility function. Since the latter implies that all income elasticities are unity, what we are reduced to is the former: the dependence of marginal rates of substitution upon current values only. Cf. Kunio Yoshihara, "An Econometric Study of Japanese Economic Development," unpublished Ph.D. dissertation (University of California, Berkeley, 1966), pp. 86-95.

and income ratios is due to the higher proportion of American income given over to expenditure, particularly throughout the lower income ranges. This manifests itself in the deficits reported for American families below $120 per capita income, while the breakeven point is $80 for British units, and even somewhat lower for French. While we must seek to explain this divergence, it does not exempt us from also trying to explain the divergent expenditure patterns.

In the second instance, current income may not measure usual, or permanent, income. The deficits accruing to low income families cannot be a continuously recurring phenomenon. As the later 1901 United States Bureau of Labor survey confirmed, such dissaving was primarily financed out of previously accumulated bank deposits or current credit.* Then the past and future history of income as well as its present level is necessary to any evaluation of current behavior. Accordingly total expenditures reflect more adequately the normal standard of living than do current receipts, at least at the lower reaches of income distribution.[6] Since, moreover, the average American industrial worker's income was higher than that of the European, and the British and French observations are more concentrated around their respective means, there is some basis for believing American current income levels to be more distorted than those for the other two countries. This would account for the large deficits observed for low American incomes, but not in France and Britain. Whether greater variance of income is a general characteristic of American urban incomes is a subject worthy of further research; it has important implications for the differential savings potentials of urban workers. For these data, in any event, support for this view can be found in the much more similar ratios of savings to income among the three countries that result from aggregating income and expenditure by industry, thereby eliminating much of the transitory component in earnings. Table 3.3 presents the savings-income ratios and per capita incomes for the industrial groups making up the basis of the 1890-91 inquiry. Figure 3.4 graphs them, along with the savings-income ratios calculated in Table 3.1 on the basis of the original income grouping. Note how the American savings ratios calculated for low average income by industry substantially exceed those derived from the heterogeneous income classification. Initial international differences are considerably compressed. Thus at an income per

---

*The 1901 inquiry showed that of 507 families reporting a deficit, 244 obtained credit, and 94 financed it out of former savings. 150 did not report the source. Unfortunately, the relative amounts involved are not specified. U.S. Bureau of Labor, Eighteenth Annual Report, 1903, p. 513.

TABLE 3.3

Savings Ratios by Industry

United States		Great Britain		France	
Per Capita Income	Savings Income	Per Capita Income	Savings Income	Per Capita Income	Savings Income
Cotton and Wool					
75	-2.8	60	-4.7	41	-11.2
95	4.6	78	3.8	47	-3.4
105	6.1	85	2.9	60	4.0
130	5.6	101	1.6	78	8.3
163	6.6	135	10.4	102	7.1
246	12.3	216	10.8	159	16.7
Glass					
126	7.3	90	3.4		
148	.3	99	3.3		
151	2.8	159	8.7		
182	7.6	184	6.7		
246	8.0				
357	13.5				
Iron and Steel[a]					
85	3.4	75	7.1		
89	1.5	79	4.6		
111	5.6	87	6.8		
142	13.1	100	5.0		
172	8.8	123	3.6		
238	6.9	187	7.1		

[a]Includes pig iron, bar iron, steel, bituminous coal, coke and iron ore.

Source: Seventh Annual Report, Vol. II, pp. 1925, 1928, 1929, 1942, 1944, and 1947.

capita of around \$120, the original French-United States deviation is 21 percent points; for the cotton-woolen industry averages the equivalent divergence is less than 5 points.

This recognition of the role of permanent income also helps explain why the British Board of Trade data are suggestive of lower American food expenditures even relative to income. This inquiry was conducted for a week's interval only, and limited to soliciting those then employed. Among the reasons for variable annual earnings are unemployment and sickness, and these are thereby implicitly excluded. Moreover, standard weekly food purchases and quantities were ascertained, and this may also have contributed to greater accuracy.

Holding permanent income and family size constant, there is therefore good reason to believe American workers spent less on food. Relative to total expenditures, they certainly did. To help us understand why, it is useful to write the demand for foodstuffs as a function of the relative price of food and real income:

$$Q_f = g\left(\frac{P_f}{\sum_i w_i p_i}, \frac{Y}{\sum_i w_i P_i + w_f P_f}\right).$$

All other commodities are assumed to be individually weak substitutes or complements and are aggregated into a composite good whose price is

$$\sum_i w_i p_i.$$

Money income Y, is deflated by a price index including that of food. Then if the price of food, P_f, varies among observations, tastes being identical, the expenditure ratios $P_f Q_f/Y$ will also differ. Price enters in three distinct ways: as multiplier of the quantity purchased, as an influence upon the quantity consumed through relative prices, and as a partial determinant of real income.

Lower food prices thus imply lower expenditures except to the extent that the price and income elasticities compensate. In the case at hand, we have taken the conversion of money incomes at the official exchange rate. Suppose that the weighted average of all other prices but food were consistent with such an exchange rate, and that the lower American price of food implies a higher real income. Americans should then consume more food on that account. If, however, the exchange rate already reflects the lower food price, then real income is properly adjusted. In that event, the only offset to reduced expenditures is the elasticity of substitution in response to lower food prices. In general, the elasticity of the food expenditure ratio

FIGURE 3.4

Savings-Income Ratios

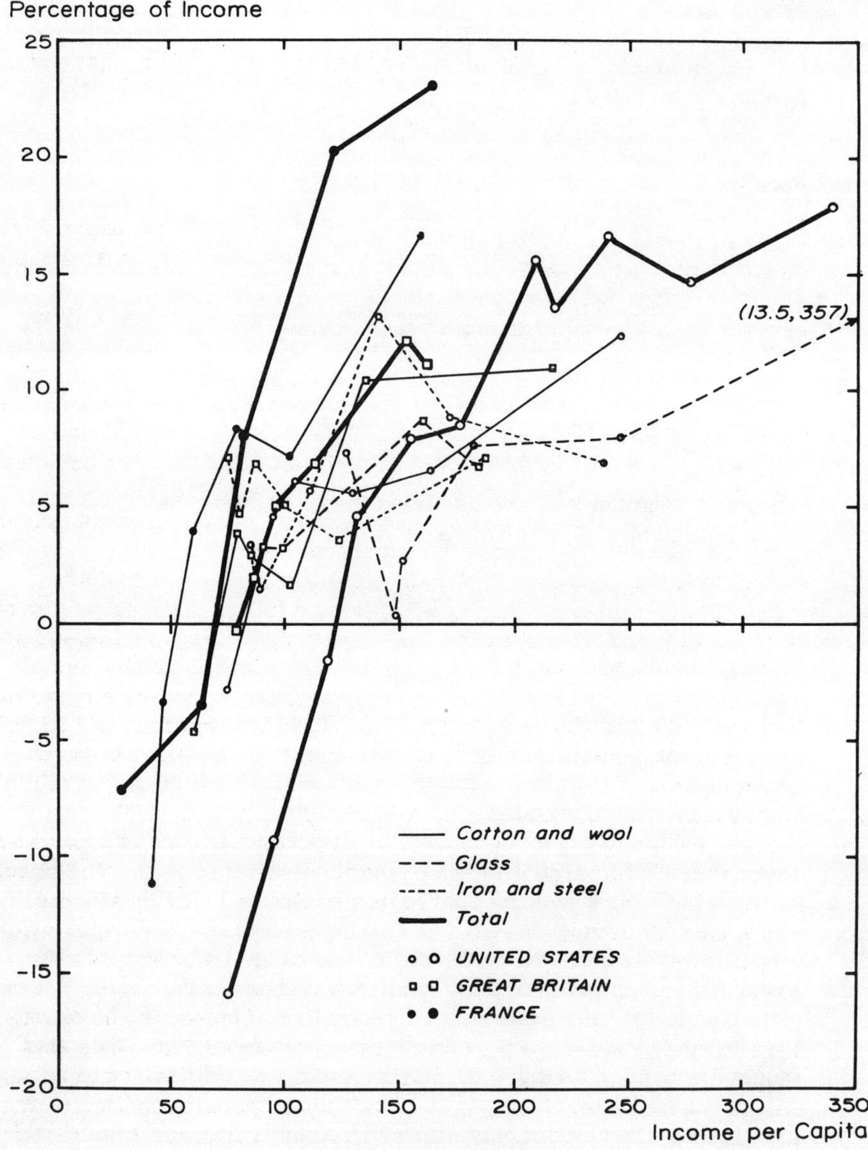

with respect to the price of food equals one minus the absolute value of the price elasticity:

$$\frac{d \log \;\; PQ_{f/Y}}{d \log P_f} = 1 - |\xi_p|.$$

The price elasticity in turn equals the sum of the income elasticity weighted by the share of food in total income and the substitution elasticity weighted by nonfood expenditures:

$$|\xi_p| = |w_f \xi_y + (1-w_f)\, \xi_s|.$$

In the case where the exchange rate already reflects the lower American food price, the first term is zero; to the extent that real incomes are influenced, it remains.

In general, $1 - |\xi_p|$ will be positive, even when there is an income term. Engel's Law does operate, and this confirms a value for ξ_y less than unity. A value of about .8, as we shall see later, seems to be characteristic of the three countries. Then, unless the elasticity of substitution exceeds unity, relative food expenditures and food prices will be positively correlated. The smaller the elasticity of substitution, and hence the lesser increased consumption, the greater the direct variations. As limited responsiveness seems to be the rule, $\langle 1 - |1\xi_p|$ may be expected to range between .5 and .8, closer to the upper limit in the absence of a real income effect.

This price phenomenon is not limited to international comparisons. It also explains some of the observed variation in 1888-91 food expenditures within the United States. Thus holding family income and size constant, and comparing relative food expenditure between Pennsylvania and the midwestern states of Ohio, Indiana, and Illinois, we find lesser outlays in the latter 45 times out of 50. The results are comparable for Massachusetts though fewer cells have sufficient observations to be used. As between Pennsylvania and Ohio, an average estimated price deviation of 14 percent produced a percentage divergence of 11 percent in the proportion spent on food. The resultant elasticity of .8 is somewhat high, considering that an income effect was operative, though it should be noted that the largest differences are to be found at the upper end of the income spectrum, where the income elasticity is smaller.

The later 1901 American investigation of incomes and expenditures is tabulated in a form that more conveniently reveals this regional effect. Table 3.4 consolidates the relevant information. Corresponding to each region are per capita total expenditures, the actual percentage spent on food, the hypothetical percentage based

TABLE 3.4

Regional Food Expenditure Ratios, 1901

	Per Capita Total Expenditure	Food Expenditure percentage	Adjusted Food Expenditure percentage	Price Index	Elasticity of Expenditure Ratio
North Atlantic	148	43.5	43.5	100	
South Atlantic	132	42.6	44.5	91	.7
North Central	144	40.9	43.7	94	.7
South Central	122	42.4	45.4	89	.6
Western	160	41.1	42.9	108	-.4

Sources: Per Capita Expenditure and Food Expenditure Percentage: U.S. Bureau of Labor, *Eighteenth Annual Report*, 1903, p. 647. Adjusted Food Expenditure Ratio: Calculated by converting observed North Atlantic food expenditures to those appropriate to levels of per capita total outlays of other regions, using .8 expenditure elasticity reported in H. Gregg Lewis and Paul H. Douglas, "Studies in Consumer Expenditures," *Studies in Business Administration*, XVII, 2 (1947). Price Index: Calculated from quantities and costs reported in *Eighteenth Annual Report*, pp. 648-49 (North Atlantic region is base). Elasticity of Expenditure Ratio: Adjusted Expenditure - Actual/Actual ÷ 100 - Price Index/Price Index.

on the North Atlantic consumption pattern but observed regional expenditure differentials, and a food price index calculated with the North Atlantic states as base. The differences between the actual and hypothetical percentages measure regional price effects adjusted for income. This difference compared to the variation in prices is the basis for the estimate of the elasticity of food expenditure with respect to the price of food. Thus for the North Central region, the actual expenditure ratio was 7 percent smaller than that anticipated, while prices were 10 percent lower, implying an elasticity of .7, somewhat high but within an *a priori* reasonable range. Values for two other regions correspond in magnitude and sign.

Only the Western states fail to conform to expectations, as a result, partially, of the frailties of index numbers. Consumption of fruits and vegetables represented almost a fourth of total expenditures in the region, compared to 10 percent nationally. Such a divergence of weights makes any comparison of prices inexact. With Western quantities determining the market basket, and with eastern prices of fruits and vegetables 20 percent greater, prices in the Western states are 2 percent lower than those in the North Atlantic region. Carrying through the calculation on the revised base of the Western states, the sign of the elasticity changes to positive, though too large (1.8). Similar regional variations seem to characterize the U.K. 1904 budgets. Forces other than price differences were also at work. But it is impressive how relevant such differentials are to the observed consumption structures.

It is possible by similar appeal to prices, to reconcile the much higher relative food expenditures reported in the 1901 survey compared to that conducted in 1888-91. Over the intervening decade relative food prices had risen appreciably. Rees's cost of living index implies an increase of 16 percent over the interval, not so much because food prices increased absolutely, but that others fell.[7] The corresponding increase in the expenditure on food, holding the income distribution constant, was 10 percent.

Prices therefore may indeed matter in the cross-section analysis of consumption patterns. It is very likely that they explain much of the late nineteenth-century international differences in consumption, after adjustment for income and family size. An index of relative food prices based upon information contained in the 1888-91 survey reveals an American advantage of perhaps 10 to 15 percent, with British prices slightly lower than the French.* Such evidence is confirmed by reference to other sources. Another and independent comparison of the retail price levels for food in the three countries in 1890 produces an index of 126 for Britain and 124 for France, with the United States equal to 100. Still a third calculation based upon the international prices collected in the 1875 Young Report yields a value of 122 for Britain and 123 for France.[8] All of the information is consistent in their lower American prices for meat—both beef and pork—and grain, and somewhat higher or equal costs for dairy products and imported groceries like coffee, tea, and sugar.

The net result, a clear differential in favor of the United States, is adequate to explain the observed deviations in expenditure patterns. The latter seldom exceed 10 percent, while prices diverge by perhaps twice as much.

---

*By 1906 the British Board of Trade reported higher American food prices, largely due to the intervening decline in the price of meat. Cost of Living in American Towns, pp. cxvi-cxvii. This phenomenon is discussed more fully in the third section of this paper.

The same applies to categories other than food. American expenditures for rent consistently exceed those in other countries. For similar size accommodations, prices were correspondingly higher: twice as great as those in Britain and higher still in relation to the cost in France.[9] In part, there is a quality as well as a price effect operating, since the physical characteristics of worker housing in the United States were generally better. As the Board of Trade report commented, in the United States was to be found a "more generous allowance of ground space per dwelling, except in congested areas, [and] . . . more modern character of a greater proportion of the fittings and conveniences of the dwelling, as illustrated by the more frequent provision of bathrooms."[10] For clothing, where roughly similar ratios prevail in both the United States and Great Britain, the prices seem to have been equivalently comparable.

The other side of the argument that the price structure rather than inherent taste characteristics caused the observed differences in expenditure is the rapid assimilation and Americanization of consumption of immigrant groups. Though foreign and native families are carefully distinguished in the 1888-91 and 1901 inquiries, little systematic difference is revealed despite the variety of origins. As the summary of the 1901 survey affirmed, "no very marked differences are noticed between the native and the foreign families in the several groups of income, but as a whole the foreign families show a little larger percentage of expenditure for rent, fuel, lighting, and food, and a little smaller percentage for clothing and sundries."[11] The relatively greater concentration of immigrants in the North Atlantic states, and therefore the slightly higher average prices for food and rent that they faced, explains some of that variation.

An equally extensive tabulation of family expenditures classified by national origins is to be found in the Board of Trade inquiry. Among the groups distinguished were Germans, Scandinavians, Southern Europeans, Slavs, Jews, and Negroes. While ethnic differences readily appear in the specifics of food consumption, the striking result is the substantial uniformity of the allocations to large categories. Figure 3.5 presents some of the Engel curves for food as an illustration.[12] Despite differential lengths of exposure to American conditions, there are no significant differences among the immigrant groups worthy of notice. It is equally revealing that out of more than 3,800 budgets of American families, only 74 were reclassified to the original ethnic groups because of distinctive national dietary habits. Immigrants adapted rapidly and definitively, not only in their patterns of expenditure, but in other ways as well.

FIGURE 3.5

Engel Curves for Food by Immigrant Group, United States

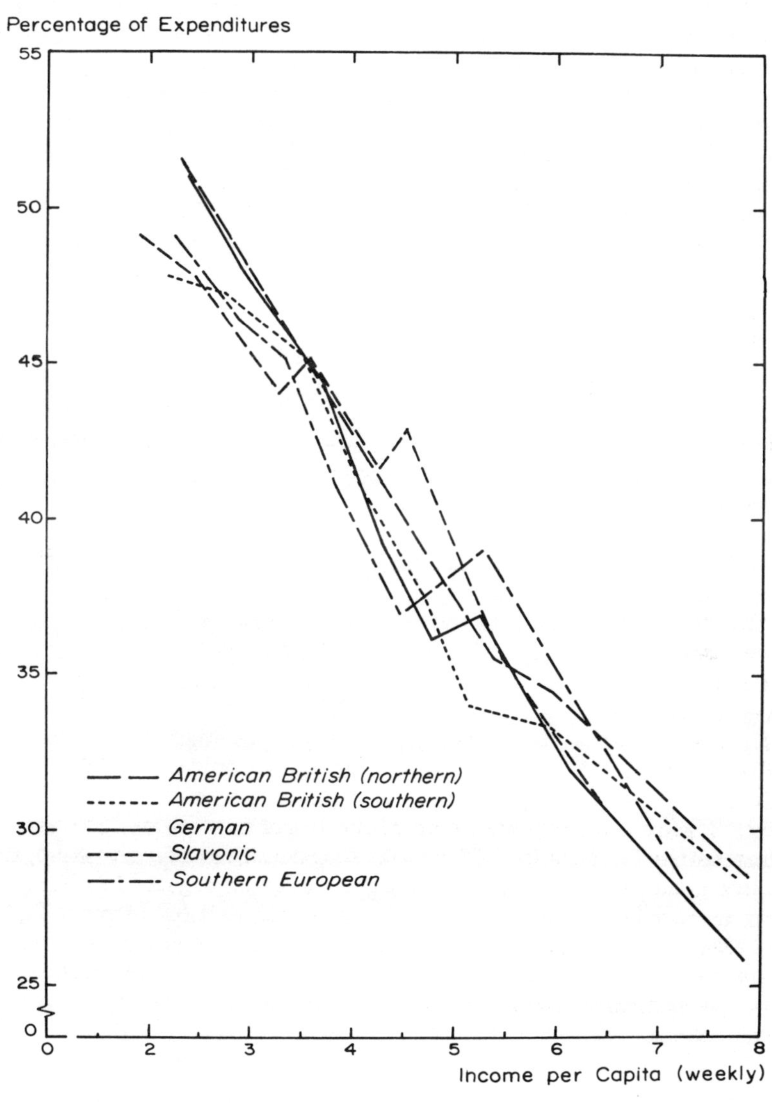

COMPARATIVE DEMAND STRUCTURES

Thus far we have concentrated upon differences in income distribution and relative prices as the factors principally responsible for the large initial international disparities in the allocation of expenditure. We now turn to an examination of taste differences more directly by calculation of demand relationships in the three countries. The resulting income and family size elasticities are tabulated in Table 3.5. Preferences may be supposed to influence the elasticities as well as the levels, while prices operate only on the latter. Hence the focus here on changes. The elasticities for rent, food, and clothing are derived from the common equation

$$\log \frac{X_i}{N} = \log A + b \log \frac{\Sigma X_i}{N} + c \log N$$

where X_i is the expenditure on category i, ΣX is total consumption, and N is family size. The residual demand for other goods and services is calculated from the budget constraint.

In the instance of "nonnormal" families, which may have boarders, consumption per capita for rent and food are defined inclusive of such persons, as are expenditures, on the assumption that payments for such services are reflected in family outlays. This is not a totally satisfactory solution, but is likely to provide better estimates than other alternatives. In such cases, the demand for clothing and other sundries is more distorted since the expenditures are made only for the nuclear family in question, but out of an average outlay that lies between the expenditure per resident and expenditure per family member. Potential error on this account has been minimized by eliminating observations with large numbers of additional residents relative to actual family members.*

---

*There are two alternative estimates $\hat{\beta}_m$ and $\hat{\beta}_n$ corresponding to the true parameters β_m and β_n. The subscripts refer to residents and family members respectively. $\hat{\beta}_m$ is a better approximation of β_m for rent and food because family purchases include outlays made on behalf of residents, and because the proportion of residents' income comprehended in the family total is large. $\hat{\beta}_m$ is an upward biased estimation of β_m because not all income of residents is recorded in family receipts. Conversely $\hat{\beta}_n$ is a better approximation to β_n because clothing outlays presumably do not contain any component corresponding to purchases of residents. It is biased downward since some incomes are overstated.

TABLE 3.5

Expenditure and Scale Elasticities[a]

	Number of Families	Rent Expendi-ture	Rent Family Size	Food Expendi-ture	Food Family Size	Clothing Expendi-ture	Clothing Family Size	Other[b] Expendi-ture	Other[b] Family Size
United States									
Normal									
Income class I[c]	55	1.25	.06	.92	-.15	.76	.74	1.18	-.22
		(5.73)	(.31)	(8.89)	(1.46)	(2.78)	(2.80)	(3.9)	(.8)
Income class II[c]	59	1.75	.10	.29	-.14	1.44	.44	1.60	-.13
		(3.60)	(.54)	(1.61)	(1.96)	(3.20)	(2.46)	(2.7)	(.6)
Income class III[c]	70	1.14	.04	.54	-.32	1.18	.39	1.36	.15
		(4.56)	(.25	(5.34)	(4.99)	(5.14)	(2.73)	(7.4)	(1.3)
Total	184	1.13	.44	.68	-.18	1.21	.49	1.29	-.24
		(13.63)	(.47	(18.00)	(4.23)	(13.69)	(4.89)	(15.4)	(2.4)
Non-Normal (Renters)									
Income class I[c]	30 (37)	1.00	-.66	1.00	-.01	.94	.58	1.05	-.13
		(1.92)	(3.75)	(5.92)	(.21)	(2.70)	(4.80)	(2.2)	(1.4)
Income class II[c]	57 (59)	.48	-.35	1.10	.09	1.75	.58	.47	-.47
		(1.06)	(3.34)	(4.53)	(1.60)	(2.68)	(3.15)	(.6)	(2.5)
Income class III[c]	52 (43)	.10	-.56	.25	-.17	1.41	.64	2.19	.07
		(.16)	(1.82)	(1.15)	(1.64)	(3.86)	(3.46)	(4.6)	(.3)
Total	139	.72	-.44	.86	.03	1.20	.54	1.23	-.24
		(5.61)	(4.50)	(17.06)	(.65)	(9.92)	(5.96)	(8.7)	(2.2)
(Owners)									
Income class I[c]	17 (21)	—	—	1.18	-.05	2.00	.40	.17	-.23
		—	—	(4.10)	(.37)	(3.02)	(1.22)	(.2)	(.6)
Income class II[c]	28 (26)	—	—	1.39	-.03	.54	.06	.74	-.04
		—	—	(3.25)	(.28)	(1.04)	(.75)	(1.3)	(.2)
Income class III[c]	29 (27)	—	—	.07	-.36	1.07	.49	1.72	.10
		—	—	(.31)	(3.20)	(3.15)	(2.26)	(7.6)	(.8)
Total	74			.72	-.04	.94	.30	1.34	-.09
				(9.19)	(.63)	(8.02)	(2.67)	(13.4)	(.9)
Great Britain									
Normal									
Income class I[c]	124	.61	-.54	.97	.10	1.18	.71	1.30	-.71
		(4.42)	(5.30)	(11.70)	(1.70)	(5.62)	(4.65)	(2.9)	(2.1)
Income class II[c]	127	.62	-.54	.80	-.05	1.56	.54	1.22	-.02
		(3.31)	(7.77)	(6.96)	(1.20)	(6.89)	(6.45)	(4.4)	(.2)
Income class III[c]	62	.86	-.24	.81	-.08	1.19	.59	1.46	-.08
		(4.39)	(1.56)	(5.63)	(.72)	(6.42)	(4.01)	(5.1)	(.4)
Total	313	.50	-.51	.87	-.15	1.30	.56	1.31	.19
		(9.75)	(9.75)	(26.06)	(.45)	(19.86)	(8.50)	(17.0)	(2.5)
France									
Normal									
Income class I[c]	94	.95	-.08	.96	.16	.79	-.17	1.23	-.18
		(11.86)	(.75)	(25.82)	(3.28)	(9.17)	(1.51)	(15.1)	(1.5)
Income class II[c]	40	.75	-.38	.75	-.12	.96	.11	1.59	.22
		(1.29)	(1.23)	(1.88)	(.56)	(1.63)	(.34)	(1.9)	(.5)
Income class III[c]	15	1.32	.18	.66	-.08	.98	.27	1.41	-.11
		(3.44)	(.32)	(3.37)	(.29)	(3.03)	(.56)	(3.6)	(.6)
Total	149	.95	-.13	.94	.07	.92	-.14	1.19	-.15
		(13.37)	(1.50)	(23.53)	(1.51)	(12.27)	(1.51)	(11.9)	(1.4)

[a] Absolute "t" values are reported in parentheses.

[b] Elasticities calculated as residual from the identity, $\Sigma w_i \xi_i = 1$, where w_i are the shares in expenditure, and ξ_i are the expenditure elasticities, and $\Sigma w_i s_i = 0$ where w_i are as before, and s_i the family size elasticities.

[c] Income class I ranges up to $89 per capita; class II to $149; class III, $150 and over. For renters and owners, where the dependent variable is divided by residents, so is expenditure. These numbers are given in parentheses.

Source: Derived from author's calculations; basic data are the same as those of Table 3.1.

The consistent technique of instrumental variables was employed to compensate for the statistical bias inherent in least squares calculation of the relationship of a component of expenditure to its total.[13] The final novelty is use of a sample of individual families from the 1888-91 survey as our set of basic observations. This enables us to examine the demands of other than normal families in the United States, to disaggregate the observations into more income classes, and to explore the implications of age structure upon consumption.

Comparison of the expenditure elasticities for normal families within the same per capita income bracket reveals considerable agreement among the three countries.* In only 4 of 36 paired comparisons of the expenditure coefficients did statistically significant differences emerge, three of them in the category of rent. This test, moreover, is biased in favor of revealing taste differences. In general, since the expenditure elasticity is equal to (dq/dy) . (y/q), and q is a function of price, calculated elasticities are themselves directly dependent upon relative prices. Only in the special case where a logarithmic demand relationship actually obtains, does independence exist. It is therefore relevant to note that the category revealing by far the largest international variation in price—housing—also contains the greatest number of deviations from the hypothesis of equality of the coefficients. Moreover, the cause of the difference—the lower British elasticity—is in a direction consistent with an influence of prices.

Yet this impression of uniformity is much blurred if we look only at the aggregate expenditure elasticities for the different commodities. Of 12 paired comparisons, half indicate statistically significant differences encompassing three of the four categories. American food elasticity is smaller compared to the French and British; British rent elasticity is correspondingly lower than those prevailing in the American and French sample; and French elasticity of demand for clothing falls below those of the other two countries. The patterns of demand for these three products exactly compensate,

---

*Paired coefficients are tested rather than the indicated and more straight-forward analysis of covariance of the pooled data for two reasons. The first is that with the method of instrumental variables, the essential property that the sum of the residual sums of squares across groups to be less than the total no longer holds. Accordingly the F. distribution affords an improper test. Secondly, the specific comparison of the coefficients enables one to focus on differences in income elasticities, rather than in the regressions as a whole.

and thereby imply very similar elasticities of residual demand in the three countries.

Two factors principally produce this aggregation error. First, there are the different income distributions of the different countries. This weighting effect has already been noted in the discussion of expenditure ratios. Yet this factor alone would be insufficient were it not for the simultaneous variation of elasticities with level of income. Table 3.5 reveals the tendencies: food elasticities fall with increasing income; clothing elasticities rise; while those for rent and sundries seem more inclined to be stationary. Higher American per capita incomes therefore automatically yield a lower aggregate food elasticity, while the converse in the French sample results in a smaller calculated elasticity for clothing. No such convenient explanation exists for the lesser responsiveness of British outlays for rent. The much lower aggregate elasticity than that found in the specific income groups is a measure of the lack of uniform minimum requirements for all income levels. A positive relationship of fertility and family income, yielding many small families in the higher income <u>per capita</u> brackets may be responsible. In any event, it is difficult to conclude other than that the English patterns of industrial housing outlays reflected in this sample differ basically and considerably from those in France and the United States, and merit more detailed study.

The lack of fidelity, in general, of the aggregate results has obvious implications. International cross-section studies have favored the logarithmic form for its convenience in avoiding problems of currency conversion. Yet if elasticities are not in fact constant, and prices can influence them as well, the results must be interpreted with care. Houthakker, in his article commemorating the centennial of Engel's Law, suggests a possible negative relationship of elasticites for food and per capita income levels, though nothing conclusive.[14] Here that finding is unequivocal if not completely continuous. Between the lowest and highest per capita incomes elasticity always declines, but its intermediate movement is not uniform in the United States sample. Even within countries, therefore, the true structure of demand may be distorted by imposing elasticity constancy, without adequately testing for variation. The practice of using group means rather than individual observations, with consequent inability to discriminate effectively among variable elasticities, may be deceptive.

The conclusion we have found of similar expenditure elasticities among comparable families in the three countries actually appears to apply less well to different types of urban industrial family composition within the United States itself. Table 3.5 includes both owners of their houses as well as renters of a less homogeneous composition. Their coefficients are sometimes not only different by large absolute amounts, but indicate divergent tendencies. Yet beyond the significantly smaller food elasticity for normal families in the $90-149 bracket, no variation exceeds the bounds that could occur by pure chance.*

Though the demands are thus not decisively different, perhaps because the limited samples make detection difficult, one common feature of the "nonnormal" results merits additional comment. This is the very substantial increase in elasticity of demand for sundries as income per capita rises from the first to the third level. For both renters and owners, increases in expenditure are almost exclusively allocated to basic necessities initially, but in much lesser proportions thereafter; food elasticities exceed unity until the highest income level. Basic requirements may therefore differ as between these less homogeneous households and the normal grouping. Owners may find alternative outlets for their outlays in the form of household furnishings, repairs, and improvements that do not present themselves to simple renters. And our "nonnormal" renters, with different composition and greater reliance upon supplementary sources of income, appear likewise to have a correspondingly different allocation of increments of receipts. These variations call attention to the necessity to broaden the traditional boundaries of inquiries into historical household consumption behavior. Normal families represent a minority of the respondents even within the classification, itself circumscribed, of urban industrial workers.**

Thus far the discussion has been confined to income elasticities. The question of family size and attendant economies of scale also merits attention. These latter are measured by the signs and magnitudes of the coefficients reported in Table 3.5. They are calibrated on a per capita scale—and thereby already compensate for the altered allocation of expenditures implied by the change in per capita income associated with the addition of another family member. On a family expenditure scale, the size coefficient $C = C' - b + 1$, where C' is the per capita size coefficient, and b, the expenditure elasticity. Hence, C will generally be positive, and less than unity, without directly indicating scale effects. Only if family composition goes beyond the income effect to alter the allocation of expenditure does scale have independent significance.

---

*Two total coefficients for renters, those for rent and food, also are at variance with those for normal families. The principal cause, however, seems to be differing income distributions.

**Of the original sample of 25,440 families included in the 1901 inquiry, only 11,156 "normal" families were represented, or less than half. The "normal" families selected seem to be the totality of that group. U.S. Bureau of Labor, <u>Eighteenth Annual Report</u>, pp. 15-18.

The array of coefficients assembled in Table 3.5 reveals evidence of possible economies of scale in housing and food consumption, and much more convincingly, diseconomies in expenditures for clothing. The latter is ubiquitous except for the case of France. In essence, clothing requirements are sufficiently fixed so that larger families with identical per capita income are impelled to spend more on them than smaller ones. Such physical requirements translate into expenditure shares because price does not greatly vary between adult and childrens' items. By contrast, in the case of food consumption, a large degree of substitutability among alternative qualities exists, as well as the capacity for marginal adjustments, which lends itself to the presence of economies of scale. In housing as well, since there is common space available unrelated to numbers, there is scope for more efficient utilization with increased family size. Both in Great Britain and for nonnormal United States renters, this phenomenon is observed. For normal American families it does not, and does so only weakly in France. Its absence in the former case is due to sampling variability, and in the latter possibly to rental scales or accommodations related more closely to family size.

It is of interest to explore the effects of family composition upon food consumption in a more detailed and disaggregated form. The coefficients thus far presented are limited to family size without allowance for the effects of age distribution. Yet it has been usual practice from Engel's day to develop equivalent scales to convert the lesser food requirements of children into a common denominator. In similar fashion, it is possible to examine actual food expenditures, discriminating among different types of families—not only in size, but age distribution, and other characteristics if desired. Basically one starts from a demand relationship in which population units are weighted rather than equated.[15] The double logarithmic form is convenient for this purpose and could be written as:

$$\frac{E_F}{\Sigma\alpha_{iPi}} = A\left(\frac{E}{\Sigma\beta_i P_i}\right)^{\xi},$$

where E_F is expenditures on food; E, total expenditures; α_i, the specifically weighted food consumption scale; β_i, the general income scale; P_i, the individuals with different characteristics i; and ξ, the income elasticity. This is a nonlinear relationship as it stands. However, if one sums across family units similar in composition and statistically estimates the equation:

$$\log E_F = \log A + \xi\ E + a_1 d_1 + a_2 d_2 + \ldots + a_n d_n,$$

where d_i are dummy variables corresponding to each separate class of family observed, ξ can be correctly determined.* The assumption required is that elasticity be identical for all family classes, and that their consumption differ by constants measured by a_i. In a second stage it is possible to estimate α_i, given β_i, by considering the linear relationship

$$E_F\left(\frac{\Sigma\beta_i P_i}{E}\right)^{\xi} = A\,(\Sigma\alpha_i P_i)$$

in which α_i can be determined up to a factor of proportionality.

It is precisely the latter we are seeking to determine, i.e., a scale, and there is no loss in this procedure. Note that α_i itself is dependent upon β_i. Corresponding to different general income scales, there will be alternative specific consumption scales.[16] The relationship between the two determine the <u>differential</u> weights associated with consumption by particular types of individuals.

In our own application we have examined three age groups—5 years and less, 6 to 14, and 15 and over—and two countries, Great Britain and the United States.** Within each country, moreover, two income per capita classes were defined, since the assumption of a single elasticity over the entire income range cannot be maintained. The first stage elasticities for the four groups, and the specific

---

*More precisely, if we write the demand relationship as

$$\frac{x_i}{\sum_j \beta_j P_{ij}} = A\left\{\frac{\Sigma x_i}{\sum_j \alpha_j P_{ij}}\right\}^{\xi}$$

where i refers to family and j to specific age groups, then by summing across n groups of identical families, we can substitute $\beta_{ik} \equiv \Sigma\beta_j P_{ij}$ and $\alpha_{ik} \equiv \Sigma\alpha_j P_{ij}$ in the above relationship. Then we estimate

$$\log x_i = \sum_k \log A\, \beta_{ik}\, \alpha_{ik}^{\;-\xi} + \xi \log X_i.$$

**Because it is desirable to have large numbers of observations to define the different family groups as identically as possible, and also because there is no evidence of economies of scale, France was excluded from this analysis.

scales corresponding to β_i equal to one, are given in Table 3.6* Their general purport, with the single exception of the upper income level United States entry, is one of little or no *differential* variation of food consumption with age relative to the income per capita scale employed.

Such a conclusion is consistent with the evidence indicated in Table 3.5 for limited economies of scale in Great Britain. Since normal families are already standardized and per capita income is used, the scale coefficients tend to reflect age distribution as well as family size effects. Most conclusively, in the first phase estimation itself, the dummy variables created to reflect family composition proved statistically significant only in the equation for higher American incomes.

The failure to find systematic effects of age composition while physical requirements are clearly not invariant is not self-contradictory. These results tell us only that families of identical size and income but of different age structures consume identically, not that food expenditure for infants is the same as for adults. If parents do not adjust their own food outlays downward with the birth of a child, but only reduce their expenditure as children grow older and demand more, that behavior will generate observations like our own. To put it another way, recall that the estimate of the specific scale depends upon a presumed general scale, taken in this instance as of per capita form. Starting the other way round, with given physical requirements, we could infer that families adjust their incomes for age composition as well. Families with small children behave as though their incomes were large, and make their allocations accordingly.

What is even more intriguing is the impli[illegible] disparity of income perceptions between lower- and higher-income families in the United States and, to a lesser extent, Great Britain. The latter do respond as if they reckoned themselves generally poorer, independently of age composition. An obvious question is whether this difference reflects itself in other behavior, including that of desired and realized family size.

---

*Use of simple least squares in the second stage of analysis leads to unbiased, but inefficient estimates because of heteroscedasticity. The error term in the original demand relationship is multiplicative, and remains so in the substitution performed in the second stage. Since Brown's results, weighted and corrected, were not greatly dissimilar, it did not seem necessary to pursue this correction here.

TABLE 3.6

Specific Food Consumption Scales

	Expenditure Elasticities	Scale		
		Over 15	6-14	Under 6
United States				
Income Class I[a]	.97	1.00	1.03	1.03
Income Class II[b]	.50	1.00	.58	.61
Great Britain				
Income Class I[a]	.91	1.00	.97	1.11
Income Class II[b]	.81	1.00	1.01	.82

[a]Up to $124 income per capita.
[b]$125 and over.

Source: Derived from author's calculations; basic data are the same as those of Table 3.1.

All of this begins to take us far afield, and on the basis of quite modest and limited findings. The point is that study of age composition effects can shed significant light on more than mere consumption patterns, extending to the question of the legitimacy of income per capita as the appropriate measure of well-being to which individuals respond.

Our analysis of demand structures thus far has been limited to our 1888-91 sample. It is useful to consider its consistency with the totality of the 1888-91 inquiry, and also with the later American 1901 survey. We are restricted in this endeavor to normal American families. For them, the correspondence is good. The income elasticities for rent, food, and clothing derived from the 1888-91 cell means are .96, .62, and 1.14 respectively. The relevant sample values are 1.13, .68, and 1.21, all larger by a factor of about 10 percent, and therefore understating the elasticity for sundries correspondingly. Of equal relevance is the parallel variation with income. Food elasticity declines from .95 for income per capita of $125 and less to .48 in the higher income bracket; the clothing elasticity rises slightly from 1.09 to 1.14; and the rent coefficient declines from 1.12 to .84. The economies of scale are equally accurately portrayed, both in the aggregate, and including the differing results for food in the upper income class.* On the whole, therefore, our sampling technique has not distorted the results for normal families, and has permitted us to enlarge our scope of comparison and include nonnormal observations.

Equally, the 1888-91 survey compares well with the later Bureau of Labor investigation. The latter was designed to sample more accurately the industrial and geographic distribution of workers in the United States and is therefore presumably more representative. Houthakker reports expenditure elasticities of .84 for rent, .71 for food, and 1.44 for clothing. The lower value for rent relative to 1888-91 is partially ascribable to his inclusion of less elastic fuel and light outlays; an estimated adjustment increases the value to .91.[17] The larger deviation is for clothing and represents a real difference in the two surveys. Relative clothing prices had fallen over the decade by about 30 percent, which only compounds the difference. Despite this anomaly, the earlier ordering of elasticities remains invariant and of comparable magnitude, and can be taken to reflect American purchasing habits at the end of the century.**

Unfortunately we cannot vouch equally for the reliability of the British and French representation. Houthakker's earliest surveys for the two countries refer to 1937-38 and 1951 respectively and therefore afford no basis for comparison. The contemporary inquiries of the Board of Trade can give some assistance though the majority of its observations lie outside a comparable range. Their general contour is consistent with the earlier data, as we have seen in Figure 3.3, and that in itself is relevant. Recall that our principal purpose in undertaking the statistical study of demand in this section was to confirm that the initial expenditure differences found in the data themselves could be explained more readily by relative prices and different income levels than by national tastes. This has been established. The international expenditure differences found in the sample are real enough. They are reflected even in Mulhall's crude estimates of consumption, as well as detected by the Board of Trade. What would controvert our results is a sample displaying similar variation in expenditures, but whose basis was a different structure of preferences.

---

*One difference in the aggregate data is that small economies of scale do appear in the rent equation. The elasticity is .14, which is significantly different from zero t-statistic of -3.91.

**Scale effects calculated from the 1901 survey, converted to a per capita basis, are also comparable with the earlier 1888-91 results. They are -.13, .45 and -.27 for food, clothing, and rent respectively.

ORIGINS OF AMERICAN INDUSTRIAL DEMAND

We have focused thus far upon the comparative consumption patterns of urban industrial workers at the end of the nineteenth century. The evidence has indicated that a higher proportion of American expenditures, at identical levels of income per capita, did go for nonfood requirements, less as a consequence of taste differences than lower food prices. These permitted a higher standard of food consumption with smaller outlays. What is now critical to the argument for larger nonfood demand is the relative price structure of these goods and services. Larger American expenditures for these items only meant greater demand if prices were not equivalently higher. All prices entering into consumption in the United States could not be inferior to those in Europe for that would violate the legitimacy of the exchange rate as a conversion factor for real incomes. And in fact they were not: the Young Report argued that clothing prices were twice as high in America, compared with Britain, with the working population of the latter enjoying lower prices than the French also.

Yet this is to exaggerate the divergence. The comparative prices of standard cotton textiles listed in the same Report reveal no such advantage. Of nine products, the New England price was lower than the London for no fewer than seven, with one equal. A more ample sample of English industrial cities and American regions makes for a less-decisive margin, but one nonetheless generally on the American side. For manufactures more generally, the qualitative adaptation to the American market through the production of standardized lines worked to keep prices down. Service prices were generally higher in the United States, and food prices could be significantly lower because the costs of transportation represented a significant increase in selling price. This structure of relative prices would have favored industrial demand. Though the evidence is far too meager to be conclusive, the potential advantage of lower food prices could well have been turned to greater initial demand for manufactures without a favorable real income differential. As such a differential developed, there was an unequivocal shift toward such products associated with an income elasticity above unity. Central to this process were the special characteristics of the rural sector in shaping demand as well as keeping food prices low. These matters take us far from our budget studies, but necessarily if we are to understand the historical evolution of the American market. It was not until 1890 that the proportion of the population engaged in agriculture amounted to less than a majority of the labor force; its share of income exceeded a fourth until approximately the same year.

American agriculture, outside the South, was both commercialized and family-sized. In conjunction, they meant a high degree of direct provision of foodstuffs and shelter, combined with market purchasing power for industrial goods. Diversified agricultural production took care of the majority of food requirements, and this even in the South. Cash outlays were limited to such essentials as salt, sugar, and coffee that were not locally available. Housing needs were similarly self-provided, though, as on the prairies, purchases of construction materials might be necessary. Farmers, like our urban owners, were thus spared allocations for rent, while at the same time enjoying a near self-sufficiency in foodstuffs.

The first extensive survey of farm operators in 1922-24 showed that even at that late date, approximately two-thirds of food consumed was directly furnished. As a proportion of total consumption, something slightly more than half passed through market transactions, depending upon the level of income. Including the imputed value of consumed production, however, the share allocated to food was higher than for industrial workers with comparable incomes per capita.[18]

Four factors, partially offsetting, determined the scope of this rural demand for manufactures. One is the lesser cash expenditures for food and shelter. The second, incorporating the findings of the later budget studies, is the partially canceling lesser demand for nonfood products. The third, equally adverse, is the smaller income per worker earned in agriculture, even allowing for the imputed value of consumption. And the last is the size of the rural sector. Their net resolution yielded a significant role for rural consumption of manufactures until the latter part of the nineteenth century. Estimates by Dorothy Brady suggest that in the 1830s farm demand represented 58 percent of the national market for clothing, 53 percent of the sales of house furnishings, and half of the outlays for reading and recreation. Small towns, many dependent for their livelihood upon an agricultural hinterland, accounted for half as much again.[19] As a share of the demand for domestic producers, their importance loomed even larger since imports catered to many of the whims of the wealthy.

In their sheer number, of course, farmers were potentially important. Realization of their importance required an income distribution that did not allocate purchasing power to the extremes. An agricultural sector composed of many laborers and few owners, even with the same productive efficiency, would have presented a different aspect. Less food would have been consumed directly. Instead the rural laborers would have expended their own salaries almost exclusively to purchase it, with little remaining for other purposes. The greater incomes of the rich would have gone for servants, for imports, for travel. The case of the plantation South was extreme. Slaves received no margin for expenditure and were allocated the merest of necessities. Large plantation owners prided themselves on their foreign, including northern, fashions. Yet in Britain itself, where no more than 4,000 owners were said to account for four-sevenths of the land in England and Wales, 85 percent of the agricultural labor force in 1851 consisted of laborers.[20] The French peasant proprietor was much more firmly established, but not without a larger number of sharecroppers and agricultural wage earners than in the United States. In 1882, tenants and sharecroppers represented a fifth of the labor force, workers a half, and occupying proprietors a residual 30 percent.[21] Including family workers, American free farm laborers made up only one-third of the nonslave agricultural labor force during the entire antebellum period, and with tenancy still being comparatively limited, proprietors made up virtually the rest.[22]

This structure influenced the quality of the market as well as its quantity.[23] Rural demands, by virtue of their absolute size, left their stamp upon supply. The enthusiastic receptivity of standardized, low-priced, and less durable commodities was a consequence in no small measure of the tradition of simple, functional design inherent in prior household manufactures. Foreigners recognized this characteristic of American demand, often with mild condescension:

> . . . a very large domestic supply of articles of wearing apparel of most descriptions is available there of standard sizes . . . though often less durable. It is evident, however, that the practice of buying clothes that are expected and intended to last for a single season only and not for two or more is much more common than in this country. In this respect an analogy may be traced to a national characteristic, noticeable not only in respect to clothing but also as regards houses in their inferior durability and, as regards machinery, in the greater rapidity with which it is either worn out or discarded. In all of these directions there appears to be a half-conscious discernment of what is regarded as "economy in spending," which, while savoring of extravagance, tends at the same time . . . to secure . . . as regards clothing, as also food, the maximum of freshness and satisfaction.[24]

The origins of such a national style would seem to lie in the rural market not only by virtue of its tastes, but also its geographic dispersion. Production could not be easily tailored to individual locales, but was soon standardized in urban centers and widely distributed through a quickly improved system of internal transportation.

Rural demand per capita was possibly less efficacious in directing production to industrial goods than the demand of urban workers, whose relative incomes were higher and food demands lesser. Nevertheless, its qualitative features were an important counterweight. Moreover, the American family structure of efficient agriculture made the rural market relatively better, compared to other nations, even in its quantitative dimensions. The absolute amount of expenditure upon manufactures for a given rural income per capita was probably greater in the United States than in Britain and France, owing to more equitable income distribution.*

As manufactures took root, and the population became more urban, the allocation of consumer expenditures progressively reinforced and accelerated the transition. Principally owing to a diminished rural sector, per capita consumption of staple foodstuffs in the United States increased but modestly in the last third of the nineteenth century, and perhaps over an interval twice as long. Between 1870 and 1900, consumption of wheat rose from 5.4 bushels per capita to 6.0; consumption of pork declined, either from 137 pounds to 72 in the semi-official version, or more plausibly, from 90 to 76 in another estimate; on the other hand, consumption of beef increased, but the gain from 64 pounds to 73 is not sufficient to increase meat intake as a whole. Over the same period, per capita income had risen 70 percent.[25] To be sure, sugar, coffee, dairy products, and other food items entered more extensively into consumer budgets, but the principal beneficiary was industrial products. Agriculture, less cotton, grew 110 percent over this interval, netting out unprocessed exports; manufactures grew 480 percent. Yet the terms of trade between foodstuffs and other products included in Hoover's cost of living index only mildly alter; values are recorded of 92 for 1851-55 and 108 for 1876-80, with 1860 equal to 100.[26] Thereafter, there is some decline likely in the 1880s and a larger rise in the 1890s.

The very fact that food prices should have been relatively lower earlier would have given them more leverage at precisely the right moment—when per capita incomes were smaller and the percentages allocated to food higher. What is significant is that they did not rise rapidly thereafter and impede the extension of the market. American food prices in the 1830s and 1840s were not only lower relative to those of a nonfood composite, but also compared to British foodstuffs. That is, British food prices fell more rapidly from 1831-50 to 1866-90 than did American, and we have already seen that American foods were absolutely cheaper at that later date.[27] Hence, the comparative

---

*Moreover, that same structure probably produced more income by the self-direction of work effort and the minimization of disguised unemployment. In combination they compensated for the greater rurality of America.

advantage the United States enjoyed was greater in the earlier period than that portrayed in Table 3.1.

Moreover, it was an advantage that not even the enlightened British policy of free trade could erode until the very end of the century. Grain from the plains of the Dakotas and the steppes of Russia could be admitted without duty and its price equalized, but that of meat could not. Technological changes did not permit substantial trade in chilled or frozen fresh beef and mutton until the late 1880s. Thereafter they largely substituted for the earlier consumption of imported pork products, in response to the lower price of the newly available imports. Between 1885 and 1900, British imports of beef per capita rose from 3.5 to 11.7 pounds, and those of mutton from 1.8 to 9.3 pounds. Prices of these products declined by more than 20 percent. Imports took over almost half the national market.[28] Not surprisingly, therefore, as we noted earlier, the Board of Trade survey found in the first decade of the twentieth century that retail prices of food in British industrial cities were then cheaper than in the United States. France reaped no such benefit. Committed to restrictionism and protection of agriculture as exemplified in the Meline Tariff of 1892, meat prices remained stationary over the last twenty years of the century and industrial workers derived no corresponding boost to their real incomes.[29]

As in so many instances, one has been forced back to the special characteristics of the American agricultural sector to understand more adequately the dimension of the nineteenth-century American market for manufactures. This rather different dual economy flourished in a way that few have emulated. Yet it is useful to reflect upon the implications of that success for present policies.

IMPLICATIONS FOR CURRENT PROBLEMS OF LDCs

The preceding discussion is germane to contemporary development problems in three respects. The first is the broader concept of the extent of the market it has conveyed. Some discussions have dismissed demand as a significant variable because there are few countries so small as not to permit of the establishment of at least a single plant of optimum size throughout a broad spectrum of industrial activity. Therefore the market is not a limiting factor in instituting industrialization. This is an entirely static view of the matter and lacks the support of history. It ignores the reciprocal influence of demand in shaping present supply, as well as the effects of potential sales in determining the introduction of new productive techniques and products. Not least of all, it ignores the conditions under which an effectively competitive structure of production can evolve.

Some of the presently developing countries that first emerged into industrialization at the beginning of the twentieth century, particularly those in Latin America, seem to have been afflicted with precisely the malady of a limited market. Textiles, shoes, and other industries initially nurtured under protective shelters were relegated to rapid technological obsolescence and lack of vigor. There was no rural sector whose demands contributed effectively to the creation of a market for manufactures, nor was there a ready and continuing supply of foodstuffs at low prices as in the United States.

This is all in the past, and cannot be undone. To generate wider markets now, we must focus upon the growth of demand, and therefore upon income elasticities. These vary with income themselves and between urban and rural settings. They are thus sensitive to income distribution and population movements, as well as quite possibly, to relative prices. Where decisions to invest represent a meaningful constraint upon development, expectations of future market expansion can be a significant factor. One of the reasons for the success of the import substitution strategy in stimulating investment, leaving aside the question of its efficiency, was the guarantee of a rapidly growing market fed by progressive reduction of the import share. Such rates of growth cannot now be repeated, but it represents a lesson in the significance of market expectations, and the extent to which these are relevant in nonsocialist economies. What has been lacking are fully effective policies for turning the rural sector simultaneously into more efficient producers and more substantial consumers of their own produce as well as of manufactures. More equal rural and urban income distributions would seem to help as well as greater emphasis upon external markets to compensate for the sometimes low urban elasticities of demand for foodstuffs. In this fashion, there is the incentive of a growing agricultural demand to stimulate productivity change, lower prices, and greater scope for nonfood expenditures among the urban poor.

It is this concern with an independent influence of demand that distinguishes this discussion from the superficially similar analysis of dual economy and marketable surplus models. This is the second area in which historical results have a bearing. Here, too, the terms of trade between agriculture and industry play a central role in maintaining the rate of growth. The reasons are, however, quite different. The purpose is to permit urban money wages to remain low, industrial profit high, with the surplus reinvested in the industrial sector to provide continuing growth. Even when an elasticity of demand is explicitly specified for manufactures, its effect is limited to determining the equilibrium growth rate, and not whether one attains it. Such models, in short, tend conveniently to abstract from the entire range of issues previously raised concerning the interrelationship of demand with supply.

The issue being joined is whether savings is the principal constraint to market-oriented development. This is not to deny that high rates of capital formation are a necessary concomitant to the growth process, but rather how they functionally evolve. The long standing inconsistency between greater equality of income distribution and high rates of investment is much mitigated if the circumstances of more vigorous market demand can evoke and channel resources more effectively. Can one yet be so certain of the structure of underlying behavioral relationships in developing countries as to rule out such a possible consumption-oriented strategy that was apparently central to the American success? Increasing empirical evidence indicates declines in domestic savings associated with inflow of foreign capital; this speaks directly to the point of constraints other than those of thrift. At the household level, a recent study in Taiwan has shown that acquisition of modern consumers' goods was associated with other behavior patterns favorable to development, including savings itself.[30]

This logically brings me to the third and concluding point: the need for more intensive micro household analysis in the developing countries. More and better surveys are now being taken. Their results must not be left at the level of description, but rather turned to the important questions of economic policy which they can illuminate. Our assigned task has been to show the relevance of microanalysis to historical questions of development. I can only hope that this discussion has been substantively revealing, and indicative of the potentialities of similar research applied to present problems.

* * *

COMMENT BY JEFFREY G. WILLIAMSON

The role of demand and the extent of the market has rarely been analyzed so effectively as by Fishlow here. Development economists have paid too little attention to demand in current dynamic general equilibrium models for developing economies. Yet recent research by Cheetham, Kelley, and myself (1971) indicates that changing demand parameters may be even more influential on growth performance than savings parameters!

Fishlow quantifies one historical relationship that deserves special emphasis:

> The evidence has indicated that a higher proportion of American expenditures, <u>at identical levels of income</u>

> per capita [italics added], did go for nonfood requirements, less as a consequence of taste differences than lower relative food prices. . . . Though the evidence is far too meager to be conclusive, the potential advantage of lower food prices could well have been turned to greater initial demand for manufactures without a favorable real income differential. As such a differential developed, there was an unequivocal shift toward such products associated with an income elasticity above unity. [p. 74]

This in itself may be an interesting explanation of the unusually rapid rate of industrialization in the nineteenth-century American economy to the extent that higher levels of industrialization imply more rapid introduction of new technology.[31] The concept of dualism is multifaceted and one well-documented aspect is rural-urban differences in demand behavior. Yet the explanation of the relatively "high preference" for foodstuffs by rural populations has most often been explained by taste differences. Perhaps such an explanation is the logical result of our conventional assumption that all households in an economic system are faced with the same set of prices. In an underdeveloped economy with high transport costs, this assumption is surely in error. As late as 1870, grain prices in New York were as much as 80 percent higher than in Iowa.[32] Whitney has shown that 90 percent of America's structural change between 1879 and 1899 is to be found with final demand.[33] Fishlow's research raises the question: To what extent did the westward population shift foster American industrialization? Given low food prices and resulting low budget shares for food in the West, how important is the population shift in accounting for the impressive American industrialization after 1870? Consider the potential impact of a population shift to a region specializing in agricultural products where the price of that product is low.[34] Let the per capita demand for agricultural products be d_A and total per capita expenditures be e. Then with a simple Cobb-Douglas specification we have:

$$d_A = P_A^{\alpha} e^{\beta}$$

or:

$$D_A = N\{P_A^{\alpha} e^{\beta}\},$$

where D_A is aggregate demand for agricultural products and N is the total population. To simplify the problem still further, assume that demand parameters are identical in the two regions. If we denote a superscript W as "West" and E as "East," then aggregate American food expenditures can be written as:

$$E_A = P_{AW} \{P^{\alpha}_{AW} e^{\beta}_{W}\} N_W + P_{AE} \{P^{\alpha}_{AE} e^{\beta}_{E}\} N_E$$

or:

$$e_A = P^{\alpha+1}_{AW} e^{\beta}_{W} \eta + P^{\alpha+1}_{AE} e^{\beta}_{E} (1-\eta)$$

where η is simply the share of population in the West. The interesting issue raised by Fishlow's research is by how much were American food expenditures, as a share in total expenditures, reduced by the relative expansion of the West? The United States budget share can be expressed as:

$$w_A = \frac{e_A}{e} = \{P^{\alpha+1}_{AW} e^{\beta}_{W} \eta + P^{\alpha+1}_{AE} e^{\beta}_{E} (1-\eta)\} e^{-1}$$

$$\frac{\partial w_A}{\partial \eta} = e^{-1} \{P^{\alpha+1}_{AW} e^{\beta}_{W} - P^{\alpha+1}_{AE} e^{\beta}_{E}\}$$

$$= e^{-1} \{P^{\alpha+1}_{AW} [e^{\beta}_{W} - Z^{\alpha+1}_{A} e^{\beta}_{E}]\} < 0,$$

where Z_A is an index of transport costs (e.g., the percentage by which New York prices exceeded Iowa prices). Engel effects are captured by $0 < \beta < 1$, while the low price elasticity of demand for agricultural goods implies, of course, $-1 < \alpha < 0$. In the 1970s, Z_A was as large as 1.8. Thus it makes no difference by how much eastern per capita income exceeds western—the shift of population to the West must have had a pronounced impact on nonfood expenditures in the United States and played some role in the rapid rates of structural change up to 1900, especially in the West itself.

Economic historians have always stressed the interaction between the distribution of income and the composition of demand. In fact, development economists are now devoting attention to their interdependence in exploring Latin American experience with labor absorption. Yet the traditional approach is to invoke the assumption that demand elasticities vary with income levels and hence to explore the impact of size distribution of income on demand structure. Fishlow now suggests another fruitful avenue for research: the changing rural-urban distribution of population may have a profound effect on demand structure to the extent that significant variance in commodity price structure exists in low income economies. Yet the direction of the impact in contemporary developing economies should be diametrically opposite to the American experience. With the shift to urban centers, Engel effects should be offset, since higher urban food prices imply lower nonfood budget shares for a given per capita income.

Finally, Fishlow's research stresses once again the importance of evaluating the Green Revolution within a general equilibrium framework where impact through demand can be fully appreciated.[35] Until recently, most research on technological change in agriculture has been focused on supply. Fishlow's historical analysis suggests equal concern with the price-induced effect on demand.

CHAPTER

4

EXPERIENCE IN GENERATING MICRO DATA IN LATIN AMERICA

Robert Ferber and
Jorge Salazar-Carrillo

The collecting of data on the behavior of economic units is especially hazardous in the case of less developed countries. Not only must one face the usual problems of specifying what is to be collected, how, when, where, and with what degree of reliability, but a whole range of additional problems enters the picture, principally relating to organization, the recruiting of qualified people, and communication.

Even in the United States and other countries with highly developed statistical survey organizations, data are obtained with errors far exceeding what would be expected purely on the basis of sampling theory—errors which at times tend to dwarf the statistics themselves. Unlike errors in other data, those in economic data do not always cancel when the data are combined into aggregate form.[1]

For these reasons, similar studies on the reliability of data collected in less developed countries are badly needed. This paper reports on experiences in collecting data from consumers, businesses, and governments in Latin America. Unfortunately, hard data are not available on the magnitude of whatever nonsampling errors and biases may be present. But the types of errors likely to be most important, and the probable effects of such errors on estimates of parameters and on their variances, are pointed out.

THE FRAMEWORK

There are various ways of classifying errors in a survey—among others, by the stages of the survey, by source, by likely magnitude, and by the type of study. For our purposes, consideration of errors by the stages of a survey would seem to be as appropriate as any other classification procedure, given the need to evaluate the likelihood of different kinds of errors and considering the scant information available on the subject.[2]

A survey can be divided into the following major stages:*

1. Specification of objectives.
2. Sample design and sample selection.
3. Questionnaire preparation.
4. Interviewer selection, training, and supervision.
5. Data collection.
6. Data reduction (including machine cleaning).

This is a broad classification, encompassing many types of error within each category. The principal types will be considered, first, with reference to a survey of consumer expenditures; second, with reference to the collection of price data; third, with reference to the collection of wages and costs in business and government establishments in Latin America.

Evaluation of the likely effects of these errors at each stage will be made with regard to two key parameters in each study: the mean and the variance. Thus the reference will be to mean expenditures per consumer unit and country, whatever the mean wage and mean price per establishment and country may be. Variances will correspond to the variances of these statistics.

CONSUMER EXPENDITURE SURVEY

The consumer expenditure study, like those to be discussed later, was carried out under the sponsorship of the Estudios Conjuntos Sobre Integración Económica Latino Americana (ECIEL), an organization of research institutes within the eleven Latin American Free Trade Association countries, brought together and coordinated by the Economic and Social Development Program of the Brookings Institution.

The purpose of the consumer expenditure study was to analyze income and expenditures of the population of the major metropolitan areas of Latin America. The cities covered in the study, by country, are listed in the stub entries of Figure 4.1.

The study was carried out at different times in the various countries—partly because of difficulties in obtaining the necessary financing, partly because of political and economic problems,

---

*Data processing and analysis are not within the scope of this paper.

FIGURE 4.1

Time Schedule for Field Work on Consumption Study

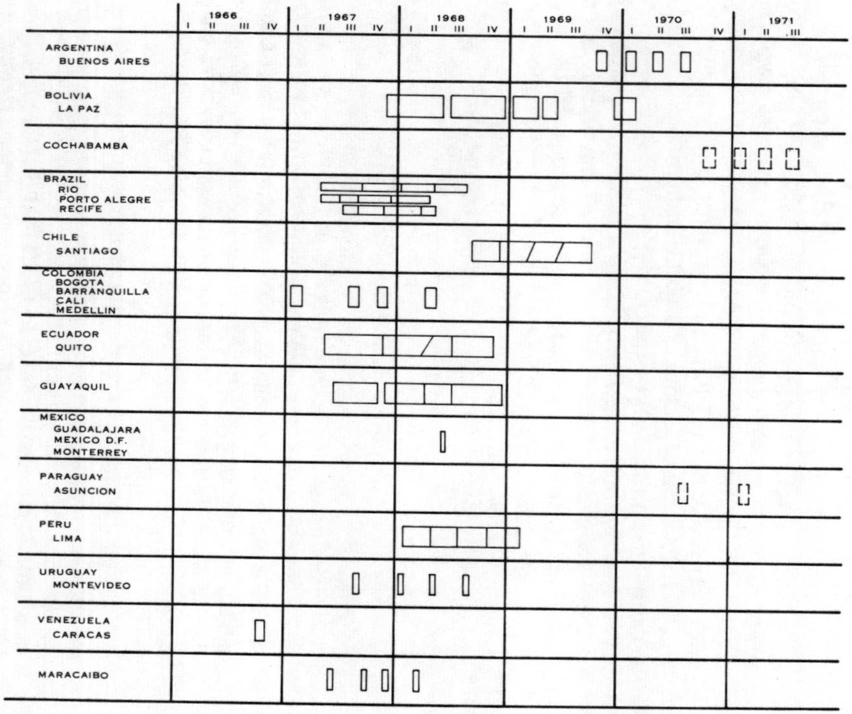

1966 I II III IV | 1967 I II III IV | 1968 I II III IV | 1969 I II III IV | 1970 I II III IV | 1971 I II III

ARGENTINA
BUENOS AIRES

BOLIVIA
LA PAZ

COCHABAMBA

BRAZIL
RIO
PORTO ALEGRE
RECIFE

CHILE
SANTIAGO

COLOMBIA
BOGOTA
BARRANQUILLA
CALI
MEDELLIN

ECUADOR
QUITO

GUAYAQUIL

MEXICO
GUADALAJARA
MEXICO D.F.
MONTERREY

PARAGUAY
ASUNCION

PERU
LIMA

URUGUAY
MONTEVIDEO

VENEZUELA
CARACAS

MARACAIBO

and partly because of differences in the survey design from one country to another. These differences will become more apparent as we review the possible sources of error at each stage of the study. The period of data collection extended from early 1966 to 1971, most countries using a panel design covering twelve months. The period devoted to field work in each city is shown in Figure 4.1, with the divisions indicating the span of each quarterly interview, where such were made.

Specification of Objectives

In the initial stages the multicountry nature of this survey caused particular problems. The principal one was that though the study, as designed by ECIEL, had a clear statement of its objectives, in most cases each country had additional objectives, partly because of the interests of its own researchers and partly because of the needs and requirements of its financing agencies.

In some cases, these objectives caused no problems, but in other cases it was necessary to redesign the questionnaire and include requests for data not germane to the main purposes of the study. Thus, if the data were to be used in preparing weights for a price index, additional information would have to be collected on quantities purchased and frequently on prices paid. This made the questionnaire a good deal longer, made it more likely that the respondent would be irritated, and, consequently, that later data would be obtained with less reliability.

The effect of these diffuse objectives is very likely to bias downward estimates of mean expenditures in these countries because of the need to collect additional data, thereby usually reducing the detail (and emphasis) in collecting expenditure data for the main study. This bias may not exist, however, where special emphasis is placed on getting more of the same type of data, as in getting weights for a price index. Variances are not likely to be much affected.

Sample Design and Sample Selection

As in other countries, the lack of trained sampling statisticians and of the necessary detailed maps were major possible sources of error in the study.* It was not difficult to devise a probability design

*Sample sizes varied substantially depending on the resources available. The range was from 200-300 in each of the Colombian cities to about 1,000 in Santiago and Caracas.

taking advantage of whatever sampling materials were available in each of the countries. However, to train people in carrying out this design was a difficult task, and there is no doubt that errors crept into the field operations associated with the sample selection.

In most instances, for example, the sample design involved prior listing work, which is difficult to do accurately even under the best of circumstances. It was even more difficult in most Latin American countries, partly because of training and supervision problems and partly because of the large number of cities with slum areas, where housing units often have no identification at all. In very poor areas, listing housing units could even be hazardous since the residents feared that this work might be connected with a police search for people without documents or for some other illegal activity.

No attempts could be made to ascertain the extent of errors connected with listing and the sample selection. These errors could have been substantial and would bias estimates of mean expenditures upward and of variances downward since families with unusually low levels of expenditures are more likely to be overlooked.

Questionnaire Preparation

If substantial groups within a population use different languages, translation of a questionnaire into those languages is usually necessary. When only a small proportion of the population uses another language, however, it is usually possible to retain the questionnaire in the original language and have the interviewer translate as he goes along. Accordingly, only Spanish and Portuguese versions of the questionnaires were prepared for this study.

Climate is especially important in a continent like South America, where types of food, clothing, and even transportation will differ from one area to another. Changes of this sort exist within the same country, as in Ecuador, where the people of Quito (at 9,000 feet and with mild temperatures) eat different foods and wear different clothing from those in Guayaquil, which is at sea level and has a hot year-round climate. Hence, questionnaires for such different cities or countries can be strictly comparable only for broad categories.

Probably the most important source of error, and the major problem in the preparation of the questionnaire for the consumer expenditure study as applied to a multicountry survey, was the choice of approach. Some countries felt very strongly that the only means of obtaining accurate data on consumer expenditures was by a diary form, while others preferred a recall-type questionnaire. A controlled preliminary test using both types of questionnaires in Chile and Uruguay yielded no significant differences in levels of expenditure.

It was impossible to get the countries to agree on a single approach, especially in the light of this test, so the choice was left open. The suggested method was a diary form for food and related products, supplemented by a three-month recall questionnaire for other types of expenditures and for income, repeated three times.

Despite the results of the pretest, it is not clear that the two approaches yield similar results. At the least, the diary approach provides much more detail on expenditures and makes the supplementary recall questionnaire easier to administer. However, the diary approach could only be used with literate families. Illiteracy in most countries of Latin America is still substantial. Attempts were made to deal with this problem by having the interviewer visit the family two or three times a week and record food expenditures on a recall basis.

A related problem was how much detail to ask on expenditures and income. Considerable resistance was encountered from local researchers when it was suggested that expenditures and income be requested by individual items, even though evidence suggests that this tends to yield better aggregative estimates. Since sample members were asked to recall these expenditures for at most three months at a time (one month for expenditures on small items and for continuing expenditures such as rent and utilities, and three months for major expenditures), the effect of varying the amount of detail may not have been large. On balance, however, it would increase the likelihood of overlooking expenditures, thereby biasing downward both means and variances.

Interviewer Selection, Training, and Supervision

Always a hazard in any personal interview survey, problems and biases arising from this source are likely to be even greater in Latin America. The pool of potential interviewers is a limited one, and career interviewers are virtually nonexistent. Interviewers had to be hired and trained from scratch, with all of the additional problems that this entailed.

Most of the interviewers were students. Though such students are generally older and more mature than their undergraduate counterparts in the United States, interviewing to them was a part-time occupation. The problem was compounded by the tendency to keep training sessions brief, not to mention the fact that experienced supervisors were not always available. Moreover, it was not possible to have the same people conduct the training sessions in different countries, with the result that there was undoubtedly substantial variation in training standards from one country to another.

For these and related reasons, it is probable that the level of training and supervision produced lower mean expenditures. Even so, variances would tend to be overestimated, due to high interviewer variability.

Data Collection

Sources of error at the stage of data collection may be classified from an operational point of view as the following:

1. Locating the correct housing unit.
2. Obtaining the necessary cooperation.
3. Obtaining data within the proper frame of reference.
4. Obtaining accurate and complete data.

As mentioned in the section on sampling problems, it was not always easy to locate the correct housing unit. From a sampling point of view, unknown biases may have been introduced by the tendency (in six of eleven countries) to have the listing work and the selection of sample units done simultaneously. This leaves the interviewer with considerable discretion and makes it easier for him to rationalize the selection of better-looking and more conveniently located housing units. No evidence is available to indicate the effect of this procedure on the results.

Obtaining the necessary cooperation is a difficult problem in a consumer expenditure survey in any country. Here it was especially difficult to obtain cooperation from high-income households, undoubtedly because of suspicion of strangers. As an example, the following tabulation presents response rates by income strata for the four Colombian cities in the study for the first wave.

	High	Middle	Low
Baranquilla	76%	82%	91%
Bogotá	69	79	82
Cali	47	67	84
Medellin	87	87	92

Though underrepresentation in terms of numbers is easily corrected by means of appropriate weights, no information is available on the extent to which families not interviewed differ in their expenditure patterns from those interviewed.

The appropriate frame of reference for the interview can be especially difficult in a consumer unit survey in Latin America because of the numerous living arrangements that exist and the ease with which they can be confused. This was no exception in the present case, even though an attempt was made to deal with this problem by taking the housing unit as the basic sampling unit and then interviewing separately all consumer units residing within a particular housing unit.

The problem, essentially, was twofold. First, what constituted a housing unit? The usual definitions based on a separate entrance, separate kitchen facilities, or separate lavatory facilities raised various problems in parts of all the cities sampled because of the large number of families sharing the same facilities. All that could be done was to establish a definition based on formal or common-law relationships among groups in the same set of rooms (or room!). Considerable discretion had to be left to the interviewer in the determination of the housing unit.

Much the same was true of the definition of the consumer unit, the second aspect, because of the complex interrelationships existing among individuals residing within a particular housing unit. Rules could be used to distinguish, for example, among married children having independent incomes, living with the parents and sharing or not sharing some common expenses, as well as what to do about other related people living in the same unit but not sharing expenses. The final determination, however, was up to the interviewer.

Obtaining the necessary data accurately and completely seemed on the whole not to introduce any severe problems other than those encountered elsewhere. Indeed, for the lower-and middle-income ranges, these data seemed to be given at least as readily as in surveys in the United States, to judge by the completeness of the questionnaires and the reports of the interviews. Most suspect would be the expenditure, and especially the income, data for high-income families, among whom reluctance to cooperate was widespread. One would suspect that expenditures were somewhat understated and incomes substantially understated by this group but by how much is an unanswered question. Variances would tend to be underestimated for the same reasons.

Data Reduction

Problems at this stage centered on the lack of trained people to do editing and coding. Fortunately, this is not a difficult training problem though it is not clear how careful training or supervision were at these stages. Cursory indicators are that in some countries the work was done at least as well as in the United States, whereas in other countries there were major shortcomings.

In view of the highly variable quality of data reduction people both within and among countries, variance estimates would very likely be overstated, though in terms of averages these errors may well cancel each other.

PRICE AND PURCHASING POWER PARITY SURVEY

The objectives of this study were to compare prices and determine purchasing power parity rates across LAFTA countries, and to provide a basis for estimating their real gross domestic product. Due to lack of resources, the survey was mostly restricted to the capital cities of these countries. Data were collected in May 1968.

Specification of Objectives

Unlike the consumer expenditure survey, this study had a clear statement of intent. Though initially the objective was somewhat confused, it was clarified in joint meetings with the participating institutions. The only way in which these ambiguities affected the project was by delaying the collection of data.

Sample Design and Sample Selection

For a large and important number of categories, the price survey relied on the sample design and materials of the consumer survey in the selection of a stratified sample of outlets in neighborhoods of different income levels. Stores were selected within neighborhoods on the basis of a probability selection of street corners. The fact that selection of a particular type of store within a neighborhood is a fairly simple problem and that very low-income areas were not considered, together with the more manageable size of the survey, reduced the magnitude of problems at this stage.

However, two other factors caused errors. One was the complex sampling structure required for a comprehensive price survey, the selection of outlets being different in most categories. The other was the tendency for interviewers to facilitate their work by picking outlets that were most obvious, or those where they thought they could find better cooperation in completing their task.

These forces tended to diminish the chances of selection of less modern, unusual, special, or lower-income outlets. Thus the country mean can be expected to be biased upward and the country variance to be biased in the opposite direction. They probably affected the different countries in a uniform fashion, and thus intercountry comparisons would remain unaffected.

Questionnaire Preparation

This time a uniform set of questionnaires was prepared by the coordinating staff at Brookings. No country variations were permitted, except for minor semantic changes to make the questionnaire more understandable in a few countries. Also, a group of specialists visited every country in the study, in the hope of achieving a comparable selection of goods and outlets and appropriate implementation of the questionnaires.

Particular problems were faced in the area of investment goods and consumer durables. There are several ways in which price and other pertinent data can be obtained for these types of goods. Though a personal interview method was suggested, some institutes found mail questionnaires more convenient. A variant of this approach was to leave a questionnaire with the firm, asking that it be completed and returned. As compared to the personal interview approach (which can involve more than one visit to the firm), the latter methods are more prone to error, especially when the amount of information requested is sizable and firms are reluctant to cooperate.*

Under these conditions, we would expect that in countries where these methods were used, errors in prices given would bias the country mean upward, with variances affected in the same way. Fortunately, few countries shied away from personal interviewing in machinery and equipment and consumer durables. Whenever this occurred, pricing errors can be expected to bias the country mean so that it would lie between the mean of effective discount prices and that of list prices.

On the other hand, construction goods prices were generally obtained by leaving the questionnaire and picking it up at a later date. The effect of this procedure (as opposed to the personal interview approach) is also to increase the country mean and variance.

Interviewer Selection, Training, and Supervision

In most cases the interviewers were already trained and experienced in price index work. Yet their degree of sophistication cannot be compared with their counterparts in developed countries. Training sessions seemed satisfactory, even if somewhat short. Not only could the study count on supervisors with price index experience,

---

*In the price survey not only did we ask for effective discount prices (rather than list prices) for machinery and equipment and consumer durables, but information was requested on certain specific brands and models and on the most important characteristics of the machines (horsepower, capacity, etc.). In the case of construction goods, a detailed questionnaire sought cost estimates for certain specifications and each of its components.

but the coordinating staff provided homogeneous supervision of the training process and conducted extra training sessions of their own.

Even though we would expect data variability to be greater than in the United States, for example, because of the lower quality of local interviewing and supervisory personnel, the elaborate checking and processing of the data at Brookings probably restricted these errors to minimal proportions.

Data Collection

Already mentioned were the problems involved in locating the correct outlet in the price survey. Lack of sampling aids, listings, maps, etc., may have biased interviewers toward selecting the most expedient and convenient outlets. For example, establishments selected for consumer price index work may have been favored. Yet, since price variability among outlets is much smaller than expenditure variation, the effect on means and variances is not expected to be as large as in the consumption study.

It was difficult to obtain the collaboration of outlets in the investment goods and consumer durables sections, particularly in certain countries.* However, this problem was surmounted in various ways.**

Data Reduction

The objectives of the price study were of a more purely international nature than those of the consumption and wage studies. This meant that each institute had a less tangible stake in the outcome of the former and could not be expected to exert as much care in the collection and reduction of data.

Accordingly, the responsibility of the central coordinating staff in the price survey was greater. Coding and editing sheets were prepared at Brookings and sent to the collaborating institutions to facilitate and reduce possible errors in this phase. Yet it still was

---

*Our experience in requesting information from United States companies on machinery and equipment prices suggests that refusals are not higher in Latin America.

**Such as by obtaining the information from a buyer rather than a seller, posing as potential customers, examining transaction records, enforcement of legal obligation to provide information, using government bid price information, etc.

deemed necessary to recode and reedit the data at Brookings. Computer listings were then sent to the institutes for verification.

Both mean prices and variances for these goods are probably overestimated in every country, as a result of the tendency to select more prominent outlets. This seems to have mostly affected the investment goods and consumer durable sections of the study, where the type of information sought was of a more complex nature.

INDUSTRIAL WAGE AND LABOR COST SURVEY

The purpose of this survey was to compare take-home pay and labor cost for the different LAFTA countries and to analyze their industrial wage structure.

The industries covered were cotton textiles, metallurgy, pharmaceuticals, auto assembly, tires, heavy household appliances, wood products, vegetable oils, and paper products.

A purposive sample of six to nine firms whose main line of production fell within any of these industries was selected in each country. Though the study was carried out during different time periods, all the data refer to November 1966.

Specification of Objectives

In theory, the wage study had the same set of objectives in each country. Unfortunately, the original methodological statements contained inconsistencies which were not cleared up by the time of the survey. This problem necessitated thorough checking, cleaning, and adjusting of the country data to ensure international comparability in the concepts. An additional difficulty was that, in contrast to the price study, the wage survey could not be adequately supervised by the coordinating group at Brookings.

It is not clear whether these problems affect the variance of wages at the establishment or country levels. They undoubtedly increased the variance if taken over all countries. Means were clearly affected. Certain less skilled occupations were not appropriately represented in the sample, and as a result the industry averages of wages and labor cost are overestimated.

Sample Design and Sample Selection

The lack of trained personnel, as well as the absence of disaggregated statistics and information on economic activity in these countries, was a major obstacle in designing a sample and selecting the firms to be interviewed. Detailed figures on production, exports, technology, etc., were required, but in many countries, up-to-date listings of firms could not be found.* This made the sample design difficult and must have affected the country's means and variances. Given these difficulties, the selection of firms was to a great extent influenced by expediency and prior knowledge by the researchers involved. As a result, some of the less conspicuous and lower wage-paying establishments were probably missed, increasing the wage mean and decreasing its variance in each country.

Questionnaire Preparation

The wage survey started with the same questionnaire for all countries and a homogeneous approach to data collection. Though uniformity was stressed, some country variation was required because word usage and conditions varied by nation. Depending on the collaboration expected from the business community and the secondary variables to be investigated, the questionnaires differed in size and depth. However, an invariant core was kept, with only semantic differences from country to country.

Yet this sensible diversity contemplated in the methodology proved to be problematic when coupled with 1) a core questionnaire obscure in certain sections and not explicit in others; 2) insufficient supervision of the data collection effort by the coordinating group. As a result, the cleaning and processing stage became complicated and time-consuming.** The major problem was the incomparability of the wage data in terms of fringe benefits concepts. Further work had to be done in the field and at Brookings to ensure better comparability.

Interviewer Selection, Training, and Supervision

Though errors in this stage would be expected to be larger in underdeveloped areas, the size of the survey and the collaboration of

---

*In Latin America, the distinction between firm and establishment or plant is very tenuous. Generally, firms do not operate more than one plant in a country.

**We should point out that the types of comparative projects undertaken by ECIEL seem to be unparalleled in economic development research. Since the wage survey was the first major data collection effort undertaken by ECIEL, it was more prone to difficulties.

institutes with certain expertise in industrial research minimize the importance of this problem as compared to the consumer survey. On the other hand, little supervision could be given by the coordinating staff. It is difficult to evaluate the significance of this type of error on the country means, but we expect the lack of centrally-directed training and supervision to have enlarged country variances significantly.

Data Collection

Location of the correct firm was not so complicated as in the price survey. Yet some errors surely crept into the selection process, as already noted. On the other hand, this is compensated by the fact that wage variability among firms is larger than price variability among outlets (though still less than the variation in the expenditures of consumer units). These errors (in the selection of units) are not expected to have a significant effect on the estimates.

The procedures used in requesting information from firms and in completing the questionnaire may have also generated errors. The original plan called for an interview with the personnel manager or his counterpart, with the questionnaire to be filled in by the interviewer and the respondent together. Two or three visits were considered necessary to complete the questionnaire. However, the interviewers seemed to have trouble with this procedure. Most institutes used one visit to deliver and explain the questionnaire and another to pick it up. The questionnaire was then to be checked for inconsistencies and inappropriate responses, with added questioning if necessary. It is doubtful that such indirect control devices were fully effective.

Given the normal tendencies to exaggerate costs and understate income and profits which afflict firms, especially in Latin America, the resulting plant and country means are probably higher than if strict personal interviewing had been followed. Moreover, the lack of direct control over questionnaire replies probably biases the variances in an upward fashion. It is reasonable to assume, however, that the magnitude of these errors is similar across countries.

Even though the institutes involved in the wage survey were well known by the industrial community, some firms refused to cooperate.* This was particularly acute in certain countries and sectors, and to a certain extent was caused by the fact that the information requested was considerable. The problem created by refusals was difficult to handle, since the number of firms in each industry

---

*Some were government institutes with legal backing for research.

was small to begin with. As an example, response rates were 71 percent in Colombia, 47 percent in Brazil, and 79 percent in Venezuela (the latter for the pharmaceutical and metallurgical industries).

Firms refusing to be interviewed would likely differ significantly from the others, probably paying lower wages and having lower labor costs per employee. Though the play of the labor market can be expected to place some bounds on wage diversity, country estimates would nevertheless be affected. This kind of bias would increase the means and lower the variances. Though the errors would be significant, they probably neutralize one another in international comparisons.

Data Reduction

Given the more manageable size of the wage survey and increased guidance by the central coordinating staff, data reduction errors do not seem to have been substantial, and in any case probably cancel out. No effect on the variance estimates is considered probable either, due largely to the fact that the coding and editing group was small, with adequate training and supervision being less difficult. Also, because of additional adjustments required in making the data comparable across countries, part of the burden of coding and editing fell on the coordinating staff, which provided additional verification of the work by the institutes.

CONCLUSIONS

It is clear that errors in surveys of this type pervade all stages and are likely to arise in many different ways, depending on the design and administration of the study. Indeed, administrative aspects would seem to be at least as important as the survey design in determining how errors arise and how critical they may be. The latter is especially true in cross-country studies involving people with little experience in this type of work.

Secondly, the likely direction and magnitude of effects of particular types of errors are not easily generalized. This is brought out by the overall summary of likely effects by stage of the survey and by study, as provided in Table 4.1. It suggests that the same source (and even type) of error may produce opposite effects on means and on variances, depending on the study. Moreover, our experience shows that the same source of error is not always likely to affect the mean and variance of an estimate in the same direction, though this may generally be the case. Even the overall effects,

TABLE 4.1

Likely Effect of Errors on Means and Variances of Three ECIEL Studies

Source of Error	Consumption Study Mean	Consumption Study Variance	Price Study Mean	Price Study Variance	Wage Study Mean	Wage Study Variance
Specification of objectives	-	0	0	0	+	+
Sample design and sample selection	+	-	+	-	+	-
Questionnaire preparation	-	-	+	+	0	+
Interviewer selection, training, and supervision	-	+	0	0	0	+
Data collection	-	-	+	+	+	+-
Data reduction	0	+	+	+	0	0
Overall evaluation	-	?	+	+	+	+?

Code: + : overstatement of parameter; 0: little or no effect; -: understatement of parameter.

shown in the last line of the table, are not necessarily consistent either among studies or between means and variances of the same study (and it should be stressed that this overall evaluation is highly subjective).

Third, the types of errors likely to be most important in these studies are no different from those likely to be most important in a comparable study in the United States—namely, selection of sampling units, interviewer training and supervision, and data collection. Their control, however, is much more difficult.

Fourth, the nature of the errors is such that, for any one study, they are likely to be much the same in all countries. For this reason, the data are likely to possess more reliability for international comparisons than as absolute estimates of means or variances in a particular country. In this sense, therefore, the multicountry nature of these studies serves to offset some of the biases encountered in survey work.

These results suggest that research is badly needed to ascertain more concretely what errors exist in the generation of micro data in the less developed countries. Virtually no research appears to have been undertaken on this subject. Yet methods are available, ranging from validation studies, such as those undertaken in the United States and a few other countries, to careful evaluation of respondents and interviewer reports while using the best reports as a yardstick for gauging accuracy and reliability. None of these methods is easy, but there is no question of their feasibility. The substantial errors that can arise in obtaining micro data should serve as an additional incentive for work of this kind.

CHAPTER

5

GENERATING MICRO DATA IN LESS DEVELOPED COUNTRIES THROUGH SURVEYS: SOME EXPERIENCE IN ASIA

Eva Mueller

Development economists are clearly aware of an increasing need to work with disaggregated data. But to deal with such data requires a broad spectrum of statistical observations at the individual, household, and firm level. Before discussing the feasibility of collecting micro data in less developed countries through surveys we must ask what kinds of microeconomic data we need most. There is an American tendency to become enthusiastic about a tool—such as the survey method—and then look for places where it can be used. I should prefer to begin by specifying major information gaps and then see whether surveys can fill them.

Benjamin Higgins has pointed to the information gap that I would rank first—information on economic behavior. As he says: "The trouble with neoclassical microeconomics was not implicit in the method; the trouble was that too little time and energy was devoted to examining the assumptions regarding behavior. . . ." One might add that even if neoclassical economists had assiduously studied economic behavior, their findings would not be transferable to today's LDC. The task of developing a set of empirically validated propositions about the nature of economic behavior and economic decisions in an LDC is still before us.

There are a number of testable hypotheses regarding economic behavior that may be cited as illustrations. One is the backward-sloping supply curve of labor. Another and more general one is the

---

The author gratefully acknowledges valuable suggestions by Frank M. Andrews and James N. Morgan of the Survey Research Center of the University of Michigan and the M. T. R. Sarma of the National Council of Applied Economic Research in New Delhi.

hypothesis advanced by Irma Adelman, who suggests that in traditional societies a primary objective of economic decisionmakers and institutions is risk reduction, subject to adequate income constraint. In modern societies, by contrast, behavior and institutional arrangements are oriented toward income or profit maximization, subject to maximum risk constraint. Another behavioral hypothesis is that business firms and households in LDCs change their behavior in response to large economic incentives but not in response to small ones. This could be true 1) because of considerations of risk; 2) because of an inadequate information system; 3) because economic behavior has a stronger habitual element in an LDC than in a MDC; or 4) because institutional arrangements are slow to respond to changes in relative prices, supply, or technical conditions. A final example of a behavioral hypothesis is that economic actors in LDCs respond to positive economic incentives but not to negative ones. The carrot is more powerful than the stick. These hypotheses are not mutually exclusive, and each may have validity under certain circumstances. We need more factual information on people's reactions to incentives and risks, in order to find out what kind of economic behavior occurs under what conditions.

Secondly, there is a need for micro data on economic stocks and flows—data on income, consumption, savings, investment borrowing and debt repayment, assets, etc. One would like to know the distribution of these aggregates in the LDCs, their determinants at the individual level, and their relation to behavior at the micro level.

Third, there is a need for data on the impact of specific development programs at the individual level. What kinds of people feel a need for or benefit from a particular program and what kinds do not? We must find out under what circumstances a program succeeds or lags. And we must learn how the program ties in with the behavior and attitudes of the economic units at which it is directed.

A good deal of microeconomic data has been collected in the LDCs. Yet most of it relates to very small microcosms—one or two villages, a single firm or a single factory labor force, particular groups of entrepreneurs in one locality and industry. Though we have gained important insights from these research activities, we need additional research to establish empirically tested generalizations on the experiences and behavior of representative groups of households, producers, and firms. For this, studies must be based on scientifically drawn samples large enough to permit the application of multivariate statistical analysis and statistical significance tests. This is where sample surveys enter the picture.

Is the collection of micro data through surveys likely to be feasible and productive in the less developed countries? Elaborate statistical analysis and significance tests may be meaningless, if the data are biased to begin with. No categorical answer to the question of feasibility is possible. Some data are much more difficult to collect than others. Some statistical projects are unrealistically ambitious, others are not. Some LDCs have survey facilities, some do not. It is surely wrong to belittle _all_ attempts to collect economic survey data in LDCs by citing a few failures. Instead we should ask what kinds of data collection are most feasible? Where has the survey method had its clearest successes, and where does it encounter its most severe limitations?

Accuracy depends on the proposed utilization of the data. Thus the question of feasibility cannot be answered independently of the question of purpose. Furthermore, sampling error is only one of the ways in which sample size influences accuracy. Obviously, feasibility depends on the manner in which data collection and access to collected data are organized in the LDC. The answer may lie in behavioral and interdisciplinary studies, and the avoidance of a practice which might be called "excessive quantification."

KINDS OF ECONOMIC DATA TO BE COLLECTED

It seems to me that the prerequisites for successful survey work are present in many LDCs. My particular experience with surveys in India and Taiwan* suggests that it is no more difficult than in the United States to hire satisfactory interviewers as long as the job involves some continuity. Able young men and women have fewer employment opportunities in such countries than in the United States and therefore can be recruited more easily for survey work. In India, practically all our interviewers had masters' degrees in the social sciences or statistics. Though their motivation may have left something to be desired, and turnover was fairly high, they had a better understanding of survey objectives and economic concepts than the average professional interviewer in the United States (usually a college trained housewife). In Taiwan, the interviewing staff, largely female and for the most part not college-trained, was highly motivated.

---

*The author has conducted surveys with the National Council of Applied Economic Research in New Delhi, and with the Taiwan Provincial Institute of Family Planning in Taichung. This field work has been supplemented by conversations with social scientists who have done surveys elsewhere and by written reports about survey work in LDCs. Generalized statements in this article are based on this admittedly limited experience. They may not be universally valid.

These women were experienced, conscientious interviewers and seldom changed jobs.

The availability of interviewers with an academic background in economics or another discipline closely related to the content of the survey may solve a thorny problem. The traditional rule that the interviewer should never rephrase the question or interpret it to respondents is hardly workable in LDCs, where educational differentials between respondents are very large. Communication with illiterate respondents with few contacts outside their village is obviously extremely difficult. It is thus desirable to give interviewers some latitude in explaining the meaning of questions to respondents, at least questions of fact. The better educated an interviewer is, and the better he or she understands the objectives and methods of the survey, the greater is the chance of performing this sensitive task in an acceptable manner.

In general, well-trained interviewers are cordially received by respondents in the less developed countries. Life is less entertaining in an Indian village than in an American town or suburb, and a visit by an interviewer is an interesting event. People have more time on their hands than in the United States, and the interviewer does not have to compete with the television set. Thus the preconditions for a successful interview exist.

In both India and Taiwan, response rates in household surveys are in the neighborhood of 95 percent—much higher than in the United States. Response rates in panel studies are also relatively high, suggesting that longitudinal studies are feasible in LDCs. In our Taiwan study, 89 percent of the husbands of an original group of married female respondents could be interviewed after 20 months. In a recent rural survey in India by the National Council of Applied Economic Research (NCAER), 95 percent of a cross-section of rural heads of household could be reinterviewed after one year. In an earlier NCAER study covering urban households as well, about 90 percent of the respondents in the first round of interviewing also provided an interview one year later.

For the most part people in LDCs are willing and able to talk about recent experiences, if these experiences have been of some importance to them. Recall is facilitated by the fact that matters pertaining to a person's work or to his economic situation are usually important to him. Thus we can obtain reliable information on a wide range of economic behavior; for example, whether the respondent used pesticides, whether he put money into certain savings media during a recent period, what kinds of home improvements he made, how much he worked, whether he bought shoes or a bicycle or went to a movie, whether in recent years he bought any equipment for his small business. Such inquiries are not difficult so long as we do not ask for exact amounts or costs involved.

Information about socio-economic characteristics of respondents is usually needed for economic studies. Absolute accuracy is not essential so long as this information is used only for purposes of classification. Sociologists have been concerned with the difficulty of classifying people according to such Western concepts as age, education, occupation, household composition, and urban versus rural background.[1] Such concerns appear to be justified in some parts of Africa and in the more backward areas in Asia. In India and Taiwan Western socio-economic and demographic concepts seem to have become familiar to most respondents.

One hears, for example, of the difficulty which people in LDCs have in reporting their age. In Taiwan reporting of the birthyear seems to be remarkably accurate. Birthdates are apparently important in the Chinese culture, and people write them down in a book or remember them. A cross-section of Taiwanese women were asked to give their husbands' birthyear in a survey. Twenty months later the husbands were interviewed and also asked for their birthyear. In 85 percent of cases, husbands named the identical birthyear; in another 9 percent, husband-wife reports were only one year apart. Education of both husband and wife was reported with an equally high degree of consistency. It is doubtful that respondents would do better in the United States! By contrast, however, a survey in Orissa, India, found that "age [of children] represents a serious research problem because it is often not known. There is often a substantial difference between the age recorded on school records, the parents' estimate, and the child's estimate."[2] Orissa is one of the least developed states of India, with little industry and low per capita incomes. It also has the highest percentage of "backward" people of any Indian state—that is, people recognized officially as belonging to scheduled (untouchable) castes or tribal groups.

One area where survey research has encountered particularly stubborn conceptual difficulties has been highlighted by Gunnar Myrdal.[3] He has rightly criticized measurements of labor force participation, employment, unemployment and underemployment in LDCs. Since unemployment is a matter of growing concern in these countries, this is indeed an area to which more attention ought to be devoted. The problem would seem to lie in the inability of Western-oriented researchers to formulate an analytical framework relevant to local institutional arrangements.

Next, attitudinal data may be considered briefly. So long as attitudinal questions are simple and are concerned with reactions to everyday experiences, they can help to interest the respondent in the interview while bringing forth useful information as well.[4] However, illiterate or poorly educated respondents have small vocabularies, are inarticulate, and are unable to handle abstract concepts.

For example, expectational questions (such as income expectations) baffle many people in LDCs. One gets such answers as "Only God knows the future" or simply "I don't know" much more often than in the United States. Similarly, many people cannot make complex or hypothetical choices between various alternatives. Both in India and Taiwan many men cannot rank-order various reasons for saving according to importance. Frank Andrews reports that in Peru, in remote but substantially populated regions of the Andes, questions like "How many children would you like to have?" are virtually meaningless to respondents. I doubt that the kind of questions sometimes asked in United States surveys to measure personality traits could be successfully asked in large-scale surveys in LDCs. On the other hand, the rather "iffy" question "If your income rose, what would you do with the extra money?" was answered readily by Indians and Taiwanese regardless of education. This was evidently something to which they had given real thought (though it is not certain that their intentions would actually predict behavior).

Attitudes of businessmen toward existing situations and policies are even more important and are likewise measurable. Such data provide some feedback on government policies affecting businessmen, whether credit programs, import regulations, or vocational training programs. I do not have in mind loosely structured conversations with businessmen, though they may be of value too. One can ask a series of questions about particular situations and policies of a sizable sample of business owners and then compare how larger and smaller owners reacted to a certain government program. One can also compare businessmen in different industries and locations or those in expanding as against static or declining firms.

In brief, much attitudinal information useful to economists can be obtained by patient and skillful questioning. However, the researcher should avoid matters to which many people have not given much thought or which they do not see as having personal relevance to them, such as plans to shift to as yet unknown agricultural techniques, opinions about the current Five Year Plan, or expectations of future income. Attempts to measure deep-seated psychological traits also may encounter considerable difficulties.

But the data in which we as economists tend to be most interested are quantitative micro data on income, savings, consumption, and business operations. Household income data are of particular importance. How feasible is it to collect such data in LDCs? The myth that it is not possible to collect worthwhile income data in such countries is incorrect. Admittedly, people in LDCs often do not know what their annual income is; however, it can usually be approximated with their help. A wage or salary earner in government or industry would know his monthly, bimonthly, or weekly pay. He would have to be questioned carefully about various supplements such as overtime, year-end bonuses, housing allowances, and the like. He also would have to be questioned in detail about layoffs and other losses of income. An agricultural wage laborer would present a more difficult case. He normally lives from hand to mouth, and the whole concept of a periodic or regular income is foreign to him. Nevertheless, one can find out from him how much work he had during the different agricultural seasons in the past year, what kind of work he did, and how much he was paid for each kind of work—in cash and kind. The questioning has to be detailed and leisurely enough to facilitate recall. Sufficient information can usually be obtained to warrant an estimate of income.

Similar considerations apply to the calculation of farm income. Most farmers know and are willing to tell how much land they have under various crops, also how much and what kind of livestock they own and have bought and sold. This is public information. One can further inquire about amounts of each crop produced, prices received, amount of labor employed, wages paid, the quantity and price of other purchased inputs. Much of this information can be checked against price and yield data for the area available from outside sources.[5] One can also ask whether the past agricultural year was an unusually good one for the respondent, unusually bad, or more or less normal and why.

In Taiwan, we checked each farm income schedule against available outside information on prices, wages, yields, fertilizer application, hog feeding costs, etc. There was a high degree of consistency between farmers' reports and the published averages for these items. It was assumed arbitrarily that if a farmer reported a "normal year," his prices, yields, and costs should not deviate by more than plus or minus 20 percent from the published averages. By this criterion 65 percent of farm interviews appeared accurate. Another 24 percent required small adjustments. For example, farmers said that they grew all their own vegetables, but the interviewer neglected to ascertain the value of this minor crop. The remaining 11 percent of farm income estimates appeared doubtful, which does not necessarily mean that all of them were inaccurate. In India one should probably expect less accurate estimates. In general, if one wishes to obtain income data of accuracy comparable to that obtained in the United States, a much more detailed and time-consuming interview is required.*

---

*In Taiwan a more detailed questionnaire regarding farm income was easier to administer than a shorter one requiring respondents to summarize some information. Length (up to two hours of interviewing time) was no barrier to cooperation from farmers. Even more lengthy interviews were conducted in India without difficulty.

In the case of wage and salary earners and farmers, the main problems are lack of knowledge and poor recall. When it comes to obtaining the income of self-employed businessmen, traders, and artisans, additional difficulties arise. Their concept of income is different from that of the economist—it tends to be a cash flow concept. In addition there may be intentional deception or secrecy. There are no good cross-checks or outside data which can be used to identify questionable business interviews. The best one can do is to examine the plausibility of the income figure in the light of the housing the self-employed occupy, the durable consumer goods they own, the kind of schools their children attend, the amount of labor employed in the business, the kinds of investments made, etc. Such checks are obviously inadequate and often inconclusive. About 20 percent of the business incomes reported in Taiwan appeared ridiculously low on the basis of such checks. The accuracy of the remaining 80 percent could not be evaluated conclusively. Many among these 80 percent were very small businessmen who were obviously in a low-income bracket; their income reports could not have had a large margin of error in absolute terms. There is no way of estimating the frequency of underreporting of income by the larger business owners.

In India, some checks on survey estimates of average total household income were made. They consisted of adjusting the survey data for differences in coverage and definition and then comparing the survey estimate of per capita household income with an estimate derived from the national income accounts. It appears that for two surveys conducted in 1960-62 by NCAER, the adjusted survey estimate is 87 percent of the national income estimate for the same period.[6] In the United States, income data have been collected by the Bureau of the Census, the Survey Research Center of the University of Michigan, and earlier by the Bureau of Labor Statistics. These surveys have produced personal income averages ranging from 82 to 92 percent of external estimates. There is no conclusive evidence then that underreporting of income is much more of a problem in India than in the United States. However, larger conceptual adjustments were made in the Indian data, and the Indian national income estimates also have a relatively large margin of error. In both countries, underreporting seems to be most frequent for the poorest and richest households and for self-employed businessmen and households with substantial property income.*

*The poorest households are most easily missed when households are listed for sample selection. When they are included, they apparently want to appear even poorer than they are.

When data on consumption and income are collected from the same sample of households, aggregate consumption universally tends to exceed aggregate income.[7] This is true even when national income data and direct survey estimates of saving indicate that household saving was on the average positive. In an Indian survey conducted in 1964-65, income and expenditure data were collected from the same national sample of respondents.[8] Expenditures exceeded income by 15 percent, though household saving (according to external estimates) may have been as high as 7 percent. Of course, the discrepancy is due partly to the understatement of income, but there seems to have been some overstatement of consumption as well. In order to facilitate recall of small expenditures, the consumption survey used the most recent day, week, month, and year preceding the inquiry as reference periods, depending on the size and frequency of the expenditure. Some error may have been introduced in the process of converting the data to a common reference period of one year. In addition, people probably tended to assign expenditures to a more recent date than was in fact correct. This phenomenon, called telescoping, has been observed in the United States as well.

While there is inconsistency in the aggregate level of income and expenditure data, it is encouraging that the distributional characteristics of the two sets of data seem to be consistent. One can subtract from Indian household income, as measured by the NCAER surveys, adjusted (and admittedly uncertain) estimates of household savings and in this way obtain an indirect estimate of consumption. One can then compute the Lorenz coefficient for the consumption data derived via household income minus savings, and for consumption data obtained by direct inquiry in the National Sample Surveys. The two Lorenz coefficients turn out to be very close.

Since the levels of household income and consumption expenditures are inconsistent, and since degree of under- and overreporting appears to be related to income, household savings cannot be derived by subtracting expenditures from income. People can be questioned directly about changes in various assets and liabilities, but the results are unsatisfactory. Household savings data collected by surveys are inaccurate in the United States as well as in LDCs, and partly for the same reason: notions of secrecy interfere with data collection. In LDCs there is an added difficulty that savings often are not monetized, taking the form of such direct investments of unknown value as home additions, construction of wells and irrigation channels, land improvements, home-made tools, etc.

One component of saving is debt—debt incurrency and debt repayment. In India, as in the United States, people feel sensitive and secretive about their debts, and they do not know how much of their repayments represent principal and how much interest. A further difficulty is created in India, and perhaps in other LDCs also, by the predisposition of lower income families to exaggerate their economic difficulties. They therefore tend to deny that they have been able to make debt repayments. If you aggregate debts incurred and debts repaid, incurrences exceed repayments by far too large a margin. Money lenders are of course even more reluctant than farmers to disclose their credit transactions. In spite of all this, there is no clear presumption that Indian debt data are more inaccurate than United States savings data obtained from surveys.

It does not follow that surveys can provide no information at all about savings behavior. One can simply ask people whether or not they have put money into a postal savings account, or cooperative shares, or life insurance, or into any number of other savings outlets during a recent period. A higher proportion will reply truthfully to such an inquiry than to questions about amounts involved. One can probably obtain a fairly accurate classification of families into those who have put money into various savings media during the past year, those who have taken money out, or both, or neither. One can construct another classification distinguishing between families who save in modern forms (bank accounts, postal savings, life insurance, pension funds, etc), those who save in traditional forms (chit funds as in India or chwa funds as in Taiwan, land, business inventories, livestock, or hiding money in the house), or both, or neither.

In Taiwan we went one step further. Having established the existence of one or more forms of saving, we asked respondents whether their present savings in all these forms amounted to as much as two months' income. When the reply was "Yes," we went on to ask "As much as half a year's income?" And if the reply was "Yes" again, we asked "As much as a year's income?" The answers to these questions gave us a classification of families into large medium, and small savers relative to income, and of course nonsavers. Something can be learned from such qualitative data about the social and economic factors associated with basic differences in savings behavior.

But at present it is not feasible to use surveys in LDCs to collect reasonably accurate data on amounts saved. We do a disservice to economists in LDCs if we do not urge them to avoid collecting data which cannot be obtained with some degree of accuracy. And we do them a further disservice if we induce them by our example to perform elaborate calculations on savings data which do not merit that kind of attention. The opportunity costs are too high, and besides there is so much other research that can and needs to be done.

Another kind of data very difficult to collect in LDCs by surveys is quantitative data on business operations, i.e., information on amounts that would go into an income statement or balance sheet, or that relate in an important way to the firm's net worth or profit position[9]. Obviously, business owners in LDCs do not think in terms of accounting concepts meaningful to economists. Detailed probing is thus required to get the desired information. Businessmen in India and Taiwan feel that it is essential to maintain secrecy vis-à-vis their competitors and the tax collector. Detailed probing makes them uneasy. To be sure, if pressed by an interviewer, they will give some figures, but these may be far from the truth. To make matters worse, we do not know how to assess the degree of accuracy of the interview. In the United States it is often possible to use published balance sheets and profit-and-loss statements, either alone or in conjunction with data from personal interviews, for microeconomic studies of business behavior. In LDCs published statements are less likely to be available, and when they are, they are seldom comparable between firms or over time.

All this does not imply that empirical studies of business firms in LDCs are unrewarding or impossible. If the researcher is content to pursue a modest goal, he may collect some worthwhile data. Interesting kinds of business behavior and decisions can be studied. For example, many more businessmen are willing to say whether or not they invested in machinery or equipment in the past year, whether they increased their inventory, or enlarged or improved their place of business, than would be willing to disclose the amounts of money involved. Similarly, many businessmen are willing to discuss important changes they made in their business operations, new products they introduced, or their methods of financing. They are also able to explain why they made certain decisions. There is a fair chance of cooperation from businessmen as long as they are not pressed for financial detail. Indeed, an assurance that there will be no inquiry about financial amounts may enhance their willingness to provide qualitative information

PURPOSES OF DATA COLLECTION

What constitutes a tolerable degree of accuracy depends on the purpose for which survey data are collected. Such data are least suitable for the derivation of financial aggregates. Taking household income as an example, the known tendency of some respondents to understate income would lead to inaccurate aggregates. The aggregates might have a sizable margin of error even if 70 percent of households reported their income correctly. It would be more hazardous still to derive aggregate saving or components of aggregate saving (such as farm investments, changes in debt, or net additions to bank accounts) from survey data. Reporting errors, together with the extreme skewness of the distribution of savings, makes sample surveys an inappropriate means for estimating aggregate savings. Likewise survey data are not accurate enough to provide us with financial aggregates relating to small or medium-sized firms in LDCs.

These negative statements are not meant to imply that surveys have equal shortcomings for other purposes. Nor do they mean that accuracy in the aggregate is the most appropriate test of survey data. Three points must be made here. The first is that errors in surveys seem to have a similar pattern over time and between countries.* For example, if in India the lowest and the highest income receivers tend to understate their income, this bias is likely to be the same from year to year; and it is likely to be similar in Pakistan. Changes in income distributions can then be evaluated on the basis of successive surveys, and comparisons of income distribution in India and Pakistan are then warranted. Secondly, if a substantial majority of people report their incomes or consumption outlays correctly, and some of the remaining errors are neither very large nor correlated with crucial explanatory variables, then functional relationships are worth estimating from survey data. Third, since our understanding of important forms of economic behavior and economic decisions in LDCs is so inadequate, it might be wise to give priority to studies involving such variables rather than financial variables which are poorly measured.

Let us now consider three kinds of analytical purposes for which survey data collected in LDCs are well suited. The first is studies of distributions, changes in distributions, and determinants of distributions. A second purpose is estimating functional relationships, and a third is program planning and evaluation.

There is, at least in Asia, a particular need for studies of income and asset distributions and their changes over time. In the last two decades, economists have been concerned largely with problems of income growth; now problems of income distribution are coming strongly to the fore. Sample surveys can be used not only to study income distributions in LDCs and their trends, but also wage distributions, consumption distributions, and the distribution of various kinds of assets—especially land, housing, and farm equipment. A series of surveys (using comparable methods and samples) can indicate which subgroups of the population benefited most from recent economic development and which least. It is essential that we learn much more than we now know about the distribution of gains in welfare brought

---

*However, it cannot be determined or tested in how far this observation can be generalized.

about by economic development. Longitudinal surveys may be particularly appropriate for that purpose. For example, there is a large three-year panel study now under way in India to investigate (among other things) the impact of the Green Revolution on the distribution of rural incomes and investments. It is unlikely that this important issue can be settled by one study in one country. By multivariate analysis of survey data we can find out what factors or combinations of factors are the most important determinants of very high and very low incomes. In the mid-1950s Kuznets had some perceptive things to say about the tendency for income inequalities to be larger in LDCs than in MDCs.[10] We still do not know much more than we knew then about the anatomy of income distributions in LDCs and how they change.

A second, and no doubt the most important, use of survey data is for the study of functional relationships. A particular advantage of the survey method is that it permits an interdisciplinary approach. Often the question arises in LDCs as to what extent behavior is dominated by noneconomic considerations and to what extent it is influenced, or subject to being influenced, by economic incentives. Surveys enable us to study the interaction of economic and noneconomic factors in relation to a given kind of behavior.

If the study of functional relationships enhances our understanding of economic behavior, it should also increase our ability to forecast economic behavior. For example, we may analyze with the help of survey data the economic and noneconomic factors that determine whether or not a person migrates from his village to an urban area. Such a study should throw light on factors which may increase or reduce the migration stream in the future. And it may identify variables which can be manipulated in order to change the migration rate. This kind of investigation represents a proper use of the survey method. It would not, however, yield a *quantitative* forecast of migration.

Similarly, surveys can be used to study the acceptance of such innovative practices as the use of high-yielding varieties of grains, of contraceptive methods, or of modern consumer goods. Economists need to know—in India, in the Philippines, in Mexico—what kinds of people accept innovations and what others adhere to traditional modes of behavior. How is nontraditional behavior associated with education, income, income change, ownership of land and other assets, perceived costs and risk, perceived gains, exposure to information, and the like? How do innovative practices spread within a village or city? Survey data can throw some light on such issues and, in doing so, can help us to assess future trends and formulate policies.

There are other research objectives using functional relationships, which, though highly desirable, demand more from the survey method than it can deliver. I am referring to the use of micro data from surveys to compute exact coefficients, such as the propensity to save in an LDC or certain demand elasticities. Attempts to forecast savings rates from micro data both ignore the poor quality of the savings data and make the mistake of assuming that all other factors which affect saving in an important way can be taken into account in the multivariate analysis. I suggest that we design surveys primarily to learn more about the conditions under which people save in LDCs, and the purposes for which they save, before we attempt precise calculations of marginal propensities and before we test the permanent income hypothesis there. We have very limited information about what farmers do with their money when they raise a larger harvest, or how saving is affected by modern forms of consumption or by the opening up of attractive investment opportunities. For behavioral studies of such issues, simplified scales may be used at the start which distinguish between large savers (relative to income), medium and small savers, and nonsavers.

Another temptation is to compute functional relationships from micro data in order to arrive at demand projections—demand for consumer goods or demand for agricultural inputs such as fertilizer. Here the major problem is the rapid transformation of tastes and production techniques characteristic of developing societies. When tastes are changing, income elasticities of demand lose some of their forecasting value, except for basic necessities (such as food-grains and cotton textiles). When techniques are changing, as when the high yielding varieties of grains (HYV) were introduced, past input coefficients no longer have much meaning. Surveys do enable us to evaluate the direction and order of magnitude of the changes which are occurring. For example, in India a study was made comparing consumption patterns of two parallel samples, one representative of the most developed urban and rural areas of the country, the other of areas which continue to be strongly dominated by traditional economic activities.[11] Another study compares consumption expenditures of HYV users with consumption expenditures by cultivators who are not HYV users.[12] Such comparisons of consumption patterns among two contrasting groups (at comparable income and educational levels) should reveal some of the shifts in consumption demand that are in progress. Similarly, a study is being conducted in India by NCAER which compares fertilizer inputs by a representative national sample of cultivators who use and those who do not use the high yielding varieties, again controlling for other variables. The aim is to gain an understanding of factors associated with suboptimal applications of fertilizer. Such studies should be of value to the planners while avoiding exact quantitative predictions.

The third potential use of survey data in LDCs is in program planning and evaluation. First of all, surveys may identify problems—

felt needs or sources of dissatisfaction. An example is a study of the *barriades* of Lima, Peru.[13] This study, besides obtaining descriptive data about people and their homes, measured attitudes toward 26 public and private services. It thus helped to set priorities for urban development projects.

Surveys can also assist in identifying attitudes and behavior patterns which have a bearing on the success of development programs. Policies often fail because they assume that the attitudes and economic behavior of a target population can be readily changed, or can be changed by small economic incentives. A better approach may be to understand and accept existing behavior patterns as a fixed condition in the short run and to design policies appropriate to them. Or else, it may have to be determined what kinds of economic incentives are necessary to bring about a desired change in behavior. In this way, administrative programs can be improved and costly mistakes minimized. Program evaluation can focus on agricultural extension work, cooperatives, small scale industry, response to export incentives, nutritional programs,[14] and family planning.[15]

SAMPLE SIZE AND FEASIBILITY

Large federated countries tend to use large samples for political and administrative reasons—to facilitate breakdowns by individual states.* The National Sample Survey in India is usually based on close to 10,000 cases. For one of the Rural Credit Surveys, as many as 80,000 households were interviewed. Though large samples minimize sampling errors, the sampling error decreases only in proportion to the square root of sample size. On the other hand, reporting errors probably increase faster than sample size. The larger the sample, the greater the task of interviewer hiring, training, and supervision. It is nearly impossible in India to communicate effectively with interviewers in the field by mail, not to speak of telephone or telegraph. If the field staff is very large, adequate supervision (i.e., frequent visiting of sampling points by the supervisory staff) tends to become more difficult. Inadequate quality controls may result not only in unnecessarily large reporting errors but also in failure to implement sample selection according to design. It is true that India is much less homogeneous than the United States as regards economy, culture,

---

*The United States Bureau of the Census is also under a great deal of pressure to provide local area data and is forced into spending large sums for that purpose.

as well as political and social environment. The same is true of other LDCs. Since sampling error depends on size of variance, a larger sample may be needed in an LDC than in the United States to obtain a given degree of accuracy. Yet there is hardly any research problem (as opposed to multiple-purpose or administrative data collection) in an LDC where the disadvantages of making a survey of more than 4,000-5,000 cases would not outweigh the advantages.*

There is nothing inherently wrong with very small sample surveys, but their use for policy guidance is surely limited. In India, there is a proliferation of such surveys already. In particular, studies of one or a few villages or agricultural areas have become common. Sometimes only a sample of households is interviewed, sometimes every household in the village. Objectives differ from survey to survey, and even when there is a common objective, questionnaires and sample design differ. Villages differ greatly from each other, which makes it difficult to generalize on the basis of what happens in one or a few villages. The total number of cases is often so small that multivariate statistical analysis is not possible. If micro analysis is to have any impact on policy matters, it cannot dwell on the unique features of particular situations. Rather, it should attempt to discover regularities in what may appear to be diverse behavior patterns on the part of individual economic units. There is no reason why economists who value the microeconomic approach should resort to the anthropologists' methodology. From a practical point of view, surveys should have enough cases, and should lend themselves to sufficiently sophisticated analysis, to have some impact on policymakers as well as on the economics profession. I believe that surveys of, say, 1,200-4,500 cases have much more potential for microeconomic research and policy planning than their present use in LDCs would suggest.

DATA ORGANIZATION AND DISSEMINATION

The last statement raises the question of survey organization. Small localized microeconomic studies can be undertaken with the help of a few graduate students and/or paid investigators hired on an *ad hoc* basis. Surveys of the size and quality needed require the

---

*One qualification is necessary. There is often a legitimate use of the sample survey *in place of* a special purpose census. In such cases it may be appropriate to go well beyond the 4,000-5,000 case limit suggested here. Obviously LDCs also face difficulties in carrying out quality census work. In such circumstances a large survey may yield better and cheaper data than a census.

services of a professional, preferably permanent, survey organization. Obviously the feasibility of collecting microeconomic data in LDCs depends on the availability of a well-trained and flexible field staff. There is no question that such a staff, with a core of permanent field supervisors, will on the whole collect more accurate data than an ad hoc group of investigators, however well motivated. A permanent survey organization would gradually learn how certain concepts are best approached and certain economic magnitudes best measured, given the constraints of local conditions and the local culture. Unemployment and underemployment measures would be a case in point. A permanent survey organization would have more reason to conduct validity studies and profit by them than a temporary survey group. Validity studies are rare in India, and in other LDCs as well. The need for quality and validity checks and for methodological studies in such countries cannot be emphasized enough. A permanent survey organization could attempt to standardize frequently used classifications, both as regards conceptualization and code categories. It could also become a collecting point for methodological findings to be gleaned from many scattered survey research endeavors carried out by other researchers in the country. And finally, the organization would acquire sophistication in the analysis of survey data, something now quite limited in most LDCs. Given adequate computing facilities, it could develop and disseminate computer programs suitable for the analysis of microeconomic data.

If LDCs want to make progress in microeconomic analysis of development related issues and problems, they need survey organizations that can make special purpose surveys for social scientists in government, the universities, or elsewhere, and make them with a trained and experienced interviewing staff. These organizations should be separated from the official data collection machinery.

One further organizational objective deserves mention—data banks. The same survey can often serve a number of research objectives, if the data are made available, and if codes and other explanatory materials are accessible without undue effort. Indian researchers are often possessive about their data and may deny them to their own Indian colleagues. Foreigners may likewise depart with their data without sharing them with their Indian collaborators. As a result, the small amount of data collected is often only partially exploited for research. Comparative studies are inhibited. Indian Ph.D. candidates either have to base their dissertations on the meager data which they themselves can collect or on published aggregate data. They therefore build too many theoretical and mathematical models to which no data at all are fitted. The same situation seems to prevail in other LDCs.

In short, if there is to be more microeconomic analysis of development problems, we need survey organizations in LDCs which can collect the desired data with the greatest possible accuracy. And we need data banks, so that available data can be made more accessible to research workers in the countries themselves and from abroad. Scholars from MDCs as consultants and providers of research money. These roles might well be used to influence research policy so that it will move toward these organizational goals.

* * *

COMMENT BY IRWIN FRIEND

The two preceding papers on generating micro data relating to economic behavior in less developed economies are both interesting and useful. Ferber and Salazar-Carillo discuss the general types of errors in estimates of economic parameters based on survey data from households and business firms, while Eva Mueller considers which types of information are feasible to collect through such surveys and argues against what she calls "excessive quantification."

Her most frequently cited example of "excessive quantification" is the collection and analysis of data on overall saving by individual households. Presumably the same strictures would apply to survey data on wealth. She states (p. 110) that " at present it is not feasible to use surveys in LDCs to collect reasonably accurate data on amounts saved. We do a disservice to economists in LDCs if we do not urge them to avoid collecting data which cannot be obtained with some degree of accuracy. And we do them a further disservice if we induce them by our example to perform elaborate calculations on savings data which do not merit that kind of attention. The opportunity costs are too high, and besides there is so much other research that can and needs to be done."

Survey data on saving and wealth do involve substantial margins of error, but the inferences drawn by Mueller from that fact are, in my view, incorrect. If an LDC (or any other country) needs the best possible estimate of the marginal propensity to save, or of the relationship of household wealth to economic behavior, the prescription would not appear to be, as Mueller suggests, to count noses on the number of households that save in a particular form or the number that surmise that their saving in all stipulated forms is high or low relative to their income. Such qualitative data are of very limited usefulness in answering important economic questions. Thus no reasonable economist questions that both monetary and fiscal policy affect the level and composition of economic activity—the issue is how large would be the impact of specific policies in dollar figures.

There is little justification for recommending that an LDC collect information which is basically of little importance simply because the information is readily available. The resources would be better spent in concentrating on the data needed, on selecting the best procedures for compiling and analyzing such data, on trying to improve procedures where necessary, and in the meantime attempting to make the best analytical use of available data, which includes a full realization of the nature and probable magnitude of the errors involved. Parenthetically, one might disagree with Dr. Mueller as to the tradeoff function between reliability and importance of data, and as to the importance of and types of error in household information on saving and wealth.

There does not appear to be any alternative approach available which would avoid the fundamental deficiencies in survey saving data in the LDCs. Actually aggregate time-series estimates of household saving in tangible form in LDCs, which is a very high proportion of their total saving, are typically either from sources no more reliable than household surveys or from the surveys themselves. Partly as a result of these data deficiencies, but also because of the relatively short time-series estimates ordinarily available in LDCs and in some cases the rapidity of changes in the economic structure, the marginal propensity to save at any point of time may be fully as well estimated from the cross-section as from the time-series data. An attempt should be made to reconcile the two sets of estimates before either can be taken seriously. In some cases, as implied earlier, the two sets of estimates will not be independent, in view of the necessity for estimating a portion of aggregate investment from survey data.

This does not mean that the survey data on saving either in LDCs, or for that matter in the United States, should be used in unadjusted form. An example of the types of adjustments required to go from unadjusted to adjusted survey estimates of aggregate or average household saving is provided by a supplement to the Review of Economics and Statistics, May 1959.[16] Similarly, the problems involved in, and the adjustments required for, estimating marginal, as distinguished from average, saving propensities from survey data are also there discussed. It is obvious that constant absolute or proportional (to income) biases in estimates of saving of households classified by income do not pose any major problems for estimation of the marginal propensity to save.

In another part of her paper (p. 113-114), Mueller derogates the usefulness of survey data for estimating the propensity to save not only because of the poor quality of the data but because it "[assumes] that all other factors which affect saving in an important way can be taken into account in the multivariate analysis." This is a strange reaction to the relative advantages and disadvantages of cross-section and time-series data. Actually, even in a country like the United States, with its comparative wealth of time-series statistics, one of the key limitations of such data is the absence of a sufficiently large number of independent observations from which one can disentangle income and correlated effects.

One of the major advantages of cross-section data in analyzing saving propensities is that they can provide the number of independent observations that will permit holding constant the effects of many other socio-economic characteristics correlated with income, as well as abstract from the major problems of simultaneity confronting time-series data. Furthermore, where there is a strong time trend in income, time-series data do not permit income effects on saving to "be adequately distinguished from those of 1) time trends in distributional variables; 2) the increasing availability of consumption opportunities through the introduction of new products, improved distribution of existing ones, and expanded credit facilities; and 3) such institutional factors as the growth of social insurance and the expansion of communications media, which may have a profound impact on the consumer's preferred distribution of disposable income. In time-series analysis, all of these are effectively impounded into the income coefficient."[17] This is not to say that survey data do not have their own problems for economic analysis, but simply that used judiciously they are a valuable supplement to time-series data, which have different but not necessarily less serious problems.[18] Survey data could be made even more useful for saving analysis by expending more resources on the collection of continuous cross-section or panel data in lieu of a series of discrete cross-sections.

Mueller indicates (especially on p. 114) her preference for developing a simple scale of saving-income ratios from survey data—viz., large, medium, and small savers—in lieu of actual estimates of total saving for the household. She mentions specifically that such information can be used to test how saving is affected by such developments as modern forms of consumption or by the opening up of attractive investment opportunities. However, without a complete enumeration of the household's saving, it is difficult to see how anything especially useful can be formulated, in view of the economic questions at issue—e.g., is saving in new investment forms more competitive with the total of <u>all</u> other forms of saving than with consumption? Useful attempts have been made to obtain answers to such questions from the data on saving survey to which Mueller objects.[19] These suggest, for example, that contractual saving is more competitive with or substitutable for consumption than is the case for other forms of saving which are largely substitutable for each other.

My reservations about the Ferber-Salazar paper are minor and may well be based on ignorance. In several instances, statements about expected biases in parameter means or variances flowing from indicated deficiencies in survey procedures did not seem entirely self-evident. However, it would be useful to know which of such statements are based on empirical evidence, no matter how scanty, and which on prejudgments.

To illustrate, the authors indicate that they would expect that in countries where mail questionnaires were used in lieu of personal interviews, errors in prices obtained from the retail outlets covered would bias upward the estimated mean prices and variances (p. 93). The sample bias toward selection of "more prominent outlets" is similarly believed by the authors to overstate mean prices and variances (p. 94). It might have been desirable to provide a little more background for these statements.

Finally, the errors in estimates of economic parameters which these three authors discuss in connection with survey data, and which may likewise characterize time-series estimates, have not received the attention in this conference that they deserve. Economists generally recognize that gross misspecification of model structure vitiates the usefulness of results. They do not appear to be so familiar with the substantially different implications that may be associated with relatively small differences in estimated parameters even with the same general model structure.

CHAPTER

6

DOMINANCE AND ACHIEVEMENT IN ENTREPRENEURIAL PERSONALITIES

Reeve D. Vanneman

INTRODUCTION

Though one would expect social psychological research on development to deal exclusively with micro-level data, the fact is that some of the most impressive empirical results have used aggregate data. For instance, the heart of McClelland's well-known research[1] was the correlation he found between the cultural level of achievement motivation (as measured in childrens' readers) and measures of national economic growth. In other research he claims to find similar relationships for ancient Greece, preindustrial Spain and England, and pre-Incan Peru. The more plausible and less controversial results using individual-level measures have, in fact, been less consistent. For instance, in one sample of managers of large United States corporations, McClelland found managers in the middle-salary bracket to be highest in Need Achievement (nAch).[2] Also, less successful life insurance salesmen were found to have slightly higher levels of nAch than more successful salesmen.[3] Of course, there are other studies which did find a positive relationship between nAch and entrepreneurial success. Nevertheless there is sufficient discrepancy to warrant reexamining the micro theory offered by McClelland.

His analysis of successful entrepreneurial behavior isolated six characteristics, five of which he claimed to be typical of those high in nAch.[4] It is the "need achievers'" superiority in these five characteristics that supposedly explains why they are more successful entrepreneurs. But the list McClelland used was developed "analytically and theoretically," primarily from the work of economic theorists and historians. A closer look at entrepreneurial behavior as it empirically occurs might have resulted in a more precise understanding of the role of psychological variables in promoting economic growth. Recent research on managerial behavior points up at least two ways in which McClelland's list might have been improved. First of all, he should have recognized the variety of behavioral patterns exhibited by successful entrepreneurs and related each pattern to factors in the firm's environment. And second, he might have given greater weight to the social and interpersonal aspects of entrepreneurial behavior. These omissions are not peculiar to McClelland's approach but tend to characterize much social psychological work on development.

Several recent studies have established clearly that the formal organizational structure associated with economic success varies depending on the environment of the firm.[5] Though the primary focus of attention in these studies has been organizational structure, it is easy to see the implications for patterns of managerial behavior. Just as there is no one best way of structuring an organization, neither is there one best managerial personality. Rather, these relationships are contingent on the environment surrounding the firm. Though the studies emphasizing the importance of the environment have concentrated on firms in highly industrialized economies, there is every reason to suspect that a similar approach would prove useful in investigating entrepreneurial behavior in LDCs.

This suggestion is not a new one. Eisenstadt[6], for instance, complained that the case for need achievement was too monolithic. Surely there are some circumstances in which no matter how much need achievement individuals possessed, it would be unlikely for much enterprise to result. In these situations we might expect that some other psychological variable would be in greater "demand." One of the objectives of social psychological research on development ought to be to identify the environmental variables which modify, enhance, or destroy the relationship between a given psychological variable and entrepreneurial success. By recognizing the complexity of environmental demands, we may understand better the inconsistencies in our present data.

In searching for other personality variables needed for entrepreneurial success, we need to pay more attention to the interpersonal aspects of entrepreneurship. Social psychological analyses of successful entrepreneurship have, for the most part, tended to focus more on its innovative or achievement aspects. Neither nAch nor "the innovative personality"[7], for instance, are especially concerned with aspects of interpersonal behavior, but more with the individual's approach to impersonal objectives and his success with task- and problem-solving activities.

And yet if, as Cole suggests, among the chief functions of entrepreneurship are "the social elements of leadership, effective coordination, human relations and the like"[8], then some of the talents and motives which the entrepreneur brings to his position must surely be social in nature. In his monograph on backwardness in southern Italy,[9] Edward Banfield singled out the lack of interpersonal trust as the principal deterrent to economic development. Albert Hirschman[10] has regretted "the one-sided . . . and traditional emphasis on the creative aspect of entrepreneurship." It is rather "the 'human relations' component of entrepreneurship, the art of agreement-reaching and of cooperation-enlisting, which will remain a critical bottleneck of . . . economic development."[11] Not infrequently the leading entrepreneur in the early development of an industry had little technical skill, made only minor contributions toward economic rationalization, and was distrustful of continued innovational development. His success was based rather on his perceived leadership and his ability and determination to play the dominant role in interpersonal situations. What is not frequently realized is that this syndrome of social dominance is psychologically distinct from achievement behavior. There is a distinction to be made between the dominance and achievement syndromes if we are to arrive at a hypothesis on the importance of both personality types in different economic environments.

Social psychological research on small groups provides a general framework within which we can identify the different kinds of entrepreneurs that are successful in different environmental circumstances. The distinction between dominance and task-instrumental behavior has been demonstrated in factor analytic studies of personality traits and small group interaction.[12] These two behavioral clusters may often be confused, as has often happens in discussions of entrepreneurship. Actually the small group studies show that the men who dominate the interaction within a group are not necessarily those who are recognized as best for instrumental tasks. As we will see, this distinction corresponds closely with patterns of entrepreneurial behavior.

Recent work by Robert F. Bales serves as an excellent example of research in this area. Bales's three-dimensional descriptive system distinguishes between the dominance dimension of social behavior (which he calls upward or "U" types) and an orthogonal task-instrumental dimension (which he calls forward or "F" types). Bales describes the dominant or "U" type in this way:

> He thrives on competition. Material success is the value most squarely in the middle of the cluster he may advocate, but he may speak in favor of social success as a worthy goal, and he is also in favor of tough-minded assertiveness as a means to social and material success.

> Power is important as a goal in itself. . . . The person in a U group role is central in the power structure, though not necessarily the most powerful, and his support is likely to be needed for the enactment of ideas put forth by other powerful members of the group. . . . He perceives himself correctly as talkative and self-confident. . . . The persistently upward moving person is likely to test high on written personality tests which measure adventurous, thick-skinned, and active and dominant traits. He may also test high on other traits which involve a major tendency to convert drives into overt action. . . . The UPB adjacent type is enthusiastic, talkative, and extroverted; and he shows poise, spontaneity, and confidence.[13]

As contrasted with this type, Bales notes the member who is preoccupied with the assigned tasks and goals of the group. "No other directional type has, to the same degree, the single-minded, persistent, undeviating devotion to the received tasks of the group." He is primarily concerned with means toward that goal rather than the creation or elaboration of new goals. "The problem of the group is to work deductively, it is felt, from the given goals, values, and rules to a definition of their proper application to the specific problem at hand. Thus, there is major emphasis on reasoning rationally from given premises and on extending action instrumentally from conclusions so derived." Furthermore, the interpersonal relations of the task-oriented type, Bales notes, are "strictly impersonal and affectively neutral."[14]

Is this distinction, discovered in the psychological literature, descriptive also of different patterns of entrepreneurial behavior? There are, of course, a host of different typologies of entrepreneurship. Distinctions between creative, adaptive, and imitative entrepreneurship, or between industrial, financial, and managerial entrepreneurship, as well as several others, are familiar in the literature. The problem with these typologies is that they relate poorly to the major dimensions of differences in interpersonal behavior identified in social psychological research. The creative versus imitative distinction, for instance, deals more with the output or effects of entrepreneurship. Financial, industrial, and managerial distinctions deal more with the principal type of resources used by entrepreneurs. As such, these typologies make distinctions between entrepreneurs whose patterns of social behavior were similar and fail to distinguish between others with unrelated patterns of behavior. For example, people who innovate in marketing are usually different types of individuals from those who innovate in manufacturing. To argue for a trait such as "innovativeness" is to engage in the fallacy of psychological reductionism. The mistake has been to take a social outcome such as innovation (or achievement) and assume there must be some analogous psychological trait which predicts it. This is what we are trying to avoid by approaching the social outcome as a product of a particular combination of psychological and environmental conditions. The typology we require therefore must be one based on the interpersonal behavior involved and not on the social and economic effects of entrepreneurship.

Fortunately, not all extant typologies are irrelevant to psychological analyses, nor is it necessary to introduce yet another. Chandler's historical work[15] though emphasizing changes in the later stages of a firm's growth, also takes note of changes in the relatively undeveloped environment. His distinction between resource accumulation and resource rationalization closely resembles a typology based on behavioral patterns. Resource accumulation refers to the process of aggregating large amounts of capital and labor for the purpose of exploiting a new and expanding market. The men who accomplished this on a national scale were the great empire builders who have attracted much of the notice and notoriety of entrepreneurial history. Rationalization refers to the development of methods, especially systematic ones, for managing these aggregates of men and capital. In making the distinction between empire-building and organization-building, Chandler recognized that these were behavioral patterns carried out by different people with different motivational and personality structures.

> In the last two decades of the nineteenth century, American industrialists concentrated their imagination and energy on the creation of these industrial empires. They became engrossed in planning the strategies of expansion and in securing the resources—the men, money, and equipment—necessary to meet the needs and challenges of a swiftly industrializing and urbanizing economy. The powerful captains—the Rockefellers, Swifts, Dukes, Garys, and Westinghouses—and their able lieutenants had little time and often little interest in fashioning a rational and systematic design for administering effectively the best resources they had united under their control. . . .
>
> On the other hand the industrialists who met these administrative challenges were rarely the men who had created the great industrial domains. . . . The formulation of designs for the government of a business empire called for different talents and a different temperament than did its acquisition.[16]

Historical examples are presented below in order to illustrate how this categorization may clarify the psychological analyses. The ten American cases were selected from a list of the twenty-five largest U.S. industrial enterprises in 1919 to represent ten different industrial classifications.[17] In most of these cases, we find that the empire-building and rationalization functions were clearly specialized among different individuals, that this specialization reflected habitual patterns of behavior and not merely responses to specific situations, and that there were consistent differences between the two types in contemporary impressions and descriptions of their character. Thus the evidence supports the hypothesis that dominance and achievement are two distinct patterns of behavior differentially demanded at different stages in the growth of firms in a developing economy. The evidence is, admittedly, only tentative but the convergence of the different areas of research is encouraging.

CASE STUDIES

General Motors[18]

The creation and growth of General Motors is virtually the paradigm of distinct empire-building and rationalizing specialization. There was a rather abrupt chronological break between the two phases of growth, associated with a turnover in corporate management. William Durant founded and promoted the great combination, but others, most notably Alfred Sloan, were forced to turn the giant combination into an effective and profitable organization.

Durant grew up in Flint, Michigan, an area where the manufacture of carriages and wagons was flourishing. In 1885, Durant began another of these firms with $2,000 capital, mostly borrowed. His greatest assets were his salesmanship and promotional abilities. He knew little of, and cared less for, the manufacturing aspects of the business. At one time the entire manufacturing process was contracted for, and later, when Durant acquired his own plant, the carriages were simply assembled there from parts, the parts being supplied by other firms. Still, Durant's success as a salesman had made his firm one of the largest in Flint by the turn of the century.

Durant's first contact with automoblies came in 1904 when a fellow Flint carriagemaker persuaded him to buy his interest in the Buick Motor Corporation. Fortunately for Durant, the Buick was already an excellently engineered car, and all the firm lacked was sufficient promotional efforts. Durant was ably suited for this, and within a few years Buick was the leading producer in its field.

Durant's first effort at empire-building in 1908, when he attempted to combine the four leading producers (Buick, Ford, Maxwell, and Reo) into one firm, did not materialize because of a shortage of cash. However, by 1910 he had succeeded in acquiring ten passenger-car and two truck companies, and a parts producer. Durant's acquisitions followed the opportunities available and represented no coherent plan of growth and consolidation. They were "a conglomeration of companies acquired because they were available rather than because they fit a pattern."[19] The acquisitions included, in fact, some questionable investments, and already in 1910 a banking syndicate was forced to step in and remove Durant from the presidency of General Motors in order to save the company.

What followed for General Motors was a brief interim of consolidation and rationalization. The new management was more concerned with internal organization, as well as research, than with external expansion.

Meanwhile, outside General Motors, Durant had returned to what he found most satisfying, the promotion and expansion of large volume business. Durant organized two new firms—the Chevrolet Motor Car Company in Detroit and another in Flint. With these firms, Durant entered into the mass market previously discovered by Ford. Chevrolet was successful, and Durant was off again on a period of expansion and acquisition. A third firm was acquired and began producing Chevrolets in 1913. With Chevrolet as a base, and with the help of Du Pont money, Durant again gained control of GM. His second administration was scarcely different from the first. Again independent firms were acquired at a rapid pace. By 1920 some twenty more had been brought into the combination. Among these were such diverse operations as refrigerators and farm machinery. Existing plants were enlarged, and Durant, certain of the continued growth in demand, gave free rein to his divisional managers to invest and expand.

Whatever systematic administration had been imposed on the firm during the hiatus was quickly loosened upon Durant's return. The general office consisted almost entirely of Durant and a few of his assistants. The multitude of parts companies which Durant had been able to get hold of were brought into the corporation in the most convenient manner. Some were integrated into the parts division, United Motors Corporation, others were maintained in the separate car divisions such as Chevrolet and Buick, still others existed as independent divisions within the corporation. Attempts at establishing a systematic accounting system were abandoned, resulting in haphazard financing and accumulation of inventories. Durant "neither exercised nor delegated authority effectively. He provided only spasmodic and haphazard co-ordination among the component parts of General Motors."[20]

Still Durant's contribution should not be negated. His irrepressible faith in the future of the auto industry had led him to aggregate the country's third largest industrial firm. The basis for the integrated firm had been laid. If the market had continued to expand as rapidly as Durant supposed, the administrative shortcomings would not have been so injurious. But in 1920, when the postwar boom was spent, Durant found himself overloaded with inventory and deeply in debt. At the height of the crisis, the Du Ponts stepped in and relieved Durant of the presidency. The responsibility for giving administrative structure to the industrial empire fell to Alfred P. Sloan.

Sloan was fascinated with just those aspects of business which Durant ignored. As early as 1918, while president of the United Motors (parts) division, Sloan had on his own initiative drafted plans for an administrative reorganization. Although not opposed by Durant, Sloan's concern and his efforts were largely ignored. Chandler relates that he had worked on "several plans in order to keep the organization lined up."[21] When Pierre du Pont moved into the presidency, Sloan's plan was accepted almost in its entirety. In the years after Durant's departure, Sloan continued his concentration on internal coordination, adjusting and modifying his plan when necessary. A general staff was created, relationships between divisions were clarified, and systematic accounting and budgeting procedures were installed.

The personalities of the two men were as different as were their effects on GM. Durant was "picturesque, spectacular, and aggressive."[22] All spoke of him with warm affection, even after the 1920 fiasco. Sloan, on the other hand, was quiet and cool. He had a precise mind that abhorred waste and inefficiency. His training had been in engineering and his original business success in production, not sales. As president of United Motors, Sloan had already emphasized exactly what would be his most important contribution to the parent company—the introduction of systematic administration. Durant's and Sloan's contributions to General Motors were much more than responses dictated by the environment and the position of the firm. Their efforts were characteristic of the type of social behavior the two men pursued throughout their careers. Durant always emphasized the need for expansion and growth, both within and outside General Motors. Not only did he give little attention to systematic administration, he actually seems to have preferred the free-wheeling methods that were curbed somewhat in the 1910-15 hiatus. Sloan, on the other hand, was always concerned with systematic organization. His plan for reorganization was developed on his own initiative and without the aid of other corporate executives. The two men were successful because their preferred dispositions coincided with the economic demands of the time. For the firm then, it was the coincidence of these personal predispositions with the appropriate economic environment which brought about its tremendous success.

Carnegie Steel[23]

Some three decades earlier, a similar pattern of transition from empire building to rationalizing occurred in steel. The change in leadership of the Carnegie steel empire was not so dramatic as with General Motors, but the shift in emphasis with the ascendency of Henry Clay Frick is well documented. Carnegie first produced steel in 1875, but his various Pittsburgh plants existed for some time as a loosely knit collection of mutually dependent companies. Rationalization at the corporate level proceeded successfully only after Frick assumed the presidency in 1889. The recorded personal differences between Carnegie and Frick are virtually the same as those observed with Durant and Sloan.

From his position as a superintendent of the Pennsylvania Railroad, Carnegie became interested in a railroad car-manufacturing company, a Pittsburgh iron mill, a blast furnace, and an iron bridge builder, all of whose fortunes were closely tied to the expansion of railroading. Carnegie's connections, and his extroverted and sociable personality, won him these companies' customers and creditors. The planning and organizing, and even the initiation of some of the firms, were left for the most part to others. Carnegie's contribution to the organizational side of these businesses was more as a charismatic authority. Even one of Carnegie's most outspoken critics acknowledges that among the various partners in these enterprises, Carnegie "was looked up to by the others because of an assertiveness in his manner which the other boys interpreted as evidence of fitness for leadership."[24]

Carnegie had been, at first, reluctant to enter the budding steel industry. Not until 1873, long after British successes with the Bessemer process, did Carnegie and eight other partners begin plans for a steel plant. As Carnegie became more convinced of the success of steel, he determined to own the controlling interest in the firm. He used the panic of 1873 to buy out some of his partners. Five years later, when the capitalization of the firm was increased, Carnegie subscribed to the entire increase himself. As a result, he had a 59 percent interest in the firm. This majority control was important to Carnegie, and in the ensuing years he never permitted his interest to slip below 50 percent.

The growth of the steel firm was dramatic. When the Edgar Thomson Steel Works began producing steel in 1875, it accounted for some 8 percent of the nation's output. By 1878 it was producing over 100,000 tons of steel annually, or 12 percent of the nation's output. Blast furnaces were added in 1880 (evidence of Carnegie's inability to mesh the interests of his steel firm with his independent interests in the blast furnaces built in 1870). In 1882 Carnegie obtained an interest in the Frick Coke Company, the largest supplier of coke to Pittsburgh, and within a year was the largest stockholder in the firm. In 1883 Carnegie acquired an important Pittsburgh competitor, the Homestead works. Throughout this expansion, he continued to hold onto his earlier investments in the iron business. There was an abortive attempt at consolidation in 1881, but the various interests remained loosely integrated until the 1890s. By encouraging competition among his subordinates, Carnegie not only neglected problems of coordination but aggravated them.

In 1889, Henry Clay Frick acceded to the chairmanship of Carnegie Brothers and Company, whose most important property was the now greatly enlarged Edgar Thomson Steel mill. It was Frick who molded the various enterprises into a coherent unit. The legal apparatus for this was established in 1892, with the incorporation of the Carnegie Steel Company, Ltd., with a $25 million capitalization. This one firm brought together the old iron mills and blast furnaces, the original steel plant, and the two important acquisitions of 1883 and 1890. Frick was in effective control of the operation of these properties, and Carnegie himself acknowledged Frick to be a "genius at management." Meetings of department heads became formalized, and minutes were recorded for the first time. Frick's biographer records the achievement.

> The various segregated plants, until then operated by dissociated and independent managements, jealous of and actually competing with one another, were assembled in masterly fashion; connecting railways were built; possession of yards which had been secured by railroad companies was regained; waste was reduced to a minimum; and young active and ambitious men headed by Schwab and Morrison were installed in authority and, while encouraged in every conceivable way, were held to strict accounting.[25]

Expansion did not cease once more attention was paid to rationalization. But an important part of this expansion was now vertical. Over Carnegie's objections, Frick gained the company an interest in the important Lake Superior ore fields. A company was organized for the transportation of ore through the Great Lakes and a railroad was built to bring the ore from the lakes to Pittsburgh. Though for various reasons these separate ventures (and the Frick Coke Company) were never entirely integrated into the firm, Frick was moving in this direction in the late 1890s. However, conflict between Frick and Carnegie led to Frick's dismissal and an end to any plans for consolidation. Instead, attention focused outward again as Carnegie prepared to begin fabricating finished steel as a challenge to the Morgan-engineered combinations dominating that industry.

Horizontal expansion had also increased in the last decade of the century. During Frick's chairmanship, the three Pittsburgh plants increased their production of steel from 536,000 tons, or about 16 percent of the nation's total production, to 2,663,000 tons, about 25 percent of the nation's production. Indeed, Frick was an empire builder in his own right before becoming involved with Carnegie, having aggregated the coke-producing ovens in the Connellsville coal region into his own Frick Coke Company. The difference, then, between the period of Frick's ascendancy and the earlier growth was the emphasis Frick placed on integrating the various firms into a smoothly functioning unit which operated according to a rationalized plan at the corporate level as well as the plant level. This shows that emphasis on expansion or on internal rationalization are not always mutually exclusive. Nevertheless, the specialization of the rationalization function, both as to time and individual, is as clear with Carnegie Steel as it was later with General Motors.

Few greater contrasts in personalities could be observed among leading industrialists than between Carnegie and Frick. Carnegie was impulsive and assertive, sometimes explaining business decisions abruptly by, "I've got the flash!" He lead an active social life and enjoyed his associations with prominent political figures of both Britain and America. Carnegie was talkative and ebullient, he exuded confidence. His engaging personality was helpful on the sales and promotion end of the business and, on a few occasions, in acquiring needed capital for the firm. But his contact with the actual management of operations was not great. In later years, Carnegie came to spend half the year in Britain, keeping in touch with company affairs by wire and letter. These communications were used primarily to exhort and discipline his various lieutenants. His approach toward subordinates was warm, personal, and often paternal. They in turn regarded him with great loyalty and even affection. He resisted the more modern forms of corporate structure, preferring the personal ties of a partnership.

Frick, however, was cold, impersonal, and formal. People had little affection for him, though all respected his managerial talents. Unlike Carnegie, Frick was reserved, always in control. This difference, between impulsiveness and control, may be basic to the specialization of the rationalizing function. One observor noted that "Frick was a patient plodding organizer. Carnegie was a brilliant erratic schemer."[26] The same could as easily have been said of Sloan and Durant.

The question of generality of these two syndromes is an important one. Not surprisingly, not all cases are so clear-cut as these. But an examination of more of the largest United States firms at the turn of the century provides further evidence for the specialization of the two functions.

Examples of Specialization Within Top Management

Henry du Pont established control of the chemical industry in the post-Civil War period.[27] Concentrating on the expansion and maintenance of his control, Du Pont never bothered with any more administrative details than he could handle through personal correspondence. As a result, only prices were controlled, and systematic coordination of purchasing, production, and distribution never developed.

In the early 1900s the Du Pont empire was simultaneously expanded and rationalized. But the two activities were specialized in different individuals. Expansion was largely the work of Coleman du Pont, while his cousin Pierre administered the firm and gave it its functionally departmentalized structure. The personality differences between Coleman and Pierre resemble the pattern we have observed with Durant and Sloan and with Carnegie and Frick. Coleman has been described as being capable of "charming the birds right out of the trees." Pierre, however, was "quiet and studious, had the rational, analytical outlook of an organization builder."[28] Moreover, Coleman's fascination with empire-building did not end with the explosives industry. He followed this with ventures in New York real estate and an attempt to build a hotel chain along the Eastern seaboard. Pierre, too, continued his organizational efforts in other contexts. In other great consolidations such as General Motors and United States Rubber, he later encouraged the creation of better-defined structures, though he did not undertake directly the organizational work involved.

The pattern of specialization within top management and a less abrupt transition between empire-building and rationalization is also noticeable in another pair of cases. Unlike Du Pont however, where Pierre emerged as the dominant force in his own right, the subordinates who created rationalized structures for McCormick Harvester Company and Armour & Company remained relatively obscure.[29] But McCormick and Armour themselves were clear-cut cases of empire-builders with relatively little interest in administrative structure.

Cyrus McCormick, famous as the inventor of the reaper, may be considered to exemplify the true entrepreneurial hero whose success depends on creative innovation. His business success, however, was not established until after his original patent expired, and it owes much more to his domineering personality than his technical expertise. Once he decided to exploit the reaper commercially, McCormick put his greatest emphasis on sales and promotion of the new machine. When not absorbed in this work, McCormick was involved in patent litigation and consequently became "as well known in Washington as . . . the most eminent public men."[30]

Since McCormick spent most of his time traveling, he left the details of manufacturing and administration to others. In the beginning this led to poor quality and a lack of coordination. The situation improved only when manufacturing was centralized in one factory under the direction of Cyrus's brother William. "Cyrus planned the work in large outlines . . . while William added the details and supervised the carrying out of the plan."[31] After William's death, another brother, Leander, followed by the general superintendent, Charles A. Spring, and finally Cyrus's son, accomplished the necessary administrative coordination. However, with the head of the company so involved in external relations, the coordination achieved was not always sufficient. One officer complained that the firm "practically had no head—every man in the office seems to do what is right in his own eyes."[32] Only in the last four years of McCormick's life was there a "new and persistent emphasis of the company upon greater economy and efficiency of operation."[33] Not accidentally, this new emphasis coincided with Cyrus's diminishing influence in the firm due to old age and rheumatism. It seems clear therefore that administrative structure was primarily the result of managers working under McCormick.

McCormick's "will to power"[34] matches the empire-building pattern we have observed. He had "an indomitable will to have his way upon any matter which came before him."[35] Not surprisingly, McCormick ran for political office several times and also purchased his own newspaper in order to editorialize to the world at large. He had none of the charm and sociability of a Carnegie or Durant, however, and so never won any of the elections he entered. He was "gruff" and sometimes "offensive," preferring "to play a lone hand."[36] He felt "slight attraction for society and the lighter side of life."[37] Nevertheless, though he had frequent quarrels with business partners, "the feeling of loyalty and friendliness . . . of the employees had from the start been unusually strong."[38] In this he was not unlike Carnegie and Durant. His need for power seems to have expressed itself also in his unrelenting emphasis on expansion, which he pushed over his brother's objections.

P. D. Armour also represents an empire-builder whose operations were structured and rationalized by subordinates. Despite his prominence in the meat-packing industry, he was known more as a great merchant and trader than as a manufacturer. He described himself as a born speculator. Armour entered the packing business early and expanded as the demand for western meat multiplied. Within five years of his permanent move to Chicago, he had established other packing houses in Omaha, Sioux City, East Saint Louis, Saint Joseph, and Fort Worth. Then he turned to building complete branch houses for receiving meat from the central packing cities and distributing it to local retailers. The man's motives fit the empire-building pattern. He is said to have "valued money . . . only as a measure of power," and he "liked to relax and play the grand and magnificent." His charismatic appeal has also been noted. "Socially he was irresistible. He got up close—invited confidence—made friends and held them."[39] "Particularly among those connected with the interests which he controlled, loyalty to him and his wishes was pre-eminent."[40]

However, from the beginning of the modern meat-packing industry, there was a critical problem of coordination among highly specialized buyers, slaughterhouses, and distribution branches.[41] These problems were solved simultaneously with the expansion of the industry and could not be delayed for a second generation of corporate leadership. Though the evidence is not altogether certain, it would seem that the empire-builder, Armour, made only minor contributions to the rationalization of this complex system of buying, slaughtering, and distribution. Instead, he "surrounded himself with good men to run the packinghouses,"[42] much as Carnegie did with his steel plants. Armour's reputation as a speculator and trader rather than a manufacturer has already been noted. He freely admitted that the economies he gained through manufacturing the by-products of the slaughterhouses were forced on him by competition.[43] The fact of specialization of empire-building and rationalization functions is thus descriptive also of Armour & Company, but in this case the specialization was less clearly associated with changes over time in the corporate leadership. Nevertheless the personality basis to empire-building specialization is here also confirmed.

Examples with Long Periods of Dominance by Empire-Builders

Several of the largest firms, especially those that approached monopolistic control, experienced considerable delays in the rationalization of their administrative structure. United States Steel, for instance, the heir to the Carnegie empire, did not adopt a consolidated rationalized structure until Myron Taylor succeeded Elbert Gary as chairman.[44] (But Gary was hardly an empire-builder, since United States Steel's share of the market decreased dramatically during his presidency.) Taylor put great emphasis on administrative reorganization, as he had done successfully in the revitalization of a group of cotton mills. As is typical of the rationalizers, Taylor is described as "formal," "not intimate," and characterized by an "aloofness that has kept him free of emotional entanglements in either business or pleasure." A contemporary report indicates that there was "no evidence that he had thought much . . . of problems larger than the simple rationalization of men and machines." His only reported diversion, the investigation of genealogies, is characteristic of the orderly, systematic mind useful to the rationalizers.

United States Rubber was put together principally by Charles Flint in 1892.[45] After launching the combination, Flint departed to engineer combinations in wool, chewing gum, electricity, and other industries. The managers of the rubber combination were also more interested in expansion than administration. Smaller companies were acquired or forced out of business, a combination of manufacturers of industrial rubber products was merged in 1905, and control of raw materials was sought. In this emphasis on expansion, the firm suffered from lack of central coordination. "Specifications and standards were not centrally controlled so that a retailer reordering a given type of footwear might be resupplied by a different manufacturing plant using the same brand name but different in quality, construction, appearance and even measurement."[46] In 1927 a syndicate of Du Ponts gained control and eventually installed F. B. Davis as president. Davis gave immediate priority to reorganization and within three months had developed a corporate structure which was to remain fundamentally intact for thirty years. Again the specialization of expansion and rationalization is evident, though in this case there is insufficient data as to a personality basis to this specialization.

Anaconda, largest of the nonferrous metal producers has been dominated for most of its history by empire-builders.[47] As a consequence, its central office and administrative structure remained loosely organized. The copper mines of Butte were first developed by Marcus Daly in 1882. From then until shortly before his death in 1900, Daly was the dominant force in Anaconda, if not in all of Montana. In addition to developing the mines, he built the first smelter in Montana, constructed a railroad to haul the ore from the mines to the smelter, and bought extensive lumber properties to protect his supplies for the mines. Daly also owned his own newspaper and spent lavish sums on it to increase his influence. While not running for office himself, he was deeply and at times notoriously involved in

Montana politics. Descriptions of Daly tally with those of other empire-builders. Observers have described his "energy and magnetism," his "great charm and wit," and "his faculty of making associates loyal friends"[48]. He personally hired many of the miners who worked for Anaconda and he enjoyed close associations with them. His sociability was, however, balanced by a more basic trait of dominance. "Although generous in his treatment of miners, he insisted on absolute obedience to his orders,"[49] and would turn his "fiery temper"[50] on anyone who disobeyed. This impulsiveness, perhaps the most central aspect of the dominance syndrome, was also reflected in Daly's decisionmaking, which, according to one source, was "often abrupt and made by rule of thumb."[51]

In 1889 Anaconda was absorbed by Amalgamated Copper, the great combination put together by H. H. Rogers. Though Amalgamated never attained the same dominant position in copper as did United States Steel in its industry, the combination succeeded in uniting the remaining copper interests in Butte. Rogers has been described as "power hungry" but possessing a "magnetic personality and genial charm."[52]

Control of the copper empire later shifted to John D. Ryan and then to Cornelius F. Kelley. If these later generations of empire-builders were not so flamboyant as Daly, it is still clear that their primary interests were expansion and dominance of the copper industry. The entire period prior to the Depression was filled with major and minor acquisitions, made "not in any logical relationship to Anaconda's Montana [holdings] but in response to the acquisitive will of Messrs. Ryan and Kelley."[53] The concentration on empire-building resulted, as we might expect, in a lack of attention to systematic coordination of the integrated empire. There was "little thought to building at the central office such staff departments as engineering, research, labor or public relations to better the co-ordination between the functional units or to improve accounting and other financial and administrative data."[54]

The Standard Oil experience is also revealing since Rockefeller did not fit the same personality pattern as Durant and Carnegie.[55] Rockefeller has been described as a "methodical," "unemotional," "restrained" individual characterized by a complete mastery of details, faultless order, and rigid economy. "Precision was a ritual, important in itself." He "never seemed aggressive, and was always serene and quiet."[56] Though this description is clearly at variance with the more typical empire-building syndrome, Rockefeller was surely one of the great empire-builders with only minor claims as a significant rationalizer. In this light, it is important to note that Rockefeller delegated to other officials many of the empire-building activities important to Carnegie and Durant. In particular, the external relationships of Standard Oil were not usually handled by Rockefeller directly. Perhaps the most significant advantage of the firm was its large railroad rebates, but these were always negotiated by an early partner, Henry Flagler. Similarly, the job of persuading competing refiners to join with Standard was handled by partners (John Archbold, the second president, being one of the most important). The great pipeline empire was the work of such men as Daniel O'Day and H. H. Rogers. These men all fit more clearly with the empire-building pattern we have discussed.[57] Flagler is described as "ambitious," but having "a keen sense of humor" and a "personal responsibility to employees that won warm respect and loyal support." Archbold was "mercurial and jovial," and "quick to make decisions and aggressive in developing plans." Rogers was "power-hungry" but possessed a "magnetic personality and genial charm." O'Day was "driving, occasionally ruthless" but also "warmhearted," and favored "close personal relations . . . that developed a cohesion among subordinates and a loyalty that would be difficult . . . to excel." Much of the empire-building activity therefore was undertaken by men who resembled the Carnegie-Durant type more than did Rockefeller himself.

Two Exceptions

There are, however, two conspicuous examples in which empire-building and administrative rationalization were performed by the same individual. James B. Duke built the American Tobacco Company first through exploitation of a technological innovation, the cigarette machine, and then through aggressive acquisition of competing firms.[58] Throughout this expansion, however, there was steady consolidation of the empire, specialization of factories and constituent firms to one product, and central control of purchasing and sales by functional departments. The evidence indicates that Duke's leadership was equally as important in both phases of the development of American Tobacco.

Charles Coffin, first with Thomson-Houston and later with General Electric is another who initiated significant empire-building and rationalization activities.[59] The emphasis on consolidation was prompted by the financial panic of 1893. Before that time Coffin's energies seem to have been directed more toward expansion and acquisition. After the panic, the district sales offices were brought under effective control and became in fact branches of the central office. The scientific factory costs system and the functional system of factory organization were transferred from Thomson-Houston to all of General Electric. Though the evidence here is not entirely clear, it seems that Coffin's contribution to the development of a more consolidated structure was equal to the role he played in expansion and acquisition. Like Duke, therefore, Coffin did not limit himself to either empire-building or rationalization at the expense of the other.

Examples from Less Developed Countries

The distinction between dominance and achievement-oriented patterns of entrepreneurship should also be useful in describing entrepreneurship in less developed countries. The evidence is scattered but indicates that the differences are not peculiar to the growth of United States firms.

Torcuato diTella, who built the Latin American industrial giant S.I.A.M. diTella, fits easily into the empire-building pattern.[60] His first successes were based on opportunistic exploitation of a change in city ordinances for bread-kneading machines. Aggressive salesmanship and the initiation of credit sales were important factors in his early success. A later growth in gasoline pump production was dependent on diTella's close personal ties to government and banking officials. Characteristically, the depression was met by expanding into new markets rather than retrenching and consolidating. DiTella became a prominent Argentine public figure, active in government and social circles. But, as we might expect, the administration of his holdings was hardly systematic. In the early years, the factory was "just a large shed and under it there was a great deal of crowding and confusion. Bread mixing and kneading machines were produced together with gasoline pumps."[61] DiTella was usually unsuccessful at developing his own products and achieved production efficiency only after arranging licensing agreements with American firms. But he resisted the more formal organizational structure urged on him by these firms. His ties with his subordinates were based on a patron-client relationship which encouraged personal loyalty at the expense of systematic, impersonal efficiency. But he operated in new and rapidly expanding markets, and the success of the firm depended more on aggressive promotion and personal favors from the government and the banks. For these reasons, DiTella's extraverted and engaging personality was a great asset that more than offset his lack of attention to systematic administration. It was only after his death that the firm began to emphasize the development of structures for quality control, cost accounting, and efficient decentralization of authority.

Other examples of empire-building specialists would not be difficult to find. Papanek's[62] study of Pakistani development reports that the entrepreneurs who aggregated huge fortunes during the 1950s and early 1960s showed little concern for the internal operations of their empires. Studies of the founding of the Japanese *zaibatsu*[63] also seem to indicate the important role of the dominance dimension of entrepreneurial behavior.

Geertz's anthropological work on two Indonesian towns describes the two different problems that must be solved for successful industrial organization.[64] "Tabanan's group approach, its pluralistic collectivism, gives it advantages in mobilizing capital, disadvantages in improving efficiency and rationality; Modjokuto's ego approach, its bazaar-economy individualism, gives it advantages in efficiency, disadvantages in capitalization."[65] These are exactly the problems that are solved by the dominance and achievement dimensions of entrepreneurial behavior.

DISCUSSION

The pattern established by these case histories should now be abundantly clear. The basic point is that empire-building and rationalization were specialized functions and were handled by very different types of individuals. They were for the individuals involved habitual patterns of behavior, as well as appropriate responses to economic conditions.

One critical difference between the two types is the internal or external orientation of the entrepreneur. The concerns of the empire-builder were by nature directed outward. His goals, expansion and industrial dominance, were measured in terms relative to the industry and environment as a whole. The personal contributions of these men were also principally in the external relationships of the firm. Durant and Carnegie were great salesmen and utilized their engaging personalities to attract customers, competitors, and creditors alike. Their nonbusiness behavior was not unlike the pattern to be observed in their business life. Prominence in society and involvement in politics were typical of their careers. Social and political activities were sometimes used to further their business interests, but they seem to have often been pursued for their intrinsic satisfaction. Even when empire-builders directed their attention inward toward the company itself, their primary concern was with persons and personalities rather than roles and responsibilities. Relationships with subordinates were diffuse instead of functionally specific, and a paternalistic concern for the subordinate's entire family was common. In this way, they helped to solve the most critical internal problems facing the early growth of their organizations, the maintenance of trust and cooperation among subordinates otherwise jealous of their respective power. It is perhaps paradoxical that dominant and power-hungry individuals are the best suited to solve the power conflicts threatening the formation and early growth of these organizations. In fact, several of these empire-builders were incapable of working with partners in a cooperative relationship. But this same strength of personality encouraged subordinates to identify with the firm and gave it sufficient cohesiveness to survive.

There were, of course, two distinct means of resource accumulation. The first was based on the exploitation of an important technological change to tap a rapidly growing market. A second mode emerged through the strategy of combining several existing firms within a larger combination. Many of the successful empire-builders utilized both methods whenever the occasion permitted. Durant with General Motors and Henry du Pont with the Gunpowder Trade Association are examples. The personal skills required by the two modes of growth were not dissimilar. In both, the external focus was characteristic, directed either toward customers and the possibilities of the new market, or toward competitors and the need to combine the various firms in the industry. Also, the ultimate goal of size and industrial dominance were the same in both methods. Because of their psychological equivalence, it is not surprising to find that the same empire-builders succeeded in both.

The rationalizers come much closer to Weber's description of the modern bureaucrat. Though respected for their talents, Sloan, Frick, and Pierre du Pont did not generate the warmth and loyalty that characterized their predecessors. Their relationships with subordinates tended to be impersonal and were certainly more functionally specific. They saw their organizations as systems of roles and functions as compared to, for instance, Carnegie who prided himself on the individuals in the organization and not on the organization itself. The rationalizers were men whose whole lives were dominated by their businesses. Their role in politics was less dramatic than the empire-builders and they indulged themselves much less in any active social life. Most characteristic of the rationalizers was their direction of attention inward toward the operations of the firm rather than outward. In focusing on the operations they stressed orderly and systematic administration based on explicit principles.

It is a mistake, however, to characterize their activity as routine. The act of creating a rationalized and efficient structure may eventually lead to bureaucratic routinization, but the organizing work itself is creative. The men who devise these organizational structures may be reducing much of their subordinates' work to a routine, but they are not themselves engaged in routine tasks. The achievement and task-oriented characteristics of their behavior would not be required by a purely routine schedule.

It should be obvious that the environments in which these two types flourished were markedly different. The empire-builders began typically by the early exploitation of a market opened up by technological or social changes. The rationalizers are more successful in established markets, in which pressures of competition focus on reduction of unit costs.

The exceptions cited may point up technological factors affecting the transition from empire-building to rationalization. For instance, the highly perishable nature of tobacco necessitated a carefully controlled structure from the beginning in the American Tobacco Company. Buyers of tobacco leaf were highly specialized and the flow of tobacco through drying, processing, and sales had to be coordinated with a precise time schedule. These technological limits may have influenced the need for the first empire-builder to be a skilled rationalizer as well. On the other hand, though meat is another perishable product requiring close coordination between purchasing, manufacture, and sales, Armour seems to have been able to build his empire by delegating the needed rationalization to subordinates. General Electric's early rationalization may have been necessitated by different considerations. Its first expansion was based on the sale of generating equipment to electric light and power companies. This type of unit production requires close coordination among the various functions and so may also favor the fusion of empire-building and rationalization. The possibility of an entrepreneur performing both functions is not ruled out by this psychological analysis. The dominance and task-oriented dimensions are orthogonal and not negatively related, and thus various combinations of the two types are to be expected.

CONCLUSIONS

The specialization of these functions has important implications for past and future work on the social psychological aspects of industrial organization in developing economies. If entrepreneurial behavior is not a unidimensional construct, then we need to know which patterns of behavior are predicted by which psychological variables. Briefly, I would like to review the implications of the distinction drawn between dominant and achievement-oriented entrepreneurship for one specifically psychological tradition of research, and then for the various quasi-psychological themes offered by three prominent economic and sociological theorists.

Need Achievement and Entrepreneurial Behavior

Work on nAch has suffered, I think, from a confusion of empire-building and rationalizing functions. It has never been entirely clear which pattern of behavior the motive is supposed to predict. Need achievement has been defined as the "urge to improve" and is measured by the frequency of thinking in terms of "competition against a standard of excellence."[66] Both of these are framed in terms of a relatively impersonal task-oriented goal and not interpersonal domination. Actual experimental work confirms that the need achiever is a highly task-oriented individual, motivated principally by the intrinsic satisfactions of the task itself and not by the extrinsic reward structure. Several experiments have shown that the correlation between nAch and performance is reduced or eliminated once immediate external rewards are offered.[67] These and other experiments suggest that nAch characterizes people for whom the means to a goal, the instrumental task-oriented behavior, has become the most satisfying aspect of the task. In short, neither the definition of nAch, the measurement method, nor the experimental behavior suggests much in common with the empire-building entrepreneurs I have described. And yet in much of the literature it is the empire builder who is most often thought to be the embodiment of achievement motivation.

For instance, McClelland's last work on achievement motivation dealt with an attempt to increase its levels among businessmen. What is of interest to us is the way in which the behavioral results of such training were measured. At one point, the different types of entrepreneurial behavior are recognized but mistakenly combined as one syndrome. Of the four activities supposedly indicative of achievement-motivated behavior, the first is most analogous to the rationalizing, improving pattern. Two of the other three are more suggestive of the empire-builders.

1. Specific action taken to improve procedures, e.g., he has simplified reports of agents so that they can be posted daily.
2. Unusual increase in firm's business due to man's activities.
3. Promotion or salary increases above 25 percent for a two-year period, which are unusual.
4. Goes into business for himself.[68]

In finally operationalizing the measures of achievement-motivated behavior, only two are selected as important, "establishing a new business" and "expansion of the firm."[69] But these are the two most clearly descriptive of the empire-building syndrome and not the rationalization dimension. Neither reflects the urge to improve but rather the urge to grow. Put simply, they are measures of "bigger" and not "better," and thus do not, I believe, reflect the nature of the achievement motive.

It seems more likely, given the task-for-its-own sake orientation of high need achievers, that the relationship between nAch and entrepreneurial success will be limited to the rationalizing type of entrepreneurship. Other motives, in particular power motives, may be more characteristic of empire-builders. Though there is less research on power motivation than on achievement motivation a useful measurement system has been devised which defines power acts as those designed to have impact on others. Insofar as we can abstract a motivational pattern from the historical data, it would be fair to say that Durant, Carnegie, and the other empire-builders were motivated by a need to have a significant impact on others.

Schumpeter, Sombart, and Weber

Schumpeter has made the distinction between entrepreneurs whose function is to combine the factors of production in new ways and managers who run existing businesses more routinely.[70] Entrepreneurs fulfill their function "more by will than by intellect . . . more by 'authority,' 'personal weight,' and so forth than by original ideas."[71] Schumpeter also recognized the role of personality in this process, in particular the role of power motives. "First of all there is the dream and the will to found a private kingdom. . . . Then there is the will to conquer, the impulse to fight. . . . Finally there is the joy of creating."[72] But in making this empire-building entrepreneur his hero of economic development, Schumpeter has ignored the Sloans and Fricks who neither ran their firms in routine ways nor dominated them by "intuition" and "personal weight."

Similarly Sombart recognized the conflict between rationality and entrepreneurial acquisitiveness.[73] But the ultimate product of progressive rationalization, the bourgeois bureaucrat, is very different from the individual who first designed the rationalized system. This is an important distinction which Sombart never entirely clarifies. As a result, his entrepreneur is both a successful organizer who achieves proper coordination through assigning specific functional responsibilities and a daring, acquisitive entrepreneur. Thus while Sombart did identify the two contradictory styles of entrepreneurship, his fascination with the empire-building aspect results in insufficient recognition of the positive contributions of the specialized rationalizer.

In contrast, Weber's much discussed theory of the origins of capitalism emphasized primarily the rationalizing behavior of entrepreneurs.[74] It was this new quality of economic life which defined the "spirit of modern capitalism." The critical consequence of this spirit was the "rational organization of formally free labor." In pointing to the behavior typical of the spirit of modern capitalism, he was indicating not the task of capital accumulation or risk-taking, but the modern capitalist's attention to improving the operations of his firm.

Critics of the Protestant ethic thesis, however, have not been so careful in specifying what constituted the spirit of modern capitalism.[75] For instance, one prominent line of attack has been to show that capitalism had its roots in the Renaissance and thus, by predating the Reformation, could not have been the result of a Protestant ethic. But Weber's thesis links the Protestant ethic not with any particular form of capitalism but with the rationalizing, systematic spirit of capitalism. Weber recognized that capitalism had existed in all civilizations. His description of the capitalistic adventurer suggests much of the dominance-oriented pattern of entrepreneurship. But what was supposedly unique about modern Western capitalism, and what he saw as linked to Calvinism, was this spirit of systematic and continuous rationalization. This capitalist spirit is described as a major dimension of interpersonal behavior, encompassing thrift, impulse control, and a concentration on instrumental tasks as ends in themselves. This personality dimension is not merely a syndrome of favorable attitudes to capitalist acquisition. In fact, Weber specifically mentions that a curbing of the impulse to make money is necessary to the rationalizing spirit. Sociologists who have addressed themselves to the normative and value aspects of the capitalist spirit have thus missed the essence of what Weber described. It is true that such an attitude was not the consequence of Calvinism, but neither was it a central element of the spirit of capitalism. Rather, it is the fundamental personality dimension of a concentration on instrumental tasks as ends in themselves which results in increasing rationalization and may be the true link between Calvinism and economic development.

* * *

COMMENT BY BERT F. HOSELITZ

Vanneman attempts to deal with two problems. The first is his argument that entrepreneurship should be divided into two categories—namely, the men who accomplish the aggregation of large amounts of capital and labor for purposes of exploiting a large and expanding market (and who were thus the great empire-builders who attracted much fame), and those men who gained the position of entrepreneurs and developed systematic methods through rationalization for managing these aggregates of men and capital. Secondly,

Vanneman, by examining the psychological dimensions of the methods developed, attempts to find the relationship and the degree of importance of the empire-builders and the rationalizers within a given system.

For Vanneman, the division of the entrepreneurial class into two categories was stated especially clearly by A. D. Chandler in Strategy and Structure, 1962.[76] But this distinction was made long ago by writers on the entrepreneurial function. For example, Veblen wrote about it in the following passage from his Engineers and the Price System:

> The effect of this move has been twofold: experience has brought out the fact that corporation finance, at its best and soundest, has now become a matter of comprehensive and standardized bureaucratic routine, necessarily comprising the mutual relations between various corporate concerns, and best to be taken care of by a clerical staff of trained accountants; and the same experience has put the financial houses in direct touch with the technological general staff of the industrial system, whose surveillance has become increasingly imperative to the conduct of any profitable enterprise in industry. But also, by the same token, it has appeared that the corporation financier of nineteenth-century tradition is no longer of the essence of the case in corporation finance of the larger and more responsible sort. He has, in effect, come to be no better than an idle wheel in the economic mechanism, serving only to take up some of the lubricant.[77]

Though this was written in 1921, Veblen had already made the same distinction in 1904 in The Theory of Business Enterprise. Anyone wishing to discover the development of Veblen's idea of empire-builders versus rationalizers should read the third chapter of this book, where it is fully described.[78]

Another author of the same distinction is Werner Sombart. In 1930 he wrote about the rationalizers as follows:

> The economic outlook has recently undergone material changes and will continue to change in the future. The capitalistic spirit at its prime was characterized by psychological strains of peculiar intensity born of the contradictions between irrationality and rationality, between the spirit of speculation and that of calculation, between the mentality of the daring entrepreneur and that

> of the hard-working, sedate bourgeois. At present this strain is relaxing. Rationalism is thoroughly permeating the capitalist spirit, and a completely rationalized mentality is no longer a capitalist mentality in its characteristic sense.[79]

The distinction made between empire-building and rationalizing entrepreneurs was not always recognized. Among earlier writers on entrepreneurship, for example, Cantillon and Say, we find nothing about a rationalizing entrepreneur and are confronted only with a man who takes risks but does not rationalize. The fact that an entrepreneur is obliged to rationalize emerged only at the end of the nineteenth century, and for particular reasons: i.e., that empire-building entrepreneurs were becoming rarer and rarer; that big firms were being administered more and more as establishments where capital rather than labor could be used; that the number of empire-building entrepreneurs tended to diminish in favor of more rationalizing entrepreneurs. Proof of this is perhaps best given by Joseph Schumpeter. When he wrote The Theory of Economic Development in 1911, he wrote on entrepreneurs as if they were all empire-builders. On page 66 of the English edition of this book, first issued in 1932, he lists entrepreneurs as almost all engaging in new empire-building strategies. The rationalization of industrial existence was almost completely neglected. It is true that he says there that entrepreneurial activity was:

> the carrying out of the new organization of any industry, like the creation of a monopoly position (for example through trustification) or the breaking up of a monopoly position[80]

but surely this passage does not indicate that the most important aspect of entrepreneurship is the rationalization of large firms. But Schumpeter lived through the 1920s and 1930s, and in this period his belief in empire-building entrepreneurship was greatly transformed. In 1942 his book Capitalism, Socialism and Democracy appeared, and here he states his belief that capitalism will come to an end because the empire-building quality of the formerly important entrepreneur has vanished. In a particularly imaginative passage, he says,

> Rationalized and specialized office work will eventually blot out personality, the calculable result, the "vision." The leading man no longer has the opportunity to fling himself into the fray. He is becoming just another

office worker—and one who is not always difficult to replace.[81]

Who can say whether this analysis of capitalism is correct? That we have capitalism even in many Western social democratic countries (for example, England and Sweden) will not be denied. That this capitalism is in its institutions much closer to socialism than it was, for example, in 1850 will also not be denied. It is, in other words, quite possible that the fate of capitalism is parallel to the prediction of Schumpeter—namely, that capitalism will eventually evolve into socialism—but the present institutions, though they retain the form of capitalism, are in reality bureaucracies where the free expression of capitalism is limited to the stock market and private meetings of corporation directors.

To come to the second point, Vanneman uses principally McClelland's example. The fact that Need Achievement is combined with entrepreneurship is known and has been proved by McClelland and his collaborators in a large number of instances.[82] In fact, it is generally believed that an increase in Need Achievement leads to an increase in entrepreneurship. A more difficult question is the amount of increase of entrepreneurial activity associated with an increase in Need Achievement. Vanneman himself admits this and should have dealt with the question in greater detail. If one takes as one example the outcome of the costly experiment made by McClelland and Winter in India, and if one studies the tremendous input involved and compares it with the relatively poor output, one might perhaps recognize the enormity of the problem.[83]

We must therefore conclude that an entrepreneurial society such as existed in Western Europe and North America after 1750 cannot recur. These two continents are thus far the only examples in history where the particular methods that we call capitalism originated and developed. Whether we can learn anything from these examples in order to make capitalism reappear in other societies is a moot question.

CHAPTER

7

EFFECTS OF POLICIES ENCOURAGING FOREIGN JOINT VENTURES IN DEVELOPING COUNTRIES

Louis T. Wells, Jr.

INTRODUCTION

The effect of foreign investment on the economies of developing nations has long been a subject of debate. Though there are still economists who would exclude all private direct foreign investment, as well as those who would favor a completely open door to the foreigner, most end up somewhere between the two extremes. The debate must focus on whether foreign investment leaves the country better off than it would be under whatever may be a feasible alternative. The conclusions depend to a great extent on situations specific to individual countries. They turn largely on the issue of what would happen without the foreign investor. Would, for example, a local entrepreneur make the investment if the foreigner did not enter? Would he turn the resources to consumption or to use in a foreign capital market if the foreigner were to invest? Does the presence of the foreigner generate more or less net entrepreneurship in the country than would be the case in his absence? The theoretical framework for handling many of these pieces of data is available.[1] Though there are some practical problems in solving the system in

---

The research on which this paper is based was financed by the Ford Foundation as part of the study of "The Multinational Enterprise and the Nation State" and by the Harvard Business School, division of Research. The findings of this research are reported in more detail in John M. Stopford and Louis T. Wells, Jr., Managing the Multinational Enterprise (New York: Basic Books, 1971). An earlier version of this paper was presented at the Harvard Development Advisory Service Conference in Dubrovnik, June 20-26, 1970.

a general equilibrium approach, it is the shortage of empirical data that delays definite answers. We simply have too little information on the very micro level at which such decisions are made. The approach for policy work has been to attempt some crude generalizations about the roles of various classes of foreign investment.[2]

The question as to whether a policy of accepting certain foreign investment brings more benefits than does some alternative policy is vigorously debated among economists. The debate becomes even more complicated when the question involves the terms under which the foreign investment is to be undertaken. If the government has the option of insisting that the foreigner take in a local partner, does this improve the outcome for the host country? Little empirical work has been done on the effects of different terms of entry. This paper is an attempt to shed some light on the results of a policy that insists on local participation in the equity of a foreign subsidiary.

A number of countries apply pressure on the foreign investor to share ownership of his subsidiary with locals. Frequently cited are the policies of Japan, Spain, Ceylon, India, Mexico, and Pakistan. The governments of many other countries take some steps to encourage local ownership when the investor enters or at some time during his stay.

The idea of encouraging joint ventures by the foreign investor is supported by U.S. Agency for International Development (AID).[3] and some international organizations, though the Pearson Commission hedged considerably on their advantages for the host country.[4]

Government policies to encourage local participation in subsidiaries of foreign firms could have a number of effects. If, for example, the foreigner is needed by the local economy but refuses to enter joint ventures, the government might be forced to retreat from its joint-venture program so often that the ownership of industry would look similar to that in a country that did not press for joint ventures. Another possible outcome is that foreign investors desiring complete ownership of subsidiaries will simply not invest in the country. In this case, the makeup of foreign investment in the country would be different from that in similar countries with less aggressive policies on local ownership. Still another pattern would result if the government is partially successful, but has to retreat from its policy for a few foreign investors who insist on complete ownership and are much needed by the host country. In this case, the ownership patterns in the country would show more local participation than in countries without joint-venture policies—the combination of investors might be somewhat similar, but the foreigners who object strongly to joint ventures would still retain complete ownership of their operations in the country.

The first section of this paper shows that strong policies encouraging joint ventures do result in a pattern of foreign investment that includes more local ownership than is found in other countries. The investment picture is not substantially different, but the few investors who rarely enter joint ventures elsewhere still do not take in local partners. The government allows them complete control of the subsidiary, or they do not invest in the country. The second section summarizes what is known about the determinants of investors' attitudes toward joint ventures.

On a different level of analysis, requirements or incentives for joint participation may lead the foreign investor to treat the subsidiary differently from the way he would treat a wholly-owned operation. The resulting policies could negate any benefits that the host country expects from its joint ventures. The multinational enterprise could, for example, choose to export from a wholly-owned subsidiary elsewhere, when it might have exported from the country in question if there were no local partner to share in the profits. The loss of potential exports would cost the country foreign exchange and employment. Another possibility is that the parent charges higher transfer prices for sales from the parent to the joint venture than it would have charged a wholly-owned subsidiary, leaving a smaller share of profits for the local partner than might have been anticipated by him or by the government. The third section examines these matters, especially the way a multinational enterprise treats its different subsidiaries, and concludes that the case for joint ventures is highly qualified.

To see what the response of multinational enterprise was to the policies of countries strongly encouraging joint ventures, the investments of 187 American enterprises were examined.* To analyze the policies that multinational enterprises follow toward their joint ventures, the investment data were supplemented by information from a number of other studies of foreign investment. These data enabled us to differentiate, to an extent, between patterns of behavior toward wholly-owned subsidiaries and those toward joint ventures. The data were drawn primarily from countries where the investor is given considerable freedom in the ownership of subsidiaries. In a few cases, the reader must exercise some caution in extending these behavioral patterns to cases where the foreign investor entered joint ventures as a result of government pressure.

---

*All the firms that appeared on Fortune's 500 list in 1967 and that had six or more manufacturing operations outside the United States in 1964 were included in the study.

TABLE 7.1

Ownership of Manufacturing Subsidiaries Entered in 1960-67 by Area, Less Developed Countries

Foreign Ownership on Entry (percent)	Ceylon		India		Mexico		Pakistan		Ceylon, India, Mexico, and Pakistan		Other Less Developed Countries	
	No. of Subs.	Percent	No. of Subs.	Percent	No. of Subs.	Percent	No. of Subs.	Percent	No. of Subs.	Percent	No. of Subs.	Percent
95-100	2	66.7	1	3.1	50	39.7	1	10.0	54	33.9	334	52.4
50-94	0	0.0	14	43.7	39	30.9	6	60.0	59	34.5	194	30.5
5-49	1	33.3	17	53.2	37	29.4	3	30.0	58	31.6	109	17.1
Total	3	100	32	100	126	100	10	100	171	100	637	100

INVESTMENT PATTERNS

Changes in Ownership

Some clues to the effectiveness of government policies that encourage joint ventures can be gathered by examining the experience of countries that have made the attempt. The data show roughly what one might expect. Those countries whose governments are frequently cited as insisting on joint ventures have a larger percentage of local ownership in foreign subsidiaries than do the other developing countries. Table 7.1 shows the ownership of manufacturing subsidiaries entered between 1960 and 1967 by the firms examined. The relatively strict policies of Ceylon, India, Mexico, and Pakistan appear to result in a larger percentage of joint ventures in the makeup of foreign investment than do the policies of other developing countries.

Table 7.1, along with Table 7.2, also hints at the existence of some complex patterns. The ownership data show that even the "strict" countries have retreated rather frequently from their insistence on joint ventures. Complete foreign ownership is not rare, even during recent years. One could build an hypothesis along the following lines: The more a country advances, the more it needs foreign investment from particular firms. Some of these are the ones that resist pressures to form joint ventures. The easy opportunities for import substitution have been filled; the need has shifted from products that require only widely available technology to more advanced products

TABLE 7.2

Ownership of Manufacturing Subsidiaries in Japan

Foreign Ownership	Subsidiaries Existing in 1966		Subsidiaries Entered in 1960-67	
	Number of Subsidiaries	Percent	Number of Subsidiaries	Percent
95-100	18	14.6	10	11.2
50-94	45	46.6	30	33.7
5-49	60	48.8	49	65.1
Total	123	100	89	100

for which only a few firms have the know-how. And some of these firms are likely to oppose local participation. Similarly, efforts on the part of the government to increase manufactured exports may require marketing or technological inputs that only certain foreign firms can supply. As the need for particular investors increases, the attractiveness of a country may also be enhanced. The larger international market which operations in a new country may open up leads some firms to be willing to relax their insistence on control if it might curtail access to the market. The net effect of these two trends on the relative bargaining powers of the firm and the government could produce the patterns indicated by the sketchy data. Countries that have very low per capita income—such as India and Pakistan—may not be forced to retreat often from their insistence on joint ventures since their requirements are not of the kind that only a small select number of investors can fulfill. The more advanced countries may need the services which only the more stubborn investors can provide, but may not have a sufficiently attractive internal market to make the potential investor retreat from his insistence on sole ownership. These countries may have to back down and allow wholly-owned subsidiaries. The data suggest that Mexico may have been in this position in recent years. However, as the attraction of the local market increases, the foreign investor may be more likely to yield than the host government. Japan is a good illustration of this case in the period examined.

Figure 7.1 shows the relationship graphically for the foreigner's use of joint ventures and the per capita income of the country, for countries that strongly encourage local partnerships. Ceylon has been excluded since it had only seven investments by the 187 enterprises. Of course, the small number of countries represented can be only suggestive of the complex relationship here examined.

It is fairly safe to conclude that strong government policies of requiring joint ventures from the foreign investor are successful in changing the ownership pattern. A much larger portion of the foreign subsidiaries in Spain, Ceylon, India, Mexico, and Pakistan have local ownership than in otherwise similar countries. Whether such patterns of investment ownership provide the host country with more benefits depends on a number of factors.

The Pattern of Foreign Investment

The shift in the ownership of subsidiaries in the "insistent" countries could result if the country frightens away a large number of firms that resist joint ventures. There are well-known cases of enterprises refusing to abandon their policy of complete ownership

FIGURE 7.1

Percentage of Subsidiaries that Were Wholly-Owned by per Capita GNP of Host Country

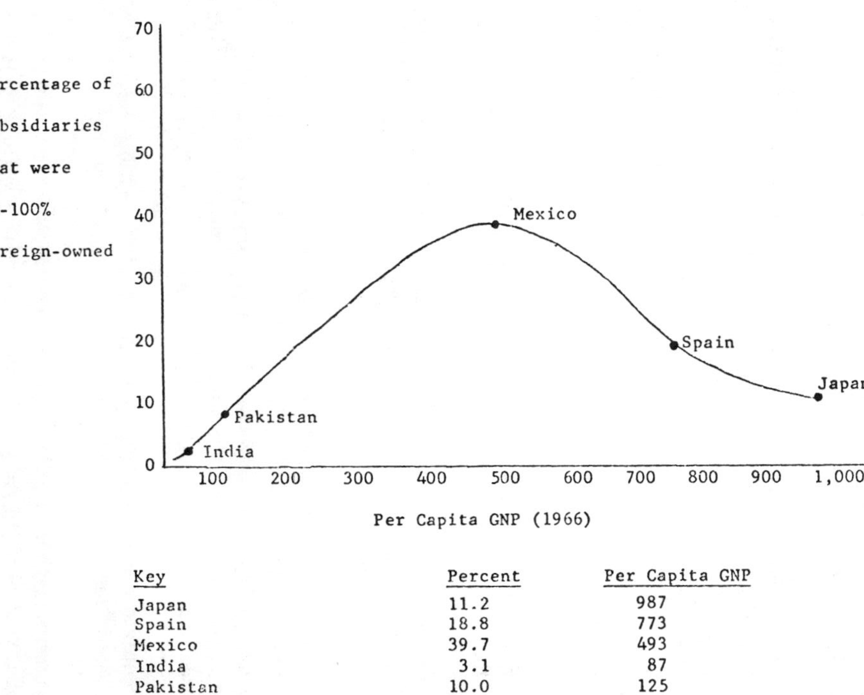

Key	Percent	Per Capita GNP
Japan	11.2	987
Spain	18.8	773
Mexico	39.7	493
India	3.1	87
Pakistan	10.0	125

of their overseas subsidiaries. General Motors, for example, supposedly refused to enter the Indian market because of India's insistence on local equity participation. If many enterprises behave in this way, it is possible that countries insisting on joint ventures will have a different combination of foreign investors than they would have in the absence of a strong ownership policy.

To test the possibility of such a difference because of a country's insistence on joint ventures, we compared the number of subsidiaries in the countries with a strong joint-venture policy to the number of subsidiaries in other less developed countries, for firms grouped by their willingness to enter joint ventures in unrestrictive countries. Tables 7.3 and 7.4 indicate that firms utilizing few joint ventures in countries where they are free to choose have approximately the same proportion of their LDC subsidiaries in countries with strong joint-venture policies as do other firms. However, of the 33 firms that had no joint ventures at all in the rest of the world in 1966, 24 percent had no investments in Spain, Ceylon, India, Mexico, and Pakistan, while only 6.6 percent of the rest of the enterprises had no such investments. The data indicate that probably only enterprises that have almost no joint ventures elsewhere avoid countries that try to enforce a joint-venture policy.

Retreating from the Policy

The ownership data show that even Spain, Ceylon, India, Mexico, and Pakistan allow a significant number of foreign investors to own all the equity in their local manufacturing subsidiaries. Since most foreign investors who prefer not to use joint ventures still invest in these insistent countries, an important question is whether these enterprises retreat from their insistence on wholly-owned subsidiaries or whether the host government backs down from its requirements of local participation for these firms.

There are many well-known cases in which the government has backed down. IBM, according to Business International, "convinced both the Indian and Japanese governments that it is better to have IBM invest on its own terms than not at all."[5] We examined the data for the 187 enterprises to see if this pattern was typical.

Thirty-six multinational enterprises had at least 90 percent of their foreign subsidiaries wholly-owned in countries without strong joint-venture policies. Only five of these firms held joint ventures in Spain, Ceylon, India, Mexico, or Pakistan in 1966. Only two had joint ventures in which they held a minority interest. Table 7.5 indicates that enterprises that oppose joint ventures elsewhere are much less likely than other firms to have joint ventures in Spain,

TABLE 7.3

Manufacturing Subsidiaries in Spain, Ceylon, India, Mexico, Pakistan, and Other Less Developed Countries Classified by Willingness of the Parent to Enter Joint Ventures Elsewhere (1960-66)

	Parent's Use of Joint Ventures Outside Japan, Spain, Ceylon, India, Mexico, and Pakistan, 1960-66 Entries*									
	None		Low		Low-Medium		High-Medium		High	
Area of Incorporation	No. of Subs.	Percent	No. of Subs.	Percent	No. of Subs.	Percent	No. of Subs.	Percent	No. of Subs.	Percent
Spain, Ceylon, India, Mexico, and Pakistan	56	23.3	40	25.8	79	23.5	86	30.2	131	27.8
Other Less Developed Countries	157	73.7	115	74.2	257	76.5	197	69.8	340	72.2

*Low = 20 percent or less joint ventures; Low-Medium = 40 percent or less, but more than 20 percent; High-Medium = 60 percent or less, but more than 40 percent; High = more than 60 percent.

TABLE 7.4

Manufacturing Subsidiaries in Spain, Ceylon, India, Mexico, Pakistan, and Other Less Developed Countries, Classified by the Parent's Holding of Joint Ventures Elsewhere (1966)

Area of Incorporation	Parent's Use of Joint Ventures Outside Japan, Spain, Ceylon, India, Mexico, and Pakistan, 1966 Subsidiaries*									
	None		Low		Low-Medium		High-Medium		High	
	No. of Subs.	Percent	No. of Subs.	Percent	No. of Subs.	Percent	No. of Subs.	Percent	No. of Subs.	Percent
Spain, Ceylon, India, Mexico, and Pakistan	29	23.9	109	23.7	98	28.9	89	32.1	67	25.7
Other Less Developed Countries	92	76.1	352	76.3	241	71.1	188	67.9	193	74.3

*See Table 7.3

TABLE 7.5

Average Ownership of Manufacturing Subsidiaries in Spain, Ceylon, India, Mexico, and Pakistan, by Parent's Ownership of Manufacturing Subsidiaries Elsewhere

	Percentage of Parent's Manufacturing Subsidiaries in Countries Other than Canada, Japan, Spain, Ceylon, India, Mexico, and Pakistan that Were Wholly-Owned in 1966						
	0	0-20	20-39	40-59	60-79	80-89	90-100
Average percentage of parent's manufacturing subsidiaries in SCIMP* that were wholly-owned in 1966	0	26.6	27.5	30.9	45.3	68.1	84.0

*SCIMP = Spain, Ceylon, India, Mexico, and Pakistan

Ceylon, India, Mexico, and Pakistan. One interpretation of the table would be that it indicates how often the host government relaxed its requirement for joint ventures. For the firms with 90-100 percent of their other subsidiaries wholly-owned, the insistent governments allowed complete ownership 84 percent of the time.

The job of the government official who negotiates with foreign investors would be eased somewhat if he knew what kind of foreign firm is likely to resist strongly pressures to form joint ventures.

DETERMINANTS OF THE ENTERPRISE'S ATTITUDE TOWARD JOINT VENTURES

An examination of the use of joint ventures by the 187 United States multinational enterprises when they go abroad provides some clues as to when the government of a less developed country may be pressured by the firm to relax its requirement for joint ventures. Certain kinds of business strategies appear to make potential interference by a local partner in decision-making hard to tolerate. Certain other strategies allow the firm to accept an outside influence at the subsidiary level if the partner provides particular contributions. One might picture the management decision in a cost-benefit framework. Local partners bring certain benefits—marketing skills, management, and capital—but wholly owned subsidiaries allow the firm more control of the operation. The decision as to which form offers the greatest net benefit depends on the need of the enterprise for the contributions of the local partner and the importance of maintaining control over subsidiaries.

Relatively undiversified firms that allow their product line to age are unable to tolerate joint ventures in many overseas manufacturing facilities. As they begin to face price or marketing competition for their mature lines,[6] the firms respond by trying to reduce costs of production by "rationalizing" manufacturing facilities around the world or by concentrating resources on generating marketing techniques to create a differentiated image for the firm's products. Both strategies result in a great deal of centralized decisionmaking.

The multinational enterprise that rationalizes manufacturing facilities usually ends up with significant trade among its subsidiaries. To obtain longer production runs, it specializes its plants by product models or by parts and cross-ships among affiliates to provide each market with a full line. Such a strategy necessitates the removal of autonomy from the individual subsidiary. Each operation can no longer operate to maximize its own profits. The center must allocate production and markets to various plants to minimize the costs of the system as a whole. As an enterprise begins to move in this direction, potential conflicts with a joint-venture partner multiply. A large portion of sales and purchases takes place with affiliates. The partner is interested in establishing transfer prices that will increase local profits. The firm may be interested in establishing prices that minimize tariffs, taxes, and costs of transferring funds. Similarly, the local partner is interested in serving more markets and, in some cases, manufacturing more items. The investor's international system may have different interests. The result is a reluctance on the part of the parent to continue to enter joint ventures. And the enterprise begins to buy out existing partners or to sell out its partial interests (an example is provided by Ford in the United Kingdom, which bought out local minority interests when it began to rationalize European production).

The firm that turns to marketing techniques to differentiate its mature products has a similarly low tolerance for joint-venture partners. For products that are mature in all the markets faced by the company, relatively little adjustment is made in the marketing approach from one area to another. The emphasis in the firm is on transferring techniques that prove successful in one market to another as quickly as possible. The result is usually a centralized organization

TABLE 7.6

Advertising Expenditure and Joint-Venture Entries[a]

Advertising as Percent of Sales	Mean Percentage of Manufacturing Subsidiaries that Were Joint Ventures (entered 1960-67, excluding Canada, Japan, and SCIMP)[b]
More than 10 percent	6.4
10 percent or less	36.6

[a]Excludes extractive firms.
[b]SCIMP = Spain, Ceylon, India, Mexico, and Pakistan.

which sends virtually complete marketing programs to the subsidiaries to be implemented locally. The contribution of a local partner that is most valued by other firms—local market information and local market access—is of little value to such an enterprise. But a local partner provides a potential source of serious conflict over marketing budgets and strategy.*

The reluctance of firms that follow a strategy of production rationalization or marketing differentiation to enter joint ventures is indicated in Tables 7.6 and 7.7. Table 7.6 demonstrates the effect of a strategy with heavy emphasis on marketing by pointing out that firms that spend a large portion of their sales revenue on advertising are less likely to enter joint ventures than are firms which spend little on advertising.

Table 7.7 is a bit more complicated. It shows the relationship between the organizational structure of the enterprise and its use of joint ventures. The area organization form is one where foreign subsidiaries report directly to a geographically organized unit—a Latin American headquarters within an international division or a Western Hemisphere division, for example. This form of organization tends to be associated with a narrow range of products, along with production rationalization or standardized marketing strategy.[7]

One other type of firm tends to avoid joint ventures: those enterprises that concentrate on developing new products for a familiar market. These firms do not need the marketing know-how of the

*Responses to a questionnaire sent to the 187 firms indicated the importance of these contributions and conflicts.

local partner, and the potential for conflict over royalties and technical fees is great. Table 7.8 shows the influence of R and D on the use of joint ventures.

In contrast to firms concentrating on marketing, production rationalization, or R and D, there are three types of firms that enter joint ventures frequently, even in countries where the host government has no policy to encourage them to do so. Firms that exercise control over raw material sources (mining firms, for example), or that avoid competition associated with mature products by constantly introducing new products, turn frequently to local partners in their manufacturing subsidiaries to provide local market information and access to channels of distribution. A firm that is relatively small in its industry turns to local partners to provide capital and management for a large foreign investment program.

The enterprise whose strategy is based on the control of raw material sources is generally faced with a high fixed cost and low

TABLE 7.7

Organizational Structure and Use of Joint Ventures

	Organizational Structure of Enterprises		
Joint Venture Entries[a]	Area[b]	Product[c]	Autonomous Subsidiaries[d]
Percentage of manufacturing subsidiaries that were joint ventures (1960-67)	25.5	38.9	53.3
Percentage of manufacturing subsidiaries that were minority or 50/50 joint ventures (1960-67)	5.9	20.8	34.9

[a]Excludes Canada, Japan, Spain, Ceylon, India, Mexico, and Pakistan.

[b]Area includes all enterprises where foreign subsidiaries report to a geographically organized unit. In the Franko terminology, these are the IIIiA, IIIA, and IIiA companies.

[c]Product includes only those firms that are organized primarily into product divisions with worldwide responsibility.

[d]Autonomous subsidiary organizations are those where subsidiaries report directly to an international division.

TABLE 7.8

R&D Expenditures and Joint Ventures[a]

Joint Venture Holdings[b]	R&D as Percentage of Sales			
	1.0% or Less	1.1 to 2.9%	3.0 to 4.9%	5% or More
Percentage of manufacturing subsidiaries that were joint ventures (1966)	44.0	33.0	28.3	21.7
Percentage of manufacturing subsidiaries that were minority or 50/50 joint ventures (1966)	24.0	21.6	17.2	11.5

[a]Excludes extractive firms.

[b]Excludes subsidiaries in Canada, Japan, Spain, Ceylon, India, Mexico, and Pakistan.

marginal costs in its extractive operations. But in an oligopolistic industry, prices tend to be higher than marginal costs. The firm is interested in assuring a large market for the output of its extractive operations. To do so, it is willing to enter joint-venture arrangements at the fabricating or distribution stage to tie a market to the source. Table 7.9 illustrates the willingness of extractive-oriented companies to accept joint-venture partners in manufacturing operations.

The firm whose strategy is based on generating a wide range of new products is faced with a diversity of markets—for products with which it has had little experience, and national markets for which the product may be in different phases of the life cycle. The firm typically does not have standardized marketing approaches. If it did, they would not be appropriate for the different national markets. To obtain the marketing know-how, such an enterprise turns frequently to local partners. Table 7.10 shows the propensity of diversified enterprises to enter joint ventures.

The third type of firm likely to enter joint ventures, even where they are not required, is one that is small in its industry. If the small company develops a new product, it may try to reap monopoly profits quickly before larger competitors can copy its innovations. To expand its operations internationally before competitors can do so, it turns to joint-venture partners to provide capital and management, the supply of which is more inelastic in the small firm than in its larger competitors. In other cases, it may seek an investment distribution that is similar to that of its larger competitor abroad. If investments are lumpy, it could again have insufficient internal resources. In either case, joint ventures would be a way of providing capital or management skills not available inside the firm. Table 7.11 shows the effect of size on use of joint ventures. Questionnaire data support the hypothesis that firms that are relatively small in their industry find a partner's contribution of capital and management more important than do large firms.

THE NATIONAL INTEREST

Knowing which firms can be most easily persuaded to take in local partners can ease the job of the government policymaker, provided he is certain that the country is better off with more joint ventures and less wholly-foreign operations. That the host country is better off with joint ventures than with wholly-owned foreign subsidiaries is almost axiomatic in developing countries. However, data that compare the behavior of the multinational system toward its joint ventures and its wholly-owned operations indicate that the host country may sometimes be better off if the foreign firm has all the equity.

TABLE 7.9

Use of Joint Ventures by Extractive Firms

	Parent Activity[a]	
Joint Venture Holdings[b]	Extractive	Nonextractive
Mean percentage of manufacturing subsidiaries that were joint ventures (1966)	48.3	30.1

[a]A multinational enterprise is classified as extractive if it has four or more extractive operations outside the United States.

[b]Excludes subsidiaries in Canada, Japan, Spain, Ceylon, India, Mexico, and Pakistan.

TABLE 7.10

Use of Joint Ventures by R&D-Oriented Diversified Firms

Diversification[a]	Mean Percentage of Manufacturing Subsidiaries that Were Joint Ventures (Entered 1961-67)[b]
Low	0.0
Medium	27.6
High	35.0

[a]Low = one 3-digit SIC industry outside U.S.; medium = 2 or 3 industries; high = 4 or more industries.

[b]Excluding Canada, Japan, Spain, Ceylon, India, Mexico, and Pakistan.

It has already been shown that for some investors the host country may have little choice, since it may not succeed in inducing the foreign firm to take in a local partner. However, for a wide range of investors, insistence on joint ventures does increase the likelihood that the firm will include a local partner in its operations. Where the government can influence the choice of ownership, it needs to know a good deal about the behavior of the multinational firm in order to make a rational decision as to whether the country will be better off with a joint venture.

Whether the investment is wholly-owned or a joint venture influences government objectives in a number of areas. The two cases are likely to have different effects on the country's balance of payments, the supply of capital, management, or technical skills, the political costs of accepting foreign investment, and the amount of control that the government can exercise over the operation.

Some of the differences in behavior of the parent toward wholly-owned and jointly-owned operations affect the timing of payments. The importance of some of these differences depends on the rate of discount that the government applies to future flows of foreign exchange. A joint venture, for example, pays a steadier stream of dividends than does the wholly-owned subsidiary, which tends to declare less dividends in the early years. Though the total of outflows over the life of the investment may be the same, if the government applies a high rate of discount to future payments, the attractiveness of the wholly-owned subsidiary would be greater on this one dimension.

Balance of Payments

The interests of the host country are affected when the multinational enterprise prices goods and services provided to a joint venture differently from the way it prices them to a wholly-owned subsidiary. Variations in the amount of investment provided from abroad, in dividend policies, and in propensities to import supplies or to export the output also affect the balance of payments of the host country.

Pricing of Goods and Services

The multinational enterprise, acting as an "economic man," has an incentive to remove profits from the subsidiary in ways that eliminate the need to share them with the local partner. Direct payments to the parent for services and higher prices on purchases from affiliates reduce the profits that have to be shared. On the other hand, it has been argued that the local partner acts as a constraint on the firm's ability to use such techniques to take funds out of the country. In the absence of a local partner, who is interested in maximizing profits in the subsidiary, the foreign firm might use transfer prices, royalties, technical fees, etc., to shift profits to lower tax jurisdictions, to avoid exchange controls, or to reduce the recorded profitability of the subsidiary so that accusations of exploitation are less likely.

TABLE 7.11

Size of Firm in Industry and Use of Joint Ventures

Relative Size of Firm in Its Industry[a]	Mean Percentage of Manufacturing Subsidiaries which were Joint Ventures (Entered 1961-67); Equal Weight to Each Industry[b]
Large	25.8
Small	34.2

[a]Large = largest to 1/2 size of largest, measured by sales. Small = less than 1/2 size of largest.

[b]Excludes subsidiaries in Canada, Japan, Spain, Ceylon, India, Mexico, and Pakistan.

TABLE 7.12

Percent Overpricing of Imports in Colombia
by Subsidiary Ownership and Industry

Ownership of Plant	Industry			
	Pharmaceuticals	Chemicals	Rubber	Electronics
100 percent foreign-owned	155	25.5	44	16-66*
Joint venture	—	20.2	—	6-50*
Local	19	22.2	0	

*Weighted price differential.

Source: Constantine Vaitsos, Transfer of Resources and Preservation of Monopoly Rents, presented at the Dubrovnik Conference of the Harvard Development Advisory Service, June 20-26, 1970.

Existing evidence comes out slightly on the side of those who claim that the local partner is effective in defending his interests. Data for Colombia indicate that joint ventures have a slightly lower "overprice" (margin over what third-party prices would be) than do wholly-owned subsidiaries. Table 7.12 shows the extent to which transfer prices differed for imports into Colombia. The data could simply show that joint ventures are more likely to appear where a firm has little oligopoly power. In these cases, it will also be less able to overcharge on its imports. However, interviews conducted with chemical firms indicated that the same firm was less likely to use high transfer prices to take profits out of joint ventures than it was for wholly-owned subsidiaries. These interviews also demonstrated the influence of local partners in another way. When a large number of joint ventures were present in a system, the parent tended to standardize its transfer price so that all subsidiaries were charged the same price.[8] With standardization went flexibility to use transfer pricing to shift funds from subsidiary to subsidiary. The standardized prices supposedly reflected market prices.

Findings for New Zealand also support the contention that the presence of a local partner tends to lower the costs of purchases. Deane found that joint ventures were more likely than wholly-owned subsidiaries to be free to purchase from nonaffiliated suppliers.[9]

Though the evidence supports the claim that transfer prices to the joint venture are generally lower than to wholly-owned subsidiaries, there is some indication that the pattern may be more complex. Deane suggests that foreign investors may charge lower prices to their wholly-owned subsidiaries initially than they charge later, perhaps to generate local cash for expansion.[10] However, he found that foreign investors with local partners are reluctant to follow this strategy, no doubt because of the difficulty of changing transfer prices at a later date when cash demands are lower.

Savings to the economy through more favorable transfer pricing may not, however, be a net gain for the host country. There is considerable evidence that the foreigner shifts some of the remittance obtained from transfer pricing in its wholly-owned subsidiaries to other techniques for the joint ventures. Charges for the provision of know-how, tradenames, and management appear to be higher for joint ventures than for wholly-owned subsidiaries. The Colombian data again provide some indication that royalty payments are higher where local equity exists. And Deane cites a managing director:

> . . . the parent "wouldn't quarrel with making a local issue but at present we do not have to worry enormously about prices of articles as to whether we have a fair profit here or overseas. . . . [This is] really more important insofar as ancillary services are concerned. For example, at present there are no technical services or royalty payments for know-how. This would have to be revised if a local issue was made."[11]

Two studies of foreign investment in Australia found that joint ventures were charged more than wholly-owned subsidiaries for services.[12] Interviews with chemical companies also indicated more frequent payment of fees for technical services from joint ventures than from wholly-owned subsidiaries. In addition, host governments are more willing to allow payments for technology in the case of joint ventures than in cases where all the equity is owned by foreigners.[13] In India, royalty payments to foreign parents were generally not allowed for wholly-foreign subsidiaries, but were allowed for joint ventures.[14]

Though the data indicate that joint ventures are charged lower transfer prices than wholly-owned subsidiaries for purchases from affiliates, it appears that the parent compensates somewhat with higher charges for technical service fees. A common royalty fee of 2.5 percent of sales would offset a reduction of over 130 percent on transfer pricing, if purchases of components and parts from the parent accounted for 4.2 percent of sales,[15] including the overpricing margin.

In the case of chemicals, where the transfer price margin was found by Vaitsos to be about 5 percent, a tiny royalty fee could cover any loss on transfer pricing. Though more work is necessary on what typical savings in transfer prices might accrue to a joint venture, the Colombian data, which are probably extreme, indicate that a multinational enterprise can easily shift payments that would have been remitted by transfer pricing to other forms, and that these shifts need not be very large in relation to the value of sales.

Investment and Dividends

The balance of payments will also differ with a joint venture and a wholly-owned subsidiary because of the differences in the amount of investment provided in foreign exchange and the dividend payments in the two cases.

If the decrease in inflow of capital because of the contribution of the local partner were offset by a proportional reduction in dividend payments abroad in later years, the problem would be relatively simple. The rate of return to the foreigner would be the same in the joint venture as in the wholly-owned case. And the government would be indifferent as to the balance-of-payments effects in the two cases so long as the rate of return is equal to what the government would consider an appropriate discount rate for future foreign exchange payments.

Though the nature of the recorded contribution of the foreign partner differs in the wholly-owned and joint-venture case, it appears to be primarily one of bookkeeping techniques and not one that affects the government's choice of ownership form. The foreigner is more likely to capitalize contribution of know-how in a joint venture than in a wholly-owned subsidiary. The chemical firms interviewed indicated an interest in joint ventures primarily when they would obtain equity for a contribution of know-how. Brash's study of United States investment in Australia reported larger proportions of know-how in the capitalization of joint ventures than in wholly-owned operations.[16] Similarly, a study of United States investment in Japan discovered that capitalization of know-how was important for joint ventures but not for wholly-owned subsidiaries.[17] Where United States ownership was 25-30 percent, the foreign capital consisted of about 50 percent know-how. Where the Americans had 50 percent of the stock, know-how accounted for 25 percent of the foreigner's contribution. In cases where the United States firm held more than half the equity, no know-how was capitalized.

It is tempting to conclude from these figures that the foreign firm acquires a claim on the profits of joint ventures disproportionate to its contribution. However, there is some evidence to suggest that this conclusion is unwarranted. When the multinational enterprise has complete ownership, it has no need to capitalize know-how and apparently does not bother to do so in many cases. On the other hand, when it goes into a joint arrangement, it must capitalize this portion of its contribution if it is to receive a return on it. The presumption is that it contributes roughly the same know-how in both cases, and is entitled to payment for the know-how. This behavior is consistent with the fact that wholly-owned subsidiaries generally report a higher return on equity than do joint ventures.[18] If wholly-owned subsidiaries do not capitalize know-how, the equity would be understated, showing a larger rate of return.

Dividend payments of the subsidiary do appear to differ between wholly-owned and joint-venture cases. For the joint venture, they tend to be larger and more stable. Joint-venture arrangements often spell out a formula for dividend payments. In the negotiations, the local partner frequently insists on regular payments. A Canadian study highlighted the variability of the foreign parent in taking out dividends from wholly-owned subsidiaries.[19] A study of Australia found that wholly-owned subsidiaries were more likely than joint ventures to declare no dividends from time to time.[20] A study of investment in New Zealand describes the variability of payments for wholly-owned operations and the demands for regular dividends by local shareholders.[21] The result of the presence of a local partner seems to be to make payments more regular.

Part of the explanation for what appear to be lower dividends for the wholly-owned subsidiary may lie in the ability of the parent in this case to find other means to withdraw profits. We have mentioned higher royalties. In addition, the parent can use debt held by affiliates to remove profits. Payments of interest and principal on these debts provide an alternative to dividends for withdrawing funds from the subsidiary. Some of these payments will escape local taxation and exchange controls. In Australia, for example, debt to affiliates was found to be higher for the wholly-foreign subsidiaries than for the joint ventures.[22]

Importing and Exporting

The balance of payments of the host country will be affected differently if joint ventures have a propensity to import parts and components that is not the same as that of wholly-owned subsidiaries. For Canada and Australia, studies found that joint ventures did have some tendency to buy locally more than did wholly-foreign subsidiaries.[23] However, the author of the Australian study cautions that the results could come from the fact that a larger percentage of the joint ventures were acquisitions of firms that had already established purchasing patterns. It is also possible that the higher imports for the wholly-owned subsidiaries represent a significant overcharge on transfer prices, rather than a greater physical quantity of goods.

The findings for Canada[24] show only a very slightly higher propensity of the joint venture to buy its inputs locally. A stronger relationship was found for New Zealand.[25] Since the joint ventures were entered primarily on the initiation of the parent, one might expect the joint ventures to be in operations that would have bought locally in any case. In some instances, the local partner may have been included—as indicated in responses to our questionnaires—primarily for the access to be provided to raw materials. Forcing more firms to enter joint ventures may not have increased local purchasing.

On the export side, the data are more consistent. Though the local partner may be interested in generating exports from joint ventures, the requirement that the profits have to be shared does, in many cases, inhibit the parent from using the joint venture as a source for third markets. Based on a purely competitive model, the foreign firm would be indifferent to exporting return on investment; it would receive only X percent of the profits from exports from a joint venture, but it would have made only X percent of the investment. Its rate of return will be identical in a wholly-owned operation and in a joint venture.

In a more realistic model, imperfect competition leads to the existence of a joint venture and a wholly-owned subsidiary, both having some unused capacity. No additional investment is required to supply exports to a third market. If the marginal costs of production in the joint venture and the wholly-owned subsidiary are identical, and transportation and tariff costs the same, the parent should choose to export from the wholly-owned subsidiary. The incremental contribution from a joint venture must be shared with a local partner, while the contribution from the wholly-owned subsidiary accrues solely to the parent.[26] There would, in most cases, have to be a fairly wide margin of production costs, transportation, and tariff differences to cause sourcing in joint ventures.

Other factors may also act to push the parent toward exporting from a wholly-owned subsidiary. The parent may know that if expansion is required in the future the partner will not be able to supply his share of new investment, even though the joint-venture arrangements frequently require that the original proportion of ownership be retained. Thus expansion may be delayed, or the parent may have to lend the partner money so that the partner can retain his share in the equity of the new investment. Secondly, the parent may feel that it has more flexibility in the future if it exports from the wholly-owned subsidiary. If it finds it cheaper to export from a third operation in the future, it can discontinue exporting from the wholly-owned subsidiary without crossing the interests of a local partner who has become used to supplying the market.

Data indicate that the parent is successful in resisting these pressures from the local partner in the majority of cases. The enterprise develops a number of techniques to control exports. Though many governments of less developed countries require that no prohibition of exports appear in joint-venture agreements,[27] sometimes the licensing arrangements provide for the use of know-how and trade names only for certain geographical areas. About 45 percent of 1,051 collaboration agreements in effect in 1964 in India had explicit restriction on exports.[28] The frequency of restrictions was higher for minority foreign participation than for cases where the foreigner held a majority of the stock.[29] Similar restrictions were found on exports from foreign subsidiaries in Australia,[30] and in Colombia and Nicaragua.[31]

Considerable caution must be exercised in interpreting these findings. If control is in the hands of the foreign firm, explicit prohibition of exports may not be necessary (and may be dangerous from the point of view of antitrust). Cutler[32] provides a lawyer's discussion of the need for agreement with partners, but of the absence of need when control is in the corporate family.

More important, and more difficult to police by the government, are the provisions that appear frequently whereby the marketing organization of the parent is responsible for all sales outside the country of operations. This organization can simply choose wholly-owned subsidiaries to supply third markets.[33]

A recent study by the Council for Latin America provides evidence of the importance to the developing country of access to the multinational system's marketing network. Two-thirds of the exports of United States subsidiaries were sold through affiliated enterprises.[34] The work of de la Torre[35] confirmed the importance of the foreign firm's marketing network in increasing the exports of manufacturers from Nicaragua and Colombia. Closing this organization to the joint venture can seriously affect the exports of the host country.

Still another technique used by the multinational enterprise to control exports within the system is to limit, in the joint-venture agreement, the size of the plant to a capacity adequate only for the local market.

Interviews with chemical firms indicated the frequency with which these devices were used to control exports. Two of the eight chemical companies placed no restrictions on exports from joint ventures. Two included in the joint-venture contract limits on the patent rights to certain areas, and two included provisions limiting access to certain market areas. The other two firms exercised control centrally, having retained a great deal of decisionmaking power over the joint venture.

Cases of exports from joint ventures are, however, not infrequent. International Computer and Tabulators, for example, agreed to export 30 percent of its production from its Indian venture.[36] It insisted on, and received, a majority of the equity in return, despite India's position that foreigners should hold a minority share. The local equity is to be sold to the public, and there will be no clearly identifiable partner. International Harvester has also begun to make its Mexican plant its sole manufacturer for certain products, even though it has agreed to sell 51 percent of the equity in the subsidiary to Mexicans.[37]

In the special case of assembly operations established by a foreigner primarily to produce for export back to his home market, one rarely finds a joint venture with a local partner. The potential conflicts with local interests—overpricing of components for assembly, of pricing sales back to affiliates, etc.—are very great. For assembly enterprises exporting to the United States, there is often an additional incentive to shift profits away from the assembly operation, creating an opportunity for conflict with a local partner, since the American tariff will be calculated on the foreign value added. Mexico has recognized the importance of control to the multinational enterprise for export-oriented assembly operations. It has relaxed considerably its insistence on joint ventures for border investments.

Skills and Training

The transfer of technical and management skills to nationals of the host countries has not been studied much. It is often asserted that more transfer is made in joint ventures than in wholly-owned subsidiaries. Little evidence on one side or the other exists.

There is some evidence that managers of United States firms believe that more know-how is picked up by local personnel in joint ventures than in wholly-owned subsidiaries. Foreign firms investing in New Zealand objected to the inclusion of local partners because the partners would receive secret information.[38] Similar objections to joint ventures were voiced by a number of managers interviewed in connection with this study. On the other hand, the parent firms seem able to withhold certain information from joint-venture partners.[39]

Evidence for Australia suggests that wholly-owned subsidiaries are more likely than joint ventures to send local employees to the United States for management training. However, local employees are likely to hold more responsible positions in joint ventures. These employees may receive some training from their holding of responsible jobs; on the other hand, they probably would have held equally responsible jobs in locally owned businesses had they not been employed by the foreign subsidiary. A study of foreign investment in Canada concludes that presidents and directors of minority subsidiaries are more likely to be Canadians than in cases where the foreign firm owns more than half of the equity.[40] This finding is consistent with what we already know: that joint ventures are more likely to be entered when the parent does not attempt to control its subsidiaries closely. Whether the same pattern would obtain if the parent were to enter the joint venture under duress is difficult to ascertain from these data. One's guess is that an attempt would be made by the parent to retain control by appointing the principal officers.

The Supply of Capital

If there is no clear assumption that the joint venture benefits the host country on the payments and training sides, similar questions exist as to its benefits from the provision of capital.

Studies indicate that joint ventures in Canada and Australia were more likely than wholly-foreign operations to borrow locally.[41] If this is the general pattern, then the joint venture will place an even heavier demand on local capital than is indicated by the decreased initial inflows. Supporting this contention is the finding that the debt-equity ratio for joint ventures was higher than that for wholly-owned subsidiaries in Japan.[42] This result may be due, at least partly, to the joint venture's need to turn to debt frequently for expansion, since the local partner is unlikely to be able to raise on his own funds to contribute to an increase in equity.

Whether local borrowing decreases capital available for other investments in the country depends, of course, on what would have happened to the funds that were borrowed had the joint venture not taken them. The foreigner may provide potential local investors with: 1) a more easily visible opportunity for direct investment; 2) complementary resources that raise the local return sufficiently for investment to take place that would otherwise not have occurred; or 3) a more active capital market that increases the opportunity for other uses of potential savings. The result may be a diversion of some funds from consumption or export to local investment. It is, however, unlikely that all the funds would have gone into consumption, or would have been exported if the joint venture had not taken them. There would then be some reduction from the first round effects in the amount of capital available for local investment.

Control and Political Factors

In spite of the lack of clear economic gain to the country from having more joint ventures, a government may still be right in its insistence that the foreigner take in local partners. If a feeling of local control over industry or the political ease of allowing foreign investment weigh heavily in the list of government objectives, joint ventures may provide advantages over wholly-foreign subsidiaries.

We have argued that loss of control is the primary disadvantage that the parent associates with a joint venture.[43] Safarian's study of foreign investment in Canada, and Deane's results for New Zealand, also reported that the foreign parent exercises less control over joint ventures than over wholly-owned operations. Joint ventures seem almost always to transfer some control from the foreign parent to the local partner.

Though the joint venture might bring more local control of the subsidiary than would be present in the wholly-owned operation, there is, of course, no guarantee that the local partner will behave in the national interest. In fact, it may be more difficult in some cases for the government to take steps to control the local than it would be to influence the foreigner against whom nationalist emotions can easily be stirred. But in the majority of cases, governments seem to behave as if they can more effectively influence a local, whose future is tied up within the border of the country, than they can a foreign investor, who is not going to lose a major part of his livelihood from the action of a single host government.

On the political side, joint ventures may be easier to sell a populace that questions foreign investment in the country. Businessmen in particular are likely to be less opposed to foreign investment if they are given opportunities to be partners with the foreigner. The opportunities for profitable partnerships with foreigners tend to fall to influential individuals. And there is no doubt that individuals with political influence have prospered from pressures in some countries on the foreign investor who is entering, or who is already in the country, to find local partners. However, any radical opposition to the government will simply include the local partners in their attack on foreign investment. This process is well underway in India and Mexico, where local partners are accused of assisting the foreigner in exploiting the country. In a book unfavorable to foreign investment in India, Kurian says: "For the Indian big bourgeoisie, this [the joint venture] gives an opportunity to strengthen their position relative to other sectors of the Indian bourgeoisie."[44]

CONCLUSION

Unfortunately, a comparison of the benefits accruing to the host country from joint ventures and those from wholly-owned subsidiaries does not lead to a simple conclusion.

A strong policy of insistence by the host country that the foreigner take in a local partner does result in more local participation in foreign subsidiaries than is found in countries that do not apply pressure for joint ventures. Firms that rarely enter joint ventures elsewhere appear to convince some governments with strong joint-venture policies that they should yield on their policy of insisting on joint ventures; where the government does not yield, the firm that almost never enters joint ventures in other countries usually does not invest in that country. Whether the government should yield probably depends on how advanced the country is. If the foreign firm has a technology that is badly needed by the country, it appears that the country will sometimes retreat from its insistence on local ownership. But if the country provides a sufficiently large internal market, the firm is more likely than otherwise to yield in its insistence on complete ownership. A government official can make reasonable guesses as to the willingness of the foreign investor to take in a local partner. The firm's emphasis on marketing, production rationalization, research and development, and raw material control, along with its diversification and size relative to other firms in its industry, seem to be important determinants of its attitude toward ownership of subsidiaries.

There is no clear evidence to suggest that joint ventures or wholly-owned subsidiaries always provide more net benefits to the host country. Whether the country gains more from partnerships, assuming that the country has a choice, depends on the objectives of the government and on the responses of the firm. For example, if the government wishes the foreign investor to export his output, it should consider the preference of the multinational enterprise for exporting from wholly-owned subsidiaries. If future foreign exchange is discounted heavily, the government might choose wholly-owned operations because they bring more immediate foreign exchange inflows and are less likely to declare dividends in their early years of operation. Similarly, other differences in the effects of wholly-owned and joint subsidiaries should be evaluated in light of the weights that the government attaches to its objectives.

Weights assigned to objectives such as balance-of-payments improvement, training, and domestic political benefits vary from country to country, and from time to time within the same country. In addition, the effects of ownership will vary from industry to industry. In an industry in which local costs are too high for exports, for example, the preference of the multinational parent for sourcing from wholly-owned operations is unimportant to the host government—presumably, the subsidiary will not export anyway. What is called for is a policy consistent with the country's development strategy and to be changed as the needs of the country change. The ideal policy will, in most cases, not be a blanket requirement for joint ventures, but will differentiate by type of industry and, perhaps on an ad hoc basis, by type of investor.

The traditional theory of the firm makes only limited contributions to an understanding of the ownership preferences of the multinational enterprise and the effects of government policies on joint ventures. The world of the multinational enterprise is one of imperfect markets. Oligopoly, limited abilities to obtain and process information, and rampant uncertainty lead to actions by the firm that are hard to explain by simple theories. Complex objective functions extending outside the purely economic sphere lead to government policies that do not reflect neat economic models. And when government meets firm, the concepts of bargaining theory must be added to the list of tools needed to analyze the role of multinational business in economic development.

* * *

COMMENT BY STEPHEN HYMER

The best way to look at Wells' article is from the point of view of a government official in a third-world country trying to increase the benefits and lower the costs of dealing with multinational corporations. Corporations have *their* experts on countries, and countries need their own to coach them in the workings of corporations. What better place to find help than from American scholars interested in promoting development and who are in a good position to know what is going on? Unfortunately, Professor Wells' contribution is not so useful as it might be, for he sees the problems and policy options from too restricted and partial a point of view.

Let us begin with the issue of equity participation. Should a country allow the multinational corporation free reign in organizing its affiliates, or should it insist on local participation—and if so, which local partners and how much participation? The record shows that American multinational corporations strongly prefer near-full ownership of their foreign affiliates. Presumably this maximizes the quasi-rents on the corporation's special advantages in marketing technology or access to capital and labor.

The question is whether a country can appropriate some of this surplus for itself by forcing local participation, progressive nationalization, and so forth. Wells seems dubious. He argues that "the case for joint ventures is highly qualified" largely because companies can take offsetting policies that "could negate any benefits that the host country expects from its joint venture." His case, however, is far from proved.

Wells shows first of all that a policy of encouraging local participation is feasible. Countries that insist on local participation get more of it than average, though they may have to retreat from their stringent policy in certain cases. On the whole, their strict attitude does not seem to frighten away any but a very few firms, since the combination of foreign investors they receive does not appear to differ significantly from that in other countries.

Unfortunately, the nature of the data, based as it is on numbers of subsidiaries rather than value of investment—it uses only a crude definition of participation and does not, for example, indicate whether the local partner is the state, another foreigner, a strong local businessman, or a weak partner—limits the confidence with which one can draw conclusions. We are left somewhat up in the air.

The same is true of Wells' next point. It is true, as he says, that "the job of the government official who negotiates with foreign investors would be eased somewhat if he knew what kind of foreign firm is likely to resist strongly pressures to form joint ventures." His data indicates that large firms in nonextractive industries that spend a high proportion of their sales revenue on advertising, do considerable research, and are associated with a narrow line of products, tend to be more resistant than others. Again the measures are crude and the conclusion hardly surprising. I would advise government officials to skip this section, despite the importance of the question. A day or two of research on the particular firm with which they happen to be negotiating can give them far subtler knowledge of whether the firm has strong preferences, if so why, and what are the chances of its giving in, than the vague generalizations to be found here.

The core of Wells' essay concerns the question of whether a policy of encouraging joint ventures may yield net benefits. His findings, crudely summarized, are as follows:

On the positive side: 1) joint ventures seem almost always to transfer some control from the foreign parent to the local partner; 2) transfer prices to joint ventures are generally lower than to wholly-owned subsidiaries; 3) joint ventures buy more local inputs than other types of enterprise.

On the negative side: 1) joint ventures are charged more for technical services; 2) know-how is capitalized at a higher rate;

3) joint ventures have a more stable dividend policy; (4) they borrow more locally; 5) they probably export less.

In addition, there are two unclassified findings: 1) Wells finds little evidence on one side or the other on the question of transfer of technology and managerial skills; 2) on political aspects he finds ". . . joint ventures may be easier to sell a populace that questions foreign investment in the country. Businessmen in particular are likely to be less opposed to foreign investment if they are given opportunities to be partners with the foreigner. . . . However, any radical opposition to the government will simply include the local partners in their attack on foreign investment." I would classify this public relations function as a negative aspect unless it were exposed by the radical opposition, but I am not sure that that was Wells' meaning.

This accounting of advantages and disadvantages is highly tentative. In almost no case is the evidence strong or the conclusion clear. Wells lists many qualifications, and his presentation reads more like a preliminary review of the literature (which on the whole is very inadequate) combined with a prospectus for future research, than like a statement of findings. The coverage of issues and the amount of data are so limited that one hesitates to draw conclusions. But, if a conclusion must be drawn from his data, I would say that—contrary to Wells' assertion—it is the case for 100 percent foreign ownership that is highly qualified. Joint ventures, it would seem, yield three important benefits, while their costs could be reduced through increased vigilance.

Wells' presentation contains a very important methodological error in the way it formulates the problem. It has been observed that the most important question about local participation is its effect on bargaining power. The multinational corporation has vastly superior knowledge, gained from long experience and world-wide connections. Third-world countries, on the other hand, are generally ignorant of important facts because they stand outside the corridors of power. A major goal of local participation is access to the inner workings of the subsidiaries of multinational corporations. Of course, the multinational corporation will take defensive action to protect its secrets. But there is little it can do in a joint venture that it cannot do without the constraint of local partnership and, in most cases, there would be a net loss in privacy.

In response to local participation, the multinational corporation can introduce regular costing of technical and managerial skills and formal charges for loans. It will be stricter on credit policy. But this more accurate accounting is the lever by which the country begins to learn, and to control what it is getting—as well as what it is paying for it. Unless the local partner is totally incompetent or corrupt, the firm cannot extract more when its control is limited than it could without constraints. Before Wells can argue that the case for joint ventures is highly qualified, he must analyze the vigilance of local partners and their ability to improve through time. Mere demonstration that the company will try to get around restrictions tells us little except that the constraints are in some way binding.

Wells' failure to view joint ventures as a strategy to overcome inequality of information and experience leads him to an overly facile policy conclusion. He observes that data that compare the behavior of the multinational system toward its joint venture and its wholly-owned operation indicate that the host country may sometimes be better off if the firm has all the equity. But his later point that governments need to know quite a bit about the behavior of multinational firm in order to make a national decision as to whether the country will be better off with a joint venture does not follow.

At the present stage, third-world countries simply do not have, and cannot easily get, much knowledge about multinational corporations. They cannot really adopt the case-by-case approach Wells recommends, their tools being too clumsy and their knowledge too sparse. Their policies have to be arbitrary, and thus inappropriate in any number of cases. They face danger from two different directions. They may be too strict and therefore lose the benefits that a more knowledgeable and flexible policy might have attracted. Call this a type 1 error. Or they may be too loose and thereby increase costs beyond what they might have been. Call this a type 2 error. What is "rational" in this case depends on <u>quantitative</u> information not <u>qualitative</u>. One cannot merely indicate that the country might "sometimes" be better off by allowing full ownership. One has to know in how many cases this would be true, and at what cost, before one can say whether a general tightening or a general loosening is required. Few third-world countries have the research resources and access to data of the Harvard Business School, and few of their officials have the knowledge and training in the subject of multinational corporations that Wells has. They may use his paper as an experiment to measure the cost of gaining precise information on the behavior of multinational corporations. The cost appears prohibitive, judging by Wells's findings. This supports the rationality of continuing to use crude instruments. They might also use the example of Japan and other strict countries to indicate that past and current policies of most third-world countries have worried too much about type 1 errors and not enough about type 2.

After reading this paper, as well as others written on this subject, one becomes convinced that too much freedom for capital movement in general, and for multinational firms in particular, is <u>one of the problems</u>, rather than the solution, of underdevelopment.

CHAPTER

8

INDUCED INNOVATION IN AGRICULTURAL DEVELOPMENT

Yujiro Hayami and
Vernon W. Ruttan

INTRODUCTION

There has been a sharp transition in economic doctrine with respect to the relative contribution of agricultural and industrial development to national economic growth during recent decades, with a corresponding shift away from an earlier "industrial fundamentalism" to an emphasis on the significance of growth in agricultural production and productivity for the total development process.

Nevertheless, the process of agricultural development itself has, with few exceptions, remained outside the concern of most development economists. Both technical change and institutional change have been treated as exogenous to their systems.

In our view, technical change represents an essential element in the growth of agricultural production and productivity from the very beginning of the development process. The process of technical change in agriculture can best be understood as a dynamic response to the

---

The research on which this paper is based was financed through grants to the University of Minnesota Economic Development Center and Agricultural Experiment Station from the Rockefeller Foundation, the Ford Foundation, and the United States Agency for International Development. The paper draws extensively on the book, Yujiro Hayami and Vernon W. Ruttan, Agricultural Development—An International Perspective, Baltimore, Md.: the Johns Hopkins Press, 1971, with permission from the publisher. The authors are indebted to John Chipman, Willis Peterson, Adolph Weber and Pan Yotopoulos for comments on an earlier draft of this paper.

resource endowments and economic environment in which a country finds itself at the beginning of the modernization process. The design of a successful agricultural development strategy in each country or region involves a unique pattern of technical change and productivity growth in response to the particular set of factor prices which reflect the economic implications of resource endowments and resource accumulation in each society. It also involves a complex pattern of institutional evolution in order to create an economic and social environment conducive to the effective response by individuals, private firms, and public agencies to the new technical opportunities.

Any attempt to develop a model of agricultural development in which technical change is treated as endogenous to the development process rather than as an exogenous factor that operates independently of other development processes must start with the recognition that there are multiple paths of technological development. Technology can be developed to facilitate the substitution of relatively abundant (hence cheap) factors for relatively scarce (hence expensive) factors in the economy.

A second consideration in any attempt to develop an adequate model of agricultural development is explicit recognition of the role of the public sector in the agricultural development process. Advances in agricultural science and technology represent a necessary condition for releasing the constraints on agricultural production imposed by inelastic factor supplies. Yet technical innovations are difficult to arrive at in a country in its early stages of economic development. Institutionalization of the process by which a continuous stream of new agricultural technology is made available to a nation's farmers is particularly difficult to achieve. In most countries that have been successful in achieving rapid rates of technical progress, "socialization" of agricultural research has been deliberately employed as an instrument of modernization in agriculture. The modernization process has involved the development of both experiment-station and industrial capacity capable of producing the biological (or biological and chemical) and mechanical (or engineering and mechanical) innovations adapted to factor-supply conditions.

This paper extends the theory of "induced innovation" to include the process by which public-sector investment in agricultural research, in the adaptation and diffusion of agricultural technology, and in the institutional infrastructure supportive of agricultural development, is directed toward releasing the constraints on agricultural production imposed by the factors characterized by a relatively inelastic supply. It then elaborates an operational model, suitable for testing the "induced innovation" hypothesis. Finally, the model is tested against the long-term agricultural development experience of Japan and the United States.

INDUCED INNOVATION IN THE PRIVATE AND PUBLIC SECTORS

There is a substantial body of literature on the "theory of induced innovation." A major controversy has centered around the existence of a mechanism by which differences or changes in factor prices affect inventive or innovative activity. This discussion has been conducted entirely within the framework of the theory of the firm. Discussions of induced innovation available in the literature offer little insight into the mechanism by which differences in resource endowments affect resource allocation in public sector research.

Induced Innovation in the Private Sector

It had generally been accepted, at least since the publication of The Theory of Wages by John R. Hicks, that changes or differences in the relative prices of factors of production could influence the direction of invention or innovation [Hicks, 1932, pp. 124-125]. Arguments have also been raised by W. E. G. Salter and others against Hicks's theory of induced innovation.[1] The argument runs somewhat as follows: Firms are motivated to save total cost for a given output; at competitive equilibrium, each factor is being paid its marginal value product; therefore, all factors are equally expensive to firms; and hence there is no incentive for competitive firms to search for techniques to save a particular factor.

The difference between our perspective and Salter's is partly due to a difference in the definition of the production function. Salter defined the production function to embrace all possible designs conceivable by existing scientific knowledge, and called the choice among these designs "factor substitution" rather than "technical change" [Salter, 1960, pp. 14-16]. He admits, however, that "relative factor prices are the nature of signal posts representing broad influences that determine the way technological knowledge is applied to production" (p. 16).

We do not deny the case for Salter's definition, but it is not especially useful in understanding the process by which new technical alternatives become available. We regard technical change as any change in production coefficients resulting from the purposeful resource-using activity directed to the development of new knowledge embodied in designs, materials, or organizations. In terms of this definition, it is entirely rational for competitive firms to allocate funds to develop a technology which facilitates the substitution of increasingly less expensive factors for more expensive ones. Using the above definition, Ahmad [1966] has shown that the

Hicksian theory of market-induced innovation can be defended with a rather reasonable assumption on the possibility of alternative innovations.

Ahmad's argument can be illustrated with the aid of Figure 8.1. Suppose at a point of time a firm is operating at a competitive equilibrium, A or B, depending on the prevailing factor-price ratio, p or m, for an isoquant, u_0, producing a given output; and this firm perceives multiple alternative innovations represented by isoquants, u_1, u_1', . . . , producing the same output in such a way as to be enveloped by a concave curve, U (Ahmad calls it an innovation possibility curve), which can be developed by the same amount of research expenditure.[2] In order to minimize total cost for given output and given research expenditure, innovative efforts of this firm will be directed toward developing Y-saving technology (u_1) or X-saving technology (u_1'), depending on the prevailing factor-price ratio, p (parallel to PP) or m (parallel to MM and M'M'). If a firm facing a price ratio, m, develops an X-saving technology (u_1'), it can obtain an additional gain, represented by the distance between M and M' compared with the case that developed a Y-saving technology (u_1). In this framework, it is clear that if X becomes more expensive relative to Y over time in an economy, the innovative efforts of entrepreneurs will be directed toward developing a more X-saving and Y-using technology compared to the contrary case. Also, in a country in which X is more expensive relative to Y than in some other country, innovative efforts will be more directed toward X-saving and Y-using than in that other country. In this formulation, the expectation of relative price change, central to Fellner's theory of induced innovation, is unnecessary, though we do not deny that expectations may work as a powerful reinforcing agent in the actual economy.

The above theory is based on the restrictive assumption that there exists a concave innovation possibility curve (U) that can be perceived by entrepreneurs. This is not so restrictive an assumption as may first appear. The innovation possibility curve need not be of a smooth, well-behaved shape as shown in Figure 8.1. The argument holds equally well for the case of two distinct alternatives. It seems reasonable to hypothesize that entrepreneurs can perceive, however vaguely, a few alternative innovation possibilities for a given R and D expenditure through consultation with staff scientists and engineers, or through the suggestions of inventors.[3]

Induced Innovation in the Public Sector

Innovative behavior in the public sector has largely been ignored in the literature on induced innovation. There is no theory

FIGURE 8.1

Induced Innovation and the Innovation Possibility Curve

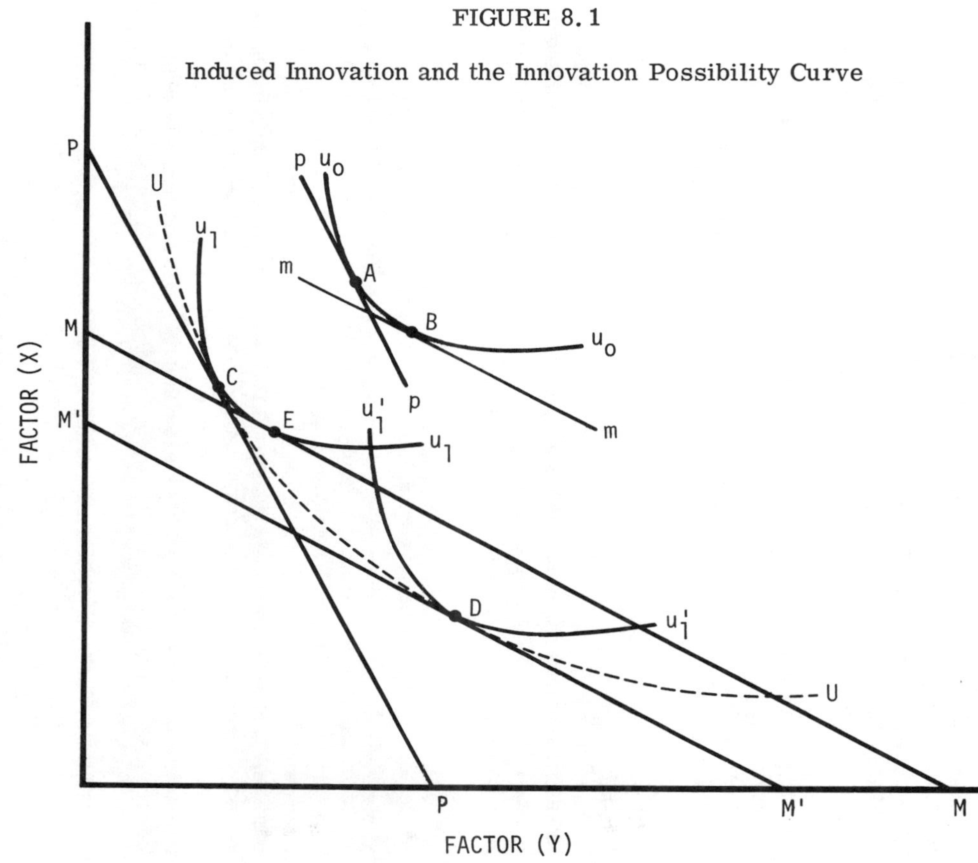

of induced innovation in the public sector.[4] This defect is particularly critical in attempting to understand the role of technical change in agricultural development, since public-sector research has represented a major source of technical innovation in agriculture.

Our view of the mechanism of "induced innovation" in public-sector agricultural research is similar to the Hicksian theory of induced innovation in the private sector. We extend the traditional argument by basing the innovation-inducement mechanism not only on the response to changes in market prices by profit-maximizing firms, but also on the response by research scientists and administrators in public institutions to resource endowments and economic change.

We hypothesize that technical change is guided along an efficient path by price signals in the market, provided that 1) prices efficiently reflect changes in the demand and supply of products and factors; 2) there exists effective interaction among farmers, public research institutions, and private agricultural supply firms. If the demand for agricultural products increases, due to growth in population and income, prices of inputs for which the supply is inelastic will rise relative to the prices of inputs for which the supply is elastic. Likewise, if the supply of particular inputs shifts faster to the right than others, the prices of these inputs will decline relative to the prices of other factors of production.

Thus technical innovations that save factors characterized by an inelastic supply, or by slower shifts in supply, become relatively more profitable for agricultural producers. Farmers are induced, by shifts in relative prices, to search for technical alternatives to save the increasingly scarce factors of production. They press the public-research institutions to develop a new technology and, also, demand that agricultural firms supply modern technical inputs to substitute for the scarcer factors. Perceptive scientists and science administrators respond by making available new technical possibilities and new inputs that enable farmers profitably to substitute increasingly abundant factors for increasingly scarce ones, thereby guiding the demand of farmers for unit-cost reduction in a socially optimum direction.[5]

The dialectical interaction among farmers and research scientists and administrators is likely to be more effective when farmers are organized into politically effective local and regional farm "bureaus" or farmers' associations. The response of the public-sector research and extension programs to the farmers' demand is likely to be greatest when the agricultural research system is highly decentralized. In the United States, for example, each state agricultural experimental station has tended to view its function, at least in part, as a challenge to maintain the competitive position of agriculture in its state relative to agriculture in other states [Tichenor and Ruttan, p. 7]. Similarly, national policymakers may regard investment in agricultural research as designed to maintain the country's competitive position in world markets or to improve the economic viability of the agricultural sector producing import-substitutes. Given effective farmer organizations and a mission- or client-oriented experimental station system, the competitive model of firm behavior can be usefully extended to explain the response of experimental station administrators and research scientists to economic opportunities.

In this public-sector-induced innovation model, the response of research scientists and administrators represents the critical link in the inducement mechanism. The model does not imply that it is necessary for individual scientists or research administrators in public institutions to respond consciously to market prices or, directly, to farmers' demands for research results, in the selection of research objectives. They may, in fact, be motivated primarily by a drive for professional achievement and recognition [Niskanen, 1968]. They may, in the Rosenberg terminology, view themselves as responding to an "obvious and compelling need" to remove the constraints on growth of production or on factor supplies. It is only necessary that there exist an effective incentive mechanism to reward the scientists or administrators, materially or by prestige, for their contribution to the solution of significant problems.[6] Under these conditions, it seems reasonable to hypothesize that scientists and administrators in public-sector research programs do respond to the need of society in an attempt to direct the results of their activity to public purpose. Furthermore, we suggest that secular changes in relative factor and product prices convey much of the information regarding the relative priorities that society places on the goals of research.

The response in the public-research sector is not limited to the field of applied science. It is not uncommon for major breakthroughs in basic science to occur as a result of efforts to solve the problems raised by research workers in the more applied fields.[7] It appears reasonable, therefore, to hypothesize, as a result of interactions among the basic and applied sciences and the process by which public funds are allocated to research, that basic research tends also to be directed toward easing the limitations on agricultural production imposed by relatively scarce factors.

We do not argue, however, that technical change in agriculture is wholly of an induced character. There is a supply (exogenous) dimension to the process as well as a demand (endogenous) one. Technical change in agriculture reflects, in addition to the effects of resource endowments and growth in demand, the progress of general science and technology. Progress in general science (or scientific innovation) that lowers the "cost" of technical and entrepreneurial innovations may have influences on technical change in agriculture unrelated to changes in factor proportions and in product demand [Nelson, 1959]. Even in these cases, the rate of adoption and the impact on productivity of autonomous or exogenous changes in technology will be strongly influenced by the conditions of resource supply and product demand as these forces are reflected through factor and product markets [Schmookler, 1966].

Institutional Innovation

Extension of the theory of "induced innovation" to explain the behavior of public research institutions represents an essential link in the construction of a theory of induced development. In the induced development model, advances in mechanical and biological technology respond to changing relative prices of factors, and to changes in the prices of factors relative to products, to ease the constraints on growth imposed by inelastic supplies of land or labor. Neither this process, nor its impact, is confined to the agricultural sector. Changes in relative prices in any sector of the economy act to induce innovative activity, not only by private producers but also by scientists in public institutions, in order to reduce the constraints imposed by those factors of production that are relatively scarce.

We further hypothesize that the institutions governing the use of technology or the "mode" of production can also be induced to change, to enable both individuals and society to take fuller advantage of new technical opportunities under favorable market conditions.[8] The Second Enclosure Movement in England represents a classical illustration. The issuance of the Enclosure Bill facilitated the conversion of communal pasture and farmland into single private farm units, thus encouraging the introduction of an integrated crop-livestock "new husbandry" system. The Enclosure Acts can be viewed as an institutional innovation designed to exploit the new technical opportunities opened up by innovations in crop rotation utilizing the new fodder crops (turnip and clover), in response to rising food prices [C. Peter Timmer, 1969].

A major source of institutional change has been an effort by society to internalize the benefits of innovative activity to provide economic incentives for productivity-raising activity. In some cases, institutional innovations have involved the reorganization of property rights, in order to internalize the higher income streams resulting from such innovations. The modernization of land-tenure relationships, involving a shift from share tenure to lease tenure and owner-operator systems of cultivation in much of Western agriculture, can be explained, in part, as a shift in property rights designed to internalize the gains of innovative activity by individual farmers.

We view institutional change as resulting from the efforts of economic units (firms and households) to internalize the gains and externalize the costs of innovative activity, and by society to force economic units to internalize the costs and externalize the gains. Where internalization of the gains of innovative activity is difficult to achieve, institutional innovations involving public-sector activity become essential. The socialization of much of agricultural research, particularly research leading to advances in biological technology, represents an example of a public-sector institutional innovation designed to realize for society the potential gains from advances in agricultural technology.

Profitable opportunities, however, do not necessarily lead to immediate institutional innovations. Usually the gains and losses from technical and institutional change are not distributed neutrally. There are limits on the extent to which group behavior can be mobilized to achieve common or group interests [Olson, 1968]. The process of transforming institutions in response to technical and economic opportunities generally involves time-lags, social and political stress, and, in some cases, disruption of social and political order. Economic growth ultimately depends on the flexibility and efficiency of society to transform itself in response to technical and economic opportunities.

AN OPERATIONAL MODEL OF INDUCED INNOVATION IN AGRICULTURE

A clear requisite for agricultural productivity growth is the capacity of the agricultural sector to adapt to a new set of factor and product prices. These changes may arise as a result of the growth of demand pressing against factor supplies, or as a result of changes in factor prices resulting from shifts in the supply functions for factor inputs. Adaptation by the agricultural sector to changes in factor-factor and factor-product price ratios involves, in the perspective outlined in the previous section, not only movement along a fixed production surface but also innovations leading to a new production surface.

For example, even if fertilizer prices decline relative to the prices of land and farm products, increases in the use of fertilizer may be limited unless new crop varieties are developed that are more responsive to high levels of biological and chemical inputs than traditional varieties. For illustrative purposes, the relationship between fertilizer use and yield may be drawn, as in Figure 8.2, letting u_0 and u_1 represent the curve of "indigenous" and "improved" varieties respectively. For farmers facing u_0, a decline in fertilizer prices relative to the product price from p_0 to p_1 would not be expected to result in much increase in the level of fertilizer use or in yield per unit area. The full impact of a decline in fertilizer price on fertilizer use and output can be fully realized only if u_1 is made available to farmers as a result of innovations leading to more responsive crop varieties.

Conceptually it is possible to draw a curve such as U in Figure 8.2, which is the envelope of individual response curves, each representing a different variety of the same crop characterized by a different degree of response to fertilizer. We identify this curve as a "metaproduction function" or a "potential production function."[9] We do not insist that the metaproduction function is inherent in nature or that it remains completely stable over time. It may shift with the general accumulation of scientific knowledge. We do consider, however, that it is operationally feasible to assume a reasonable degree of stability for the time range that is relevant for many empirical analyses, because shifts in the metaproduction function are much slower than adjustments along the surface, or to the surface from below the metaproduction function.

Our basic hypothesis that adjustments in factor proportions, in response to changes in relative prices, represent "nonneutral" movements along the isoproduct surface of a metaproduction function is further illustrated in Figure 8.3.

U in Figure 8.3 represents the land-labor isoquant of the metaproduction function which is the envelope of less elastic isoquants such as u_0 and u_1 corresponding to different types of machinery or technology. A certain technology represented by u_0 (e.g., reaper) is created when a price ratio, p_0, prevails for a certain length of time. When the price ratio changes from p_0 to p_1, another technology represented by u_1 (e.g., combine) is induced in the long run, which gives the minimum cost of production for p_0.

The new technology represented by u_1, which enables enlargement of the area operated per worker, generally corresponds to higher intensity of power per worker. This implies the complementary relationship between land and power, which may be drawn as a line representing a certain combination of land and power [A,M]. In this simplified presentation, mechanical innovation is conceived as the substitution of a combination of land and power [A,M] for labor (L) in response to a change in wage relative to an index of labor and machinery prices, though, of course, in actual practice land and power are substitutable to some extent.

FIGURE 8.2

Shift in Fertilizer Response Curve along the Metaresponse Curve

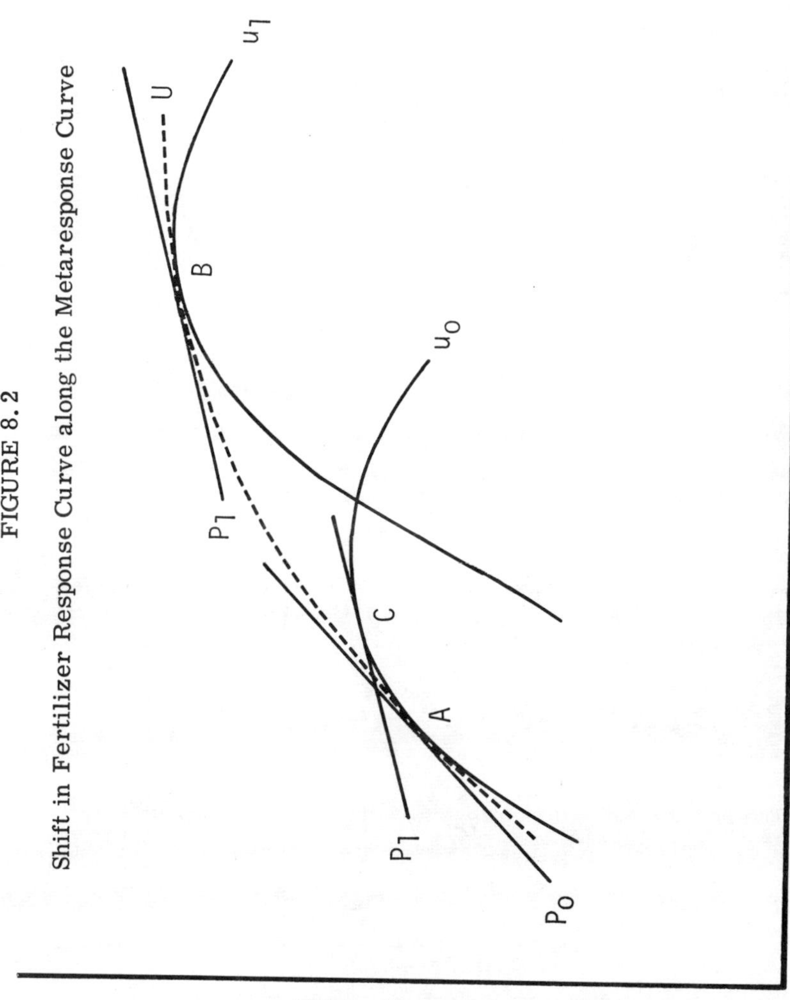

FIGURE 8.3

Factor Prices and Induced Technical Change

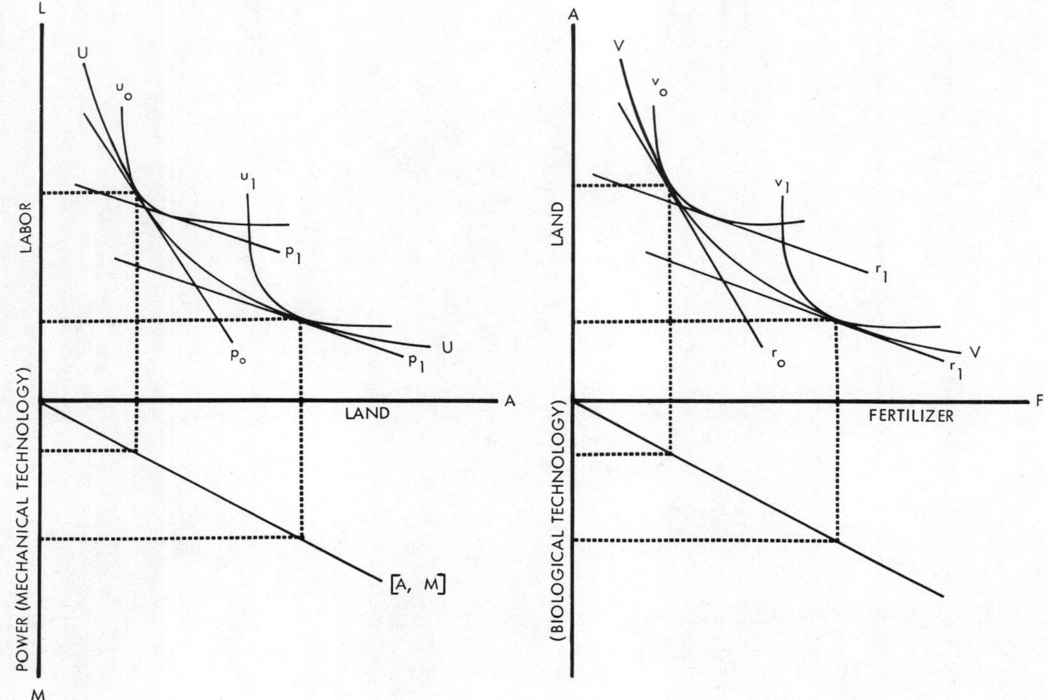

In the same context, the relation between the fertilizer-land price ratio and biochemical innovations represented by the development of crop varieties that are more responsive to application of fertilizers is illustrated in Figure 8.3. V represents the land-fertilizer isoquant of the metaproduction function, which is the envelope of less elastic isoquants such as v_0 and v_1 corresponding to varieties of different fertilizer responsiveness. A decline in the price of fertilizer relative to the price of land from r_0 to r_1 makes it more profitable for farmers to search for crop varieties described by isoquants to the right of v_0. They also press public research institutions to develop new varieties. Through a kind of dialectic process of interaction among farmers and experimental station workers, a new variety such as that represented by v_1 will be developed.

All mechanical innovations are not necessarily motivated by labor-saving incentives, nor are all biological innovations necessarily motivated incentives to save land. For example, in Japan, horse plowing was initially introduced as a device to permit deeper cultivation so as to increase yield per hectare. In the United States in recent years, attempts have been made to develop crop varieties suitable for mechanical harvesting. At the most sophisticated level, technological progress may depend on a series of simultaneous advances in both biological and mechanical technology. In the case of the mechanization of tomato harvesting, the plant breeding research and the engineering research were conducted in conjunction with each other, in order to invent new machines capable of harvesting tomatoes specifically bred to facilitate mechanical harvesting [Rasmussen, 1968]. In our judgment, however, the dominant factor leading to the growth of labor productivity has been progress in mechanization, and the dominant factor leading to growth in land productivity has been progress in biological technology.

TESTING THE INDUCED INNOVATION HYPOTHESIS

The plausibility of the induced innovation hypothesis is reinforced by the data on the relationship between fertilizer-rice price ratios and yields per hectare in Japan and other Asian countries shown in Table 8.1. It shows 1) that the higher Japanese rice yield per hectare over Southeast Asian countries is associated with a considerably lower price of fertilizer relative to the price of rice; 2) a high inverse correlation between the rice yield per hectare and the fertilizer-rice price ratio in the Japanese time series data; 3) a substantial decline in the fertilizer-rice price ratio from 1955-57 to 1963-65 in other Asian countries, associated with only small gains

TABLE 8.1

Fertilizer-Rice Price Ratios and Rice Yields Per Hectare in Selected Asian Countries and in Japan, 1883-1962

Country	Currency Unit	Price of Fertilizer Per Metric Ton of Nitrogen (1)	Price of Rice Per Metric Ton of Milled Rice (2)	Fertilizer-Rice Price Ratio (1)/(2)	Rice Yield Per Hectare Metric Ton of Paddy (3)
Cross-country comparison 1963-65					
India	rupee	1,750	595[a]	2.9	1.5
			723[b]	2.4	
Pakistan (East)	rupee	1,632	780	2.1	1.7
Philippines	peso	1,048	530	2.0	1.3
Thailand	U.S. dollar	229	70	3.3	1.6
Japan	1,000 yen	97	99	1.0	5.0
1955-57					
India	rupee	1,650	417[a]	4.0	1.3
			505[b]	3.3	
Pakistan (East)	rupee	1,322	511	2.6	1.4
Philippines	peso	962	352	2.7	1.1
Thailand	U.S. dollar	393	79	5.0	1.4
Japan	1,000 yen	119	77	1.5	4.8
Japan's time series					
1958-62	1,000 yen	100	85	1.2	4.9
1953-57	1,000 yen	113	75	1.5	4.2
1933-37	yen	566	208	2.7	3.8
1923-27	yen	1,021	277	3.7	3.6
1913-17	yen	803	125	6.4	3.5
1903-07	yen	815	106	7.7	3.1
1893-97	yen	670	69	9.7	2.6
1883-87	yen	450	42	10.7	

[a]Price at Sambalpur (Orissa).

[b]Price at Bombay. 1) Price paid by farmers. Cross country data: average unit price of nitrogen contained in ammonium sulphate; 1963-65 data are the averages for 1962/63-1964/65; 1955/57 data are the data of 1956/57; government subsidies of 50 percent for 1963-65 and of 40 percent for 1955-57 are added to Pakistan's original data. Japan data: average unit price of nitrogen contained in commercial fertilizers. 2) This is the wholesale price at milled rice basis. Japan data are converted from brown rice basis to a milled rice basis assuming 10 percent for processing cost. 3) Japan data are converted from a brown rice basis to a milled rice basis assuming 0.8 for a conversion factor.

Sources: Cross-country data: FAO, Production Yearbook, various issues. Japan data: Kazushi Ohkawa, et. al., eds., Long-term Economic Statistics of Japan, Vol. 9 (Tokyo: Toyokeizaishimposha, 1966), pp. 202-3; Nobufumi Kayo, ed., Nihon Nogyo Kisotokei (Tokyo: Norin Suisangyo Seisankojokaigi, 1958), p. 514; Toyokeizaishimposha, Bukku Yoran (Tokyo, 1967), p. 80; Institute of Developing Economies, One Hundred Years of Agricultural Statistics in Japan (Tokyo, 1969), p. 136.

in rice yield per hectare; 4) fertilizer-rice price ratios in the Southeast Asian countries today that are much more favorable than those that prevailed in Japan at the beginning of this century and earlier.

It seems reasonable to infer that the considerable differences in the rice yield between Japan and the Southeast Asian countries represent different positions on the metaproduction functions. The consistent rise in rice yield per hectare accompanied by the consistent decline in fertilizer-rice price ratio in the historical experience of Japan can be interpreted as reflecting movement along the metaproduction function.

Why, then, did rice yields per hectare of the Southeast Asian countries not increase significantly from 1955-57 to 1963-65, despite the substantial decline in the fertilizer-rice price ratio? Also, why did rice yields in these countries remain low in spite of a price ratio more favorable than in Japan at the beginning of this century? This must be attributable to the time-lag required to move along the metaproduction function, which tends to be extremely long in the absence of adequate institutions and human capital to generate the flow of new techniques. In terms of Figure 8.2, countries in Southeast Asia seem to have been trapped at the point of tangency of p_1 and u_0.

The development of fertilizer responsive rice varieties requires substantial investment in research before more responsive varieties become available to farmers. By the late 1960s more responsive varieties were becoming available throughout South and Southeast Asia [Dana C. Dalrymple, 1969]. We would expect the effect to be reflected in the new data that will become available in the early 1970s.

The plausibility of the induced innovation hypothesis is further strengthened by the data plotted in Figure 8.4. The data show the relation between fertilizer input per hectare of arable land and the fertilizer-arable land price ratio. In spite of enormous differences in climate and other environmental conditions, as well as the differences in social organization, the relationship between these two variables is essentially identical in both the United States and Japan. Given our knowledge of the fertilizer response curve for individual crop varieties, it is not plausible to assume that these observations could have been generated by movement along a common long-run production function that has been available to farmers in both countries over the 1880-1969 period.[10] The only explanation that seems plausible is that the downward drift in the fertilizer-land price ratio has induced the development of more fertilizer responsive crop varieties. In terms of Figure 8.2, it seems plausible that the data presented in Figure 8.4 were generated by shifts in individual fertilizer response curves along a common "metaproduction function" in response to a decline in the fertilizer-land price ratio.

FIGURE 8.4

Fertilizer and Arable Land, United States and Japan, 1880-1960

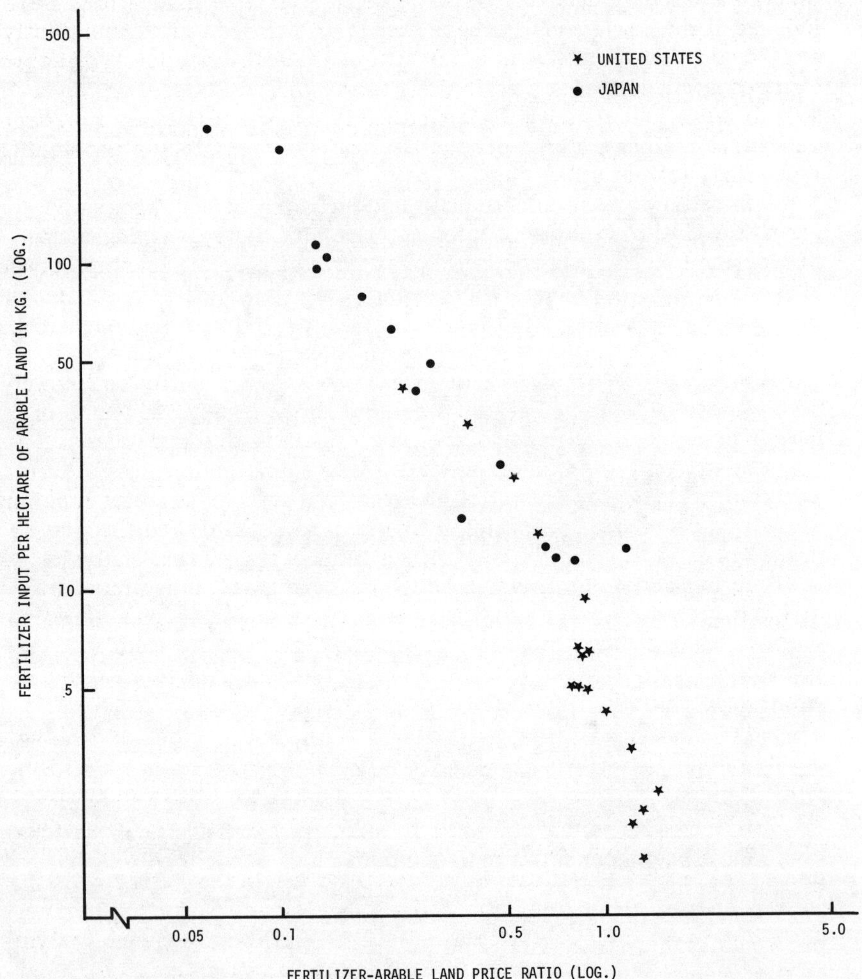

As an additional test of the induced innovation hypothesis, we have tried to determine the extent to which the variations in factor proportions, as measured by the land-labor, power-labor, and fertilizer-land ratios, can be explained by changes in factor price ratios in Japanese and United States agriculture for 1880-1960. In a situation characterized by a fixed technology, however, it seems reasonable to presume that the elasticities of substitution among factors are small, and this permits us to infer that innovations were induced if the variations in these factor proportions are consistently explained by the changes in price ratios.[11] The historically observed changes in these factor proportions in the United States and Japan are so large that it is hardly conceivable that such changes represent substitution along a given production surface describing a constant technology (Table 8.2).

In order to have an adequate specification of the regression form, we have to be able to infer the shape of the underlying meta-production function and the functional form of the relationship between changes in the production function and in factor-price ratios. Because of a lack of adequate *a priori* information, we have simply specified the regression in log-linear form with little claim to theoretical justification.[12] If we can assume that production function is linearly homogeneous, the factor proportions can be expressed in terms of factor-price ratios alone and are independent of product prices.

Keeping in mind the crudeness of data and the purpose of this analysis, we used quinquennial observations (stock variables measured at every five years' interval and flow variables averaged for five years) instead of annual observations for the regression analysis. A crude form of adjustment is built into our model, since our data are quinquennial observations and prices are generally measured as the averages of the past five years preceding the year when the quantities are measured (e.g., the number of workers in 1910 is associated with the 1906-1910 average wage).

The results of regression analyses are summarized in Tables 8.3 and 8.4. Table 8.3a presents the regressions for land-labor and power-labor proportions for the United States. In these regressions we originally included the fertilizer-labor price ratio as well. But, probably due to high intercorrelation between machinery and fertilizer prices, either the coefficients for the fertilizer-labor price ratio were insignificant or resulted in implausible results for the other coefficients.[13] This variable was dropped in the subsequent analysis.

In Table 8.3a more than 80 percent of the variation in the land-labor ratio and in the power-labor ratio is explained by the variation in their price ratios. The coefficients are all negative and are significantly different from zero at the standard level of significance except the land-price coefficients in Regressions (2) and (4). Such

TABLE 8.2

Changes in Output, Productivity, and Factor-Factor Ratios in Agriculture: the United States and Japan, 1880-1960[a]

	1880	1900	1920	1940	1960	Annual Compound Rate of Growth 1880-1960 (percent)
United States						
Output index (1880 = 100)[b]	100	155	180	232	340	1.5
Productivity index (1880 = 100)						
Total productivity[c]	100	112	105	128	179	0.7
Output per male worker	100	125	141	217	680	2.4
Output per hectare of arable land	100	91	72	94	143	0.4
Factor-factor ratios						
Arable land area per male worker (hectare)	10	13	18	22	46	2.0
Power per male worker (horsepower)[d]	1.8	2.2	3.0	6.7	40.9	3.9
Fertilizer per hectare (kilogram in $N + K_2O_5 + P_2O$)	1.5	3.3	5.0	9.5	41.6	4.1
Japan						
Output index (1880 = 100)[b]	100	149	232	264	358	1.6
Productivity index						
Total productivity[c]	100	142	195	208	229	1.0
Output per male worker	100	152	238	326	453	1.9
Output per hectare of arable land d d	100	135	184	205	280	1.3
Factor-factor ratios (1880 = 100)						
Arable land area per male worker (hectare)	0.61	0.68	0.79	0.96	0.97	0.6
Power per male worker (horsepower)[d]	0.15	0.16	0.17	0.29	1.01	2.4
Fertilizer per hectare (kilogram in $N + K_2O_5 + P_2O$)	13	17	63	115	260	3.8

[a]Flow variables such as output and fertilizer are five-year averages centering on years shown. Stock variables such as land and labor are measured in years shown.

[b]Gross output net of seeds and feed.

[c]Output divided by total input.

[d]Sum of draft animal power and tractor power.

Source: Yujiro Hayami, "Resource Endowments and Technological Change in Agriculture: U.S. and Japanese Experiences in International Perspective," American Journal of Agricultural Economics, LI (December 1969), p. 1294.

results indicate that in American agriculture the marked increases in land and power per worker over the past 80 years have been closely associated with declines in the prices of land and of power and machinery relative to the farm wage rate. The hypothesis that land and power should be treated as complementary factors is confirmed by the negative coefficients. This seems to indicate that in addition to the complementarity along a fixed production surface, mechanical innovations that raise the marginal rate of substitution of power for labor tend also to raise the marginal rate of substitution of land for labor.

The results of the same regressions for Japan (Table 8.3b) are much inferior in terms of statistical criteria. This is probably because the ranges of observed variation in the land-labor and in the power-labor ratios are too small in Japan to detect any significant relationship between factor proportions and price ratios. It may also reflect the fact that mechanical innovations developed in Japan were motivated by a desire to increase yield rather than as a substitute for labor.

The results of regression analyses of the determinants of fertilizer input per hectare of arable land for the United States are presented in Table 8.4a. They indicate that variations in the fertilizer-land price ratio alone accounts for almost 90 percent of the variation in fertilizer use. It is also shown that the wage-land price ratio is a significant variable, indicating a substitution relationship between fertilizer and labor. Over a certain range, fertilizer input can be substituted for human care for plants (e.g., weeding). A more important factor in Japanese history would be the effects of substitution of commercial fertilizer for labor allocated to self-supplied fertilizers.

A comparison of Table 8.4b with Table 8.4a indicates a striking similarity in the structure of demand for fertilizer in the United States and Japan. The results in these two tables seem to suggest that, despite enormous differences in climate and initial factor endowments, the agricultural production function, the inducement mechanism of innovations, and the response of farmers to economic opportunities have been essentially the same in the United States and Japan.[14]

Overall, the results of the data from Japan and the United States examined in this section are consistent with the induced innovation hypothesis. Agricultural growth in the United States and Japan during the period 1880-1960 can best be understood when viewed as a dynamic factor-substitution process. Factors have been substituted for each other along a metaproduction function in response to long-run trends in relative factor prices. Each point on the metaproduction surface is characterized by a technology that can be described in terms of specific sources of power, types of machinery, crop varieties,

TABLE 8.3a

Regressions of Land-Labor Ratio and Power-Labor Ratio on Relative Factor Prices: United States, 1880-1960 Quinquennial Observations

Regression Number	Dependent Variables	Coefficients of Price of: Land Relative to Farm Wage	Coefficients of Price of: Machinery Relative to Farm Wage	$\bar{R}^2$	$\bar{S}$	d
	Land-labor ratio:					
(1)	Agricultural land per male worker	-0.451 (0.215)	-0.486 (0.120)	.828	.0844	1.29
(2)	Arable land per male worker	-0.035 (0.180)	-0.708 (0.101)	.882	.0706	1.37
(3)	Agricultural land per worker	-0.492 (0.215)	-0.463 (0.120)	.828	.0789	1.34
(4)	Arable land per worker	-0.077 (0.182)	-0.686 (0.102)	.879	.0713	1.41
(5)	Power-labor ratio: Horsepower per male worker	-1.279 (0.475)	-0.920 (0.266)	.827	.1865	1.33
(6)	Horsepower per worker	-1.321 (0.474)	-0.898 (0.265)	.828	.1863	1.36

Note: Equations are linear in logarithms. Inside of the parentheses are the standard errors of the estimated coefficients.

TABLE 8.3b

Regressions of Land-Labor Ratio and Power-Labor Ratio on Relative Factor Prices: Japan, 1880-1960 Quinquennial Observations

Regression Number	Dependent Variables	Coefficients of Price of: Land Relative to Farm Wage	Coefficients of Price of: Machinery Relative to Farm Wage	$\bar{R}^2$	$\bar{S}$	d
	Land-labor ratio:					
(7)	Arable land per male worker	0.159 (0.110)	-0.219 (0.041)	.751	.0347	1.17
(8)	Arable land per worker	0.230 (0.049)	-0.155 (0.019)	.914	.0156	1.71
	Power-labor ratio:					
(9)	Horsepower per male worker	-0.665 (0.261)	-0.299 (0.685)	.262	.2191	0.60
(10)	Horsepower per worker	-0.601 (0.236)	-0.228 (0.620)	.266	.1982	0.61

Note: Equations are linear in logarithms. Inside of the parentheses are the standard errors of the estimated coefficients.

and animal breeds. Movements along this metaproduction surface involve innovations. These innovations have been induced, to a significant extent, by long-term trends in relative factor prices.

CONCLUSION

The results of this study indicate that the enormous changes in factor proportions that have occurred in the process of agricultural growth in the United States and Japan are explainable in terms of changes in factor price ratios. Despite strong reservations regarding data and methodology, when we relate the results of the statistical analysis to historical knowledge of the progress in agricultural technology, we conclude that the observed changes in factor input ratios represent a process of dynamic factor substitution accompanying changes in the production surface induced by the changes in relative factor prices.

This conclusion, if warranted, represents a key to the understanding of the success of agricultural growth in Japan and the United States. In both countries agricultural growth was associated with contrasting changes in land-labor price ratios. Prices of agricultural inputs such as fertilizer and machinery supplied by the nonfarm sector tended to decline relative to the prices of land and labor. Such trends induced farmers, public research institutions, and private agricultural supply firms to search for new production possibilities to offset the effects of relative price changes. Mechanical innovations of a labor-saving type were thus induced in the United States, and biological innovations of a yield-increasing type in Japan. After the 1930s the decline in fertilizer prices was so dramatic that innovations in American agriculture shifted from a predominant emphasis on mechanical technology to the development of new biological innovations, in the form of crop varieties highly responsive to the lower cost of fertilizer.

Rapid growth in agriculture in both countries could not have occurred without such dynamic factor substitution. If factor substitution had been limited to substitution along a fixed production surface, agricultural growth would have been severely limited by the inelastic supply. Development of a continuous stream of new technology, which altered the production surface to conform to long-term trends in factor prices, was the key to success in agricultural growth in the United States and Japan.

Such inducement of technological change was not attained without cost. The United States and Japan are among the few countries that have made a substantial national effort in agricultural research and extension for the past 100 years. The history of agricultural research

TABLE 8.4a

Regressions of Fertilizer Input Per Hectare of Arable Land on Relative Factor Prices: United States, 1880-1960 Quinquennial Observations

Regression Number	Coefficients of Prices of: Fertilizer Relative to Land	Labor Relative to Land	Machinery Relative to Land	$\bar{R}^2$	$\bar{S}$	d
(11)	-1.622 (0.200)	1.142 (0.275)	0.014 (0.286)	.950	.1042	2.08
(12)	-1.615 (0.134)	1.138 (0.255)	—	.954	.0968	2.09
(13)	-1.951 (0.166)	—	—	.895	.1406	.77
(14)	-1.101 (0.184)	1.134 (0.173)	-0.350 (0.214)	.969	.0816	1.38
(15)	-1.357 (0.102)	1.019 (0.168)	—	.970	.0832	1.15
(16)	-1.707 (0.154)	—	—	.884	.1481	.84

Note: Equations are linear in logarithms. Inside of the parentheses are the standard errors of the estimated coefficients.

TABLE 8.4b

Regressions of Fertilizer Input Per Hectare of Arable Land on Relative Factor Prices: Japan, 1880-1960 Quinquennial Observations

Regression Number	Coefficients of Price of Fertilizer Relative to Land	Labor Relative to Land	Machinery Relative to Land	$\bar{R}^2$	$\bar{S}$	d
(17)	-1.437 (0.238)	0.662 (0.244)	0.236 (0.334)	.973	.0865	2.45
(18)	-1.274 (0.057)	0.729 (0.220)	—	.974	.0810	2.45
(19)	-1.211 (0.071)	—	—	.953	.1036	1.52
(20)	-1.248 (0.468)	1.217 (0.762)	-0.103 (0.708)	.878	.1820	1.76
(21)	-1.313 (0.131)	1.145 (0.556)	—	.888	.1670	1.79
(22)	-1.173 (0.126)	—	—	.860	.1794	1.52

Note: Equations are linear in logarithms. Inside of parentheses are the standard errors of the estimated coefficients.

and extension in the United States is relatively well known. Japan's efforts to develop agricultural techniques were no less significant than those of the United States.[15] The important point, in the context of this paper, is that in both countries such efforts were directed appropriately in terms of relative factor prices.

For both the United States and Japan, vigorous growth in the industries supplying machinery and fertilizers at continuously declining relative prices has been an indispensable element in the process of agricultural growth. The development of effective research and extension systems to exploit the opportunities created by industrial development has also been of critical importance. In the absence of fertilizer-responsive crop varieties, only limited economic gains could have been realized from lower fertilizer prices. The success in agricultural growth in both the United States and Japan seems to lie in the capacity of their farmers, research institutions, and farm supply industries to exploit new opportunities according to information transmitted through relative price changes.

Our findings reinforce the emerging perspective that major advances in the understanding of economic development processes and in the design of development policies must be more solidly based on an understanding of microeconomic process and behavior. The pervasive impact of economic forces on the direction of innovative activity on the part of farmers, the firms that supply the industrial inputs to agriculture, and the public-sector research and extension institutions that produce and disseminate the new knowledge leading to technical change, is of particular significance. The theory of induced innovation in the public sector remains somewhat uncertain. The model presented here does not possess formal elegance. Yet it has added significantly to our power to interpret the process of agricultural development in Japan and the United States. In both countries, the public-sector research and education institutions designed to serve agriculture have responded effectively to economic forces in directing their activities to releasing the constraints on agricultural growth imposed by inelastic factor supplies.

REFERENCES

Ahmad, Syed. "On the Theory of Induced Invention." The Economic Journal, LXXVI (June 1966), pp. 344-57.

________. "Reply to Professor Fellner." The Economic Journal, LXXVII (September 1967), pp. 664-65.

________. "A Rejoinder to Professor Kennedy." The Economic Journal. LXXVII (December 1967), pp. 960-63.

Barker, Randolph. "Economic Aspects of New High Yielding Varieties of Rice: IRRI Report," in Agricultural Revolution in Southeast Asia: Impact on Grain Production and Trade, Vol. I. New York: Asia Society, 1970, pp. 29-53.

Bober, Mandel Morton. Karl Marx's Interpretation of History. Cambridge, Mass.: Harvard University Press, 2d. ed. rev., 1948.

Brown, Murray. On the Theory and Measurement of Technological Change. Cambridge, Eng.: the University Press, 1966, pp. 95-109.

Bronfenbrenner, Martin. "Production Functions: Cobb-Douglas, Interfirm, Intrafirm." Econometrica, XII (January 1944), pp. 35-44.

Chipman, John S. "Induced Technical Change and Patterns of International Trade," in Raymond Vernon, ed., The Technology Factor in International Trade. New York: Columbia University Press, 1970, pp. 95-127. (A conference of the Universities—National Bureau Committee for Economic Research.)

Dalrymple, Dana C. Imports and Plantings of High Yielding Varieties of Wheat and Rice in the Less Developed Nations. Foreign Agricultural Service, U.S. Department of Agriculture, in cooperation with Agency for International Development, Washington, D.C., November 1969.

David, Paul A., and Th. von de Klundert. "Biased Efficiency Growth and Capital-Labor Substitution in the U.S., 1899-1960." American Economic Review, LXVI (June 1964), pp. 357-94.

Fellner, William. "Two Propositions in the Theory of Induced Innovations." The Economic Journal, LXXI (June 1961), pp. 305-8.

________. "Comment on the Induced Bias." The Economic Journal, LXXVII (September 1967), pp. 662-64.

Fishel, Walter L., ed. Resource Allocation in Agricultural Research. Minneapolis: University of Minnesota Press, 1971.

Griliches, Zvi. "Notes on the Role of Education in Production Function and Growth Accounting," Report 6839. Center for Mathematical Studies in Business and Economics, University of Chicago, 1969(a) (mimeo).

________. "A Note on Capital-Skill Complementarity," Report 6905. Center for Mathematical Studies in Business and Economics, University of Chicago, 1969(b) (mimeo).

Hayami, Yujiro, and Vernon W. Ruttan. Agricultural Development—An International Perspective. Baltimore: the Johns Hopkins Press (1971).

________. "Factor Prices and Technical Change in Agricultural Development: The United States and Japan, 1880-1960." Journal of Political Economy, LXXVIII (September-October 1970), pp. 1115-41.

Hicks, John R. The Theory of Wages. London: Macmillan, 1932, pp. 124-25.

_______. A Theory of Economic History. London: Oxford University Press, 1969.

Kennedy, Charles. "Induced Bias in Innovation and the Theory of Distribution." The Economic Journal, LXXIV (September 1964), pp. 541-47.

_______, "Samuelson on Induced Innovation." Review of Economics and Statistics, XLVI (November 1966), pp. 442-44.

_______, "On the Theory of Induced Invention—A Reply." The Economic Journal, LXXVII (December 1967), pp. 958-60.

Marx, Karl. Capital, A Critique of Political Economy. Frederick Engels, ed. New York: The Modern Library (reprinted from Vol. I of the first American edition, Chicago: Kerr), 1915.

Nelson, Richard R. "The Economics of Invention: A Survey of the Literature." The Journal of Business, LII (April 1959), pp. 101-27.

Nelson, Richard R., Merton J. Peck, and Edward D. Kalachek. Technology, Economic Growth and Public Policy. Washington, D.C.: The Brookings Institution, 1957.

Niskanen, William A. "The Peculiar Economics of Bureaucracy." The American Economic Review, LVIII (May 1968), pp. 293-305.

North, C. Douglass, and Robert Paul Thomas. "An Economic Theory of the Growth of the Western World." Economic History Review, XXIII, 1 (second series, 1970), pp. 1-17.

Ohkawa, Kazushi. "Policy Implications of the Asian Agricultural Survey—Personal Notes." Regional Seminar on Agriculture, Papers and Proceedings. Makati, Philippines: Asian Development Bank, 1969, pp. 23-29.

Olson, Mancur, Jr. The Logic of Collective Action: Public Goods and the Theory of Groups. New York: Schocken Books, 1968.

Peterson, Willis L. "The Allocation of Research, Teaching and Extension Personnel in U.S. Colleges of Agriculture." American Journal of Agricultural Economics, LI (February 1969), pp. 41-56.

Rasmussen, Wayne D. "Advances in American Agriculture: The Mechanical Tomato Harvester as a Case Study." Technology and Culture, IX (October 1968), pp. 531-43.

Rosenberg, Nathan. "The Direction of Technological Change: Inducement Mechanisms and Focusing Devices." Economic Development and Cultural Change, XVIII (October 1969), pp. 1-24.

Salter, W. E. G. Productivity and Technical Change. Cambridge, Eng.: the University Press, 1960, pp. 43-44.

Samuelson, Paul A. "A Theory of Induced Innovation Along Kennedy-Weisacker Lines." Review of Economics and Statistics, XLVII (November 1965), pp. 343-56.

________. "Rejoinder: Agreements, Disagreements, Doubts, and the Case of Induced Harrod-neutral Technical Change." Review of Economics and Statistics, XLVI (November 1966), pp. 444-48.

Schmookler, Jacob. Invention and Economic Growth. Cambridge, Mass.: Harvard University Press, 1966, pp. 165-78.

Schultz, Theodore W. "Institutions and the Rising Economic Value of Man." American Journal of Agricultural Economics, L (December 1968), pp. 1113-22.

Timmer, C. Peter. "The Turnip, the New Husbandry, and the English Agricultural Revolution." The Quarterly Journal of Economics, LXXXIII (August 1969), pp. 305-411.

Tichenor, Philip, and Vernon W. Ruttan. Resource Allocation in Agricultural Research: The Minnesota Symposium. St. Paul: University of Minnesota Agricultural Experiment Station, 1969.

* * *

COMMENT BY PATRICK YEUNG

Hayami and Ruttan (or H-R) apply the concept of induced innovation in both the private and public sectors in the United States and Japan to explain the two countries' agricultural performance during the period 1880-1960. The theory of induced innovation treats technological changes as endogenous to the development process. Since the publication of J. R. Hicks' Theory of Wages, the theory of induced invention or innovation has taken on a number of additional dimensions, such as, for example, William Fellner's learning or expectational and market imperfection considerations,[16] and Charles Kennedy's consideration of relative factor shares.[17] Arguments have been raised against the induced invention or innovation hypothesis by W. E. G. Salter, K. J. Arrow, and others.[18] H-R consider the kind of argument raised by Salter (which is briefly recounted in their paper and will therefore not be repeated here) as "not especially useful in understanding the process by which new technical alternatives become available." The particular version of the theory of induced innovation in H-R's paper is primarily of the Hicksian vintage, though some of the elaborations of Syed Ahmad have been added.[19] Simply stated, this version says that the direction of invention or innovation is influenced by changes or differences in relative factor prices.

Since changes in relative factor prices themselves have to be explained, H-R give changes in relative factor scarcities as the reason. However, this tends to be tautological when it is realized that relative scarcities are often measured by relative prices.[20] Furthermore, changing relative scarcities in productive factors may themselves be consequences of (or induced by) technological changes. For this reason, unless some clarification of these points (especially in the light of the general equilibrium nature of the problem) is made, there appears to be some circularity in the H-R argument.

Their argument may be loosely summarized by extending the use of the following algebraic relationship found elsewhere in their work.[21]

$$Y/L = A/L \cdot Y/A \tag{1}$$

where Y = output
L = labor
A = land area.

As Griliches argues, growth in land area per worker A/L and growth in land productivity Y/A are "somewhat independent, at least over a certain range."[22] If this view is accepted, then equation 1 says that labor productivity Y/L may increase due to an increase in either land area per worker or in land productivity or both. By extending the implications of equation 1, each of the latter two ratios may be further decomposed as follows:

$$A/L = M/L \cdot A/M \tag{2}$$

and

$$Y/A = F/A \cdot Y/F \tag{3}$$

where M = some index of mechanical technology
F = fertilizer.

(All the above symbols are the same as those used by H-R.)

Equation 2 may be used to explain the situation depicted on the left side of H-R's Figure 8.3. Briefly, the constraint due to the relative scarcity of L (hence L is relatively expensive) may be alleviated by induced innovation of a mechanical nature (e.g., a new power source) which is complementary to the use of more land, leading ultimately to greater yield. Equation 3 may be used to explain the situation depicted on the right side of H-R's Figure 8.3. Here the constraint due to the relative scarcity of A (hence A is relatively expensive) may be alleviated by induced innovation of a biochemical nature resulting in the greater use of fertilizer and in yields.

One would agree that the situation derived from the above interpretation of equation 2 is somewhat descriptive of the United States, but not of Japan, due to the very limited expansion of land in Japan. Turning to H-R's empirical findings, one's expectations appear to be generally borne out by the contents of their Tables 8.2 and 8.3—but surprisingly H-R seem to be looking for something different for the case of Japan from their discussion of their Table 8.3b. On the other hand, one would expect the situation derived from the above interpretation of equation 3 certainly to be descriptive of Japan, but not of the United States, since land in America does not constitute a scarcity constraint for the induced biochemical innovation argument to apply. However, the empirical results contained in H-R's Figure 8.4, as well as their Table 8.4, generally appear to substantiate the situation depicted by equation 3 for both Japan and the United States indiscriminately.*

Be that as it may, H-R's approach is understandable in view of their praiseworthy attempt at parallel treatment of the United States and Japan as equals in agricultural development. However, some of the details of their argument require at least some qualification.

While the market-induced innovation hypothesis may be eminently plausible, H-R's exposition of it contains some technical problems which require rectification or qualification.

1. The term "metaproduction function" used to identify curve U in their Figure 8.2 is a misnomer. It makes output a function of fertilizer alone, which is inconsistent with the number of inputs identified elsewhere in their paper (as in their Figure 8.3). Curve U shows only a partial relationship between yield and fertilizer, not the whole production function. The form of their metaproduction function needs to be more rigorously specified.

2. It should be pointed out that there is no necessary reason why curve U in their Figure 8.2 should itself be convex or be an envelope of the series of response curves in order to be consistent with the induced innovation hypothesis. Being simply the locus of sequential points of tangency between the response curves and corresponding relative price lines, it is sufficient for it to slope upward. Likewise, Ahmad's innovation possibility curve, which H-R use to support their argument, need not, for a similar reason, be an envelope concave curve—it is sufficient for it to slope downward.

*Note, however, that in their Figure 8.4, the Japanese cluster appears to be situated somewhat to the northwest of the United States cluster.

3. Since over time the quality of an input changes, representing its quantity graphically should be qualified, so that one does not take it to imply factor homogeneity over time.

4. Since the curve U in their Figure 8.2 is defined not only by the price of fertilizer but also the price of the output, this gets entangled with an identification problem between what properly belongs to the supply side and what to the demand side. The task of disentangling it remains to be done. (In this connection, the evidence presented in their Table 8.1 can at best be described as circumstantial, for though the data show that rice yield per hectare is inversely correlated with the fertilizer-rice price ratio, the latter variable involves an element of demand which contaminates what is supposed to be a supply relationship.)

5. H-R's theory should be extended beyond the convenient assumption of continuous technological change to cover also the more realistic experience of discrete changes.

Finally, there are some questions on how useful the H-R hypothesis of induced innovation can be. Supposing that one accepts their theory as a good explanation of the historical development of United States and Japanese agriculture, one may still question whether it has general applicability. Can their hypothesis be readily applied to explain also the development of agriculture in LDCs?* Moreover, a theory of induced innovation such as that of H-R implies that it can be used for prediction purposes by simply observing a country's relative factor scarcity. One would like to know, therefore, whether H-R's market-induced innovation theory can help to predict the direction of technological change in LDCs. If it can, it would lend much to the fashioning of farsighted economic policies in LDCs for the proper channeling of economic development forces.

---

*In this connection, one is reminded of Leibenstein's statement: "Relative input scarcity and related prices are not sufficient to determine the desirability of shifting (or not shifting) from one technique to another." Harvey Leibenstein, "Notes on X = Efficiency and Technical Progress," this volume.

CHAPTER

9

MICRO FUNCTIONS IN A MACRO MODEL: AN APPLICATION TO AGRICULTURAL EMPLOYMENT AND DEVELOPMENT STRATEGIES

Lawrence J. Lau and
Pan A. Yotopoulos

INTRODUCTION

The purpose of this paper is to present a framework for the study of agricultural development that incorporates both microeconomic and macroeconomic relations. The model will lead to the determination of four variables endogenously—namely, of agricultural output quantity and price, of labor employed, and the wage rate. The final objective is to study agricultural development under the impact of changes in a number of variables usually considered exogenous to the agricultural sector—such as government price policies, terms of trade, foreign agricultural imports (including P. L. 480 imports), agricultural taxation, agricultural land, and capital policies.

The microeconomic model pertains to a representative agricultural household which both produces and consumes. The behavior of the household will be analyzed under the decision rules already familiar from similar studies [Nakajima 7] [Sen 10] [Jorgenson and Lau 2].

From the production side the household can be visualized as a firm that maximizes profits from agriculture. We can assume that the existing institutional structure in agriculture implies that the quantity of land, and to a lesser extent the quantity of fixed capital, cannot be substantially altered for any individual farm. (Later we shall examine such changes as government policy instruments.) We

---

The authors wish to thank W. O. Jones, A. S. Manne, B. F. Massell, R. R. Nelson, and V. W. Ruttan for helpful comments and K. Somel and W. Lin for computational assistance. Financial support for Lau's participation from the National Science Foundation through Grant GS-2874 is gratefully acknowledged. Responsibility for errors remains with the authors.

thus focus on labor, which in the agriculture of many developing countries is the most important, if not the only, variable input.* Under these assumptions, the firm's management problem becomes that of profit-maximization subject to a given technology (the production function) and given the quantities of land and capital and the prices of the variable factors of production. By solving the maximization problem we obtain the behavioral equations of output supply and of labor demand at the level of the household firm.

From the consumption side we may visualize the household as a source of labor supply, or alternatively, as a consumer of leisure.[1] We then derive the agricultural labor supply as a function of the wage rate, the asset income of the agricultural household and the available agricultural labor force (stock of laborers) of the household.

The fact that the household participates in the labor market substantially simplifies our conceptual approach. It has been shown, by Jorgenson and Lau [2], for instance, that in such cases the optimal production decision may be taken independently of the consumption decision. In particular, this implies that at any given wage rate, the quantity of labor utilized on the household farm itself is independent of the quantity of labor that the household is willing to supply.

A number of the assumptions inherent in our microeconomic approach may be challenged within the context of a specific country. Such demurrals, however, should be weighed against the basic advantage of the microeconomic approach: the fundamental assumption underlying the theory of the firm and of the household, namely that the firm and the household behave as if they were pricetakers, is more tenable. Consequently, one can neglect the effect of any one farm's (or household's) decisionmaking on the prices faced by the firm—prices of variable inputs and of output. Econometrically, this means that one can assume that the prices are exogenous variables in the estimation of these various functions. The first model that we examine is the household micro equilibrium model. It is completely determined by the output supply, the labor demand, and the labor supply functions for given output price, wage rate, capital, land, number of workers in the household, and asset income.

However, in the agricultural sector taken as a whole, factor prices can no longer be considered exogenous—though the output price may still be given exogenously, e.g., by the government. The equilibrium in the agricultural sector is achieved if the total labor demanded is equal to the total labor supplied. This equilibrium determines simultaneously the aggregate quantity of labor and the wage rate for

---

*Our analysis, of course, can be extended to include many variable inputs—and for that matter many variable outputs.

the agricultural sector. This model with endogenous wage rate and exogenous output price will be called the partial macro equilibrium model. In practice this model is most relevant for purposes of development planning, as in many developing economies the price of output often becomes a policy instrument determined directly by government price policies.

Finally, and for the sake of completeness, we shall also consider the model of an economy in which there is no output price control. Besides the aggregate output supply, labor demand and labor supply functions, we also specify an aggregate demand function for agricultural output which we estimate with aggregate time series data.[2] The four functions close the general macro equilibrium model. This equilibrium determines simultaneously agricultural output, output price, agricultural employment, and wage rate.

In the sections that follow, by gradually releasing the relevant assumptions, we construct sequentially each of the three models: the micro equilibrium model of the household, the partial macro equilibrium model of the agricultural sector (with price of output determined exogenously), and the general macro equilibrium model. As an illustration of our approach to micro-macro equilibrium models we calculate the impact of changes in exogenous variables by using parameters estimated from Indian agricultural data. We should emphasize that our results are to be treated as illustrative only. Incomplete and unavailable data sets have made some improvisation necessary, resulting in possibly unreliable parameter estimates.

THE MICRO MODEL

Factor Demand Function and Output Supply Function as Derived from Profit Function[3]

Consider a firm with a production function with the usual neoclassical properties

$$V = F(X_1, \ldots, X_m; Z_1, \ldots, Z_n) \tag{1}$$

where V is output, X_i represents variable inputs, and Z_i represents fixed inputs of production. The profit (defined as current revenues less current total variable costs) can be written

$$P' = pF(X_1, \ldots, X_m; Z_1, \ldots, Z_n) - \sum_{i=1}^{m} c_i' X_i \tag{2}$$

where P' is profit, p is the unit price of output, and c_i' is the unit price of the ith variable input. The fixed costs are ignored since, as it is well known, they do not affect the optimal combination of the variable inputs.

Assume that a firm maximizes profits given the level of its fixed inputs. The marginal productivity conditions for such a firm are

$$p \frac{\partial F(X; Z)}{\partial X_i} = c_i', \quad i = 1, \ldots, m. \tag{3}$$

By defining $c_i \equiv \frac{c_i'}{p}$ as the normalized price of the ith input, we write (3) as

$$\frac{\partial F}{\partial X_i} = c_i, \quad i = 1, \ldots, m. \tag{4}$$

By similar deflation we can rewrite (2) as (5) where we define P as the "Unit-Output-Price" profit, or UOP profit

$$P = \frac{P'}{p} = F(X_1, \ldots, X_m; Z_1, \ldots, Z_n) - \sum_{i=1}^{m} c_i X_i. \tag{5}$$

Equation (4) may be solved for the optimal quantities of variable inputs, denoted X_i^*'s, as functions of the normalized prices of the variable inputs and of the quantities of the fixed inputs,

$$X_i^* = f_i (c, Z), \quad i = 1, \ldots, m. \tag{6}$$

By substitution of (6) into (2) we get the profit function,[4]

$$\Pi = p \left\{ F(X_1^*, \ldots, X_m^*; Z_1, \ldots, Z_n) - \sum_{i=1}^{m} c_i X_i^* \right\} \tag{7}$$

$$= G(p, c_1', \ldots, c_m'; Z_1, \ldots, Z_n).$$

The profit function gives the maximized value of the profit for each set of values $\{p, c', Z\}$. Observe that the term within square brackets on the right hand side of (7) is a function only of c and Z. Hence we can write

$$\Pi = p\, G^*(c_1, \ldots, c_m; Z_1, \ldots, Z_n). \tag{8}$$

The UOP profit function is therefore given by

$$\Pi^* = \frac{\Pi}{p} = G^*(c_1, \ldots, c_m; Z_1, \ldots, Z_n). \tag{9}$$

Observe also that maximization of profit in (2) is equivalent to maximization of UOP profit in (5) in that they yield identical values for the optimal X_i^*'s. Hence Π^* in (9) indeed gives the maximized value of UOP profit in (5). We employ the UOP profit function Π^* because it is easier to work with than Π. It is evident that given Π^* one can always find Π, and vice versa. Furthermore, on the basis of *a priori* theoretical considerations, we know that the UOP profit function is decreasing and convex in the normalized prices of variable inputs and increasing in quantities of fixed inputs. It follows also that the UOP profit function is increasing in the price of the output.[5]

A set of dual transformation relations connects the production function and the profit function.[6] The most important one, from the point of view of our application here, is what is sometimes referred to as Shephard's [11] Lemma, namely,

$$X_i^* = -\frac{\partial \Pi^*(c,Z)}{\partial c_i}, \quad i = 1, \ldots, m, \tag{10}$$

$$V^* = \Pi^*(c,Z) - \sum_{i=1}^{m} \frac{\partial \Pi^*(c,Z)}{\partial c_i} c_i , \tag{11}$$

where V^* is the supply function. Equations (10) and (11) form the basis for our microeconomic formulation of the agricultural labor demand function and of the supply function of agricultural output.

Once a specific functional form is chosen for the profit function, then the output supply function and the labor demand function may be directly estimated, jointly, from microeconomic data. Note that specification of one profit function implies the specification of both the output supply function and the labor demand function. Furthermore we note that since

$$\Pi^*(c,Z) = V^*(c,Z) - \sum_{i=1}^{m} c_i X_i^*(c,Z)$$

by the profit identity, only (m + 1) of the (m + 2) functions, the UOP profit function, the output supply function, and the m factor demand functions may be independently estimated. It is equally clear, however, that one can always derive the remaining function in a trivial manner.

We will make our model operational by casting the analysis within the framework of the Cobb-Douglas production function. The Cobb-Douglas production function with decreasing returns in variable inputs is given by

(12) $$V = A \prod_{i=1}^{m} X_i^{\alpha_i} \prod_{i=1}^{n} Z_i^{\beta_i},$$

where $$\mu \equiv \sum_{i=1}^{m} \alpha_i < 1 .$$

The UOP profit function for this Cobb-Douglas production function is[7]

(13) $$\Pi^* = A^{(1-\mu)^{-1}} (1 - \mu) \left\{ \prod_{i=1}^{m} \left(\frac{c_i}{\alpha_i} \right)^{-\alpha_i (1-\mu)^{-1}} \right\} \left\{ \prod_{i=1}^{n} Z_i^{\beta_i (1 - \mu)^{-1}} \right\}$$

Taking natural logarithms of (13), we have

$$\ln \Pi^* = \ln A^* + \sum_{i=1}^{m} \alpha_i^* \ln c_i + \sum_{i=1}^{n} \beta_i^* \ln Z_i$$

where $$A^* \equiv A^{(1-\mu)^{-1}} (1 - \mu) \left\{ \prod_{i=1}^{m} \alpha_i^{-\alpha_i (1 - \mu)^{-1}} \right\}$$

$$\alpha_i^* \equiv -\alpha_i (1 - \mu)^{-1} < 0 \qquad i = 1, \ldots, m$$

$$\beta_i^* \equiv \beta_i (1 - \mu)^{-1} > 0 \qquad i = 1, \ldots, n.$$

For our specific case of one variable input, labor, and two fixed inputs, fixed capital and land, the UOP profit function is given by

o

(14) $$\ln \Pi^* = \ln A^* + \alpha_1^* \ln w + \beta_1^* \ln K + \beta_2^* \ln T$$

where w is the real wage rate, K is the quantity of fixed capital, and T is the quantity of land.

The derived demand functions are given by (10), i.e.,

(15) $$X_i^* = -\frac{\partial \Pi^*}{\partial c_i} \qquad i = 1, \ldots, m.$$

Multiplying both sides of (15) by $-c_i/\Pi^*$ we have

$$-\frac{c_i X_i^*}{\Pi^*} = \frac{\partial \ln \Pi^*}{\partial \ln c_i} \qquad i = 1, \ldots, m$$

which for the Cobb-Douglas profit function becomes

$$-\frac{c_i X_i^*}{\Pi^*} = \alpha_i^* \qquad i = 1, \ldots, m.$$

We can write then the derived demand function for input i

$$X_i^* = -\frac{\alpha_i^* \Pi^*}{c_i} \qquad i = 1, \ldots, m.$$

For the specific case of one variable input, labor, and after transforming into natural logs, we have

(17) $$\ln L_D = \ln(-\alpha_1^*) + \ln \Pi^* - \ln w$$

where L_D is quantity of labor employed and w is the real wage rate.

We have defined UOP profit, Π^*, as total revenue minus total variable costs, divided by the price of output. We can thus write for the supply of agricultural output

(18) $$V^* = \Pi^* + \sum_{i=1}^{m} c_i X_i^*$$

and by substitution from (16)

$$(19) \qquad V^* = \Pi^* + \sum_{i=1}^{m} c_i \left(- \frac{\alpha_i^* \Pi^*}{c_i}\right) = \left(1 - \sum_{i=1}^{m} \alpha_i^*\right) \Pi^*.$$

For the specific case of one variable input and after transforming into natural logs we have

$$(20) \qquad \ln V_S = \ln (1 - \alpha_1^*) + \ln \Pi^*.$$

Equations (17) and (20) are the structural equations for the demand for labor and for the supply of output. Their parameters are derived from a joint estimation of the UOP profit function and the labor demand function.

The Labor Supply Function

It is possible to derive the labor supply function from utility maximization of a consumer unit, by treating leisure explicitly as a consumption commodity, as in Nakajima [7], Sen [10] and Jorgenson and Lau [2], to name only a few. Here we specify instead the labor supply function directly as a function of the wage rate, the price of agricultural output, nonlabor agricultural income, fixed obligations less other asset income, and the number of workers in each household.[8] The wage rate and the prices are the actual prices faced by each household. Nonlabor agricultural income is assumed to consist entirely of the profits, net of the imputed wages for the household's own supply of labor, from agricultural operations. Other asset income may include rentals received for land owned (but not cultivated) and fixed obligations include actual rental payments made on land cultivated (but not owned) as well as land revenue taxes, and other fees. Moreover, it is assumed that the effect on consumption of leisure of the two items of incomes may be different.[9] The labor supply function may be written as

$$(21) \qquad L_S = f_3(w', p, \Pi, 0, N_a)$$

where

L_S = Total labor supplied by the household (including both labor applied on the household farm and labor hired out).
0 = Fixed obligations less other asset income.
w' = Money wage rate.
N_a = Number of workers in the household.

At this point it is not necessary to distinguish between whether the labor hired out is for agricultural or nonagricultural activities so long as the real net rate of compensation is the same in both types of activities. Observe that labor supply should be invariant with respect to a proportional change in the wage rate, prices of commodities consumed, money profits, and fixed obligations. Hence it must be homogeneous of degree zero in w', p, Π, and 0. This implies that the sum of the elasticities of labor supply with respect to the money wage rate, money price of output, profits, and fixed obligations must be zero, i.e.,

$$\frac{w'}{f_3}\frac{\partial f_3}{\partial w'} + \frac{p}{f_3}\frac{\partial f_3}{\partial p} + \frac{\Pi \partial f_3}{f_3 \partial \Pi} + \frac{0}{f_3}\frac{\partial f_3}{\partial 0} = 0 .$$

Now once a specific functional form is chosen, the labor supply function may be directly estimated from microeconomic data. Observe that while the production decisions may be made independently of the consumption decisions, the consumption decisions do depend on the outcome of the production decisions, specifically, on the level of profits from the farm operation. In other words, the model for the farm household is a block recursive one, in which the household may be visualized to make first the production decisions according to the profit-maximization principle, and then subject to the level of planned profits determine the optimal choice of leisure, work, and consumption. Given this recursive structure, the appropriate estimation procedure consists of first estimating the parameters of the production block, and then using the fitted value of the profits in the estimation of the labor supply function.

Micro Equilibrium

For any given values of the money wage rate, the money price of output, the quantity of fixed capital, the quantity of land, the quantity of fixed obligations, and the workers per household, the three functions above describe the complete micro equilibrium of the household. Note that the labor demanded is not necessarily the same as the labor supplied, because of the existence of hired-in and hired-out labor. Nevertheless, as far as the household is concerned, there is no incentive to change any of the decision variables—output, labor demand, labor supplied—unless the exogenous conditions change. Given the three functions, it is possible to compute directly the changes in the micro equilibrium values of output, labor demanded, and labor supplied for the household as a result of change in the exogenous variables.

Yet while the micro equilibrium is interesting in itself and also conveys important information on the behavioral modes of the representative agricultural household, it is not directly useful for the analysis of many policy issues. We thus turn our attention to two macro equilibrium models.

THE MACRO MODELS

The first macro model that we consider is one of partial equilibrium in the agricultural sector. For any given price of agricultural output and wage rate, the labor demanded and the labor supplied need not be the same for any one particular household. However, overall, the total labor demanded in agriculture must be equal to the total labor supplied. The macro labor demand function is given by the micro demand function times the total number of households in the agricultural sector—say, n.[10] Likewise, the macro labor supply function is also given by n times the labor supply function.[11] For partial macro equilibrium, the total demand must be equal to total supply, with the equilibrium wage rate also determined in the process. The aggregate output supply, of course, is also given by n times the output supply function. Thus, in a state of partial macro equilibrium, one has aggregate output, nV_S, aggregate labor services, $nL(= nL_D = nL_S)$, and money wage rate, w', simultaneously determined as functions of the output price, fixed capital, land, fixed obligations, and the number of workers (all expressed on a per household basis). With these reduced form functions, one can then compute the effects of governmental policies on output price, land, interregional migration, agricultural taxes, etc. on output supply, labor services, and the wage rate. This model is especially appropriate for the analysis of countries with government price control programs.

Partial macro equilibrium, however, does not lead to a clearing of the market in agricultural output. Consequently, output price adjustments may become necessary. In order to analyze this, we need to add to our partial macro equilibrium system a demand function for agricultural output.[12] It may be written as

$$V_D = f_4(p, p_n, Y, N, M) \qquad (22)$$

where

V_D = total quantity of agricultural output demanded.
p_n = price of non-agricultural commodities.
Y = national income.

N = total population.
M = net imports of agricultural commodities.

In this paper we do not require that imports and domestic output be perfect substitutes.

This demand function may be estimated from time-series macroeconomic data. It will then be appended to the partial macro equilibrium model to form the general macro equilibrium model. In this model, the output market must clear. Hence, we have

$$nV_S = V_D = V$$

and p is then determined endogenously. We further observe that the demand function must be zero degree homogeneous in p, p_n, and Y, as any consumer demand function should be, that is

$$\frac{p}{f_4}\frac{\partial f_4}{\partial p} + \frac{p_n}{f_4}\frac{\partial f_4}{\partial p_n} + \frac{Y}{f_4}\frac{\partial f_4}{\partial Y} = 0.$$

By imposing the general macro equilibrium condition, one can now determine V, L, w, and p simultaneously as functions of fixed capital, land, fixed obligations, number of workers (all on a per household basis), national income, the price of nonagricultural commodities, and net imports of agricultural commodities. It is with these reduced form functions that one can explore the general equilibrium effects of various government policies.

SPECIFICATION OF FUNCTIONAL FORMS

The Cobb-Douglas UOP profit function for the agricultural household as given in (13) above is

$$\Pi^* = A^*\left(\frac{w'}{p}\right)^{\alpha_1^*} K^{\beta_1^*} T^{\beta_2^*}$$

or

$$\ln \Pi^* = \ln A^* + \alpha_1^* \ln w' - \alpha_1^* \ln p + \beta_1^* \ln K + \beta_2^* \ln T \tag{23}$$

where w' is the money wage rate and p the prices of agricultural output. Similarly, labor demand, as given in (16) above is

$$\frac{w'}{p} L_D = -\alpha_1^* \Pi^*$$

or

(25) $$\ln L_D = \ln(-\alpha_1^*) + \ln \Pi^* - \ln w' + \ln p.$$

The output supply function is then given by

(26) $$\begin{aligned} V_S &= \Pi^* + \frac{w'}{p} L_D \\ &= \Pi^* - \alpha_1^* \Pi^* \\ &= (1 - \alpha_1^*) \Pi^*. \end{aligned}$$

Thus we have for the output supply function and the labor demand function,

(27) $$\begin{aligned} \ln V_S = {} & \ln(1 - \alpha_1^*) + \ln A^* + \alpha_1^* \ln w' - \alpha_1^* \ln p \\ & + \beta_1^* \ln K + \beta_2^* \ln T. \end{aligned}$$

(28) $$\begin{aligned} \ln L_D = {} & \ln(-\alpha_1^*) + \ln A^* + (\alpha_1^* - 1) \ln w' - (\alpha_1^* - 1) \ln p \\ & + \beta_1^* \ln K + \beta_2^* \ln T. \end{aligned}$$

For the household labor supply function, we specify the following constant elasticity form.

(29) $$\begin{aligned} \ln L_S = {} & \ln \gamma_0 + \gamma_1^* \ln w' + \gamma_2^* \ln \Pi + \gamma_3^* \ln 0 \\ & - (\gamma_1^* + \gamma_2^* + \gamma_3^*) \ln p + \gamma_4^* \ln N_a \end{aligned}$$

where the condition of zero degree homogeneity in prices and income has been imposed. By substituting

$$\begin{aligned} \ln \Pi &= \ln p + \ln \Pi^* \\ &= \ln p + \ln V_S - \ln(1 - \alpha_1^*) \end{aligned}$$

into (29), using (26), we have

$$\ln L_S = \ln \gamma_0^* - \gamma_2^* \ln (1 - \alpha_1^*) + \gamma_1^* w' + \gamma_2^* \ln V_S$$

$$+ \gamma_3^* \ln 0 - (\gamma_1^* + \gamma_3^*) \ln p + \gamma_4^* \ln N_a.$$

Rewriting the output supply, the labor demand, and the labor supply functions for the household in matrix form, putting the three endogenous variables on the left hand side, we have

$$\begin{bmatrix} 1 & 0 & 0 \\ 0 & 1 & 0 \\ -\gamma_2^* & 0 & 1 \end{bmatrix} \begin{bmatrix} \ln V \\ \ln L_D \\ \ln L_S \end{bmatrix}$$

$$= \begin{bmatrix} \ln (1-\alpha_1^*) + \ln A^* & \alpha_1^* & -\alpha_1^* & \beta_1^* & \beta_2^* & 0 & 0 \\ \ln (-\alpha_1^*) + \ln A^* & \alpha_1^* - 1 & -(\alpha_1^* - 1) & \beta_1^* & \beta_2^* & 0 & 0 \\ \ln \gamma_0^* - \gamma_2^* \ln(1 - \alpha_1^*) & \gamma_1^* & (\gamma_1^* + \gamma_3^*) & 0 & 0 & \gamma_3^* & \gamma_4^* \end{bmatrix} \begin{bmatrix} 1 \\ \ln w' \\ \ln p \\ \ln K \\ \ln T \\ \ln 0 \\ \ln N_a \end{bmatrix}$$

This can be solved to yield the micro equilibrium reduced form, reproduced in Table 9.1.

Partial macro equilibrium requires that the labor market be cleared, that is,

$$nL_D = nL_S = L$$

and in this process the money wage rate is determined for any given exogenous price of agricultural output. The three endogenous variables V ($= nV_S$), L, and w' may then be solved simultaneously as functions of the exogenous variables. Rewriting the equation in matrix form, we have

$$\begin{bmatrix} 1 & 0 & -\alpha_1^* \\ 0 & 1 & -(\alpha_1^* - 1) \\ -\gamma_2^* & 1 & -\gamma_1^* \end{bmatrix} \begin{bmatrix} \ln V \\ \ln L \\ \ln w' \end{bmatrix}$$

$$= \begin{bmatrix} \ln(1-\alpha_1^*) + \ln A^* + \ln n & -\alpha_1^* & \beta_1^* & \beta_2^* & 0 & 0 \\ \ln(-\alpha_1^*) + \ln A^* + \ln n & -(\alpha_1^* - 1) & \beta_1^* & \beta_2^* & 0 & 0 \\ \ln \gamma_0^* - \gamma_2^* \ln(1-\alpha_1^*) + \ln n & -(\gamma_1^* + \gamma_3^*) & 0 & 0 & \gamma_3^* & \gamma_4^* \end{bmatrix} \begin{bmatrix} 1 \\ \ln p \\ \ln K \\ \ln T \\ \ln 0 \\ \ln N_a \end{bmatrix}$$

We note that if and only if $-\gamma_1^* - \alpha_1^* \gamma_2^* + \alpha_1^* - 1 \neq 0$, the matrix on the L.H.S. can be inverted to provide estimates of the partial macro equilibrium reduced form coefficients. These are reported in Table 9.2.

Estimates of the profit function have already been obtained in Lau and Yotopoulos [4]. The labor supply function is estimated from

TABLE 9.1

Reduced Form Coefficients of the Micro Equilibrium Model

Exogenous Variables	Intercept	p	K	T	0	N_a	w'
Endogenous Variables							
V_S	23.127	1.166	-0.224	1.224	0	0	-1.166
L_D	22.507	2.166	-0.224	1.224	0	0	-2.166
L_S	3.617	-1.781	0.224	-1.224	0.615	1.367	1.166

Note: All variables are in natural logarithms. For sources and variable definitions see Appendixes A and B.

TABLE 9.2

Reduced Form Coefficients of the Partial Macro Equilibrium Model

Exogenous Variables	Intercept	p	K	T	0	N_a
Endogenous Variables						
V	16.5166	-0.2152	-0.0672	0.3673	0.2152	0.4784
L	10.2273	-0.3998	0.0672	-0.3673	0.3998	0.8886
w'	5.6693	1.1846	-0.1345	0.7347	-0.1846	-0.4103

Note: All variables are in natural logarithms. For sources and variable definitions see Appendixes A and B.

data of the same Farm Management Studies [20] as used in Lau and Yotopoulos [5]. Note that our estimates of the profit function parameters indicate that there is constant returns to scale, that is, $\beta_1^* + \beta_2^* = 1$.

Now for the general macro equilibrium model, we would have to specify the demand function for agricultural output of (22)

$$\text{(30)} \quad \ln V_D = \ln \delta_0^* + \delta_1^* \ln p + \delta_2^* \ln Y - (\delta_1^* + \delta_2^*) \ln p_n + \delta_3^* \ln N + \delta_4^* \ln M$$

where once again zero degree homogeneity in prices and income has been imposed. When this equation is added to the partial macro equilibrium model, we obtain a very different reduced form as output price has now become endogenous. General macro equilibrium implies that

$$V = V_D = nV_S$$

$$L = nL_D = nL_S.$$

One can write the four equations in matrix form

$$\begin{bmatrix} 1 & 0 & -\alpha_1^* & \alpha_1^* \\ 0 & 1 & -(\alpha_1^* - 1) & \alpha_1^* - 1 \\ -\gamma_2^* & 1 & -\gamma_1^* & (\gamma_1^* + \gamma_3^*) \\ 1 & 0 & 0 & -\delta_1^* \end{bmatrix} \begin{bmatrix} \ln V \\ \ln L \\ \ln w' \\ \ln p \end{bmatrix}$$

$$= \begin{bmatrix} \ln(1-\alpha_1^*) + \ln A^* + \ln n & \beta_1^* & \beta_2^* & 0 & 0 & 0 & 0 & 0 & 0 \\ \ln(-\alpha_1^*) + \ln A^* + \ln n & \beta_1^* & \beta_2^* & 0 & 0 & 0 & 0 & 0 & 0 \\ \ln \gamma_0^* - \gamma_2^* \ln(1-\alpha_1^*) + \ln n & 0 & 0 & \gamma_3^* & \gamma_4^* & 0 & 0 & 0 & 0 \\ \ln \delta_0^* & 0 & 0 & 0 & 0 & \delta_2^* & -(\delta_1^* + \delta_2^*) & \delta_3^* & \delta_4^* \end{bmatrix} \begin{bmatrix} 1 \\ \ln K \\ \ln T \\ \ln 0 \\ \ln N_a \\ \ln Y \\ \ln p_n \\ \ln N \\ \ln M \end{bmatrix}$$

Once more, if the matrix on the L.H.S. is nonsingular, the system can be solved for the reduced form. The necessary and sufficient condition for singularity is

$$-\alpha_1^* \gamma_3^* + \delta_1^* (\gamma_1^* + \alpha_1^* \gamma_2^* - \alpha_1^* + 1) = 0.$$

Some sufficient conditions are:

(i) $\alpha_1^* = \delta_1^* = 0$, i.e., both the wage rate elasticity of profit and the price elasticity of demand are zeroes,

(ii) $\gamma_3^* = \delta_1^* = 0$, i.e., fixed obligations elasticity of labor supply and the price elasticity of output demand are both zeroes.

The reduced form coefficients are reported in Table 9.3.

AN APPLICATION TO INDIAN AGRICULTURE

As an illustration we use data from the Farm Management Studies[13] of the Indian Ministry of Food and Agriculture [20] to estimate jointly the UOP profit function and the labor demand function

TABLE 9.3

Reduced Form Coefficients of the General Macro Equilibrium Model

Exogenous Variables	Intercept	K	T	O
Endogenous Variables				
V	-23.0786	0.1098	-0.6002	-0.3516
L	-63.3264	0.3961	-2.1646	-0.6532
w'	223.6096	-1.1090	6.0601	2.9353
p	183.9822	-0.8227	4.4956	2.6338

Note: All variables are in natural logarithms. For sources and variable definitions see Appendixes A and C.

conditional on the given quantities of cultivable land and fixed capital. The two functions are sufficient to determine the output supply function, as per equation (26). Also from data of the Studies, we estimate the household labor supply function. From aggregate time series data, we estimate the output demand function. The four functions, labor demand, output supply, labor supply, and output demand, are used to estimate the household micro equilibrium model and the two macro equilibrium models.

The results of the estimation of the basic regressions are reported in Appendix A. The partial macro equilibrium model and the general macro equilibrium model are presented respectively in Appendix B and Appendix C, in Tables 9.1, 9.2, and 9.3.

The reduced form coefficients for the micro equilibrium of the household are reported in Table 9.1. The exogenous variables are price of output, wage rate, capital, land, fixed obligations, and workers per household. Endogenous variables are output supplied, labor demanded, and labor supplied. It is interesting to note that the household, the elasticity of the labor supply with respect to output price is negative. The reason is that an increase in the price of output leads to an increase in profits which raises asset income and shifts the

N_a	Y	N	p_n	M
-0.7815	1.4807	2.6338	-1.1291	-0.0432
-1.4518	2.7506	4.8926	-2.0975	-0.0802
6.5246	-8.1501	-14.4968	6.2148	0.2377
5.8543	-6.8802	-12.2380	5.2464	0.2007

labor supply to the left. A similar interpretation applies to the negative coefficient of labor supply with respect to land. The coefficients of output and labor demand are positive for both prices of output and quantity of land and negative for wage rate. Increases in both workers in the household and fixed obligations, i.e., taxes, lead to increases in labor supplied.[14] All results are plausible and consistent with economic theory. The only exception appears in the reduced coefficients for capital. This result, which consistently appears also in the other tables, can probably be attributed to errors in measurement of the capital input.[15]

The reduced form coefficients reported in Table 9.2 for the partial macro equilibrium model pertain to the simultaneous determination of aggregate output, V, (under the assumption that $V = nV_S$) aggregate labor services, L (under the market-clearing assumption that $nL = nL_D = nL_S$), and the partial macro equilibrium wage rate, w'.[16] The exogenous variables are the same as in the household micro equilibrium model, with the exception of the wage rate. An increase in the price of output leads, at the household micro level, to an increase in output, profits, and labor demanded, and a decrease in the labor supplied. These effects combine at the partial macro model to produce the negative coefficients of output and equilibrium labor and the positive coefficient of wage with respect to price of output. The increase in the wage rate follows directly from the increase in labor demand and the decrease in labor supply at the household level. Observe that the elasticity of labor supply with respect to the wage rate is zero and that with respect to profits is negative (see Appendix A). The increase in the wage rate thus leads to a lower equilibrium quantity of labor. This situation is shown in Figure 9.1 where labor demand shifts to D', labor supply to L', and the wage rate increases to w_1'. As a result of these changes, the equilibrium quantity of output also declines.

An increase in the quantity of land, e.g., through reclamation projects, has the same effects on the wage rate and equilibrium quantity of labor as an increase in profits. Nevertheless, equilibrium output does not decline because the decrease in labor is more than compensated for by the increase in land—which is not surprising since in a two-factor production function we rule out a relationship of complementarity between two inputs.

An increase in agricultural taxation (fixed obligations) or workers per household does not enter the production side, thus does not affect labor demanded. It shifts the labor supply to the right and, with given labor demand, the converse effects of the price of output follow. Figure 9.1 shows this situation in terms of the wage rate w_2'.

It is worth noting the difference in the results between the micro equilibrium model of the household and the partial macro equilibrium model. There is a difference not only in magnitude but also in coefficient sign. Shifts in the household demand and supply of labor which are entirely predictable with wage rates given exogenously, when aggregated to determine an equilibrium level and an endogenous wage rate, may lead to radically different results. The object lesson is that formulating policy on the basis of partial equilibrium micro models may be a precarious exercise.

The reduced form coefficients of the general macro equilibrium model, as reported in Table 9.3, extend the simultaneous determination also to the price of output (under the market-clearing assumption $V = nV_S = V_D$). Besides the exogenous variables that appeared in the partial macro equilibrium model (price of output excluded), we add national income, total population, price of nonagricultural commodities (i.e., terms of trade), and agricultural imports.

From the partial macro equilibrium model we have established that the aggregate supply elasticity of output with respect to price is negative. So is the elasticity of demand with respect to price (see Appendix A). An increase in the quantity of land that shifts the output supply to the right[17] leads to an increase in the price and a decrease in the quantity of output. This situation is depicted in Figure 9.2 in terms of a shift of S to S' and the resulting move to V_1 and p_1. The

FIGURE 9.1

The Labor Market

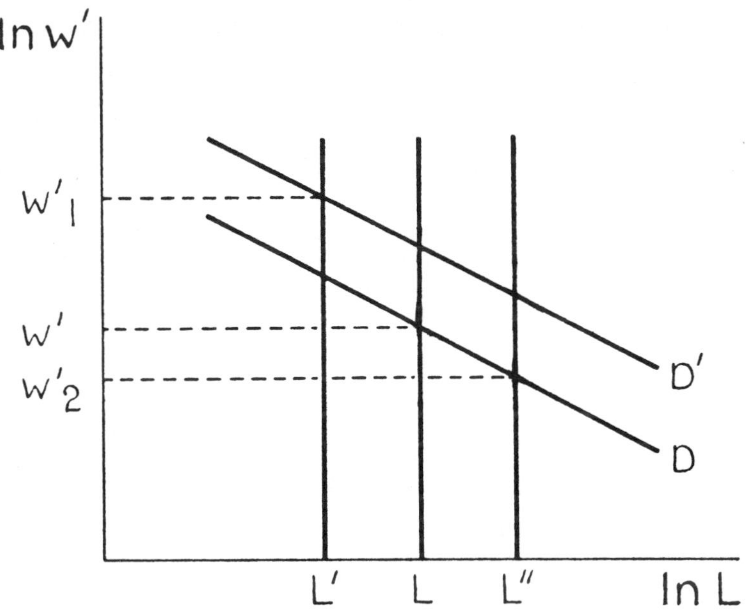

same increase in the quantity of land shifts the demand curve for labor to the right and, given the increase in the price of output and profits, shifts the labor supply to the left. Hence the increase in the equilibrium wage rate.

The explanation of the impact of changes in agricultural taxation and workers per household is traced in an analogous way as the increase in land through shifts in the aggregate supply curve of output. The impact of the other exogenous variables, national income, total population, terms of trade, and agricultural imports is analogous to the previous discussion only in that it is traced through shifts in the demand curve, instead of the supply. Consider, for example, an increase in imports of agricultural commodities, through PL 480 programs. By shifting the demand for domestic output to the left, we have an increase in price of output to p_2 and a decrease in quantity to V_2. As a result of the higher price of output, and thus profits, the labor supply shifts to the left. The final outcome is decrease in the equilibrium quantity of labor and increase in the equilibrium wage rate. We may point out that a general equilibrium macro model is more appropriate for examining the displacement effects of PL 480 imports—which have been discussed in the literature extensively but only within a partial supply equation.[18] An increase in total population[19] may be examined analogously by considering the shift of demand to D'' in Figure 9.2.

Our macro models differ sharply as to the impact of various government policy variables included in both models, such as capital, land, fixed obligations, and workers per household. These differences emanate from alternative assumptions about price of output—being fixed by government policy in the partial macro model as opposed to being an endogenous variable in the general macro model. The object lesson is that one should judge the relevance of his models within the institutional context of the economy. It is most important to know which variables are subject to control and which are to be determined as a result of market forces.

FIGURE 9.2

The Output Market

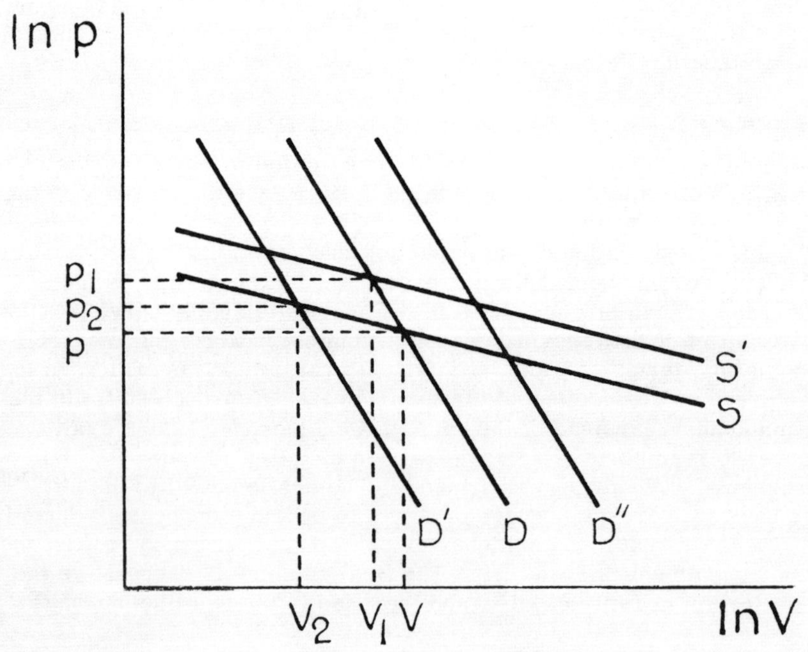

CONCLUSIONS AND CAVEATS

The important feature of this paper is that it sets out a theoretical framework for the analysis of interactions of micro functions in macro models. It then shows how the approach may be empirically implemented by combining micro data which are commonly supplied by farm management studies, together with aggregate time series data which can be obtained readily, to study the macro equilibrium of variables that are endogenous to the agricultural sector—output and labor and their equilibrium prices and wages. Such an approach may be most valuable for ascertaining the effects of alternative agricultural development strategies.

The basic problems of aggregation involved in going from micro data to macro equilibria are well discussed in the literature. Following a long line of previous researchers, we choose to ignore them. Another assumption in our model is the separability of production and consumption decisions of the household. The fact that in our sample, all households, even the ones at the bottom of the land distribution, actively participate in the market constitutes evidence in favor of this assumption. Our model, however, can easily accommodate objections to this assumption also—at the cost of increased complication. Nonseparability means that output and labor demand are not independent of asset income and number of workers in the household, while labor supply is not independent of fixed factors of production, capital, and labor. One can then include these arguments in the three equations and solve simultaneously. Macro equilibrium models, by their very nature, refer to equilibrium values of economic variables. The existence of a single equilibrium wage rate (or the clearing of the labor markets) may appear to be a disturbing assumption in certain less developed countries.[20] However, it is clear that one can always modify the concept of a wage rate to take account of the differential probabilities of employment and the differential time and age profile of earners, as well as other pecuniary and nonpecuniary costs. A step has been made in this direction by Todaro [12] and others, but it is obvious that more work is needed.

Finally, we want to reiterate that the numerical estimates presented are only illustrative because of data limitations. The main contribution of our paper is its conceptual framework, which is eminently suitable for empirical applications should better data become available. Depending on the data and the relevant institutional arrangements, one or the other of the equilibrium models of our general framework may become relevant.

APPENDIX A: STRUCTURAL EQUATIONS*

Joint Estimation of the Profit Function and the Labor Demand Function

$$\text{(i)}\quad \ln \Pi = \ln A^* + \sum_{i=1}^{4} \alpha^*_{0i} D_i + \alpha^*_1 \ln w' + \beta^*_1 \ln K + \beta^*_2 \ln T$$

$$\text{(ii)}\quad -\frac{w' L_D}{\Pi} = \alpha^*_1$$

There are two restrictions: $\alpha^*_1 = \alpha^*_1$, $\beta^*_1 + \beta^*_2 = 1$.

The Zellner's method estimates are:

$\ln A^* =$	4.415 (0.194)	$\alpha^*_1 =$	-1.166 (0.376)
$\alpha^*_{01} =$	0.776 (0.377)	$\beta^*_1 =$	-0.224 (0.153)
$\alpha^*_{02} =$	-1.133 (0.497)	$\beta^*_2 =$	1.224 (0.153)
$\alpha^*_{03} =$	-0.310 (0.238)	$\alpha^*_1 =$	-1.166 (0.376)
$\alpha^*_{04} =$	-0.111 (0.383)		

Variables are Π: profit including rent, land revenue, and interest on fixed capital
D_i: regional dummies (WB, MAD, UP, MP)
K: interest on fixed capital
w': money wage rate
T: land, average farm size
L_D: total labor days

---

*Numbers in parentheses under the coefficients are standard errors.

Estimation of the Labor Supply Function

$$\text{(iii)}\quad \ln L_S - \gamma_2^* \ln \Pi = \ln \gamma_0^* + \gamma_{01}^* D_1 + \gamma_{04}^* D_4 + \gamma_1^* \ln w' + \gamma_3^* \ln 0 + \gamma_4^* \ln N_a$$

$\ln \gamma_0^* = 8.075$ (0.523)		$\gamma_1^* = 0.000$
$\gamma_{01}^* = -1.051$ (0.305)		$\gamma_2^* = -1.000$
$\gamma_{04}^* = -0.048$ (0.327)		$\gamma_3^* = 0.615$ (0.175)
		$\gamma_4^* = 1.367$ (0.574)

Variables are L_S: family labor supply, net of hired-in and hired-out labor, in days
0: fixed obligations less nonfarm asset income
N_a: workers per household

γ_1^* is constrained to be zero after initial regression results show it to be insignificantly different from zero. γ_2^* is estimated by nonlinear methods constraining its value between -1 and 0.

Estimation of the Demand for Output Function

$$\text{(iv)}\quad (\ln V_D - \delta_3^* \ln N) = \ln \delta_0^* + \delta_1^* (\ln p - \ln p_n) + \delta_2^* (\ln Y - \ln p_n) - (\delta_1^* + \delta_2^*) \ln p_n + \delta_4^* \ln M$$

$\ln \delta_0^* = 0.148$ (0.066)	$-(\delta_1^* + \delta_2^*) = -0.429$
$\delta_1^* = -0.134$ (0.186)	$\delta_3^* = 1.000$
$\delta_2^* = 0.562$ (0.144)	$\delta_4^* = -0.016$ (0.016)

Variables are V_D: index of agricultural production [Government of India, 19] p: index of food articles' prices [Government of India, 19]

Y: index of net national product at constant prices [Government of India, 18]

p_n: index of manufactured articles' prices [Government of India, 18]

N: index of population; the coefficient is constrained to 1.0 to express demand in per capita terms [Government of India, 18]

M: index of imports of rice and wheat [Government of India, 19].

All indexes = 100 in 1952-53

APPENDIX B: PARTIAL MACRO EQUILIBRIUM RELATIONSHIPS

$$\text{(i)}\quad \ln V = \ln(1 - \alpha_1^*) + \ln A^* + \alpha_1^* \ln(w'/p) + \beta_1^* \ln K + \beta_2^* \ln T$$

$$\text{(ii)}\quad \ln L_D = \ln(-\alpha_1^*) + \ln A^* + (\alpha_1^* - 1)\ln(w'/p) + \beta_1^* \ln K + \beta_2^* \ln T$$

$$\text{(iii)}\quad \ln L_S = \ln \gamma_0^* - \gamma_2^* \ln(1 - \alpha_1^*) + \gamma_1^* \ln(w'/p) + \gamma_2^* \ln V_S + \gamma_3^* \ln\left(\frac{0}{p}\right) + \gamma_4^* \ln N_a$$

The endogenous variables are V, L, w'.
The model in matrix form is

$$\begin{bmatrix} 1 & 0 & -\alpha_1^* \\ 0 & 1 & (1 - \alpha_1^*) \\ -\gamma_2^* & 1 & -\gamma_1^* \end{bmatrix} \begin{bmatrix} \ln V \\ \ln L \\ \ln w' \end{bmatrix} = A\,\underline{\underline{Y}}$$

$$= \begin{bmatrix} \ln(1-\alpha_1^*) + \ln A^* + \ln n & -\alpha_1^* & \beta_1^* & \beta_2^* & 0 & 0 \\ \ln(-\alpha_1^*) + \ln A^* + \ln n & (1-\alpha_1^*) & \beta_1^* & \beta_2^* & 0 & 0 \\ \ln \gamma_0^* - \gamma_2^* \ln(1-\alpha_1^*) + \ln n & -(\gamma_1^* + \gamma_3^*) & 0 & 0 & \gamma_3^* & \gamma_4^* \end{bmatrix} \begin{bmatrix} 1 \\ \ln p \\ \ln K \\ \ln T \\ \ln 0 \\ \ln N_a \end{bmatrix}$$

$$= B \; \underline{\underline{X}}$$

The intercepts have been increased by ln n to account for macro equilibrium. (n = 61,780,000, estimated number of operational holdings in India, 1953-54) [Government of India, 19, p. 46].

$$A = \begin{bmatrix} 1 & 0 & 1.166 \\ 0 & 1 & 2.166 \\ 1 & 1 & 0 \end{bmatrix}$$

$$B = \begin{bmatrix} 23.127 & 1.166 & -0.224 & 1.224 & 0 & 0 \\ 22.507 & 2.166 & -0.224 & 1.224 & 0 & 0 \\ 26.744 & -0.615 & 0 & 0 & 0.615 & 1.367 \end{bmatrix}$$

In the reduced form $\underline{\underline{Y}} = (A^{-1} B) \underline{\underline{X}}$.

The reduced form coefficients matrix A^{-1} B are reported in the main text in Table 9.1.

APPENDIX C: GENERAL MACRO EQUILIBRIUM RELATIONSHIPS

(i) $\ln V = \ln(1 - \alpha^*) + \ln A^* + \alpha_1^* \ln(w/p) + \beta_1^* \ln K + \beta_2^* \ln T$

(ii) $\ln L_D = \ln(-\alpha_1^*) + \ln A^* + (1 - \alpha_1^*) \ln(w/p) + \beta_1^* \ln K + \beta_2^* \ln T$

$$\text{(iii)}\ \ln L_S = \ln \gamma_0^* - \gamma_2^* \ln (1 - \alpha_1^*) + \gamma_1^* \ln (w/p) + \gamma_2^* \ln V + \gamma_3^* \ln \left(\frac{0}{p}\right) + \gamma_4^* \ln N_a$$

$$\text{(iv)}\ \ln V = \ln \delta_0^* + \delta_1^* \ln p + \delta_2^* \ln Y - (\delta_1^* + \delta_2^*) \ln p_n + \delta_3^* \ln N + \delta_4^* \ln M$$

The endogenous variables are V, L, w, p.
The model in matrix form is

$$\begin{bmatrix} 1 & 0 & -\alpha_1^* & \alpha_1^* \\ 0 & 1 & (1 - \alpha_1^*) & -(1 - \alpha_1^*) \\ -\gamma_2^* & 1 & -\gamma_1^* & \gamma_1^* + \gamma_3^* \\ 1 & 0 & 0 & -\delta_1^* \end{bmatrix} \begin{bmatrix} \ln V \\ \ln L \\ \ln w \\ \ln p \end{bmatrix} = A \, \underline{\underline{Y}}$$

$$\begin{bmatrix} \ln (1 - \alpha_1^*) + \ln A^* + \ln n & \beta_1^* & \beta_2^* & 0 & 0 & 0 & 0 & 0 & 0 \\ \ln (-\alpha_1^*) + \ln A^* + \ln n & \beta_1^* & \beta_2^* & 0 & 0 & 0 & 0 & 0 & 0 \\ \ln \gamma_0^* - \gamma_2^* \ln (1 - \alpha_1^*) + \ln n & 0 & 0 & \gamma_3^* & \gamma_4^* & 0 & 0 & 0 & 0 \\ \ln \delta_0^* & 0 & 0 & 0 & 0 & \delta_2^* & \delta_3^* & -(\delta_1^* + \delta_2^*) & \delta_4^* \end{bmatrix} \begin{bmatrix} 1 \\ \ln K \\ \ln T \\ \ln 0 \\ \ln N_a \\ \ln Y \\ \ln N \\ \ln p_n \\ \ln M \end{bmatrix}$$

$$= B \, \underline{\underline{X}}$$

The intercepts of the first three regressions are increased by ln n to account for macro equilibrium. (n = 61,780,000, estimated number of operational holdings in India, 1953-54) [Government of India, 19, p. 46].

$$A = \begin{bmatrix} 1 & 0 & 1.166 & -1.166 \\ 0 & 1 & 2.166 & -2.166 \\ 1 & 1 & 0 & 0.615 \\ 1 & 0 & 0 & 0.134 \end{bmatrix}$$

$$B = \begin{bmatrix} 23.127 & -0.224 & 1.224 & 0 & 0 & 0 & 0 & 0 & 0 \\ 22.507 & -0.224 & 1.224 & 0 & 0 & 0 & 0 & 0 & 0 \\ 26.744 & 0 & 0 & 0.615 & 1.367 & 0 & 0 & 0 & 0 \\ 1.983 & 0 & 0 & 0 & 0 & 0.562 & 1.000 & -0.428 & -0.016 \end{bmatrix}$$

In the reduced form, $\underline{\underline{Y}} = (A^{-1} B)\underline{\underline{X}}$.

The reduced form coefficients matrix $A^{-1} B$ are reported in the main text Table 9.2.

REFERENCES

[1] J. S. Bhagwati and S. Chakravarty, "Contributions to Indian Economic Analysis: A Survey," Am. Econ. Rev., LIX (September 1969, Supplement), pp. 1-73.

[2] D. W. Jorgenson and L. J. Lau, "An Economic Theory of the Agricultural Household," paper presented at the Far Eastern Meeting of the Econometric Society, Tokyo, June 1969.

[3] L. J. Lau, "Applications of Profit Functions," in D. L. McFadden, ed., The Econometric Approach to Production Theory, Amsterdam: North Holland Publishing Company, 1971, forthcoming.

[4] ________, and P. A. Yotopoulos, "Profit, Supply and Factor Demand Functions," American Journal of Agricultural Economics, LIV (February 1972), pp. 11-18.

[5] ________, "A Test for Relative Efficiency and an Application to Indian Agriculture," Am. Econ. Rev., LXI (March 1971), pp. 94-109.

[6] D. L. McFadden, "Cost, Revenue, and Profit Functions," in D. L. McFadden, ed., The Econometric Approach to Production Theory, Amsterdam: North Holland Publishing Company, 1971, forthcoming

[7] C. Nakajima, "Some Theoretical Models of Subjective Equilibrium" in C. R. Wharton, Jr., ed., Subsistence Agriculture and Economic Development, Chicago: Aldine Publishing Company, 1969.

[8] Q. Paris, "The Farmer and the Norms of a Market Economy in Developing Countries: An Analysis of Case Studies, Part 1," The Farm Economist, XI, 11 (1970), pp. 493-510.

[9] ______, "The Farmer and the Norms of a Market Economy in Developing Countries: An Analysis of Case Studies, Part II," The Farm Economist, XI, 12 (1970), pp. 556-70.

[10] A. K. Sen, "Peasants and Dualism With or Without Surplus Labor," J. Polit. Econ., LXXIV (October 1966), pp. 425-50.

[11] R. W. Shephard, Cost and Production Functions, Princeton, N.J.: Princeton University Press, 1953.

[12] M. P. Todaro, "A Model of Urban Migration and Urban Unemployment in Less Developed Countries," Am. Econ. Rev., LIX (March 1969), pp. 139-48.

[13] H. Uzawa, "Duality Principles in the Theory of Cost and Production," Intern'l Econ. Rev., V (May 1964), pp. 216-20.

[14] S. Wellisz (with B. Munk, T. P. Mayhew, and C. Hemmer), "Resource Allocation in Traditional Agriculture: A Study of Andhra Pradesh," J. Polit. Econ., LXXVIII (July-August 1970), pp. 655-84.

[15] P. A. Yotopoulos, "From Stock to Flow Capital Inputs for Agricultural Production Functions: A Microanalytic Approach," J. Farm Econ., XLIX (May 1967), pp. 476-91.

[16] ______, Allocative Efficiency in Economic Development: A Cross Section Analysis of Epirus Farming, Athens: Center of Planning and Economic Research, 1968.

[17] A. Zellner, "An Efficient Method for Estimating Seemingly Unrelated Regressions and Tests for Aggregation Bias," Jour. Am. Stat. Assoc., LVII (June 1962), pp. 348-68.

[18] The Government of India, Central Statistical Organization, Cabinet Secretariat, Statistical Abstract of the Indian Union, 1953-54, 1961, 1965.

[19] The Government of India, Directorate of Economics and Statistics, Ministry of Food, Agriculture, Community Development and Cooperation, Indian Agriculture in Brief, Sixth and Eighth Editions, 1961, 1967.

[20] The Government of India, Ministry of Food and Agriculture, Studies in the Economics of Farm Management, Delhi, 1957-62. Reports for the year 1955-56: Madras, Punjab, Uttar Pradesh, West Bengal; Report for the year 1956-57: Madhya Pradesh.

CHAPTER

10

THE EMPLOYMENT PROBLEM IN DEVELOPMENT

Benjamin Higgins

INTRODUCTION

It is becoming increasingly clear that the major problem of the Second Development Decade will be unemployment. In recognition of this fact, the International Labor Organization is in the course of organizing a World Employment Program, to match the World Food Program launched by the Food and Agriculture Organization during the First Development Decade. A recent United Nations Expert Group Meeting on Social Policy and Planning concluded:

> The dualism created through the existence of heavy and rising unemployment in town and countryside seems to us particularly ominous. In our view it should be considered as the problem of the Second Development Decade.[1]

Of all forms of sociological dualism, the most serious cleavage in the next few years will be between those who are more or less fully employed and those who are not. The same report states bluntly:

> Provision of employment should be the major goal of the Second Development Decade. Employment is the basis for improvements in nutrition, education, and health. The major form of "dualism" emerging at the present time is the enormous gap between those who are employed and those who are not, whether in village or in city.[2]

In developing countries, open unemployment and underemployment average around 25 percent of the labor force. The present prospects are that in the absence of a drastic shift in the orientation of development plans and programs this figure could rise to 50 percent by the end of the 1970s. Add seasonal unemployment and low-productivity employment ("disguised unemployment"), and the aggregate figures could be much higher.

What makes the outlook for the Third World still more disturbing is the fact that much of this unemployment will appear in cities, rather than in the countryside where it might be relatively easily handled by traditional village social security systems and "shared poverty." The push from the countryside and the lure of the cities remain strong, despite the failure of the urban industrial sector to expand fast enough to absorb all those seeking urban employment. The result is both increasing unemployment and underemployment in the cities and a transfer of low-productivity employment from agriculture to the urban services sector.

Judging by the best informed estimates now available, there is little or no prospect of an absolute reduction in numbers seeking a livelihood on the land in developing countries as a whole. Take, on the one hand, current rates of population growth and the still higher rates of growth of the labor force, and on the other, the increasingly capital-intensive and labor-saving nature of industrial investment and the limited opportunities for productive employment in urban services; make any reasonable estimate of the probable amount of industrial investment; and the inescapable conclusion is that much if not most of the increase in the labor force will be obliged to remain on the land. Many developing countries cannot even hope for a reduction in the proportion of the labor force engaged in agriculture. Others may succeed in shrinking the relative size of the agricultural sector only at the cost of increasing unemployment, underemployment, and low-productivity employment in the cities.

What all this boils down to is that we have made disappointingly little progress in raising levels of welfare in the Third World during the Decade of Development (the mere fact that it has now become the "First" Development Decade is a measure of the disappointment), despite rates of growth of national income that were high in comparison to previous rates of growth in the same countries, high in comparison to growth rates of advanced countries during their periods of industrialization, and quite respectable even in terms of growth rates of advanced countries during the same decade. Unless the efforts of developing and donor countries alike are substantially increased, and if they are not redirected from income-oriented planning to employment-oriented planning, the prospects for the Second Development Decade are grim indeed: swelling unemployment, aggravated population pressure on the land, increased concentration of poverty in the cities, where it assumes its most distressing form;

growing gaps between rich and poor regions and social groups within poor countries; and growing gaps between rich and poor countries. What is particularly disturbing is that all this can take place with rates of growth of national income that will look most impressive by comparison with those recorded by the now advanced countries in their periods of rapid industrialization.

Why has it taken so long to come to grips with the true nature of the development problem? Many of us have been reluctant to face all the implications of the population explosion. It is not simply that rates of population growth are much higher in developing countries today than they were in the advanced countries during the eighteenth and nineteenth centuries, or in the same less developed countries between 1850 and 1950. It is also that the recent drops in death rates have resulted in extremely young populations. As a consequence, dependency ratios are much higher in the LDCs than in the advanced countries. The employment problem is aggravated by the fact that numbers of entrants into the labor force are even greater than increases in total population. But the demographic situation contributes to the employment problem in a more subtle way. In countries where anything up to half the total population may be of school age, the burden of education is crushing; and the absence of the essential ingredient of trained personnel limits employment opportunities for those at lower levels of skill.

Secondly, so far as economists are concerned, even those who are well acquainted with developing countries have shied away from the conflict between raising national income on the one hand and raising employment and welfare on the other. Most of the planning models currently in use are refinements of aggregative Keynesian models. Basically they assume that the way to reduce unemployment is to raise national income, and that the way to raise national income is to accelerate the rate of capital accumulation. We have known in our bones that neither of these assumptions could stand up to the facts in most LDCs, but the implications were so appalling, and the difficulty of constructing more realistic models so forbidding, that we have treated the ache in our bones with the palliative of mathematically elegant models.

Third, most of us—whether economists or other social scientists—have suffered from the "Colin Clark syndrome." From Colin Clark and others we had learned that the historical development of the now advanced countries took the form of structural change with the gradual shrinkage of the relative size of the primary sector (farming, fishing, and forestry) and the transfer of the labor force to the secondary (industrial) sector, as well as the later growth of the services sector, accompanied by a further decline in the relative importance of agriculture. This process, together with capital accumulation and technological advance, assured rising productivity and incomes. Unemployment existed, but was regarded as a result of the instability produced by growth and of the imperfections of the monetary system. Much development theory and most development planning has been based on the assumption that development in the LDCs should and would take this same form, even though no such process had taken place in the past in most LDCs, and despite lack of clear evidence that it was taking place currently. We knew, of course, that progress à la Colin Clark had not taken place in most LDCs in the past; instead, investment in the modern sector had produced the phenomenon of "technological dualism." But somehow we associated the failure of capital accumulation and technological advance to bring prosperity to LDCs with the evils of colonialism, and felt that things would surely be different with a deliberate international effort to raise living standards of the indigenous populations of the LDCs. We were blinded by our own good intentions to the fact that the kind of development strategies we were promoting involved no fundamental change in the development process inherited from the past, and that aggravation of dualism was the inevitable result.

Finally, we have been slow to recognize—or to admit—that the nature of technological change and shifts in product-mix taking place in LDCs are of a sort that heighten, rather than reduce, the conflict between income and employment. True, our textbooks refer to the choice of technology and of product-mix, and state the desirability of adapting both of these to the factor-endowment. But few of us have insisted that finding efficient techniques or suitable product-mixes that would raise the ratio of increases in employment to investment is a critical necessity for the success of the international development effort; and few indeed are the official development plans and programs that make changes in technology and product-mix so as to reduce the investment-employment ratio, the keystone of development strategy.

All this may seem obvious, but it is neglected even in so fundamental a document as the Pearson Report.[3] The Report seems to suggest that solving the problems of LDCs is a matter primarily of still more rapid capital accumulation, so as to generate a still more rapid growth of national income. How is it possible for so sophisticated a group to begin its report with a section entitled "Crisis In Aid," to report that the target growth rate of 5 percent per year was achieved during the 1960s, and then to state that a growth rate of 6 percent per year "would transform the economic outlook in a developing Country"? The growth rate of 5 percent per year clearly did not transform the Third World, and in many countries economic and social conditions have deteriorated despite the high growth rates. How then could a mere increase in growth rates of national income from 5 percent to 6 percent bring a revolution in the position of the

LDCs during the 1970s? The authors are not unaware of the facts, nor of the complexity and enormity of the problems; nonetheless the whole vast subject of unemployment and urbanization together is dismissed in three pages. Yet it is precisely here that the major problems of the Second Development Decade lie.

To reiterate, it is becoming clear that with conventional development planning, average unemployment and underemployment in all LDCs combined is likely to rise during the Second Development Decade, and could well reach 50 percent of the labor force by the end of the period. The unemployment will be concentrated among young people, many of them with some education. Given the limits to investment in the secondary (manufacturing) sector and the increasingly capital-intensive techniques utilized in this sector, there is no hope of absorbing more than a fraction of the increase in the labor force in that sector. Meanwhile the push from the villages and the pull toward the cities remain strong. The drift to the cities, and the transfer of poverty and disguised unemployment from the agricultural, rural sector to the urban, services sector will continue. Yet the migration from village to city will not be sufficient to prevent increasing population pressure on the land. Absolute numbers in agriculture will continue to grow, and many developing countries will fail even to reduce the proportion of the labor force engaged in agriculture. All this can take place with increased rates of capital accumulation, and with growth rates of national income of 6 percent per year.[4]

CAUSES OF UNEMPLOYMENT

What are the reasons for the seeming intractability of the employment problem in LDCs? Why is it so much more serious than was the employment problem in the now advanced countries during their period of industrialization? In a recent statement,[5] Hans Singer suggests five major factors:

1. The relentless increase in population, and the even higher rate of growth of the labor force. We might add that in some LDCs, though not all, the density of population is already much higher than the population densities in Europe, North America, and Australasia when industrialization was launched in these regions.

2. The overwhelming concentration of science and technology in the richer countries has resulted in rapid increases in the overall capital intensity of "modern" techniques, and the lack of real incentive toward the creation of a labor-intensive technology. Here I would add that in the modern sector—or much of it—technical coefficients are either fixed or are regarded as being so, with the result that abundant labor does not result in substitution of labor for capital.

3. The "quantum leap" in labor productivity when modern technologies are imposed on age-old traditional techniques. Technological displacement, in other words, is on a much larger scale when modern techniques are introduced in traditional, long stagnant societies than was the case during the Industrial Revolution in Europe.

4. The preference for urban life and the sizable gap between urban and rural wage levels, which makes urban underemployment preferable to agricultural employment.

5. Social structures that deprive a high proportion of the rural population of land and other inputs necessary to utilize new agricultural techniques.

There is, however, a sixth source of unemployment which, where it is operative, creates the highest levels of unemployment of all: the rainfall cycle in arid zone countries. In North Africa, for example, unemployment among farmers and particularly among seminomadic raisers of livestock, can reach 80 percent during a drought year. This unemployment, moreover, becomes open and highly visible as the population converges on the cities in search of work or relief. This type of unemployment is the exact reverse of "Keynesian" unemployment—it is not effective demand that collapses but supply. People are unemployed because there is no longer any production process to engage in (the crops fail and the animals die), and there are no resources with which labor can be combined. From an economic point of view, drought-stricken land is not land at all. Spiethoff caught a glimpse of this possibility, but stressed imbalance in industrial production, especially of capital goods, rather than total collapse of the sector employing the bulk of the population. Jevons and Moore, of course, stressed the importance of the rainfall cycle as a cause of economic fluctuations, but directed their attention to the impact on advanced countries through international trade rather than to the much more serious impact on the LDCs themselves.

Nor is the impact of rainfall cycles limited to the agricultural sector. There is a kind of "cobweb" involved. Under drought conditions, the real cost of employing labor rises because food is scarce. Money wage rates in the industrial sector, which represent the cost of a subsistence level of living in the countryside plus a fairly fixed premium, may rise rather than fall. Demand for industrial products falls at the same time, and unemployment spreads to the industrial sector as well.

THE ROLE OF MICROECONOMICS

Given this situation, it is clear that macroeconomic planning must be supplemented by intensive planning for individual sectors, regions, cities, industries, villages—with the closest attention to conditions actually prevailing in these microcosms of the economy and of the society. But planning without theory is even worse than measurement without theory. If we are to do micro planning with any degree of competence we must have micro theories. But the assumptions regarding behavior underlying these micro theories must conform to the actual behavior in the microcosms under consideration. The challenge to the economist interested in development is to find ways of introducing into his analysis the knowledge we have regarding socio-cultural frameworks, and of individual behavior within those frameworks, gleaned by other kinds of social scientists in the course of their investigations. Efforts to bring off such "shotgun weddings" through macro models (such as the theoretical models implicit in Everett Hagen's theory of social change) have not been successful. Let us see what we can do with micro models.

As a consequence of the disillusionment with neoclassical microeconomics during the great Depression, and the apparent success of Keynesian macroeconomics in dealing with the economic problems of war and reconstruction, many of us have thrown out the baby with the bath water. The trouble with neoclassical microeconomics was not implicit in the method—it was that too little time and energy were devoted to examining assumptions regarding behavior, and that too little thought was given to problems of aggregation. With these major defects removed micro theory can be extremely helpful. The remainder of this paper is devoted to some illustrations of the manner in which micro models may be built to deal with particular situations in particular countries, with special emphasis on the problem of employment.

The Modern Sector

I shall not repeat here all the description of the modern sector that is presented in my book, Economic Development.[6] Let us assume that technical coefficients are fixed, or nearly so, and that technological progress in the sector tends to be labor-saving and capital-absorbing, so that capital-labor ratios tend to rise through time. We shall also assume that there are a series of "traps" at various levels of development, each requiring discontinuous leaps in the volume of investment in order to outrun population growth.

We shall assume, too, that the supply curve of labor to the modern sector resembles that shown in Figure 10.1. At any point of time, the supply curve bends backward at some level of income where leisure seems more desirable than any use of further income within the limit of existing tastes and wants. However, the supply curve shifts to the right because of population growth as we move through

FIGURE 10.1

The Labor Market, Modern Sector

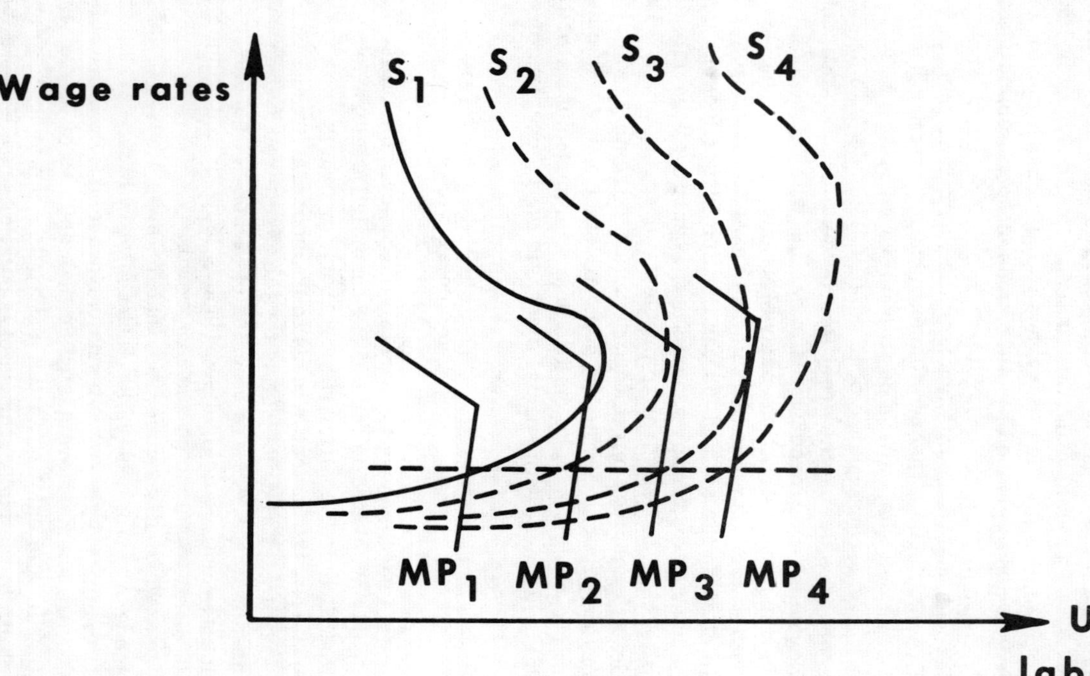

time, giving the illusion of an "unlimited supply of labor" at a wage rate not far above the level of per capita income in the traditional sector, unless and until the rate of expansion in the modern sector and consequent increase in labor requirements outruns population growth. For "modern sector" we may also read "rich region," and for "traditional sector" "poor region." Under these circumstances there will be a more or less constant gap between wage rates in the modern sector and wage rates or incomes in the traditional sector.

At any point of time, the stock of capital in the rich region is given. The marginal productivity curves or demand curves for labor look like those in Figure 10.1, because of the low elasticity of substitution of labor for capital and the "lumpiness" of investment. The short-run supply of additional capital is a function of profitability of investment in the modern sector (rich region) but falls off sharply at the point where domestic savings are all absorbed and the rate of return on new investment falls to "r + x," where "r" is the rate of return on investment elsewhere (in the case of colonies, the mother country; in the case of Canada today, the United States) and "x" is the premium needed to cover additional risks attached to investment outside of the investors' own country. The marginal productivity of labor in the modern sector may be raised by capital accumulation, growth of the market, improved terms of trade, and possibly by innovation, depending on its nature (its intensity, and the degree to which it is labor-absorbing or labor-releasing). Recast in these dynamic terms, the Fei and Ranis model becomes very useful.[7] In this context their basic equation—

$$\eta L = \eta K + \frac{B_L + J}{\epsilon LL}$$

where ηL is the rate of labor absorption, ηK the rate of capital accumulation, B_L the degree of labor-absorbing bias of innovation, J the "intensity" of innovation (rate at which productivity is raised through time), and ϵLL the rate at which marginal productivity of labor falls as the ratio of labor to capital is raised (shaped of the marginal productivity curve)—becomes very significant. The trick is to reach the "turning point" where wages begin to rise in both regions (sectors) and to sustain growth thereafter, despite the squeeze on profits implicit in wage increases as such.

The Traditional Sector (Poor Region)

In the traditional sector, isoquants are relatively "well behaved," though, as we shall see below, this statement is less clearly true if we adhere to a rigorous neoclassical production function, with no changes in technique or in ratios of capital to land. As good land gives out with population growth, if absorption into the modern sector (rich region) does not outrun population growth, the ratio of labor to land-and-capital tends to rise. Failing innovations of a neutral or labor-absorbing type in the traditional sector itself, marginal productivity of labor in the poor sector and region tends to fall sharply. In many developing countries, there has been a progressive shift from slash-and-burn shifting agriculture (a device for combining much land with relatively little labor) to stable and irrigated agriculture. This shift involved labor-absorbing innovation and postponed the drop in average and marginal productivity of labor for some time, but with continued population growth and absence of further innovation of a labor-absorbing or neutral kind, falling per capita incomes in the poor region (traditional sector) become inevitable. If incomes were previously above subsistence level—and there is evidence that with slash-and-burn agriculture they often were—the result may be a drop in wage rates in the rich region to subsistence wage plus a constant margin, permitting some increase in employment in that sector. However, wages cannot drop below subsistence levels for long in the poor region, and therefore cannot drop continuously in the rich region either.

At this point let us introduce Yong Sam Cho's basic diagram, since variations on his original theme will serve us well.[8] In Figure 10.2 we measure hours of work per week on the horizontal axis to the right of the origin and number of men employed to the left of the origin. The curve w-l (wage-labor) shows the locus of wage rates (or incomes) needed to provide sufficient nutrition to permit people to work the corresponding number of hours per week. Each wage rate has a corresponding marginal productivity curve. At low rates, the marginal productivity curve for additional men starts low, since each man brings few hours; but for the same reason marginal productivity of additional men falls slowly. Conversely, at high wage rates, each man can work longer hours; marginal productivity begins high, but falls rapidly, since each additional man brings many hours of additional labor supply to work with the fixed stock of land-and-capital. Having established these premises, let us examine a few specific cases.

Case 1: The Capitalist Landlord

Let us consider first the case of the "capitalist landlord," who owns a substantial amount of land-and-capital and hires labor for wages. Equilibrium will be established with N_1 workers employed

FIGURE 10.2

Marginal Productivity and the Wage-Labor Curve, Traditional Sector

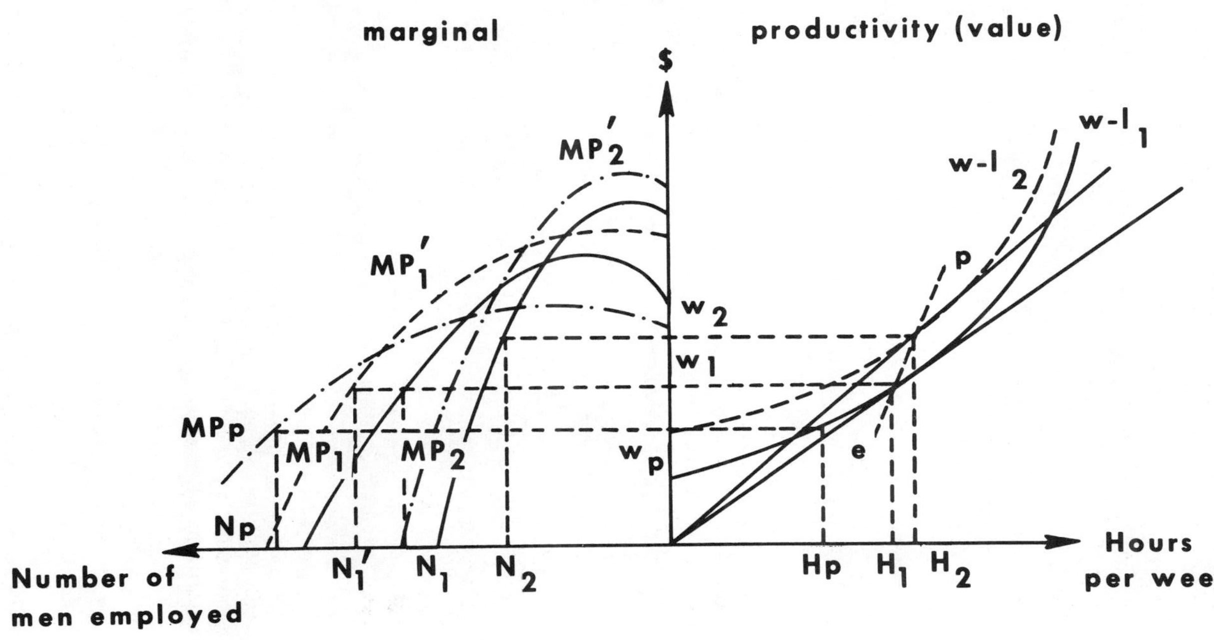

at a wage of W_1, each man working H_1 hours per week. The tangency point of the w-l curve with a straight line through the origin (indicating the hourly wage rate) is a maximum-profit position, since it minimizes costs per man-hour, or maximizes output per unit of wages. The market is assumed to be purely competitive, a reasonable enough assumption if we are talking about staple products of the traditional sector. It is also assumed that product per man-hour is the same for each hour worked. If the labor force exceeds ON_1, there will be open unemployment equal to the excess over ON_1.

The W-L Curve

In Figure 10.2 we have reproduced the w-l curve in the same form in which Cho first presented it, for lack of convincing evidence that its shape should be different. Let us remember that the curve rests on physiological, not psychological, data. As drawn, it suggests that nutritional requirements rise at an increasing rate as hours of work per week increase. There is some evidence that such is the case. Colin Clark, in a recent paper,[9] presents data that suggest that for adult males in India caloric requirements per day rise by 151 per hour when the working day is increased from zero to four hours, by 151 again for the fifth hour of work, and by 251 for the sixth. For adult women, assumed to do half as much hard physical work as the males, caloric requirements rise by 60 per hour for the first four hours, by 66 for the fifth hour and by 67 for the sixth. Estimates for another part of India show marginal caloric requirements of 72 when hours increase from four to five per day, and 78 for the sixth hour per day, as an average for the whole population. Cho himself presents only data on caloric requirements in Korea as "degree of labor" changes from "light, ordinary, heavy, very heavy, and extremely heavy." The marginal caloric requirements are 300, 500, 500, and 500 respectively. These data might suggest a shallow "S" shape for the w-l curve, rising steeply for the first hours per day, less steeply thereafter and then more steeply again. Obviously the curve must become vertical at some point. No amount of food will permit, say, twenty hours of work per day indefinitely. Since the tangency point with the lowest wage line would always occur within the range where the w-l curve is convex downwards (so long as caloric requirements do not actually fall over any range as hours increase) the flattening-out of the curve over the middle range of increases in hours would not change the results of the analysis.

Cho refers to the w-l curve as "the supply curve of labor." There is a sense in which this description is correct; the curve shows increases in hours worked per man as wages rise. But it is not a "supply curve" in the sense of the locus of tangency points of indifference curves with wage lines. The w-l curve has no psychological significance in itself. People are badly off, getting just enough to eat to permit them to go on working the equivalent number of hours, anywhere on the curve. What might be the relationship of the w-l curve to the lowest indifference curve on the chart? Could the w-l curve itself be considered the lowest indifference curve? Below it people die, normally the least preferred situation. At first it may seem that working short hours at low wages might be preferable to working long hours at high wages, since leisure is preferred to work. But in the situation described by the w-l curve, leisure has little or no value. By definition, no active use of leisure, requiring energy expenditure and thus additional calories, is possible. When people are working twenty hours a week, "leisure" is really underemployment and rather boring. There are at least two reasons why longer hours and more income and better nutrition may be preferred:

1. Eating itself contributes to welfare. Having two or three meals a day with a varied diet, as distinct from one meal a day with a restricted and monotonous diet, would be regarded by most workers and peasants as an improvement in their standard of living. If the only sacrifice is a certain amount of useless leisure—underemployment—moving along the w-l curve is likely to bring a move to higher indifference curves.

2. In peasant societies, higher output provides better insurance against risk. If crops are disappointing, hours of work can be reduced, but once a crop is planted, acreage and hours of work cannot be quickly expanded to compensate for bad weather, another child, or the arrival of some member of the extended family.

On the other hand, it is clear that peasant societies need not be far above a bare subsistence level to derive satisfaction from leisure: engaging in conversation, watching traditional dance and theatre, listening to traditional music—none of which require much expenditure of effort except for the performers, who frequently have higher real incomes than the average. When the desirable and undesirable features of working longer hours and having higher income are all taken into account, it seems likely that the lowest indifference curve would not depart very far from the w-l curve. On balance, however, in poor societies where the working week is short, it seems likely that most people would experience some increase in satisfaction in moving up the w-l curve. If workers want to work as much as possible and eat as well as possible, while employers want to maximize profits, the equilibrium at the tangency point of the w-l curve and the wage (equal rate of profit per man-hour) line is a sort of Pareto optimum.

It is important to understand that once the w-l curve is introduced there are two maximization processes instead of one. The capitalist, profit-maximizing employer first maximizes profits in terms of wage rates and hours of work, and then in terms of numbers of workers and value of marginal product. It is no longer a matter of choosing the optimal total number of man-hours to combine with his land-and-capital, because it is no longer a matter of indifference as to how he gets his additional man-hours. Two hundred men working 20 hours are not the same thing as 100 men working 40 hours, since the cost per man-hour will be different depending on which combination is chosen. In terms of output, under Cho's implicit assumptions, more men are always a perfect substitute for more hours per man, but in terms of cost per man-hour, and thus in terms of cost per unit of output, they are not.

Let us therefore drop Cho's two simplifying assumptions (pure competition, identical output for each hour worked) one by one.

Introducing Monopoly Power

If we relax the assumption regarding pure competition, and introduce some degree of monoply power, the curve of value of marginal product of labor will, of course, be marginal product times marginal revenue instead of marginal product times price. The curves will accordingly fall off more steeply as employment increases. However, this change in assumptions (which may or may not be a move toward reality, since much of the modern sector in LDCs of the real world is selling exports in a highly competitive world market) does not change the basic analysis. So long as all man-hours are identical and more men are a perfect substitute for more hours per man-week, it will still pay the entrepreneur to minimize cost per man-hour, and then add men to his work force until the value of the marginal product is equal to the wage rate.

Variable Output Per Hour

What does change the analysis is dropping the assumption that output is steady throughout the working day. Let us suppose that Adam Smith is right, and that the normal worker takes a while to warm to his task and tires toward the end of the working day. The curve of hourly output as the working day is lengthened would rise and then fall. But more men are no longer a perfect substitute for longer hours; there is for any level of employment an optimum number of hours which maximizes output per hour, and this optimum may not be achieved at a wage rate that minimizes wages per hour. Minimizing wages per hour is no longer the same as maximizing output per hour, and the relationship between dO/dH and dW/dH becomes a relevant consideration for the entrepreneur. So long as the slope of dO/dH exceeds that of dW/dH it will pay the entrepreneur to raise wages and increase hours up to the point where hourly output is maximized, and once again to add workers until value of marginal product equals that of wage rate. The equilibrium must still be on the w-l curve, but it need no longer be at the tangency point with the wage-line through the origin.

In Figure 10.2 this change of assumptions shows up in two ways. On the left side of the diagram, there will be among the family of MP curves, each corresponding to a particular wage rate, on that maximizes profits. In the right, the wage line (straight line through the origin) is no longer a curve showing equal rates of profit per hour or per unit of output. The equal-rates-of-profits curve, will now have a shape reflecting the shape of the hourly output curve. Equilibrium will still be established, however, where an equal-rate-of-profit curve is tangent to the w-l curve.

Is there any escape from unemployment and the subsistence-level equilibrium trap under these conditions? If the rich region expands fast enough to permit transfer out of the poor region faster than the labor force grows it will be possible first to eliminate open unemployment and then to reduce the numbers of men employed in the poor region (traditional sector), while raising wage rates and lengthening the working week. In the process, we will move from $w\text{-}l_1$ to $w\text{-}l_2$. Whether or not the $w\text{-}l_1$ curve may be thought of as the lowest possible indifference curve of the workers as we move upwards to $w\text{-}l_2$, $w\text{-}l_3$, etc., we are moving into a zone of welfare where workers can choose between additional income and leisure, which is the essence of increased welfare at this level of development. There is, of course, no advance in welfare entailed in moving along any one of these indifference curves; only a move upward along the expansion path (e-p) involves an increase in welfare. If employment can be reduced to N_2, wages can rise to w_2 and the marginal productivity curve will rise to MP_2, with no technological advance in the poor region. However, this rise in wages in the poor region will raise wages in the rich region as well, and this rise in wages in the rich region will tend to choke off the transfer of workers from poor to rich region.

There is good reason to suppose that the w-l curves will flatten as higher levels of welfare are attained. That is, the additional wage income required to bring forth additional hours of work per week will be less when only "psychic" requirements must be met rather than physiological ones. Historically, at any rate, hours of work have tended to lengthen in the traditional sector (poor region) as technological progress has taken place. The higher wage at zero hours of work reflects the increased capacity of the society to sustain any one of its members in idleness as overall productivity rises.

Can a cumulative process of development be launched through some improvement within the poor region? Let us suppose that there is a significant improvement in technology in the traditional sector—high-yield seed strains, or improved fertilizers and pesticides. Let us also assume that the capitalist landlord is willing and able to make the necessary investments—an important consideration, since investments are always required for the introduction of such innovations. The marginal productivity curves all shift upward, MP_1 to MP'_1, MP_2 to MP'_2, etc. If there is unemployment or underemployment in the poor region, the capitalist landlord will tend to increase the number of workers employed, while leaving wages and hours the same. There will be an increase in welfare for those brought into employment. If the original w-l curve included the share of output formerly used to sustain unemployed villagers, there will also be an increase in welfare for those formerly employed, and they may now consume the whole of their own income themselves. It is even possible that they may shift to $w\text{-}l_2$. However, it is hard to see how a cumulative process could be launched by a once-over improvement of this kind. The poor region may now have some capacity for saving, but there is no place to invest savings except in the once-over improvement itself. Moreover, if wages begin to rise in the poor region they will rise in the rich region too; unless there is an offsetting improvement in productivity of the rich region as well, the result will be a return to the villages of people formerly employed in the rich region (modern sector) and we may end up just as badly off as when we started. With an expanded world market for the output of the poor region and improved terms of trade, a similar process would be launched, with the same kind of restraints.

It is, of course, conceivable that wages, hours, and employment could rise together in the poor region, through some improvement in technology of the traditional sector. It is hard to envisage a continuous rise in employment, in excess of the growth of the labor force, while wages and hours also increase, without a discontinuous "quantum leap" in productivity or a sharp fall in the rate of population growth. Even then, the process is likely to be brought to a halt by the squeeze on profits in the rich region and consequent release of workers from that region (and modern sector), unless there is simultaneous improvement in productivity in the rich region as well. Of course the terms of trade between rich and poor regions may turn in favor of the rich region, which might prevent a rise in real wages all around and so prevent contraction of the rich region. But that would hardly be to the benefit of the poor region.

The Low-Level Employment Trap

It should be noted that with the introduction of the w-l curve we have a microeconomic explanation of unemployment. In traditional neoclassical micro theory, if unemployment appears, the supply curve of labor should fall until wage rates are once again equal to the value of the marginal product at full employment. Once we introduce the relation between wage rates and hours of work, however, this solution is no longer possible even for an individual firm. Reducing wage rates will also reduce hours of work, shift the curve of value of marginal product downward, and reduce profits instead of raising them. So long as profits are maximized, there is no solution within the enterprise for the unemployment shown in Figure 10.2. Full employment would occur only by accident, if the maximum profit combination of hours per man and number of men employed should happen to absorb the entire labor force. Even then there could still be underemployment in the sense that the working week would be shorter than that regarded as normal in advanced countries. The construction presented here, in fact, provides an explanation of the underemployment typical even of the modern sector of developing countries (especially in the modern agricultural subsector), as well as of unemployment.

Case 2: Peasant Proprietors

We turn now to the case of peasant proprietorship in the poor region (traditional sector). Holdings will typically be small, but they will be at the disposal of the families who work them. The case is common enough. In Southeast Asian societies, for example, while land often belongs nominally to the village, a particular family has the right to work a particular holding so long as it continues to do so. Greece, Brazil, and a good many other LDCs have peasant proprietors as well. The poorer farming and fishing enterprises, woodlot operations, and even some retailing operations (the family country store) in the poorer areas of Canada and the United States also have many of the characteristics of peasant proprietorship: small holdings of land-and-capital, labor surplus, low productivity, and income at or below subsistence levels so that government transfer payments are required. We shall distinguish between two basic cases: where free land is still available, so that "slash-and-burn" agriculture is possible, and where land has become scarce.

To approach this case we need to link the Cho diagram with the

FIGURE 10.3

Wage-Labor Equilibria in the Production Function, Peasant Proprietors

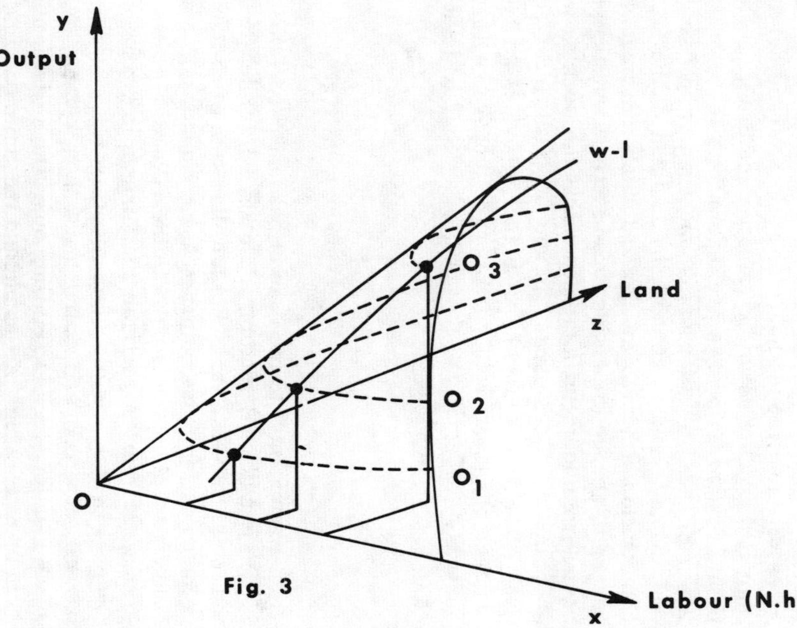

Fig. 3

FIGURE 10.4

The Wage-Labor Curve in
a Two-Dimensional Production Function

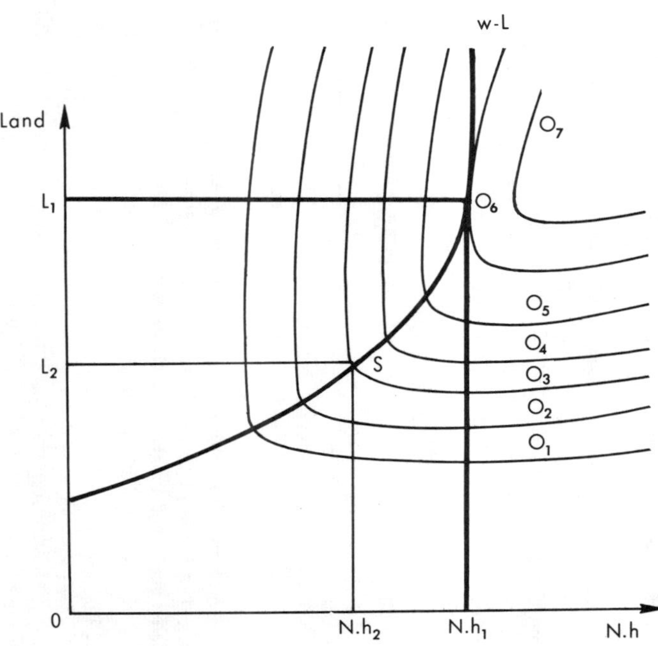

production function. In Figure 10.3, total output is measured on the vertical axis, land-and-capital on the y-axis and labor (number of men times hours-per-week-per-man) on the x-axis. On each isoquant, there will be one point representing a "Cho" equilibrium—that is, a point where the amount of income earned (output produced) is just enough to meet the physiological or psychic requirements for the corresponding number of hours of work and level of employment. In village societies of the Asian variety, the level of employment will be full employment, open unemployment is not permitted, and income is shared by sharing work. Equilibrium on the Cho diagram (Figure 10.2) is determined by the balance between income and hours when all workers are employed. The number of men employed is N_p. The wage will be W_p, hours will be H_p, the relevant marginal productivity curve will be MP_p. Thus the increase in labor utilized as we move along the x-axis in Figure 10.3 represents mainly an increase in hours. The w-l curve is then the locus of all points of "Cho" equilibrium for "Cho" different levels of output per man.

In Figure 10.4 the w-l curve is transposed to a two-dimensional diagram, with output now in the unmeasured third axis. Before proceeding to analyze the case of the peasant proprietor with the help of this diagram, it is necessary to say something about the nature of the curves shown in Figure 10.4.

The Production Function

Let us first consider the nature of the production function. We have described the isoquants in the traditional sector as being "relatively well behaved." At this point we need to pin down what "relatively" means. There is some obscurity in the earlier literature as to just what is held constant as one moves along an isoquant, or from one isoquant to another. For analysis of development of poor countries this question becomes important. If we insist on a highly rigorous neoclassical definition, and permit no change in technique whatsoever within a particular production function, and no change in the ratio of capital to land as the ratio of labor to land is changed, it is highly doubtful that the isoquants are "well behaved" in LDCs. It is almost never possible to add more land to a given amount of labor (in the sense of number of men actually employed multiplied by number of hours actually worked) and increase output, without some change in technique. In the narrow, static sense, technical coefficients are probably fixed even in the traditional sector of LDCs. In reality, however, movements along the production function take place through time and represent changes in the technology (or at least in the technology-mix), and sometimes in the ratio of capital to land. The shift from slash-and-burn to stable, irrigated agriculture as the ratio of labor to land is increased is an example of the first, and the shift to mechanized agriculture as labor becomes scarce at advanced stages of industrialization is an example of the second. The production function can be made more meaningful and more useful if choices among known techniques in response to changes in availability of factors of production, and changes in capital-land ratios directly linked to labor-land ratios, are included in the function itself. Genuine changes in technique, in the sense of new knowledge and innovation, would then constitute a change in the production function.

Even with this broader concept of the production function, however, the isoquants will not be completely well behaved. Moving along an isoquant, increasing the ratio of labor (N.h) to land, might mean a shift from pure slash-and-burn to a mixture of slash-and-burn and *sawah* (stable, irrigated rice culture), perhaps with a fish pond and a poultry yard thrown in. It is certainly possible that some variation in such mixes is possible, with different ratios of land to labor, and the same total output. But it is unlikely that the range of choice is wide. More important, in a completely "well-behaved" production function, it is possible to hold labor constant, and move up a vertical line such as $N.h_2$ - O_6 in Figure 10.4, adding more land and raising total output over a considerable range before the point of zero marginal productivity of land is reached. But if, in a poor peasant society engaged in traditional agriculture, we add land to a fixed amount of labor (N.h), even if we permit a shift back toward a larger proportion of slash-and-burn in the mix, it is unlikely that output will increase over any considerable range. Substituting slash-and-burn for stable, irrigated culture with the same amount of labor will hardly raise total output, nor will the sacrifice of the fish pond and the poultry yard. It is true that there are known cases where societies have shifted back to slash-and-burn after a substantial and rapid reduction of population through emigration, but this response probably reflects discontinuities in the production function. A small reduction in the labor-land ratio with stable agriculture, with no fall in output, is not possible. Thus the technology must be changed altogether if output per head is to be maintained.

Accordingly, we have drawn the curves in Figure 10.4 with a short range that is "well-behaved" near the point of actual operations, becoming vertical or horizontal, and then turning away from the axes. This shape seems to conform most closely to actual conditions in the traditional sectors of LDCs.

What shape will the w-l curve have when transposed to the production function in Figure 10.4? Retaining our assumption that marginal caloric requirements increase with hours of work, each additional hour requires a larger increase in output, which can be translated into a greater increase in land available so long as we are operating within the "well-behaved" portion of the curves. Thus the w-l curve retains the concave downward shape of Figure 10.2.

For a peasant proprietor living close to the subsistence level while working only a few hours per week, the marginal utility of pure leisure (underemployment) may be taken as zero. As pointed out above, under these circumstances moving up the w-l curve brings improvements in welfare. Having more to eat and a more varied diet is preferred to more underemployment, and family security is better protected by working more land (or working land more intensely) and devoting more hours per week to working, with a consequent increase in total output, than if one worked less and produced less. Indeed, the rational thing to do under these conditions is to maximize total output, and the behavior of peasants in Asia and Africa suggests that they are in fact trying to do so. Maximizing output would mean, in formal terms, reducing the marginal productivity of both land and labor to zero, but this the peasant proprietor cannot do. Only if technical coefficients are completely fixed can marginal productivity of both labor and land be zero, at the corner of each isoquant. But even then, output cannot be maximized in the sense of moving up the ridge line, adding both labor and capital so long as output increases. If he does not run out of land, he will nonetheless reach a point where working more land and expending more hours will not raise output enough to enable him to work still longer hours.

If land is freely available, the proprietor will move up the w-l curve until it is tangent with an isoquant, as at O_6. Here the marginal productivity of land in the formal neoclassical sense is zero, and the w-l curve has become vertical. The family is working as much as it possibly can, and no further increase in food intake will permit them to work longer hours. The marginal productivity of labour is nonetheless still positive.

Now let us assume that population grows and land becomes scarce. The supply of land for this particular family is reduced to OL_2. Now the proprietor is unable to set the marginal productivity of either land or labor at zero. With only OL_2 units of land-and-capital, the best he can do is to operate at point S, where available land is fully utilized and the w-l curve cuts an isoquant. Not surprisingly, output and income are lower, and the number of hours worked fewer, than was the case when land was more abundant. Output per man-hour is raised, but total output is reduced. In short, an *improvement* in technology is now necessary to maintain output and income per capita at the same level that was attained by abundant land and slash-and-burn agriculture. Historically, this improvement of technology has been achieved by adding to stable agriculture and irrigation such innovations as fertilizer, improved seeds, pesticides, rodent control, etc. But with continued population growth in the poor region, all these have been needed to offset the continued reduction in quantity of land per family. In densely populated areas like Java, peasant incomes have fallen despite such innovations.

It is worth noting that in analyzing the case of peasant proprietors, the average product curve replaces the marginal productivity curve in the Cho diagram. Total income per worker will be equal to average productivity with full employment. Hours of work, similarly, will be determined by total income per worker, not wages.

Where now is the escape? Neutral or labor-saving innovations (improved seed or fertilizer, perhaps) may raise levels of welfare, while hours are shortened as the population grows. Labor-absorbing innovations (improved irrigation) may permit longer hours and increased output, but any such once-over improvement will soon be swamped by population growth. Improved terms of trade will have a similar effect. Once again, it is hard to see any escape without a reduction in numbers in the traditional sector (poor region), and this requires expansion in the rich region fast enough to outrun population growth. An increase in exports from the rich region to the world might raise marginal productivity there and permit absorption of labor from the poor region. But unless the expansion of employment exceeds the growth of the labor force, there will be no change in wages in either sector. Total income in the poor region also remains stagnant, and only profits in the rich region will rise.

The Constant Wage Gap

The above analysis leans somewhat heavily on the concept of a more-or-less constant gap between wages in the modern sector and wages or incomes in the traditional sector. The concept of a constant gap between peasant incomes or wages and wages paid to unskilled workers in the modern industrial sector (including plantation agriculture) was introduced into the literature by W. Arthur Lewis and has remained there ever since.[10] For the most part, the assumption has gone unchallenged, since it seems to conform well enough to reality, though some questions have been raised as to the size and stability of the gap. For purposes of the present analysis, the actual size or degree of stability of the gap is not fundamental—what matters is only that when wages or incomes in the traditional sector (poor region) rise, wages in the modern sector (rich region) rise, too.

What are the reasons for the gap? Generally speaking, writers who have used the idea in their analytical models have assumed, explicitly or implicitly, one or more of the following conditions:

1. The modern industrial sector requires longer hours of work, and thus higher nutritional standards and higher wages.
2. The modern industrial sector is concentrated in urban centers

where costs of living are higher, and these must be offset by higher wages.

3. In moving from village to city, peasants give up the built-in social security systems of village societies, face higher personal risks arising from possible unemployment or underemployment, and enter an unknown and therefore frightening world. To compensate for these disadvantages of moving from farm to factory, wages must be significantly higher.
4. An additional factor is that in many LDCs, the modern sector is also substantially foreign, and foreign enterprises are easy prey to governmental or trade-union pressure to raise incomes of employees.

It is assumed, of course, that in order to expand, the modern sector must attract workers from the villages. In the early stages of development of the modern sector, this condition holds almost by definition—at the outset, this sector has no labor force and thus no natural growth of the labor force. Expansion is possible only through migration from the villages. It is worth asking, however, what will be the outcome of improvements in the traditional sector if the modern sector is already big enough to meet its labor requirements through natural rate of growth of population in the modern (rich region) alone. One can find cases, such as São Paulo and the east central region of Brazil, that come close to this condition. In advanced countries, one can find such rich regions as the Pacific Coast of the United States or the Province of Ontario in Canada that come even closer to being able to sustain growth on the basis of population growth within the region. However, such a situation is not consistent with satisfactory development of the economy as a whole, and for the following reasons:

1. The aggregate growth even of the modern sector is likely to be slow, limited as it is to the natural rate of population growth (which cannot long exceed 3 percent per year) plus technological progress and structural change within the modern sector (rich region). Given the "lumpiness" of many kinds of innovations, investment is likely to be hampered by the inadequacy of the labor supply. Thus a modern sector (rich region) that relies on self-sustained growth without net immigration is likely to be a relatively stagnant one.
2. Thus if substantial and rapid improvements in productivity are achieved in the traditional sector (poor region)—introduction of high yield seed strains—the terms of trade are likely to turn against the traditional sector (poor region).
3. If the traditional sector is producing foodstuffs and raw materials, as is likely, it will find the income elasticity of demand of the modern sector (rich region) to be low. This

fact, together with the slow growth of income in the rich region, will tend to result in unmarketable surpluses in the poor region, once demand within the region for these products is satisfied. There remains the world market, but similar problems are likely to arise there.

The net outcome of such a situation is likely to be an aggravation of dualism rather than general economic development.

We might also ask what the outcome might be if the gap between wages in the modern sector and incomes or wages in the traditional sector can be squeezed, so that an increase in productivity in the traditional sector does not automatically raise wages in the modern sector. Here the difficulties of launching a cumulative process of development based on initial improvements in the traditional sector are much the same as in the previous example. Some improvements in welfare in the traditional sector (poor region) can be obtained by raising the level of consumption of products of the sector. If there are simultaneous improvements in techniques in more than one field of economic activity, fairly substantial increases in welfare may be possible by expanding trade within the sector—for example, through exchange of beef for millet in West Africa. But clearly such exchange is no recipe for sustained development. Once marketable surpluses appear, the lack of expansion in the modern sector (or of world markets) tends to put a stop to the process of growth. Terms of trade will turn against the traditional sector. Surpluses can be disposed of only by selling at a low price and buying output of the rich region at prices that are made higher by the very increase in demand from the poor region. Thus improvements in technique in the traditional sector are converted into increases in welfare in the modern sector. This sequence is a common enough phenomenon, but once again it tends to aggravate technological and regional dualism rather than leading to sustained and generalized development.

It does not seem, then, that there is any "up by the bootstraps" strategy for promoting prolonged and widespread development by improvements in the traditional sector alone. Productivity, incomes, and employment must expand in the modern sector as well, so as to provide both a market for the surpluses of the traditional region and opportunities for migration of labor from poor to rich region, traditional to modern sector.

Case 3: The Village Landlord

A case of particular interest is that which might be called "the village landlord." It often occurs in Southeast Asia, and may well exist in other societies as well. Here we have a small landlord (in

FIGURE 10.5

Employment by Village Landlord

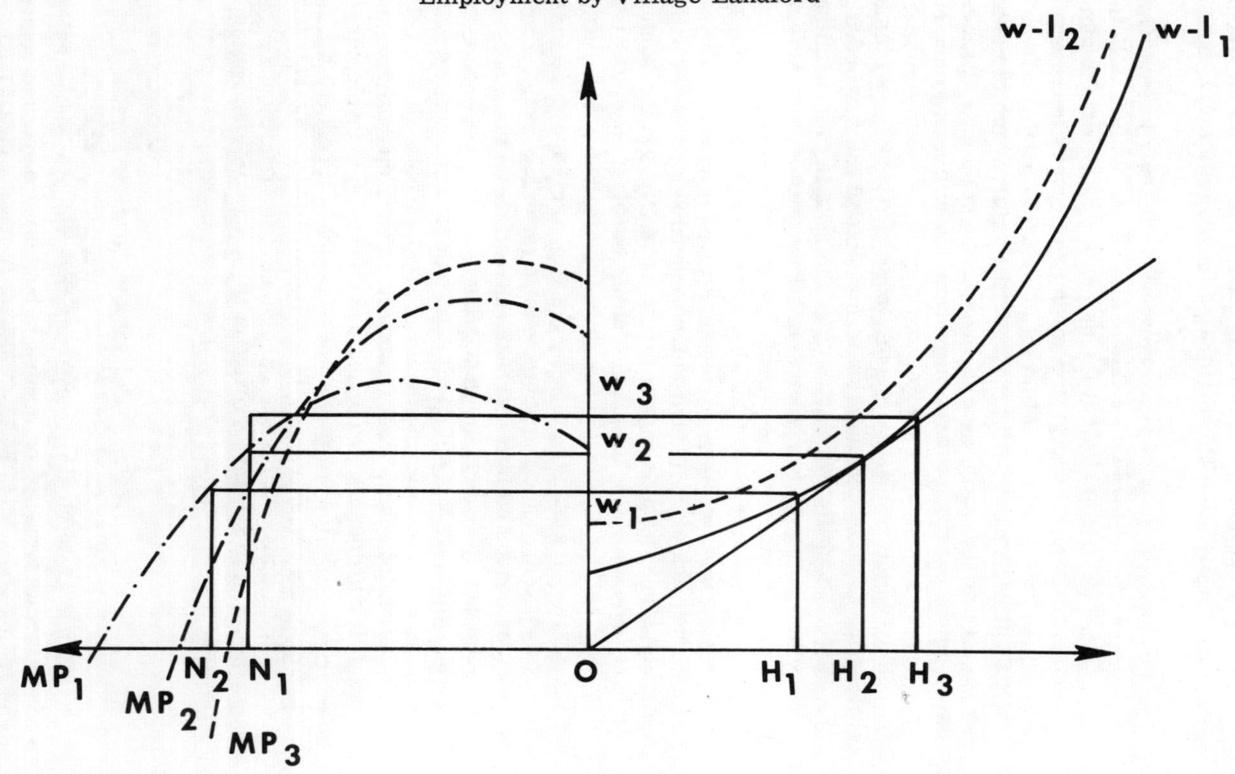

Indonesia, it might mean owning 10 to 50 acres) who therefore, with the existing labor-intensive technology, is obliged to hire labor to work his land. Or he may be the proprietor of a small traditional industry, such as a batik factory. In the framework of Southeast Asian village society, he is no longer a true "capitalist" landlord, no longer being free to maximize profits as he pleases. On the contrary, the village as a unit decides, in discussion with the landlord (or small capitalist) what the landlord's proper contribution to provision of employment and income in the village should be. The social sanctions are such that the village landlord is obliged to absorb into his employ some share of the low-productivity employment (disguised unemployment) of the village. He will be left a profit that is considered "just." If the landlord-capitalist is from another ethnic group (overseas Chinese in Southeast Asia), his bargaining position is at once stronger and weaker than if he were a member of the majority ethnic group. He will be less sensible to the daily approval or disapproval of the village, but the ultimate sanctions for failing to accept the views of the village as to what is "just" with regard to employment and profits are much more drastic—including, it would seem from recent Indonesian experience, being murdered.

Here then we begin with the level of employment N_1 in Figure 10.5. This is the level of employment suggested by the village and accepted by the landlord. But for this level of employment we have a whole family of possible wage rates and corresponding marginal productivity curves and hours of work. At wage w_1 the village landlord will obtain H_1 hours of work per man and the marginal productivity curve will be MP_1. At wage w_2, he will get H_2 hours of work per man and the marginal productivity curve will be MP_2, and so on. One of these combinations will be most profitable for the landlord.* As we have drawn the curves, the most profitable wage rate will be w_2. As population grows, however, the pressure on the landlord to increase the number of villagers in his employ will increase. If employment is raised from N_1 to N_2 with no offsetting increase in productivity, work must be spread, just as it is in the peasant proprietorships. The weekly wage rate will be reduced and the hours of work diminished. This process can be offset by technological progress within the traditional sector, such as introduction of higher yield seed strains. But for such technological progress to offset continuous population growth, it too must be continuous, or at least intermittent. Obviously, for workers in village landlord enterprises to move to a higher indifference curve, such as $w\text{-}I_2$, despite continuing population

---

*Generally speaking there will be one maximum profit position, but the possibility of multiple equilibrium is also clear.

growth, technological progress in these enterprises must be both continuous and dramatic. Once again real hope lies outside the poor region and traditional sector, in a rate of expansion in the rich sector that will permit reduced numbers in the poor region.

The Transitional Sector in Developing Countries

In many developing countries there are intermediate regions characterized by predominance of the transitional sector, with medium-sized agricultural or small industrial enterprises, utilizing traditional techniques and relatively little capital. Examples would be the smallholders' rubber enterprises in Indonesia and Malaya, copra enterprises in Sulawesi (Indonesia), the Italian farming areas in Southern Brazil, olive groves and refineries in Greece, etc. The operation of these enterprises sometimes resembles that of the "village landlord," but frequently the enterprise is large enough, while still using traditional labor-intensive techniques, to escape the social sanctions of the village and move more closely to the "capitalist landlord" mode of operation. The wage rate paid to hired labor in these enterprises tends to be somewhere between the income of peasant proprietors and wages paid in the rich region. Frequently workers can accept employment in transitional enterprises without leaving their village, and even if they have to move from one area to another, the mode of life changes less than if they move into the rich region and modern sector. Thus the premium that must be paid to attract workers from the villages is somewhat lower than in the rich region.*

The interactions between transitional and traditional sectors (or regions) do not differ much from those between modern and traditional sectors. Technological improvements, capital accumulation, or improved terms of trade may raise marginal productivity in the transitional region. The result will be some increase in employment in the transitional region, initially at the prevailing wage. Consequently the numbers in the poor region can be (momentarily) reduced. Such a reduction will permit higher wages in the poor region and longer hours. However, the rise in wages in the poor region will also raise wages in the transitional region, tending to choke off the transfer of labor from poor to transitional regions.

The main reason for adding the transitional region to the analysis is that the technologies used in transitional enterprises tend to be

---

*Caloric intake usually rises with a move from traditional to transitional or modern sector, but the increased nutritional requirements are more a reflection of longer hours than of increased energy-expenditure per hour.

much more labor-intensive, and somewhat less education-intensive, than in modern enterprises. With a given development budget and existing levels of skills, therefore, a more rapid rate of development may emerge, and a "ratchet effect" may be more easily produced, if investment is concentrated in the transitional region rather than in either the rich or the poor region. The potential contributions of transitional sectors and regions have been somewhat neglected in the development plans and programs of developing countries.

Transitional Regions in Advanced Countries

As pointed out above, advanced countries do not have regions of any size that can be regarded as "poor" in the same sense as the poor regions of less developed countries. The difference lies not so much in levels of welfare—the "poor" of Gaspésie, Quebec, may well be fundamentally worse off than the "poor" of Bali—but in economic structure. We simply do not find in countries like Canada or the United States regions of any size—even of the size of the administrative regions of Quebec—with two-thirds of the labor force engaged in peasant agriculture, using little or no capital, and consuming a significant proportion of their own produce. We may indeed find small pockets, perhaps whole counties, where conditions are not very different from those of poor regions or traditional sectors of developing countries, but the proportion of the total population living in such regions is very small.

We are thinking, then, of regions like the East of Quebec, Prince Edward Island, northern New Brunswick, Appalachia, parts of the American Southwest, parts of Mississippi and Alabama, and generally of the retarded regions of North America. Levels of per capita income are significantly below those of the rich regions of the same country. Depending on how small the regions are, the gap may exceed 100 percent, as in the case of Gaspésie versus the metropolitan region of Montreal, or even more for individual counties. Modern enterprises exist within these regions, but their share in total employment is small. Most workers will be engaged by "capitalist landlords" (or "capitalist employers") in transitional enterprises, including low-productivity services. Some will be engaged under conditions not dissimilar from those of peasant proprietors in developing countries, except that they will as a rule be on a w-l curve where the choice between output and leisure is determined by psychological rather than physiological factors.

From here on the analysis proceeds in much the same way as for interactions between rich and poor regions in developing countries. Expansion in the rich region, whether due to innovations, capital accumulation, or improved terms of trade (growth of markets as such would require capital accumulation to meet increased demand), will permit a transfer of labor from transitional to rich region. But if the result is a rise in wage rates in the transitional region, the expansion of the rich region may be choked off. If, on the other hand, progress begins in the transitional region, any increase in wage rates there will also raise wages in the rich region, leading to release of workers from the rich region. These will tend to seek employment in the transitional sector and region, since isoquants are more "well-behaved" there. Increased numbers in the transitional region will tend to prevent any rise in wages and welfare, despite the initial rise in productivity. Expansion of the rich region offers more hope than anything that can happen in the transitional region alone. Given population growth as well, improvement in the transitional region is virtually hopeless without expansion in the rich region.

It should perhaps be pointed out that the transitional regions of advanced countries do not as a rule have any phenomenon comparable to either the "village landlord," or the case of peasant proprietorship with a convention of spreading income by spreading work with the consequent reduction of average hours and productivity. Instead, open unemployment and underemployment appear, together with low-productivity employment with nominally standard hours of work. (The clerk in the corner store may be there all day, but serve few customers and read a comic book to pass the time). Government transfer payments replace village social security systems.

A THREE-REGION MODEL

Borrowing a leaf from the Fei and Ranis book, we can now pull this analysis together by showing the rich, poor, and transitional regions simultaneously on the same diagram. This device is, however, somewhat awkward, and we shall confine ourselves to one or two simple cases for illustrative purposes.

In Figure 10.6 we show the rich region (modern sector) in the upper third of the diagram, the poor sector and region in the lower third, and the transitional one in between. The total labor force is divided between the rich, poor, and transitional regions. If the "poor" region is truly poor and traditional, and if it has the common convention of work-spreading, we begin our analysis of it with the number of workers left over from the rich and transitional regions, N_p. Weekly wage rates (incomes) will be $w^{P}{}_1$, hours will be $H^{P}{}_1$, the hourly wage rate $\bar{w}$. In the rich region, employment is determined by wage rates and marginal productivity, with technical coefficients close to being

FIGURE 10.6

A Three Region Model

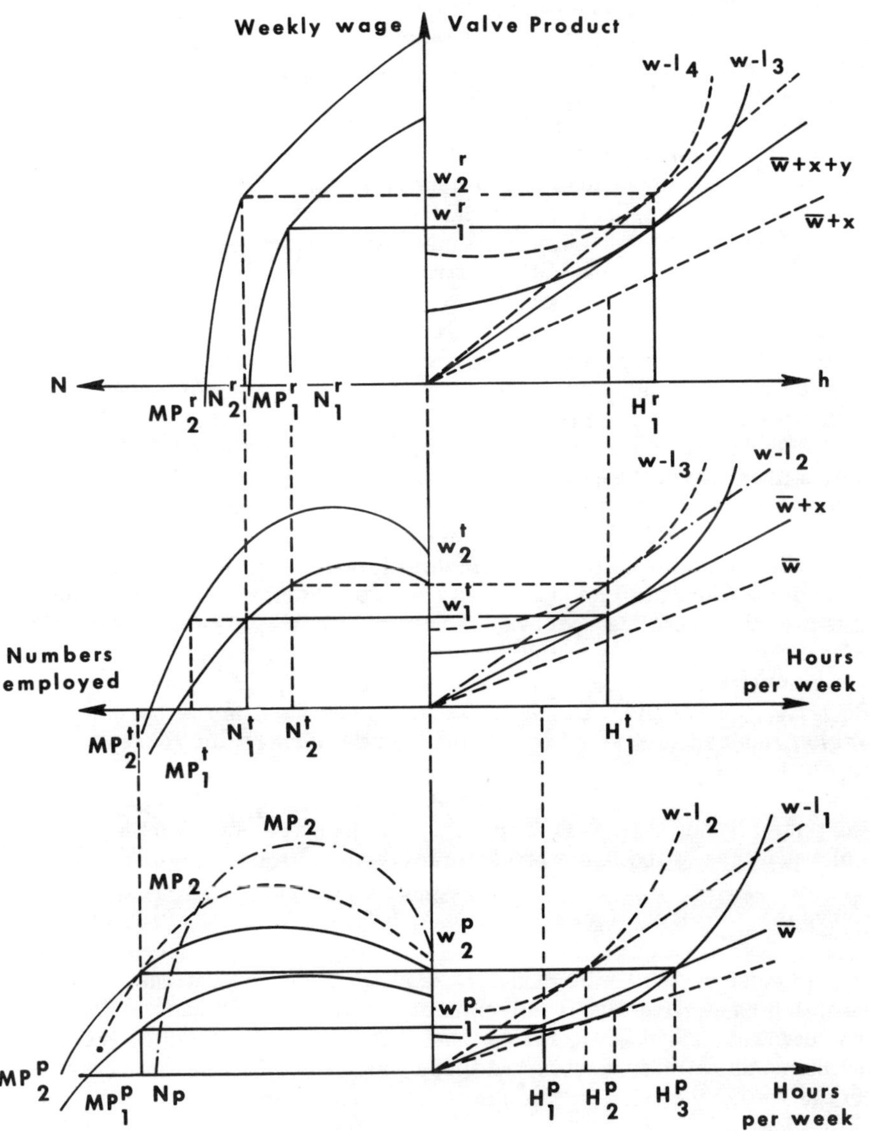

fixed except in the neighborhood of equilibrium.*

If we are concerned only with the transitional and rich regions of an advanced country, employment will be at the maximum profit position for capitalist employers in both regions. In the transitional region, the isoquants are reasonably well behaved and the marginal productivity curves are of "normal" shape. The w-l curves in both sectors will then be above the minimum, with psychological rather than physiological factors determining the choice between income and leisure. The weekly wage rate in the transitional region will be $w^t{}_1$, hours will be $H^t{}_1$, the hourly wage rate $\bar{w} + x_1$, the relevant marginal productivity curve $MP^t{}_1$, and employment $N^t{}_1$. In the rich region, the original weekly wage rate will be $w^r{}_1$, the hourly wage rate $\bar{w} + x + y$, hours $H^r{}_1$, and employment $N^r{}_1$.

Now let us assume that productivity increases in the modern sector and rich region. The marginal productivity curve shifts upward to $MP^r{}_2$. More workers will be attracted from the transitional to the poor region at the constant wage. As soon as open unemployment and underemployment in the transitional sector are wholly absorbed, employment in the transitional sector can be reduced. (More accurately, once all unemployed and underemployed willing to move have been absorbed into the modern sector, employment in the transitional sector can fall. Cho's concept of "marginal men"—those willing to shift either way in response to marginal changes in employment conditions—is pertinent for transitional regions just as for poor regions.) Government transfer payments replace village social security systems in making it possible for the unemployed, underemployed, and disguised unemployed to choose to stay where they are. However, when this "turning point" is reached, w^t will rise to $w^t{}_2$. The consequent increase in wage rates in the rich region will tend to put an end to the cumulative expansion, unless there are further increases in productivity. In our diagram, we end with employment in the transitional region reduced to $N^t{}_2$ and employment in the rich region increased to N_2.

Let us now assume that the initial improvement takes place in the poor region. In a work-spreading traditional sector, employment must continue at the same level (or increase with population growth). The initial shift from $MP^p{}_1$ to $MP^p{}_2$ permits a rise in wages and an increase in hours. Hours may rise to $H^p{}_3$ with no overall improve-

---

*Most modern enterprises have a number of operations, some of which have virtually fixed technical coefficients and some of which do not. Thus the Stanvac refinery at Bombay, when visited by the author, was fully automated and there was no use for additional men in the refinery itself—but the lawns were cut by hordes of coolies with sickles.

ment in welfare, or to $H^p{}_2$ with an increase in welfare. However, the increase in hours worked per week brings a secondary shift in the marginal productivity curves, from $MP^p{}_2$ to MP''_2, if there is no rise in welfare, or to MP'_2 if there is. Not even a village society will wish to add one man-week of employment if the man must eat more than he produces; the alternative is a reduction of hours of work, with no reduction of income, all around. As we have drawn the diagram, $H^p{}_3$ is an untenable position—the new equilibrium will be established at $H^p{}_2$.

But the process does not stop there. The rise in wages in the poor region will raise wages in both transitional and rich regions as well. The result will be a release of workers from both of these regions, and particularly from the transitional region where isoquants are relatively well behaved. In the rich region or modern sector, substantial numbers of workers can be released in the short run only by creating excess capacity, but increasing wage rates will stimulate still further the search for labor-saving innovations in the rich region. Once again it is clear that opportunities for rising levels of living in the traditional sector are extremely limited without expansion of either the transitional sector or the modern sector, or both. This statement becomes even more pertinent when population growth and an inherent tendency toward labor-saving innovation in the modern sector are added.

Similar conclusions are reached if we begin the process with the transitional sector. Here we shall assume, for the sake of convenience, that we have only "capitalist landlords." The initial wage rate is $w^t{}_1$ and employment is $N^t{}_1$. The marginal productivity curve shifts from $MP^t{}_1$ to $MP^t{}_2$. At the given wage rate, employment can expand by drawing on the traditional sector. (Wages are higher in the rich region, and while some "marginal men" may prefer to move back to the transitional region with improved working conditions, they are not likely to be large in numbers in most true situations.) Any rise in wage rates in the transitional sector will raise wage rates in the modern sector as well. The result will be some release of workers in the rich region (or, in a dynamic situation with population growth and capital accumulation, failure to absorb the increase in the labor force). Some of the workers released (or some of the addition to the labor supply) will seek employment in the transitional sector, stopping the process of rising welfare there. If there is a poor region, some of the workers released from the modern sector (or some of the increase in labor supply) will seek employment there, where isoquants are most "well behaved," bringing absolute declines in levels of welfare.

Once again the importance of expansion in the rich region and modern sector is clear.

CONCLUSION: NEED FOR AN INTEGRATED APPROACH

Our major conclusion is that there is little hope of solving the problems of poor regions and traditional sectors, or even of transitional regions and sectors, by measures confined to those regions and sectors alone. Raising incomes and employment together is virtually impossible unless the modern sector is expanding. Given population growth and a tendency for innovation to be labor-saving, the expansion of the modern sector must be even more vigorous to permit solution of problems in poor and transitional regions. In developing countries, solutions consist of implanation of elements of the modern sector in the poor region, thus bringing structural change to the poor region, or migration out of the poor region to the transitional or rich region. In advanced countries with no truly "poor" region, the solution may lie either in implanting a modern sector in the transitional regions or in encouraging migration from these regions and providing employment elsewhere.

It is clear enough that a solution that entails migration is much easier, from a purely economic point of view, than a solution consisting only of implanation of elements of the modern sector in the poor or transitional regions. There are good reasons for modern enterprises being where they are. In the case of Quebec, for example, there is reason to believe that in trying to pull the modern sector eastward from Montreal, we would be fighting not only the polar attraction of Montreal, but the whole line of developmental force—as yet little understood—running from Chicago through Detroit and Windsor, Western Ontario and Toronto. At the moment, Montreal seems to be the end of this line.

Implanting enough of a modern sector, in the form of key industries, to convert a small stagnant city into a *pôle de croissance*, or even a center of attraction, strong enough to eliminate unemployment and raise per capita incomes in transitional or poor regions is a formidable task. The locational disadvantages, in terms of remoteness from major markets, strategic raw materials, and cheap power, and limitations on public services are often overwhelming. For the scientifically-oriented industries that comprise today's category of footloose industries, the first three of these deficiencies may not be insuperable barriers, but all that we know about such industries suggests that the major locational advantages lie in the presence of educational and research institutions, cultural activities, varied recreational facilities, and a general atmosphere of scientific, intellectual, and cultural excellence that makes a particular center attractive to the scientific, technical, and managerial personnel who constitute the "scarce factor" for such enterprises. Such a list of advantages is hardly a description of small towns that exist as centers of poor or transitional regions.

* * *

COMMENT BY NATHANIEL H. LEFF

The paper by Lawrence J. Lau and Pan A. Yotopoulos is a significant theoretical contribution. These comments are simply suggestions for possible improvements in the specification of the model to make it an even richer and more useful tool for analysis in the specific area of the employment problem in less developed countries.

In its present form, the model is, explicitly, a short-run equilibrium model concerned with the optimal combination of the variable input labor with a given stock of capital. However, if one is interested in intermediate and long-run conditions affecting employment, a model that includes the effects of capital accumulation would be more appropriate. This is especially the case if technical change is embodied in new capital goods.

One is struck by the authors' treatment of agricultural unemployment. As I understand the model, given the assumption that total labor demand in agriculture must be equal to the total labor supplied, what some observers or policymakers might call unemployment is here simply called leisure. Another disturbing feature is the assumption that as total population increases, the population in agriculture is somehow held constant. These assumptions come dangerously close to sweeping key aspects of the employment problem under the rug.

One might also raise the possibility of modifying the specification of some of the model's equations. For example, might not the supply of labor in the agricultural sector also be affected by wages or employment opportunities (or both) in the nonagricultural sector? In addition, a key feature of many firms in the agricultural sector is that they are also households. Might not the family nature of these firms lead them to a set of optimizing conditions different from those of a strictly commercial enterprise?

Lau and Yotopoulos might well have specified a far richer model related to the employment problem. As their model now stands, they consider the size of the population in the agricultural sector as exogenously determined. In a long-run context, however, they might include and estimate the micro decisionmaking process which determines the birth rate and thus affects the growth of population. Recent work by Paul Schultz[11] and Maurice Wilkinson[12] has demonstrated the utility of such an approach to the determination of fertility behavior.

These comments and suggestions, however, are not intended to detract from the analytical contribution that Lau and Yotopoulos have here given us.

Turning now to Higgins's very interesting paper, I should like to make some brief comments on its general approach.

The employment problem in development is not in fact a discovery of the Second Development Decade. The basic analytics of the problem were presented by Richard Eckaus in his classic paper of 1955[13]. Aside from the work of Todaro[14], very little has been added since. Moreover, planning models focusing on employment have also been around since at least the early 1960s, which is to say that, for some time now, we have known why the employment problem arises and what are some of the things that could be done to ameliorate it. If these measures have not been implemented by policymakers in the less developed countries, the blame does not lie with development economists.

The factor-market distortions created by government policies are well known. Even if the elasticities of factor-substitution may not be so great as might be hoped, this is no reason not to take the fullest advantage of such possibilities as do exist for a given vector of final demand. Moreover, government policies affecting expenditure have rarely focused on generating demand for activities with the greatest employment-creating effects. For example, few of the activities singled out by a recent study as having the greatest employment-generating effects for India rank high on the Government of India's list of priority industries[15]. Similarly, government allocation policies have all too often favored the "modern" sector with capital, import, and credit allocations, while denying these to the "transitional" sector which, as Higgins points out, may have higher labor-output coefficients.

One might also question the role attributed by Higgins to technology as a source of the employment problem. Though their results can be interpreted in different ways, the international estimates for two-digit industries by Arrow, Chenery, Minhas, and Solow surely did not demonstrate the existence of fixed coefficients[16]. Moreover, it is also not clear that the total effect of the biases in technical progress has been to reduce employment. In United States manufacturing, technical change has had a labor-augmenting bias[17]. However, as Salter has shown, because of its effects on costs, relative prices, demand, and output, the effect of such productivity increase has generally been to increase employment.[18]

More generally, focusing attention on the supposed employment-reducing characteristics of modern technology developed in economically more advanced countries is counter-productive from the standpoint of ameliorating the employment problem in less developed countries. First, it fosters the belief that if only more conferences would call for the creation of a new technology "better suited to the needs of LDCs" the employment problem would miraculously be resolved. Secondly, this emphasis on "technology" gives intellectuals and policymakers in the less developed countries a convenient scapegoat to castigate for their employment problem, and diverts attention from the policy measures—well within their reach—that could alleviate it.

Apart from policy actions in the areas cited above, one must mention policies that supposedly deal with the most obvious culprit and source of the employment problem—high rates of population increase. Given current rates of saving and capital formation in less developed countries—themselves lowered by high birth and dependency rates[19]—no less developed country can hope to deal adequately with its long-run employment problem so long as population is growing at annual rates of 2-3 percent. Under these conditions, it is no service to the less developed countries to focus on "technology," and divert attention from other conditions more amenable to policy action.

Finally, it is surprising to find Higgins ending his paper with the conclusion that resolution of the employment problem depends essentially on developments in the "modern" sector. Surely this emphasis on growth in the modern sector is precisely what we have had during the past two decades, with the disappointing employment results which he himself has recounted. One suspects that to the extent that the employment situation can be significantly ameliorated despite high rates of population growth, it will depend largely on conditions and policies adopted with respect to the "transitional" and backward sectors.

One final comment. Both papers take the micro decisions affecting employment as being determined largely by conditions exogenous to the micro unit. This approach is a plausible one, but it underlines again the need for sensible macro policies in this area.

CHAPTER

11

MICROECONOMIC THEORY AND ECONOMIC DEVELOPMENT: REFLECTIONS ON THE CONFERENCE

Richard R. Nelson

NEOCLASSICAL PRICE THEORY AND ECONOMIC DEVELOPMENT

A dialogue, sometimes heated, sometimes searching, ran through both days of the conference. It was concerned with the relevance of neoclassical price theory to the modeling of microeconomic development problems and patterns. Several papers were consciously presented as, and others later taken to be, inconsistent with the neoclassical model. On the other hand, several participants consistently took the point of view that neoclassical theory was broad enough to encompass the phenomena in question. The discussion surrounding Leibenstein's paper was particularly sharp. Whether a particular phenomenon is consistent with neoclassical theory or not clearly depends on what one takes that theory to be. It is apparent that there are at least two views.

A number of conference participants articulated and defended the ability of the neoclassical theory to encompass and absorb a tremendous variety of things from quality variables associated with factors of production, to firms that maximize things other than profit, to perhaps even firms that maximize nothing at all because it is costly to do so. From this perspective, the theory is seen as a set of coat hangers and organizing concepts enabling people within the economics community to talk with and understand each other through a common language. All readers of Thomas Kuhn understand this kind of a role for theory and recognize that it extends to fields like physics that purport to have much tighter notions of theory than do we economists. Clearly this is one important role. But this perspective on theory has some difficulties. In particular the "broad paradigm" concept conflicts with another notion of what a theory is—a set of statements that are in principle refutable. It is not at all clear what evidence those who take the broad view would accept as evidence to refute the theory. What will stop us from—as Kuhn has described in physics—endlessly adding epicycles to the theory to patch it up?

Those at the conference who argued that neoclassical theory did not fit well took a narrower view of theory. This view was never spelled out. One might try to do so by articulating a sharper version of the theory, a version that we sophisticates may not believe in but which we tend to employ in our formalisms. I would argue that there are three assumptions in the neoclassical theory in its simple and pristine, eminently refutable, and therefore powerful form. One is the hypothesis of a production function that exists for all firms in all countries. A production function exists in the sense that if you look across firms or countries and observe different combinations of inputs and outputs, these are to be interpreted as points on that function. In the simple version of the theory, there are no costs of attaining or moving along the function. A firm is simply on it.

Second, firms are viewed as competent, and common. They are competent in that they know how to operate this production function. They are competent also in that they can and do optimize. Since all firms are competent, like clerks they are interchangeable. No firm has any particular occult capabilities with respect to technique or managerial ability. This is implicit in the simpleminded and sharp version of the theory.

Third, industries are in equilibrium in the explicit sense that all units are in a position of their individual optimum, given what the other units are doing. We also usually invoke the subsidiary assumption that the equilibrium is that of a competitive market. While this is not essential, we tend to have analytic trouble when we abandon it, and so we generally make the subsidiary assumption. From the subsidiary assumption, plus all the others, flows our ability to associate factor price with factor marginal productivity, etc.

Something like this version of the theory is implicit or explicit in what we teach our undergraduates and first-year graduate students, and it dominates the formal theory literature. If this is accepted, it should be apparent that this theory will not do to characterize economic development. It is an open question whether the phenomena discussed can be squared with a neoclassical theory viewed broadly enough so as to include general utility maximization, costs of change, costs of decisionmaking, R and D as investment, etc. It may be that the required broadening and complicating of the theory is so cumbersome that it may be worthwhile to look for another basic theory. In any case, with few exceptions, the papers at the conference were not within the traditional narrow price theory paradigm.

For example, Hayami and Ruttan (H-R) worked with the concept of a metaproduction function, not a production function of the traditional kind. It is worth considering why they felt compelled to use the new terms. Clearly their production function is not a production function in the traditional textbook sense. To move along the function, to apply more fertilizer or increase mechanization without drastically diminishing returns, new seeds or new machines must be created. At the least, the creation of a new part of the production function takes resources, and it may take creativity and luck as well. This is consistent with an "R and D as investment" extension of the paradigm. However, once one introduces research and development as a form of investment, one has to be concerned with problems of externalities to a much greater extent than in the narrow version of the theory. In addition to the research and development costs of creating a new point on the production function, H-R discuss other resource costs and problems involved in getting to the new part of the production function. Finus Welch, and earlier Edmund Phelps and I, have developed models in which education is important as a factor of production because the production function is changing. The returns to education in these models are largely a dynamic phenomenon. Yet while the H-R metaproduction function differs in significant respects from the production function of simple neoclassical theory, H-R nevertheless argue that the patterns of inputs and outputs that they observed in the United States and Japan are consistent with and explainable by the kind of factor substitution mechanisms usually associated with movement along a traditional production function.

Leibenstein's paper is an explicit assault on the "competent clerk" vision of the firm, but most of the other papers were also inconsistent with that image. Several stressed that firms were often incompetent. Others viewed the firm in terms of innovation. Innovation is simply not a clerklike activity. Schumpeter has stressed that building a new road and walking along it are entirely different things. This is not to deny that there are a number of sectors in a developing economy where the competent clerk image is appropriate. I understand that several studies have suggested that peasant agriculture looks much like the circular flow world of Schumpeter's Chapter I. But this is not the cutting edge of development. At the cutting edge we apparently are observing very unclerklike behavior. Somehow our economic theory of the firm in a less developed country will have to come to grips with the kind of discussion presented by Vanneman on the personal style of resource accumulators and rationalizers. One whole session was predicated on the assumption that there is something special about subsidiaries of foreign firms, particularly American firms, another explicit departure from the traditional view that firms are interchangeable clerks.

Uneasiness with viewing a sector as in equilibrium was less explicit in the papers. However, it is surely awkward to view a sector where significant innovation is taking place as being in equilibrium in any traditional sense. It is not clear whether the type of sectoral analysis that Higgins has developed should be interpreted as equilibrium. But then one can be confused as to how to interpret Ranis-Fei. Still it does not seem plausible to characterize sectors undergoing rapid change as being in equilibrium. It may be useful to refer briefly to the development of manufacturing industry in Colombia. It is apparent that there is now, and has been for some time, a vast dispersion among firms in Colombian industry in terms of their profitability. Profitable firms are expanding and unprofitable ones tending to contract. The movement of manufacturing development is describable in terms of movement toward equilibrium. But the state of conditions is not characterizable as an equilibrium state nor is it safe to bet that any meaningful equilibrium will be achieved in a short period of time.

If all this is basically correct, a large share of the papers presented and discussed at this conference have broken away from the simple form of the neoclassical allegory. The papers have described a world in which new technologies are unfolding; firms are innovating, adopting, and responding; industries are moving toward a moving equilibrium, squeezing out the old and bringing in the new, but not in equilibrium.

KEY QUESTIONS IN A DYNAMIC MICROECONOMICS OF ECONOMIC DEVELOPMENT

Viewing development in this way poses a number of key questions that do not receive adequate treatment within the traditional framework of microeconomic theory. One is the question of what is involved in technology transfer. Second, what is the role of indigenous research and development? Third, what is the connection between the structural changes taking place in the less developed countries and the rate of unemployment?

In manufacturing industry, in many of the major social service industries like power and transportation, and even to a lesser degree in agriculture, the development process involves to a considerable extent introducing and learning to use effectively technologies that have been employed for some time in a developed country. Once we have freed ourselves from the concept of a simpleminded cross-country production function, it is apparent that what is taking place transcends less developed countries, simply moving up the production function as their physical and human capital resources are augmented. The technology transfer process involves transfer of information in an explicit sense. It seems important to understand and to develop a model to handle the kinds of information and processes at work.

The international corporation is surely an important vehicle to study. A key research task is the careful specification of what a company in the United States knows that a person establishing a company in Colombia would not know. Anyone can specify this at a superficial level. Can we learn to treat it in the context of a formal model? Similarly, it seems important to know more about who gains from technology transfer through the route of the international corporation, and how. The traditional argument is that the international corporation benefits from the profits, and the host country benefits from the labor income, taxes, and so on. The consideration of labor income in the calculation usually stems from the observation of high unemployment in the host country. But there are serious problems as to whether the advent of modern technology in a developing country actually increases employment. But once we admit that the international corporation brings a new kind of knowledge and experience into the host country, then specific attention should be given to hunting down and identifying spill-over benefits. To what extent do people in the host country receive training and experience working in the international corporation that they then apply elsewhere in the economy? If this factor is considerable, who pays for the training? To what extent does the presence of a subsidiary of, say, an American corporation provide stimulus and the model for technological and managerial updating of domestic firms? We know much less than we ought to about these questions.

We also should know much more than we do about substitutes for international corporations as vehicles for picking up foreign technology. The Japanese, of course, have largely resisted the foreign-owned corporations and worked largely through licensing arrangements. What are the costs and what are the benefits of these two routes? Were there special resource attributes that enable the Japanese to take the second route? How much of the required technological knowledge is imparted to students of engineering and management in the course of their formal college curriculum? Do they need to study in an advanced country to acquire this knowledge? Is the role of scientific and technical formal education to enable one to learn advanced technology quickly, but only when one has practical experience with it? These all are important questions.

To what extent must or can technological borrowing be augmented by domestic research and development? The H-R paper argues persuasively that agricultural development requires more than simple technological borrowing. Soil type, temperature, rainfall conditions, etc., tend to be unique to the area and subarea in question, and seeds, fertilizers, and practices suitable for one place (particularly the developed countries) may be ill-adapted to another. In the H-R case study, the returns to research and development were clearly high. The same kinds of conditions most likely apply with respect to medicine. The less developed countries cannot simply borrow but must establish their own research capabilities.

In manufacturing and modern communications and transportation, development seems to proceed by a much less adulterated process of technology transfer. What works in the developed countries works in the underdeveloped countries. However, the fact that it works and is profitable does not mean that it cannot be improved upon. A considerable literature has developed around the idea that the special circumstances of a local environment—in particular, small scale of operation, high cost of capital, lack of skills in the work force, and nuances of local materials—make technology modification desirable. That statement, of course, hinges on some implicit assumptions about the cost of doing the needed research and development. Little industrial research and development of the implied kinds appears to be taking place in the less developed countries. Nor has there been much study of the output and costs of the industrial research and development that has been undertaken. Such a study should be high on any priority list of research topics. More broadly, it seems important to examine the extent to which a national industrial research and development policy and availability of local engineers and applied scientists can reduce dependence upon foreign corporations for modern technology, the relative effects of these two means on incomes of nationals, exports, etc. Here the Japanese case seems particularly worth examining in detail, and also Mexico's and India's experience with publicly supported applied industrial research and development.

A third major set of questions relates to unemployment and income distribution as a consequence of structural transformation, a topic hardly discussed at this conference. Once again, it may be useful to refer to Colombia. Much of the urban unemployment in that country can be diagnosed as the result of structural transformation. To oversimplify, in Colombia one can identify two groups of firms. One group, generally newcomers or a few old firms that have transformed themselves, consists of firms roughly similar to typical firms in the same industry in the more developed countries—somewhat smaller, with somewhat lower value added per worker, capital per worker, and labor quality—but using more or less the same kind of technology and recognizable as the same kind of animal. The other group is comprised of traditional small craft firms using significantly less in the way of modern equipment, quite different skills, and creating a far lower value added per worker. As development has proceeded, the modern sector has expanded relative to the traditional sector. This is the principal source of the observed productivity growth. In many sectors, modern enterprise seems to be expanding at the expense of traditional enterprise, driving the latter out of business. While employment in the modern sector is expanding, employment in the traditional sector is contracting. This is why employment growth has been so slow and sometimes even negative, and why a significant unemployment problem has emerged. One may speculate on why the price and market system has not coped adequately with the situation. However, this kind of phenomenon is clearly a high priority one for research on the microeconomics of development.

HOW MUCH PSYCHOLOGY AND SOCIOLOGY DOES DEVELOPMENT ECONOMICS NEED?

A number of discussions during the conference explicitly or implicitly posed the question: Does traditional economic analysis need to be extended to encompass more psychology and sociology than it does at present? It must surely be apparent that once one abandons the simple version of the neoclassical theory and considers explicitly innovation, adaptation, adjustment costs, frictions, and firms with a variety of possible motivations, one has let psychology and sociology in through the back door. We no longer have a model that can rely on the simple behavioral hypothesis that firms and consumers correctly maximize profits. We must now deal with considerations of what opportunities they perceive, when they perceive them, the risks they are willing to bear, the constraints and norms they face, and the kinds of benefits and costs involved. The question is do we treat these variables implicitly or explicitly, and if explicitly in what way?

A good case can be made that though economists must recognize that these factors are important, and that a simpleminded profit-maximizing model is not an adequate description of behavior, they need not work with them explicitly. In many of the microeconomics models admitting utility functions that include arguments other than profits, the signs of the partial derivatives of the decision variables with respect to external market variables remain the same as they do in the profit-maximizing theory. It is possible that while psychological and sociological factors influence the magnitudes of the coefficients of structural equations, they do not influence their signs, nor do they cause them to be unstable.

The case that economic modeling must take explicit account of the psychological and sociological variables would seem to rest on two arguments. One is that these noneconomic variables have a life of their own, and can vary over time. Thus the economist must be aware of their magnitude at any time and understand how changes in their magnitude can change the economic structural equations.

The second is that in tracing through the consequences of proposed policy changes or predicted economic changes, the conclusions one reaches are dependent upon whether and how one treats psychological and sociological factors. Both of these arguments are plausible. However, they do not weigh the costs of more complex modeling. What is particularly unclear is how the economist should begin augmenting his models to take into account these other classes of consideration.

One possibility is simply to try to develop measures of the appropriate variables and to build these into our structural systems. This is what Irma Adleman has tried to do empirically, and a considerable portion of Herbert Simon's work of a decade ago was concerned with just this. In terms of this kind of modeling, it would seem that the first steps should be to build various political structure variables into the model. Economists have to learn to understand better than we do at present the impact of various policies on economic development. We also need to understand better the effects of various kinds of economic developments on politics and hence on future economic policy.

One suspects that it is more promising to try to build explicitly behavioral models of firms in the spirit of Cyert and March and of governmental organizations following the lead of Crecine. In these models there is no explicit distinction between economic variables or variables of any other kind. The models permit, indeed call for, detailed specification of habitual behavior. Into these models one can also build a relatively rich analysis of goals, aspirations, and norms. The tricky part is specification of what triggers innovative behavior and the nature of the search process. Perhaps this makes this kind of modeling particularly suitable for the microeconomics of economic development. Perhaps the most important effect of the conference has been in making us focus on processes and patterns of innovation.

Detailed behavioral modeling at the micro unit level runs into difficulties when there is considerable diversity among the micro units. And the micro unit modeling approach, unless complemented by analysis on a more macro level, misses the fact that what really matters may be better describable in terms of distributions of attributes and dynamic properties of those distributions. Was a certain successful entrepreneur particularly important? If he had not existed, would other men have done roughly the same thing? Thus, for analysis of innovation within a sector, we might want to proceed by trying to characterize the relative number of innovative firms in the sector, the extent of which innovators tend to expand or are constrained from expanding, the lags involved and the extent to which other firms imitate the innovators, etc. In turn, these characteristics may possibly be traced back to the psychological and sociological environment.

CHAPTER

12

CURRENT STATE AND DESIRABLE DIRECTIONS IN ECONOMIC DEVELOPMENT RESEARCH

(Summary of Exchanges by Participants)

At the conclusion of the conference the participants were asked to react to the conference in general and to Nelson's reflections in particular, as well as to suggest desirable directions for research. These comments were taped during the last session of the conference or mailed soon after its conclusion. The following is a summary of the major themes.

THE RÔLE OF MICROECONOMIC THEORY

One suggestion (by Yotopoulos) was that the path for micro research on economic development to follow should be similar to the one laid out by macroeconomics, where Keynes's "simple, pristine, eminently refutable and powerful models" provided the foundation, and Kuznets indicated what data should and could be gathered to test these models. The work that followed resulted in a better understanding of macroeconomics, including increased sophistication of the models.

A similar path could prove beneficial in the study of micro aspects of development. Instead of everyone having his own simple model, we might start with the "neoclassical" model in the public domain. In searching for proper and usable data, we might also find a Kuznets along the way and end up with more understanding of development, as well as making the models more sophisticated and consistent with the real world.

Leibenstein did not agree that this was the best way to approach problems of development, since the pristine neoclassical model does not fit our experience. The point can be clarified by distinguishing between two elements of the model—rationality and substitution.

Since nobody would assert that his model or ideas are "irrational," focusing on the rationality element is not especially helpful. A more fruitful exposition could be achieved by showing that in development one can get something without giving up something else (as with innovation), thereby negating the basic element of substitution in the neoclassical model, where you cannot get something without giving up something else. Since by now it is obvious that there is no clear-cut association between the rate of investment and the rate of economic growth, i.e., that a substantial part of development does not involve substitution, the neoclassical model would not be the appropriate one to employ.

Higgins referred to the difficulties created by the equilibrium feature of neoclassical theory. In development we are interested in cumulative growth, and policymakers should not be concerned with equilibrium or with moving from one equilibrium to another. Fishlow was also skeptical whether the general equilibrium type of pursuits in the context of bettering the theory of the firm, as suggested by Nelson, "is the way in which micro analysis ought to go in terms of the problem of development."

Leff's response to Leibenstein's statements focused on the apparent absence of massive shifts in the production functions of LDCs (reported by Bruton), which *a priori* development theory would lead one to expect. He suggested that the explanation may not lie in a lack of capabilities in LDCs (as implied by Leibenstein), but rather in the economic environment created by government policies, as suggested by Bruton.

THE ROLE OF GOVERNMENT

Several participants emphasized the importance of government, both in creating the framework and environment within which micro units operate and in its direct participation in economic activity, especially investment.

Sjaastad lamented the lack of attention to the public sector. In many LDCs, some 50 percent of all investment is done by the public sector, yet, in spite of this, and in spite of the fact that such investment is subject to the same sort of micro conditions faced by private-sector investment, we do not know what the rate of return has been.

Fishlow followed this up by calling attention to the distortions of prices by the public sector through the setting of exchange rates, prices of public utilities, and policies leading to inflation. These may explain the alleged unsatisfactory contribution of firms to development.

Nelson concurred in the importance of the public sector. Further, he maintained that the social and political environment seems to be responsible for generating innovative behavior.

DESIRABLE DIRECTIONS FOR RESEARCH

As might be expected, most participants considered the research they were engaged in, both in term of topic and approach, as highly desirable. This is already reflected in the discussion summarized above. Following are some of the more explicit proposals.

Dissatisfaction with the current state of development economics and the results of the First Development Decade is reflected in some of the proposals. In some cases, it took the form of downgrading growth (measured in per capita income) in favor of concentrating research and policy measures on employment (Higgins), income distribution, and welfare (Fishlow). Adelman warned that going to the other extreme of ignoring economic growth entirely may produce disastrous consequences. Unemployment in many LDCs is largely a result of policy distortions in favor of capital intensity and cannot be blamed on the goal of economic growth.

Most participants seemed to agree that some "compromise objective function"—to use Adelman's phrase—that combines concern with growth with some of the other goals would be the best course to pursue.

Sjaastad suggested that more study of the successful LDCs—e.g., Mexico—would put us in a better position to understand the causes of both success and failure in others. In this he was joined by Nelson. Similarly, we need more work on the quantitative consequences of policies. This, of course, ties in with Adelman's comments mentioned above. The high capital-labor ratio in many industries in the LDCs has resulted from such government measures as underpricing of capital and overpricing of unskilled labor.

There are other government contributions deserving study besides its share in total investment and its effect on factor proportion. Ruttan emphasized the important role of government experimental stations in inducing technological change. While he and Hayami are already studying this aspect for the agricultural sector, similar work should be done in fields such as health and environmental sciences and the related technologies.

The second important goal of research emphasized by Ruttan was the international diffusion of research and development capacity. This had been, of course, at the back of the minds of other participants, and development economists in general. Multinational firms are often considered vehicles for such diffusion. Higgins advocated "engineering pilot plant research" of factor endowments and desirable factor proportions in LDCs, as is now being contemplated under the sponsorship of the Canadian government. Much of the literature on entrepreneurship attempts to deal with this question primarily from the point of view of the availability of indigenous adapters and innovators.

Some participants mentioned the desirability of further research on entrepreneurship in general. Hoselitz reminded us that in spite of general agreement on the importance of entrepreneurship, we still know practically nothing about how it grows or the psychological and sociological factors responsible for it. Leibenstein also acknowledged that much of economic growth ultimately depends on the efficiency and diligence of individual entrepreneurs and their workers. Other participants seemed to disagree with the importance of studying the personal characteristics of firm owners and managers. There are always firms that demonstrate entrepreneurship in LDCs, some maintained. Nelson raised the possibility that the analysis of a businessman's innovativeness and form of management may tell us more about his society than about himself.

At least two participants underlined the importance of further research on the household. Fishlow argued for such study on two grounds: because private saving is more important than public saving, and because we need to know more about the welfare aspects of development. Moreover, we know too little about income distribution, which has not only welfare implications but is also a determinant of the structure and level of demand—this, in turn, affecting the development process. Ferber further emphasized the importance of studying household behavior, both for verifying how it accords with economic theory, and for determining how it affects business behavior. There is a clear interrelationship that remains to be brought out.

Most participants mentioned, of course, the study of firms. Salazar-Carrillo proposed empirical studies on the micro level. Instead of "armchair theorizing," there should be operational hypotheses and testing. Fishlow discounted the notion that we can learn much by proceeding on the unrealistic assumption that what we are studying is in the context of a market economy and then wondering why firms are making the "wrong" responses. We have to study empirically both the firms and the framework within which they operate. One can conceive of a situation where firms are operating at a constant level of inefficiency yet move in the right direction with regard to accumulation and production of "the right kinds of goods."

Since both Nelson's reflections in Chapter 11 and the discussion on the role of micro theory reported above were largely related to the theory of the firm, there is no need to elaborate further on this theme.

CONCLUSION

It is hoped that the reader can discern from this summary at least part of the fruitful discussions that took place throughout the conference. It has not been our purpose to reproduce the vigorous and extensive exchanges that followed the presentation of some of the papers. These discussions were joined by not only the participants but often by the guests (mostly faculty members from midwestern universities). Written and verbal comments received during and after the conference were most encouraging and confirmed the high level of the proceedings. More important, the theme of the conference—micro aspects of development—has proved to be even more timely than was anticipated at the time it was initiated.

INTRODUCTION

1. Benjamin Higgins, Economic Development, Problems, Principles, and Policies, rev. ed. (New York: W. W. Norton, 1968), p. x.

2. Stephen Enke, "Economics and Development: Rediscovering Old Truths," Journal of Economic Literature, VII, 4 (December 1969), 1125.

3. Lloyd Reynolds, "The Content of Development Economics," American Economic Review, Papers and Proceedings, May 1969, pp. 401-8.

4. Ibid., p. 408.

5. Center for East Asian Studies, Stanford University, Program on East Asian Local Systems, February 1970, p. 1.

6. Ibid.

CHAPTER 1

1. Irma Adelman and George Dalton, "A Statistical Analysis of Modernization in Village India," Studies in Economic Anthropology (Spring 1971).

2. Irma Adelman and Cynthia Taft Morris, Society, Politics and Economic Development—A Quantitative Approach (Baltimore: Johns Hopkins Press, 1967) and Irma Adelman and George Dalton, loc. cit.

3. Leonard J. Savage, The Foundations of Statistics (New York: John Wiley, 1954), especially Chapter 10.

4. Lawi Odero-Ogwell, "A Programming Analysis of Kenyan Agriculture in the Nyere Region of Kenya," (Ph.D. thesis, London School of Economics, 1968).

5. See, for example, Theodore W. Schultz, Transforming Traditional Agriculture (New Haven: Yale University Press, 1964) and the studies therein.

6. Clifford Geertz, Peddlers and Princes (Chicago: University of Chicago Press, 1963), pp. 36-37.

CHAPTER 2

1. Harvey Leibenstein, "Organizational or Frictional Equilibria, X-Efficiency and the Rate of Innovation," Quarterly Journal of Economics, LXXXIII, (November 1969). The theory sketched here is not to be viewed as one in competition with the

neoclassical theory of the firm for all purposes. Even theories inconsistent with each other may be useful simultaneously. Some may be appropriate for some purposes, some for others.

2. A. A. Walters, An Introduction to Econometrics (New York: W. W. Norton, 1968) pp. 296 ff. Also, M. J. Farrell, "The Measurement of Productive Efficiency," Journal of the Royal Statistical Society, Series A, 1957, pp. 253-81. Other references in this field have been omitted for lack of space.

3. Cf. Kenneth Arrow, "The Economic Implications of Learning by Doing," Review of Economic Studies (June 1962).

4. A. B. Atkinson, and J. E. Stiglitz, "A New View of Technological Change," Economic Journal (September 1969).

5. In an old and obscure paper by the author (H. Leibenstein, "Technical Progress, the Production Function and Dualism," Banca Nazionale del Lavoro Quarterly Review (December 1960) a concept similar to the Atkinson and Stiglitz notion of localized technological change was introduced to explain comparative technological stagnation.

6. In an interesting study of 4,000 Massachusetts plants (data for 1935-59) T. Y. Shen found that: "while the data are generally consistent with a diffusion model, there exists a further systematic influence that affects the change of input output combination of the average plant . . . the observed empirical behavior pattern can be explained by the prevalence of 'X-efficiency' but not by substitution . . . this tentative finding is put to a further test by a perusal of the nature of factor intensity change. Once more the X-efficiency hypothesis turns out to be more consistent with the data. The conclusion is thus reached that a technological change model based on diffusion requires the estimation and incorporation of X-efficiency." T. Y. Shen, "Technology Diffusion, Substitution and X-Efficiency," Department of Economics, University of California, Davis, Working Paper Series No. 3, April 1970, p. 3.

7. Ann Kruger, Economic Journal, LXXXII, 311 (September 1968), 641-58.

CHAPTER 3

1. See, for example, the discussion in David S. Landes, The Unbound Prometheus (Cambridge: University Press, 1969), pp. 47-50; William N. Parker, "Slavery and Southern Economic Development: An Hypothesis and Some Evidence," in Parker, ed. The Structure of the Cotton Economy of the Antebellum South (Washington: Agricultural History Society, 1970) pp. 115-25; "The Growth and Decline of Import Substitution in Brazil," Economic Bulletin for Latin America, XI (March 1964), 1-60.

2. Two recent models which introduce demand in this fashion are Russell J. Cheetham, Allen C. Kelley, and Jeffrey G. Williamson, "Consumer Tastes, Engel Effects and Structural Change in a Dualistic Model of Growth" (unpublished); and Paul Zarenbka, Toward A Theory of Economic Development (unpublished), Chap. 2.

3. Harold F. Williamson, "Mass Production, Mass Consumption, and American Industrial Development," First International Conference of Economic History (Paris: Mouton, 1960), p. 138.

4. As quoted in Carle C. Zimmerman, Consumption and Standards of Living (New York: Van Nostrand, 1936), p. 51.

5. For a discussion and summary of early budget studies see George Stigler, "The Early History of Empirical Studies of Consumer Behavior," Journal of Political Economy, Vol. 62 (1954), pp. 95-113.

6. Milton Friedman has given formal expression to the concept of permanent income in his A Theory of the Consumption Function (Princeton: Princeton University Press, 1957).

7. Albert Rees, Real Wages in Manufacturing, 1890-1914. (Princeton: Princeton University Press, 1961), p. 74.

8. The commodities included in all three comparisons, not always for all countries, consist of beef, pork, lard, bread, wheat flour, milk, butter, cheese, eggs, potatoes, sugar, tea, and coffee. These represent the bulk of food purchases. Weights are based upon the American expenditure distribution reported in the 1888-91 survey; a European allocation reduces the difference, but not greatly. For the 1890 prices see, Great Britain Board of Trade, Report on Wholesale and Retail Prices in the United Kingdom (London: His Majesty's Stationary Office, 1903); Jean Fourastié, Documents pour L'Histoire et La Theorie des Prix, Vols. I and II (Paris: Librairie Armand Colin, 1958 and n.d.); and U.S. Bureau of Labor, Eighteenth Annual Report, Part II. For the Young Report, Labor in Europe and America, House Exec. Doc. No. 21, 44th Congress, 1st Session, 1876, pp. 371 ff., pp. 452 ff., and p. 810.

9. Board of Trade, Cost of Living in American Towns, p. lxi; Cost of Living in French Towns, p. xxxiii.

10. Cost of Living in American Towns, p. lxii.

11. U.S. Bureau of Labor, Eighteenth Annual Report, pp. 100-101.

12. Their source is Cost of Living in American Towns, pp. lxxxi-xc. The groups were selected on the basis of their importance. The others are not more deviant.

13. The method of instrumental variables guarantees consistency. For a discussion of its direct application in this context,

see Nissan Liviatan, "Errors in Variables and Engel Curve Analysis," Econometrica, Vol. 29 (1961), pp. 336-62.

14. H. S. Houthakker, "An International Comparison of Household Expenditure Patterns, Commemorating the Centenary of Engel's Law," Econometrica, Vol. 25 (1957), p. 542.

15. For a more detailed description of the method, see J. A. C. Brown, "The Consumption of Food in Relation to Household Composition and Income," Econometrica, Vol. 22 (1954), pp. 444-59.

16. F. G. Forsyth shows that because of the budget constraint, it is impossible to estimate both the general income and specific expenditure scales on the basis of budget data. The general scale is not independent of the specific ones. Nonetheless, it still seems useful to maintain their conceptual separation, and therefore not to lump them together into a single composition effect as he suggests. F. G. Forsyth, "The Relationship Between Family Size and Family Expenditure," Journal of the Royal Statistical Society, Series A, Vol. 123 (1960), pp. 367-97.

17. The normal family results for 1901 are reported in Houthakker, "International Comparison," p. 541. The adjustment made for the exclusion of fuel and lighting consisted of using the ratio of the aggregate total elasticity for rent alone, without adjustment for family size, to a comparable total elasticity for the two categories weighted together. These total elasticities are found in H. Gregg Lewis and Paul H. Douglas, "Studies in Consumer Expenditures," Studies in Business Administration, Vol. 17 (No. 3), Table V.

18. As reported in Lewis and Douglas, "Consumer Expenditures," Table III.

19. Dorothy Brady, "The Content of the National Product," Chap. 2 of A New Economic History of the United States (New York: Harper and Row, forthcoming).

20. John H. Clapham, An Economic History of Modern Britain, Vol. II (Cambridge: Cambridge University Press, 1952), p. 253; Phyllis Deane and W. A. Cole, British Economic Growth, 1868-1959 (Cambridge: Cambridge University Press, 1964), p. 144.

21. John H. Clapham, The Economic Development of France and Germany, 1815-1914, 4th ed. (Cambridge: Cambridge University Press, 1955), p. 161.

22. Stanley Lebergott, Manpower in Economic Growth (New York: McGraw-Hill, 1964), p. 511.

23. Dorothy Brady makes and elaborates this point quite forcefully in her chapter.

24. Board of Trade, Cost of Living in American Towns, pp. lxxxiv-lxxxv.

25. For food consumption, see Neal Patter and Francis T. Christy, Jr., Trends in Natural Resource Commodities (Baltimore: Johns Hopkins Press, 1962), pp. 176, 204, 216, 223. The alternative pork consumption series is based upon production estimates by William N. Parker that allow for a smaller, and increasing, slaughter-inverting ratio. Earlier series estimated for 1840 and on imply no increase in meat consumption between 1840 and 1870, and only a 25 percent increase in wheat intake. The former results, at least, do not seem entirely creditable. Underlying data are in Marvin Towne and Wayne D. Rasmussen, "Farm Gross Product and Gross Investment in the Nineteenth Century," in Trends in the American Economy in the Nineteenth Century, Studies in Wealth, Vol. 24 (Princeton: Princeton University Press, 1960), pp. 283-84, 294. (Live weight was adjusted to meat yield.) Per capita income growth can be ascertained in Robert E. Gallman, "Gross National Product in the United States, 1834-1909," Output, Employment, and Productivity in the United States After 1800, Studies in Income and Wealth, Vol. 30 (New York: Columbia University Press, 1966), p. 9.

26. For the basic information used to derive sectoral growth rates, see R. E. Gallman, "Commodity Output, 1838-1899," in National Bureau of Economic Research, R. Ruggles, Chairman, Trends in the American Economy in the Nineteenth Century (Princeton, N.J.: the University Press, 1960), p. 43, pp. 46-68, and U.S. Bureau of the Census, Historical Statistics of the United States, Washington, 1960, pp. 544-48. The cost of living index is found in Ethel D. Hoover, "Retail Prices After 1850," in Trends in the American Economy, pp. 142-43.

27. The Warren-Pearson index of United States wholesale food prices is presented in Historical Statistics, p. 115. The corresponding British index is that of Rousseaux, reported in B. R. Mitchell and Phyllis Deane, Abstract of British Historical Statistics (Cambridge: Cambridge University Press, 1962), pp. 471-72.

28. Statistical Abstract of the United Kingdom, Vol. 40 (1892), pp. 74-75, 136-41; Vol. 48 (1900), pp. 82-83, 148-53; F. W. Hirst, ed., Porter's Progress of the Nation (London: Methuen, 1912), pp. 439-42.

29. Annuaire Statistique, Vol. 15 (1892-94), pp. 340-41; Vol. 22 (1901), pp. 92-93.

30. Cf. Deborah S. Freedman, "The Role of Consumption of Modern Durables in Economic Development," Economic Development and Cultural Change, Vol. 19 (1970), 25-48.

31. As indeed it does. See Russell J. Cheetham, Allen C. Kelley, and Jeffrey G. Williamson, "Consumer Tastes, Engel

Effects and Structural Change in a Dualistic Model of Growth" (1971, unpublished).

32. Jeffrey G. Williamson, Fictional History: American Regional Economic Development, 1870-1910 (work in progress), Chap. 3.

33. W. G. Whitney, The Structure of the American Economy in the Late Nineteenth Century (1971, unpublished).

34. What follows is taken directly from the present writer's Fictional History: American Regional Economic Development, 1870-1910, Chap. 3 and Appendix 3.4.2.

35. Allen C. Kelley, Jeffrey G. Williamson, and Russell J. Cheetham, "Biased Technological Progress and Labor Force Growth in a Dualistic Economy," Quarterly Journal of Economics (August 1972).

CHAPTER 4

1. See Robert Ferber, The Reliability of Consumer Reports of Financial Assets and Debts (Urbana: University of Illinois, Bureau of Economic and Business Research, 1967).

2. This is not to say that no previous studies have been made of errors in surveys in the less developed countries. Most such studies, however, have either focused on sampling problems (such as W. E. Deming, R. H. Blyth, Jr., R. K. Jessen, and O. Kempthorne, "On a Population Sample for Greece," Journal of the American Statistical Association, Vol. 42, September 1947, pp. 357-84) or have covered aspects other than economic data (such as H. W. Boyd, Jr., R. E. Frank, W. F. Massy, M. Zoheir, "On the Use of Marketing Research in the Emerging Economies," Journal of Marketing Research, Vol. 1, November 1964, pp. 20-23). The present study differs from the others essentially in its focus on errors in economic data collection in Latin America and in its attempt to provide a fairly systematic appraisal of their effect.

CHAPTER 5

1. Alifeyo Chilivumbo, "Social Research Methods in Malawa: A Look at Some Mostly Used Methods," University Social Sciences Conference, Nairobi, Kenya, 1969 (unpublished).

2. David G. Mathiasen, "Measuring Children as a Means of Evaluating Public Nutrition Programs," paper presented at the annual meeting of the American Statistical Association, Detroit, 1970.

3. Gunnar Myrdal, Asian Drama (New York: Pantheon Books, 1963), especially Appendix 16.

4. E. Scott Maynes, "Obtaining Data on Consumption and Saving in Underdeveloped Countries," Proceedings of the Social Statistics Section, American Statistical Association, Washington D.C., 1960, pp. 5-15.

5. There is, however, some question about the cost and price figures which are most appropriate for imputing values to nonmarket transactions. See Walter Neale, "Economic Accounting and Family Farming in India," Economic Development and Cultural Change, VII, 1 (April 1959), 236-301.

6. National Council of Applied Economic Research, Urban Income and Saving, New Delhi, 1962, especially pp. 102-4; All India Rural Household Survey, Vol. II: Saving Income and Investment, New Delhi, 1965, especially pp. 36-38.

7. Dorothy Cole, and J. E. G. Utting, "Estimating Expenditure, Saving, and Income from Household Budgets," Journal of the Royal Statistical Society, CXIX, Series A (General), Part IV (1956), pp. 371-92. U.S. Bureau of Labor Statistics, "Survey of Consumers' Expenditure in 1950: Interpretation and Use of the Results," Monthly Labor Review, LXXV (1952), pp. 425-28.

8. NCAER, All India Consumer Expenditure Survey, Vol. II, New Delhi, 1967, especially pp. 46-47.

9. A striking example is Rozental's study of Thai enterprises. The author reports: "In the first place the total of assets does not fit with the total of liabilities. This embarrassing result came about despite the determination of interviewers to reconcile the respective answers, even going so far as to make estimates of the value of intangibles such as good will. Moreover, cross check questions, such as an estimate of the market value of the business, yielded results vastly different from those of net asset valuation or net worth." Alek A. Rozental, Finance and Development in Thailand (New York: Praeger Publishers, 1970), p. 257.

10. Simon Kuznets, "Economic Growth and Income Inequality," American Economic Review, XXXXIV (March 1955), 1-28.

11. NCAER, 1967, op. cit.

12. NCAER, Additional Rural Incomes Survey (unpublished report), New Delhi, 1970.

13. Frank M. Andrews, and George W. Phillips, "The Squatters of Lima: Who They Are and What They Want," Journal of Developing Areas, IV (January 1970), 211-24.

14. E.g., Mathiasen, op. cit.

15. Eva Mueller, "Attitudes Toward the Economics of Family Size and Their Relation to Fertility" (unpublished), 1970.

16. Irwin Friend and Stanley Shor, "Who Saves," Review of Economics and Statistics, May 1959.

17. Jean Crockett and Irwin Friend, "Tastes and the Income Elasticity of Consumption: New Estimates of Consumer Demand Relationships for the U.S." (mimeo.).

18. Ibid.

19. E.g., see Irwin Friend and Robert Jones, "The Concept of Saving," Consumption and Saving, Vol. 2, University of Pennsylvania, 1960.

CHAPTER 6

1. David C. McClelland, The Achieving Society (Princeton: Van Nostrand, 1961), Chap. 3.

2. Ibid. pp. 268-69.

3. Ibid. p. 264.

4. Ibid. Chap. 6. The six characteristics are moderate risk-taking, energetic or novel instrumental activity, individual responsibility, knowledge of results of decisions, anticipation of future possibilities, organizational skills. The last was not hypothesized to be related to nAch.

5. Paul R. Lawrence and Jay W. Lorsch, Organization and Environment, Managing Differentiation and Integration (Homewood, Ill.: Irwin, 1969); Joan Woodward, Industrial Organization: Theory and Practice (London: Oxford University Press, 1965).

6. S. N. Eisenstadt, "The Need for Achievement," Economic Development and Cultural Change, No. 11 (1963), pp. 420-31.

7. Everett E. Hagen, On the Theory of Social Change (Homewood, Ill.: Dorsey, 1962).

8. Arthur H. Cole, Business Enterprise in its Social Setting (Cambridge, Mass.: Harvard University Press, 1959), p. 12.

9. Edward C. Banfield, The Moral Basis of a Backward Society (Glencoe: Free Press, 1958).

10. Albert O. Hirschman, Strategies of Economic Development (New Haven: Yale University Press, 1958).

11. Ibid. pp. 18, 19.

12. A recent, quite thorough analysis of the dimensions of small group behavior can be found in Robert F. Bales, Personality and Interpersonal Behavior (New York: Holt, Rinehart and Winston, 1970). Some important papers in this field are Edgar F. Borgatta, L. S. Cottrell, Jr., and J. H. Mann, "The Spectrum of Individual Interaction Characteristics: An Inter Dimensional Analysis," Psychological Reports, No. 4 (1958), pp. 279-319; Launor F. Carter, "Recording and Evaluating the Performance of Individuals as Members of Small Groups," Personnel Psychology, No. 7 (1954), pp. 477-84; and Arthur S. Couch, "Psychological Determinants of Interpersonal Behavior," unpublished doctoral dissertation, Harvard University, Cambridge, Mass., 1960.

13. Bales, op. cit., pp. 193-207.

14. Ibid., pp. 193-207.

15. Alfred D. Chandler, Jr., Strategy and Structure (Cambridge, Mass.: M.I.T. Press, 1962).

16. Ibid., pp. 43, 44-45.

17. The list used is from A. D. H. Kaplan, Big Enterprise in a Competitive System (Washington: Brookings Institution, 1964). The choice of 1919 was somewhat arbitrary, but does not, I believe, bias the selection in favor of the hypothesis. The strategy used in investigating each case was to trace the firm's history and follow it through its first periods of expansion and consolidation. With two firms, U.S. Steel and International Harvester, it was necessary to return to the history of the largest of the constituent firms which combined to form the corporation existing in 1919.

18. Principal sources for this discussion: were John B. Rae, "The Fabulous Billy Durant," Business History Review, No. 32 (1958), pp. 255-71, and Chandler, op. cit. pp. 138-99.

19. Rae, op. cit., p. 260.

20. Ibid., p. 264.

21. Chandler, op. cit. p. 160.

22. Rae, op. cit., p. 270.

23. Sources for this section were James H. Bridge, The History of the Carnegie Steel Company (New York: Aldine, 1903); George Harvey, Henry Clay Frick, the Man (New York: Scribner's, 1928); Burton J. Hendrick, The Life of Andrew Carnegie, 2 vols. (Garden City, N.Y: Doubleday); and Joseph F. Wall, Andrew Carnegie (New York: Oxford University Press, 1970).

24. Bridge, op. cit., p. 15.

25. Harvey, op. cit., p. 99.

26. John K. Winkler, Incredible Carnegie (New York: Vanguard, 1931), p. 179.

27. Principal sources used were Chandler's review, op. cit., pp. 63-137; William S. Dutton, Du Pont—One Hundred and Forty Years (New York: Scribner's, 1942); Marquis James, Alfred I. du Pont—the Family Rebel (New York: Bobbs-Merrill), 1941.

28. Chandler, op. cit., p. 390, p. 64.

29. Sources for McCormick were Herbert N. Casson, Cyrus Hall McCormick; His Life and Work (Chicago: McClurg, 1909); W. T. Hutchinson, Cyrus Hall McCormick, 2 vols. (New York: Appleton-Century, 1930, 1935); for Armour, "Philip D. Armour—Know the Facts and Act," in The National Provisioner, The Significant Sixty (January 1961); U.S. Commissioner of Corporations, Report on the Beef Industry (Washington, D.C.: Government Printing Office, 1905).

30. Hutchinson, op. cit., Vol. 1, p. 100.
31. Casson, op. cit., p. 182.
32. Hutchinson, op. cit., Vol. 2, p. 688.
33. Ibid, p. 690.
34. Hutchinson, op. cit., Vol. 1, p. 228.
35. Hutchinson, op. cit. Vol. 2, p. 628.
36. Hutchinson, Vol. 1, pp. 133, 250.
37. Ibid, p. 457.
38. Casson, op. cit. p. 200.
39. All of these observations are from Elbert Hubbard, Philip Armour (East Aurora, N.Y.: Roycrofters, 1909), pp. 160, 151, 156.
40. R. A. Clemen, The American Livestock and Meat Industry (New York: Ronald Press, 1923).
41. U.S. Commissioner of Corporations, op. cit. p. 21.
42. The National Provisioner, op. cit.
43. Ibid.
44. A thorough account of Taylor's contribution is found in Fortune, No. 13 (1936), pp. 117-20, from which following quotes are taken.
45. This account is based on Glenn D. Babcock, History of the United States Rubber Company, Indiana Business Report No. 39 (Bloomington, Ind.: Indiana University Graduate School of Business, 1966).
46. Ibid., p. 107.
47. Sources include C. P. Connolly, The Devil Learns to Vote: The Story of Montana (New York: Covici, Friede, 1938); Ira B. Joralemon, Romantic Copper: Its Lure and Lore (New York: Appleton-Century, 1934); H. Minar Shoebotham, Anaconda: Life of Marcus Daly the Copper King (Harrisburg: Stackpole, 1956); K. Ross Toole, Montana: An Uncommon Land (Norman: University of Oklahoma Press, 1959), and articles in Fortune, LI (January 1955), p. 89, and Copper Curb and Mining Outlook, VI, 16, pp. 12-13.
48. Joralemon, op. cit., p. 74, and Toole, op. cit., p. 177.
49. Connolly, op. cit. p. 96.
50. Montana Department of Agriculture, Labor and Industry, Montana: A State Guide Book (New York: Viking Press, 1939).
51. Ibid.
52. Ralph W. Hidy and Muriel E. Hidy, Pioneering in Big Business (New York: Harper, 1955), p. 30.
53. Fortune, December 1936, p. 83.
54. Chandler, op. cit., p. 406.

55. Principal sources used were Ralph W. Hidy and Muriel E. Hidy, Pioneering in Big Business (New York: Harper, 1955) and Allan Nevins, John D. Rockefeller, the Heroic Age of American Enterprise (New York: Scribner's, 1940).

56. Nevins, op. cit., Vol. I, pp. 110, 236, 72, 156.

57. These descriptions are taken from Hidy and Hidy, op. cit., pp. 25-26, 31, 30, 77, 387.

58. Principal sources used were U.S. Commissioner of Corporations, Report on the Tobacco Industry (Washington, D.C: Government Printing Office; 1909); John W. Jenkins, James B. Duke, Master Builder (New York: Doran, 1927); Richard B. Tennant, The American Cigarette Industry (New Haven: Yale University Press, 1950); Albert C. Muhse, "Disintegration of the Tobacco Combination," Political Science Quarterly. XXVIII, 2, (1913), pp. 249-78.

59. Principal sources were Arthur A. Bright, The Electric Lamp Industry (New York: Macmillan, 1949); John T. Broderick, Forty Years with General Electric (Albany, N.Y.: Fort Orange Press, 1929); and Annual Report of the General Electric Company, January 31, 1894.

60. Thomas C. Cochran and Ruben E. Reina, Entrepreneurship in Argentine Culture (Philadelphia: University of Pennsylvania Press, 1962).

61. Ibid., p. 173.

62. Gustav F. Papanek, Pakistan's Development: Social Goals and Private Incentives (Cambridge, Mass.: Harvard University Press, 1967).

63. For example, Kozo Yamamura, "The Founding of Mitsubishi: A Case Study in Japanese Business History," Business History Review, No. 41 (1967), pp. 141-60; Kozo Yamamura, "A Re-examination of Entrepreneurship in Meiji Japan (1868-1912)," Economic History Review, 2nd Series, No. 31 (1968), and Johannes Hirschmeier The Origins of Entrepreneurship in Meiji Japan (Cambridge, Mass.: Harvard University Press, 1964).

64. Clifford Geertz, Peddlers and Princes (Chicago: University of Chicago Press, 1963).

65. Ibid, p. 127.

66. See McClelland, op. cit., and D. C. McClelland and D. G. Winter, Motivating Economic Achievement (New York: Free Press, 1969).

67. Elizabeth G. French, "Some Characteristics of Achievement Motivation," Journal of Experimental Psychology, No. 50 (1955), pp. 232-36; Elizabeth G. French and F. H. Thomas, "The Relation of Achievement Motivation to Problem-Solving Effectiveness," Journal of Abnormal and Social Psychology, No. 56 (1958),

pp. 45-48; W. J. McKeachie, "Motivation, Teaching Methods and College Learning," in M. R. Jones, ed., Nebraska Symposium on Motivation (Lincoln: University of Nebraska Press, 1961), pp. 111-42; and H. Heckhausen, The Anatomy of Achievement Motivation (New York: Academic Press, 1967), p. 138.

68. McClelland and Winter, op. cit., p. 81.

69. Ibid., p. 211.

70. Joseph A. Schumpeter, The Theory of Economic Development (Cambridge, Mass.: Harvard University Press, 1936).

71. Ibid., p. 88.

72. Ibid., p. 92.

73. Werner Sombart, "Capitalism," in E. R. A. Seligman, ed., Encyclopaedia of the Social Sciences (New York: Macmillan, 1937). I am indebted to Bert F. Hoselitz for this reference.

74. Max Weber, The Protestant Ethic and the Spirit of Capitalism (New York: Scribner's, 1958).

75. These are reviewed in S. N. Eisenstadt, The Protestant Ethic and Modernization, (New York: Basic Books, 1968).

76. Chandler, op. cit.

77. Thorsten Veblen, The Engineers and the Price System (New York: Viking Press, 1921).

78. Thorsten Veblen, The Theory of Business Enterprise (New York: Scribner, 1904), pp. 20-65.

79. Sombart, op. cit., p. 207.

80. Joseph Schumpeter, The Theory of Economic Development (New York: Oxford University Press, 1961).

81. Joseph Schumpeter, Capitalism, Socialism and Democracy (New York: Harper, 1942), p. 133.

82. Juan B. Cortés, S. J., "The Achievement Motive in the Spanish Economy Between the 13th and 18th Centuries," Economic Development and Cultural Change, IX, 2 (January 1961), and Norman Bradburn and David E. Berlew, "Need for Achievement and English Industrial Growth," Economic Development and Cultural Change, X, 1 (October 1961).

83. McClelland and Winter, op. cit.

CHAPTER 7

1. See, for example, Daniel Schydlowsky, "Benefit/Cost Analysis of Foreign Investment Proposals: The Viewpoint of the Host Country," presented at the Harvard Development Advisory Service Conference in Dubrovnik, June 20-26, 1970, and Michael Bruno, "The Optimal Selection of Export-Promoting and Import-Substituting Projects," Report on the External Sector: Techniques, Problems and Policies, Report on the First Interregional Seminar on Development Planning in Ankara, (New York: United Nations, 1967), pp. 88-135.

2. For policy recommendations based on some shaky intuitive leaps, but argued in much the same framework as the Bruno and Schydlowsky approach, see Raymond Vernon and Louis T. Wells, Jr., "Some Proposals for Ghana's Industrialization Policies," Economic Development Report #134, Harvard Development Advisory Service (1968).

3. See, for example, Michael W. Gordon, "Joint Business Ventures in the Central American Common Market," Vanderbilt Law Review, Vol. 21 (1968), p. 318, and Leland L. Johnson, "U.S. Private Investment in Latin America: Some Questions of National Policy," Memorandum RM-4092-ISA, prepared for the Office of the Assistant Secretary of Defense/International Security Affairs, The Rand Corporation (July 1964), p. 63.

4. Lester B. Pearson, Partners in Development (New York: Praeger Publishers, 1969), p. 112.

5. Pros and Cons of Joint Ventures Abroad, Management Monograph No. 18 (New York: Business International, 1964), p. 4.

6. See the literature on the product life cycle. A summary is provided in Rolando Polli and Victor Cook, "Validity of the Product Life Cycle," Journal of Business, Vol. 42 (October 1969).

7. Lawrence G. Franko, "Strategy Choice and Multinational Corporate Tolerance for Joint Ventures with Foreign Partners" (unpublished doctoral thesis, Boston, Harvard Graduate School of Business Administration, 1969).

8. See also Lloyd N. Cutler, "Joint Ventures with Foreign Business Associates, Investors and Governments," Institute on Private Investments Abroad (Dallas: Southwestern Legal Foundation, 1959), p. 276.

9. R. A. Deane, "Foreign Investment in New Zealand Manufacturing" (unpublished doctoral thesis, Vol. 1, Wellington, Victoria University of Wellington, 1967).

10. Ibid., p. 236. See also p. 95.

11. Ibid., p. 95.

12. D. T. Brash. U.S. Investment in Australian Manufacturing Industry (Cambridge, Mass.: Harvard University Press, 1966), p. 77, and W. P. Hogan, "British Investments in Australian Manufacturing: The Technical Connection," Manchester School of Economics and Social Studies, Vol. 35 (May 1967), pp. 145-46.

13. Cutler, op. cit., p. 264.

14. K. Mathew Kurian, Impact of Foreign Capital on Indian Economy (New Delhi: People's Publishing House, 1966), p. 303.

15. This was the average ratio of purchases from the parent to total sales for all manufacturing subsidiaries, as reported by C. G. Hufbauer and Michael Adler, Overseas Manufacturing

Investment and the Balance of Payments, Tax Policy Research Study, No. 1 (Washington, D.C.: U.S. Treasury Department, 1965), p. 25.

16. Brash, op. cit., p. 88.

17. Whatarangi Winiata, "United States Managerial Investment in Japan, 1950-1964, An Interview Study" (doctoral dissertation, Ann Arbor, University of Michigan, 1966). The data were not well controlled for differences in industries, but the strength of the relationship indicates that it might hold if more controls were applied.

18. See, for example, Brash, op. cit., p. 248, and Foreign Collaborations in Indian Industry (Bombay: Reserve Bank of India, 1968).

19. M. H. Watkins, (Head of Task Force), Foreign Ownership and the Structure of Canadian Industry (Ottawa: Privy Council Office, January 1968), p. 220.

20. Brash, op. cit., p. 98.

21. Deane, op. cit., Chap. 4, p. 96.

22. Brash, op. cit., p. 90.

23. A. E. Safarian, "Country of Ownership and Performance of the Firm," Economic Record (March 1968), pp. 85-86, and Brash, op. cit., p. 206.

24. A. E. Safarian, Foreign Ownership of Canadian Industry (Toronto: McGraw-Hill of Canada, 1966), p. 262.

25. Deane, op. cit., p. 236.

26. See, for example, Brash, op. cit., p. 233.

27. India, recently, for example. See I. A. Litvak and C. J. Maule, Foreign Investment: The Experience of Host Countries (New York: Praeger Publishers, 1970), p. 295.

28. Litvak and Maule, ibid., p. 293.

29. See Foreign Collaborations in Indian Industry, pp. 101, 106.

30. Brash, op. cit., p. 228.

31. José de la Torre, "Exports of Manufactured Goods from Foreign Developing Countries: Marketing Factors and the Role of Foreign Enterprise" (unpublished doctoral thesis, Boston, Harvard Graduate School of Business Administration, 1970).

32. Cutler, op. cit., p. 261-84.

33. Brash, op. cit., p. 229, mentions this vehicle of control.

34. Herbert May, The Effects of United States and Other Foreign Investment in Latin America (New York: Council for Latin America, January 1970), pp. 34, 36.

35. de la Torre, op. cit.

36. Kurian, op. cit., p. 317.

37. "Significant Corporate Moves," Business International, June 19, 1970, p. 199.

38. Deane, op. cit., p. 96.
39. Deane, op. cit.,
40. Safarian, "Country of Ownership and Performance of the Firm," op. cit., pp. 85-86.
41. Ibid., p. 240, and Brash, op. cit., pp. 83-84.
42. Winiata, op. cit., p. 118.
43. For a more complete argument on this point, see John M. Stopford and Louis T. Wells, Jr., Managing the Multinational Enterprise (New York: Basic Books, 1971).
44. Kurian, op. cit., p. 110-11.

CHAPTER 8

1. See W. E. G. Salter [1960, pp. 43-44]. For the major landmarks in the discussion generated by Salter, see Syed Ahmad [1966, Sept. 1967, Dec. 1967]; John S. Chipman [1970]; William Fellner [1961, 1967]; Charles Kennedy [1964, 1966, 1967]; Paul A. Samuelson [1965, 1966].
2. Whether the innovation possibility curve is exogenously determined or is dependent of a past innovation does not affect the present discussion, though it is a crucial problem in developing a theory of distributed shares. See discussions by Kennedy [1967] and Ahmad [1967].
3. Nathan Rosenberg [1969] has suggested a theory of induced technical change based on "obvious and compelling need" instead of relative factor scarcity and relative factor prices. In the Rosenberg model, research is directed toward removing constraints that limit growth. C. Peter Timmer has pointed out to us in a letter that the Rosenberg model is consistent with the model outlined here since, in a linear programming sense, the constraints represent the "dual" of the factor prices.
4. There is a growing literature on public research policy. Much of this literature tends to be normative rather than analytical. For a recent survey see Richard R. Nelson, Merton J. Peck, and Edward D. Kalachek [1967, pp. 151-211]. They view public-sector research activities as having arisen from three considerations: 1) fields where the public interest is believed to transcend private incentive (such as health and aviation); 2) industries where the individual firm is too small to capture the benefits from research (agriculture and housing); 3) broad scale support for basic research and science education.
5. The literature on research resource allocation in agriculture is relatively limited. See, however, Walter L. Fishel [1971] and Willis L. Peterson [1969].
6. The issue of incentive is a major issue in many developing economies. In spite of limited scientific and technical manpower,

many countries have not succeeded in developing a system of economic and professional reward that permits them to have access to, or make effective use of, the resources of scientific and technical manpower that are potentially available to them.

7. The symbiotic relationship between basic and applied research can be illustrated by the relation between work in 1) genetics and plant physiology, 2) plant breeding at the International Rice Research Institute. The geneticist and the physiologist are involved in research designed to advance understanding of the physiological processes by which plant nutrients are transformed into grain yield, and of the genetic mechanisms or processes involved in the transmission from parents to progenies of the physiological characteristics of the rice plant that affect grain yield. The rice breeders utilize this knowledge from genetics and plant physiology in the design of crosses and the selection of plants with the desired growth characteristics, agronomic traits, and nutritional value. Work in plant physiology and genetics is responsive to the need of the plant breeder for advances in knowledge related to the mission of breeding more productive varieties of rice.

8. At this point we share the Marxian perspective on the relationship between technological change and institutional development. [Karl Marx, p. 406n; Mandel Morton Bober]. We do not accept the Marxian perspective regarding the monolithic sequences of evolution based on clear-cut class conflicts. For two recent attempts to develop broad historical generalizations regarding the relation between institutions and economic forces, see John Hicks [1969] and Douglass C. North and Robert Paul Thomas [1970].

9. The "metaproduction function" can be regarded as the envelope of commonly conceived neoclassical production functions. In the short run, in which substitution among inputs is circumscribed by the rigidity of capital and equipment, production relationship can be described by an activity with relatively fixed factor-factor and factor-product ratios. In the <u>long run</u>, in which the constraints exercised by existing capital disappear and are replaced by the fund of available technical knowledge, including all alternative feasible factor-factor and factor-product combinations, production relationships can be adequately described by the neoclassical production function. In the <u>secular period</u>, in which the constraint given by the available fund of technical knowledge is further relaxed to admit all potentially discoverable possibilities, production relationships can best be described by a metaproduction function that describes all conceivable technical alternatives that might be discovered. For further discussion of short-run,

long-run, and secular production processes see Murray Brown [1966, pp. 95-109]. The relationship between U and u_i's of Figure 8.2 is somewhat similar to the interfirm envelope of a series of intrafirm production functions as discussed by Martin Bronfenbrenner [1944, pp. 35-44].

10. See, for example, Randolph Barker [1970].

11. A discussion of this test and the data used are reported in greater detail in the article by Jujiro Hayami and V. W. Ruttan [1970].

12. A direct test of the induced innovation hypothesis would involve a test for nonneutral change in the production surface. A possible approach is suggested by David and Klundert [2].

13. Derivation of factor demand functions from a multifactor production function with different elasticities of substitution, as attempted by Zvi Griliches [1964 (a) and 1969 (b)], seems to suggest a possibility for improving the present specification. Our regressions are similar to Griliches's, but our factor prices do not measure the costs of factor services other than fertilizer.

14. The possibility of structural changes in the metaproduction function over time, as suggested by some of low Durbin-Watson statistics in Tables 8.2 and 8.3, was tested by running regressions separately for 1880-1915 and 1920-60. The results, in Hayami and Ruttan [1970], do not suggest that any significant structural change occurred between those two periods. The inference from this test is relatively weak, however, because of the small number of observations involved.

15. The role of agricultural research in the economic development of Japan and the United States is reviewed in Hayami and Ruttan [1971].

16. William Fellner, "Two Propositions in the Theory of Induced Innovations," Economic Journal, LXXI (June 1961), pp. 305-8.

17. Charles Kennedy, "Induced Bias in Innovation and the Theory of Distribution," Economic Journal, LXXV (September 1964), pp. 541-47.

18. W. E. G. Salter, Productivity and Technical Change (Cambridge, Eng.: the University Press, 1960), pp. 43-44. Kenneth J. Arrow, "Comment" on John S. Chipman's paper on induced technical change and patterns of international trade, in Raymond Vernon, ed., The Technology Factor in International Trade (New York: Columbia University Press, 1970), pp. 128-32. In the same vein, one might quote Paul A. Samuelson: " . . . we must recognize that any invention which lowers cost of production can benefit the first competitor who introduces it. Furthermore, since the relative share of wages in total costs has been approximately constant for a century, any employer who is planning his research expenditures

over the coming years will reasonably take this into account and will do well to spend now the same number of pennies on experimentation designed to save a dollar of future cost, whatever its source." See his Economics, 6th ed. (New York: McGraw-Hill, 1964), pp. 738-39.

19. See his "On the Theory of Induced Invention," Economic Journal, LXXVI (June 1966), pp. 344-57.

20. See, for instance, Bo Sodersten, International Economics (New York: Harper & Row, 1970), pp. 66-68.

21. See their "Factor Prices and Technical Change in Agricultural Development: The United States and Japan, 1880-1960," Journal of Political Economy, LXXVIII (September/October), pp. 1115-41.

22. Zvi Griliches, "Agriculture: Productivity and Technology" in International Encyclopedia of the Social Sciences, I (New York, 1968), p. 242.

CHAPTER 9

1. It is possible to analyze the complete range of consumption choices without limiting it to leisure, as is done in Jorgenson and Lau [2]. However, for our present purpose, it is simpler to focus on labor supply alone.

2. Since the nonagricultural sector is a substantial consumer of agricultural output, one can no longer derive the demand function for agricultural output from microeconomic household data.

3. For further development of this derivation, see Lau and Yotopoulos [4] and [5].

4. This is sometimes called the partial profit function because some inputs are held fixed.

5. See Lau [3] for a proof of these results.

6. These relations are given and proven in McFadden [6] and Lau [3].

7. See Lau [3] or McFadden [6] for a proof.

8. In fact, we here assume that the number of workers in each household is determined more as a demographic phenomenon rather than as an economic phenomenon, at least in the short and the intermediate run.

9. One reason is possibly the transactions costs involved in converting the second type of income and expenditure into consumable items and cash, respectively.

10. Implicit here is the assumption that all households are identical, an assumption which is very strong, but nevertheless, not unusual in macro analysis. Ideally, the macro demand function should be derived by integrating the micro demand functions over the distribution of the households in the relevant dimensions.

However, if the distribution is sufficiently concentrated at the mean, the error incurred by our approximation will be small. Alternatively, one can justify the present approach by appealing to the useful paradigm of a "representative household."

11. To the extent that there exist landless laborers, the number of households included in deriving the micro labor supply function may be different from that of the number of households included in deriving the macro labor demand function. Even if this discrepancy occurs, our analysis is almost completely unaffected, except for a change in the constant term, as long as we maintain the hypothesis that the utility functions of the landed and landless laborers are identical despite differences in the endowments.

12. Ideally, we would like to have the nonagricultural sector's net demand function of agricultural output as a function of the price of agricultural output, the nonagricultural sector's income, the price of nonagricultural commodities, the nonagricultural population, and imports, and add a net supply function to nonagriculture from micro data. However, unavailability of data, especially those of the nonagricultural sector's income and nonagricultural population and micro consumption data preclude such an attempt. The alternative approach assumes that the tastes of the agricultural and nonagricultural populations are identical.

13. The Studies cover on a cost-accounting basis 2,962 holdings in the six states of India over a period of three years (1955-57). The data for only three states included sufficient information to be suitable for this study. All the data of the Studies are reported in terms of land-size cell averages. For detailed discussion of the data see Lau and Yotopoulos [4] and [5].

14. The fact that fixed obligations and household workers do not affect the production decisions, i.e., output supply and labor demand, is a direct consequence of our block recursive assumption.

15. See the discussion in Yotopoulos [15], [16] and in Lau and Yotopoulos [5].

16. The impact coefficients that we are discussing in the partial and the general macro equilibrium models refer to the case that all adjustments are completed. In a dynamic context, of course, such adjustments are not instantaneous.

17. This supply curve is not to be confused with either the micro supply curve of the household or the aggregate supply curve for the agricultural sector obtained by summing across households. It is instead the locus of all values of output and price of output that satisfy the partial macro equilibrium model.

18. For a review of the literature, see Bhagwati and Chakravarty [1] and also Paris [8] [9].

19. The impact of N in the general macro equilibrium model represents only the change in total population. This has to be combined with the resulting change in N_a in order to study the total effect of demographic factors.

20. There exists, however, evidence that even in Indian agriculture one observes equilibrium wage rates See Wellisz [14].

CHAPTER 10

1. Report of the Expert Group on Social Policy and Planning (New York: United Nations, E/CN.5/445, December 11, 1969).

2. Ibid, p. 27

3. Commission on International Development (Lester B. Pearson, Chairman), Partners in Development (New York: Praeger Publishers, 1969).

4. Cf. Report of the Expert Group on Social Policy and Planning, op. cit.

5. Mimeographed statement of April 1970.

6. Benjamin Higgins, Economic Development: Problems, Principles, and Policies (New York: W. W. Norton, 1968), Chap. 14.

7. John C. H. Fei and Gustav Ranis, Development of the Labor Surplus Economy, Theory and Policy (Homewood, Ill.: Richard D. Irwin for the Yale Economic Growth Center, 1964), p. 93.

8. The original Cho diagram appeared in Yong Sam Cho, Disguised Unemployment in Underdeveloped Areas, With Special Reference to South Korean Agriculture (Berkeley, University of California Press, 1963) p. 38.

9. Colin Clark, "The Extent of Hunger in India" (Clayton, Australia: Institute of Economic Progress, Monash University, 1972), mimeo. For the most part, nutritionists have not addressed themselves to the relationship of hours of work to nutritional requirements as such. M. C. Latham, for example, in his monograph, Human Nutrition in Tropical Africa (Rome: FAO, 1970), gives figures of calory and protein requirements for men and for women of specific body weight, according to whether they are "sedentary, active, or very active." For men, the calory requirements per day are 2,200, 2,500, and 3,000—as far as they go, these figures support the thesis of increasing marginal requirements. For proteins the figures are 60, 65, 70—constant marginal requirements. For women, the calory requirements are 1,800, 2,200, and 2,500—which is counter to the thesis. The protein requirements are 55, 60, 65 (p. 243). He also presents figures

for two kinds of working day: eight hours rest in bed, eight hours sitting or minor activities, and then either 1) eight hours of light work, or 2) five hours of light work and three hours of hard work. The marginal caloric requirement is 270, but a single figure doesn't help as much (p. 57).

10. W. Arthur Lewis, "Economic Development with Unlimited Supplies of Labour," The Manchester School (May 1954).

11. T. Paul Schultz, "An Economic Model of Family Planning and Fertility," Journal of Political Economy, March 1969.

12. Maurice Wilkinson, "An Econometric Analysis of the Determinants of Fertility in Sweden and the United States, 1870-1965" (mimeo., 1969).

13. R. S. Eckhaus, "The Factor-Proportions Problem in Underdeveloped Areas," American Economic Review, September 1955.

14. M. Todaro, "A Model of Urban Migration and Urban Unemployment in Less Developed Countries," American Economic Review, March 1959.

15. B. R. Hazari and J. Krishnamurty, "Employment Implications of India's Industrialization: Analysis in an Input-Output Framework," Review of Economics and Statistics, May 1970.

16. K. Arrow, H. B. Chenery, B. S. Minhas, and R. M. Solow, "Capitalization Substitution and Economic Efficiency," Review of Economics and Statistics, August 1961.

17. Maurice Wilkinson, "Factor Supply and the Direction of Technical Change," American Economic Review, March 1968.

18. W. E. G. Salter, Productivity and Technical Change, 2d. ed. (Cambridge, Eng.: Cambridge University Press, 1968), pp. 123-24, 128-55.

19. N. H. Leff, "Dependency Rates and Savings Rates," American Economic Review, December 1969.

ABOUT THE AUTHORS

ELIEZER B. AYAL, editor of this volume and initiator and organizer of the conference on which it is based, is currently Visiting Professor of Economics at the University of Illinois, Chicago Circle. He previously served on the faculties of the University of Michigan, Harvard, University of the Philippines, and University of Illinois (Urbana-Champaign). His publications in economic development include works on export taxation, models of development, and socio-political factors. His main geographic area of research has been Southeast Asia, especially Thailand and the Philippines, where he spent more than four years. He has served in various editorial and advisory capacities.

IRMA ADELMAN is currently Professor of Economics, University of Maryland. She has served on the faculties of the University of California (Berkeley), Stanford University, Johns Hopkins, and Northwestern. She has published extensively on economic development, concentrating recently on econometric analysis of socio-economic-political factors, as well as the analysis of Korean economic economic development. She has been a consultant for various institutions, including AID and IBRD.

ROBERT FERBER is Research Professor of Economics and Business Administration at the University of Illinois at Urbana, and director of its Survey Research Laboratory. He is also Coordinating Editor of the <u>Journal of the American Statistical Association</u> and an advisor to the Programa de Estudios Conjuntos de Integración Económica Latinoamericana. The latter is a joint research program of approximately 22 research institutes in Latin America. He has also served as an advisor to AID on Latin America.

ALBERT FISHLOW is Professor of Economics, University of California, Berkeley. From 1965 to 1970 he was director of the Brazilian Development Assistance Program. He has numerous publications in economic history. His work on development has been primarily related to his research in Latin America.

MARVIN FRANKEL is Professor of Economics, University of Illinois, Urbana, and was chairman of the department from 1967 to 1971. His publications related to economic development deal primarily with production function analysis. He has served as consultant to various agencies, including AID and ILO.

IRWIN FRIEND is Richard K. Mellon Professor of Finance and Professor of Economics and Finance, Wharton School of Finance and Commerce, University of Pennsylvania. He is also director of the Rodney L. White Center for Financial Research, as well as president of the American Finance Association. He has had extensive research and publication experience, especially in finance and economic statistics. His recent work includes participation in all stages of basic work on savings in India.

YUJIRO HAYAMI is Professor of Economics at Tokyo Metropolitan University. He received his Ph.D. from Iowa State University in 1960. In 1968-69 and 1969-70 he was Visiting Professor in the Department of Agricultural and Applied Economics, University of Minnesota.

BENJAMIN HIGGINS is _professeur titulaire en sciences économiques_ and Director of Projects, Center for Research in Economic Development, University of Montreal. His previous academic positions include membership on the faculties of the Universities of Texas, McGill, and Harvard. He has served in senior advisory positions in less developed countries throughout the world, especially Indonesia and Francophone Africa. He has published numerous books and articles in various fields of economics, concentrating primarily on economic development during the last two decades.

BERT F. HOSELITZ is Professor of Social Science at the University of Chicago. For many years he has been Director of the Research Center in Economic Development and Cultural Change at that university, and editor of its journal, _Economic Development and Cultural Change_. He is the author of many essays on economic theory and history, entrepreneurial studies, and economic development.

STEPHEN HYMER is Professor of Economics, Graduate Faculty of the New School for Social Research. He previously taught at Yale and MIT. He has written extensively on various aspects of the operations of multinational firms in particular and economic development problems in general. He is currently interested in the political economy of economic development.

LAWRENCE J. LAU has been Assistant Professor of Economics, Stanford University, since 1967. His publications have been primarily on the economy of China and the application of econometric methods to development problems, lately focusing on the profit function that he has developed with Pan A. Yotopoulos.

NATHANIEL H. LEFF is Associate Professor at the Graduate School of Business, Columbia University. He was previously Research Associate of the Harvard Center for International Studies. His books analyze the capital goods industry and economic policymaking in Brazil. He has published numerous articles on economic development.

HARVEY LEIBENSTEIN is Andelot Professor of Economics and Population, Harvard University. He was for many years on the faculty of the University of California at Berkeley. He has published extensively on various aspects of economic analysis in general and economic development in particular. His works in such fields as investment criteria, underemployment, and X-efficiency have been widely cited in the literature. His theory of economic-demographic development was among the first (1954) to relate demographic development to economic factors.

EVA MUELLER is Professor of Economics at the University of Michigan and Research Associate at the Population Studies Center. She has extensive survey experience in India and Taiwan, working on household surveys of income, consumption, saving, the impact of the Green Revolution, and the economic correlates of fertility.

RICHARD R. NELSON is Professor of Economics at Yale University. He previously served with the Rand Corporation. He has published extensively on economic analysis in general, and economic development in particular, lately primarily on production function analysis and structural change. He serves as consultant to various institutions, including the Urban Institute, the Atomic Energy Commission, and the Office of Management and the Budget.

VERNON W. RUTTAN is Professor in the Department of Agricultural Economics at the University of Minnesota and director of its Economic Development Center. He was previously on the faculty of Purdue University. He is president of the American Agricultural Economics Association and from 1965 to 1970 served as the head of the Department of Agricultural Economics at the University of Minnesota. His research and publications have been primarily on the economics of technical change and on agricultural and economic development. He has also served with the Council of Economic Advisers and the International Rice Research Institute (Philippines).

JORGE SALAZAR-CARRILLO is Senior Fellow at the Brookings

Institution and a coordinator of the Programa de Estudios Conjuntos de Integracion Economica Latinoamericana (ECIEL). He is also on the editorial boards of the Review of Income and Wealth and the Handbook of Latin American Studies. He is a professorial lecturer at Georgetown University and advisor to the OAS.

LARRY A. SJAASTAD is Associate Professor of Economics, University of Chicago. He served on the faculty of the University of Minnesota and various Latin American universities. His publications are primarily on migration and cost-benefit analysis. He has also been a consultant to various governmental organizations, especially in Latin America.

REEVE D. VANNEMAN is currently a graduate student in the Department of Social Relations at Harvard University. During 1972-73 he is in India at the Institute of Management, Ahmedabad, doing field work on organizational structures in Indian industry. This research is an extension of the work reported in the conference paper. In addition to work on organizational aspects of development, he is interested in research and theory on relative deprivation and social protest.

LOUIS T. WELLS, JR., is Associate Professor of Business Administration, Harvard Graduate School of Business Administration. His publications focus on the ramifications of multinational firms and the product life cycle model. He has advised governments in less developed countries on the subject of negotiations between foreign investors and host governments.

JEFFREY G. WILLIAMSON is Professor in the Economics Department at the University of Wisconsin, Madison. He has published extensively, especially in the areas of economic history and quantitative analysis of aspects of economic development. His current work is on a general equilibrium analysis of late nineteenth-century America, and an analytical history of Meiji Japanese development.

PATRICK YEUNG is Assistant Professor of Economics, University of Illinois, Urbana. His main interest has been in international economics. His publications in economic development include work on the effects of foreign and entrepôt trade. He is joining the economics staff of the International Bank for Reconstruction and Development.

PAN A. YOTOPOULOS is Professor of Economics, Food Research Institute, Stanford University. He was previously on the faculties of the University of Wisconsin (Milwaukee), and the niversity of Hawaii. His books are primarily on the application of conomic analysis to development problems in Greece. His articles :over various aspects of economic development.